WHY NATIONS FIGHT

Four generic motives have historically led states to initiate war: fear, interest, standing, and revenge. Using an original data set, Richard Ned Lebow examines the distribution of wars across three and a half centuries and argues that, contrary to conventional wisdom, only a minority of these were motivated by security or material interest. Instead, the majority are the result of a quest for standing, and for revenge – an attempt to get even with states who had previously made successful territorial grabs. Lebow maintains that today none of these motives are effectively served by war – it is increasingly counterproductive – and that there is growing recognition of this political reality. His analysis allows for more fine-grained and persuasive forecasts about the future of war as well as highlighting areas of uncertainty.

RICHARD NED LEBOW is James O. Freedman Presidential Professor at Dartmouth College and Centennial Professor at the London School of Economics and Political Science. He is the author of, among other books, *A Cultural Theory of International Relations* (Cambridge, 2008) which won the 2009 American Political Science Association Jervis and Schroeder Award for the Best Book on International History and Politics as well as the British International Studies Association Susan Strange Book Award for the Best Book of the Year, and *The Tragic Vision of Politics* (Cambridge, 2003) which won the 2005 Alexander L George Book Award of the International Society for Political Psychology.

T0384723

WHY NATIONS FIGHT

Past and Future Motives for War

RICHARD NED LEBOW

CAMBRIDGE
UNIVERSITY PRESS

CAMBRIDGE UNIVERSITY PRESS
Cambridge, New York, Melbourne, Madrid, Cape Town,
Singapore, São Paulo, Delhi, Tokyo, Mexico City

Cambridge University Press
The Edinburgh Building, Cambridge CB2 8RU, UK

Published in the United States of America by
Cambridge University Press, New York

www.cambridge.org
Information on this title: www.cambridge.org/9780521192835

First published 2010

A catalogue record for this publication is available from the British Library

Library of Congress cataloguing in publication data
Lebow, Richard Ned.
Why nations fight : past and future motives for war / Richard Ned Lebow.
p. cm.
ISBN 978-0-521-19283-5 (hardback)
1. War – Causes. I. Title.
U21.2.L386 2010
355.02´7–dc22
2010005504

ISBN 978-0-521-19283-5 Hardback
ISBN 978-0-521-17045-1 Paperback

To the memory of three friends and collaborators

Alexander L. George (1920–2006)
Gregory Henderson (1922–1980)
Alexander Stephan (1946–2009)

CONTENTS

FIGURES

TABLES

PREFACE AND ACKNOWLEDGMENTS

War was a defining feature of the twentieth century. A vast percentage of the people of the last century were participants or victims in one way or another of the endless stream of civil and interstate wars that characterized this era. These wars and their consequences were accompanied by unprecedented levels of ethnic cleansing and genocide. I am just old enough to remember World War II, which had a profound impact on my choice of career, discipline and research agenda. I have authored numerous books and articles on various aspects of conflict management and resolution. I have written about intelligence failures and bad crisis management responsible for wars. More recently, in *A Cultural Theory of International Relations*, I use the origins and dynamics of ancient and modern wars to elaborate and evaluate a broader set of arguments about systematic variation in the propensity and character of cooperation, conflict and risk-taking. In this book, I turn to war itself, with the goal of analyzing its causes in the past and the likelihood that they will diminish as motives for war in the future.

In 2009, when I wrote *Why Nations Fight*, I was James O. Freedman Presidential Professor of Government at Dartmouth College and Centennial Professor of International Relations at the London School of Economics and Political Science. I want to thank colleagues at both institutions with whom I discussed the premise and arguments of the book and from whom I received useful feedback on the manuscript. They include Stephen Brooks, Christopher Coker, Michael Cox, Daryl Press, Benjamin Valentino, Odd Arne Westad and William Wohlforth. Ben Valentino helped me prepare a list of wars fought since 1945, and, in conjunction with a co-authored critique of power transition, measured the respective power of rising and great powers since 1945.[1]

---

[1] Richard Ned Lebow and Benjamin Valentino, "Lost in Transition: A Critique of Power Transition Theories," *International Relations*, 23, no. 3 (September 2009), pp. 389–410.

David Lebow, Rajan Menon and two anonymous readers for Cambridge University Press read the manuscript and provided helpful criticism and suggestions. As with two of my previous books, the John Sloan Dickey Center at Dartmouth College hosted seminars to review chapters. My presidential fellows at Dartmouthy, Reyad Allie and Josh Rosselman, did yeoman's service checking facts and proofreading. Ken Booth and his colleagues at the University of Wales, Aberystwyth, invited me to present the core argument of my book as the 2009–2010 E. H. Carr Lecture and provided thoughtful feedback. For the same reason, thanks go to Rick Herrmann and the Mershon Center, Felix Berenskoetter and the School of Oriental and Asian Studies (SOAS) and Brendan Sims and the Centre of International Studies, University of Cambridge. Once again, I express my gratitude to John Haslam, my editor and collaborator on three books. Finally and foremost, thanks to Carol Bohmer for putting up with all too many "could we do this later, I'm working on my book."

PART I

Introduction

1

Introduction

War is a poor chisel to carve out tomorrow.

Martin Luther King[1]

Organized violence has been the scourge of humankind at least as far back as the Neolithic era.[2] The twentieth century suffered through two enormously destructive world wars, each of which gave rise to major postwar projects aimed at preventing its reoccurrence. The victors of World War II were largely successful in making Europe a zone of peace, but not in staving off the fifty plus interstate wars fought in other parts of the world during the last six decades. These "small" wars wasted lives and resources that might have been more profitably directed to education, welfare and development. Anglo-American intervention in Iraq is estimated to have caused anywhere from 600,000 to one million lives and will cost the US upwards of US$3 trillion if veteran benefits and health are included.[3]

There is a consensus among scholars that interstate war – in contrast to intrastate violence – is on the decline. Figure 1.1 shows the number of ongoing interstate, colonial and civil wars across the decades since 1945. Wars of colonial independence end in the 1980s and civil wars show a sharp drop after the end of the Cold War. However, several nasty civil conflicts, including the rounds of violence associated with the breakup of Yugoslavia, were sparked by the end of the Cold War, the dissolution of the Soviet Union and the collapse of other communist regimes. Interstate wars, relatively few in number, show a slight decline.

If we take a longer historical perspective, the frequency of war has been dropping throughout the modern era.[4] The decades since 1945 have been

---

[1] Black, *Quotations in Black*, p. 260.   [2] Keeley, *War Before Civilization*.
[3] Wikipedia, http://en.wikipedia.org/wiki/Iraq_casualties/ for a review of diverse attempts to assess casualties. Stiglitz and Bilmes, *Three Trillion Dollar War*.
[4] Wright, *A Study of War*, vol. 1, pp. 121, 237, 242, 248, 638; Levy, *War in the Modern Great Power System*, p. 139; Holsti, *Peace and War*; Hamilton, "The European Wars: 1815–1914."

Armed conflicts (25 + deaths per year)

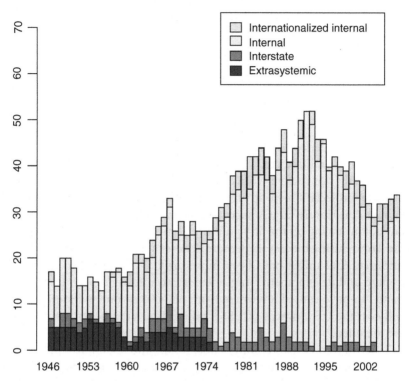

Figure 1.1   Wars by year, 1946–2007. The data are for wars that resulted in at least 1,000 deaths, military and civilian, in every year in which they are counted. I am indebted to Kristian Skrede Gleditsch for the table

the most peaceful in recorded history in terms of the number of interstate wars and the per capita casualties they have produced.[5] This encouraging finding needs to be evaluated against the pessimistic truth that the major wars of the twentieth century were often far more costly than their predecessors. World Wars I and II were the costliest wars in history, resulting in at least 10.4 and 50 million dead respectively.[6] The economic blockade of Germany and its allies in World War I seriously weakened

---

[5] Holsti, "The Decline of Interstate War."
[6] Tucker, *Encyclopedia of World War I*, pp. 272–273; Tucker and Roberts, *Encyclopedia of World War II*, pp. 300–301.

the resistance of civilian populations to the influenza pandemic that came hard on its heel, which is estimated to have killed another 1.1 million Europeans.[7] The Indochina War (1964–1978) killed perhaps 1.2 million Vietnamese, and 58,000 Americans lost their lives.[8] The Iran–Iraq War (1980–1988) produced upwards of 1.1 million casualties.[9] We judge the lethality of pathogens not on how frequently they infect populations but on the percentage of people they kill. By this measure, war became more lethal in the twentieth century even if it broke out less often. If we include intrastate war, domestic purges, and political and ethnic cleansing, the incidence and lethality of political violence increases considerably. Robert McNamara estimates that 160 million people died violent deaths in the twentieth century.[10] Our reassuring empirical finding is not so reassuring after all.

Against this pessimism, we can muster a powerful counterfactual: the number of people who would have died in a superpower nuclear war. In the 1950s, when the Cold War was at its height, US nuclear weapons were targeted on Soviet and Chinese cities. The first Single Integrated Operational Plan (SIOP), prepared by the Strategic Air Command, was expected to inflict 360–525 million casualties on the Soviet bloc in the first week of war.[11] With the increased accuracy of delivery systems, the superpowers could use less powerful warheads to destroy targets and shifted their emphasis from population to military assets and economic infrastructure. Not that this made much difference in practice. In the late 1970s, the US target deck included the 200 largest Soviet cities and 80 percent of Soviet cities with populations above 25,000 by virtue of their co-location with military and industrial targets. An all-out counterforce attack was expected to kill between 50 and 100 million Soviets, a figure that does not include casualties from attacks on Eastern Europe.[12] The number of nuclear weapons in superpower arsenals peaked at about 70,000 in the mid-1980s; a full-scale nuclear exchange would have been

---

[7] Phillips and Killingray, *Spanish Influenza Pandemic of 1918–19*, p. 7.

[8] Cook and Walker, *Facts on File World Political Almanac*, p. 325; McNamara, *Argument Without End*, p. 1, maintains 3.8 million Vietnamese died.

[9] Cook and Walker, *Facts on File World Political Almanac*, p. 325; Chubin and Tripp, *Iran and Iraq at War*, p. 1, estimate 1.5 million.

[10] McNamara, *Fog of War*, p. 233.

[11] Brown, *DROPSHOT*, on the early 1950s and Richelson, "Population Targeting and US Strategic Doctrine," on the SIOP.

[12] United States Arms Control and Disarmament Agency, *The Effects of Nuclear War*; United States Congress, Office of Technology Assessment, *The Effects of Nuclear War*; Richelson, "Population Targeting and US Strategic Doctrine."

more devastating still.[13] Some scientists, notably Carl Sagan, worried that such a war might threaten all human life by bringing about a nuclear winter.[14] Viewed in this light, war-avoidance in the late twentieth century seems an impressive achievement indeed.

War may be on the decline but destructive wars still occur. When I began this book, Israel was conducting military operations in Gaza, and India and Pakistan were reinforcing their border in the aftermath of a deadly terrorist attack in Mumbai. Three of the four protagonists in these conflicts possess nuclear weapons, making any war which they might fight that much more of an horrendous prospect. The study of interstate war accordingly remains important for humanitarian and intellectual reasons. The more we know about the causes of war the better able we are to design strategies and institutions to reduce its likelihood.

International-relations scholars have advanced a number of different but generally reinforcing reasons for the decline of war in the short and long term. These include economic development, the increasing destructiveness of war, the spread of democracy, growing trade and interdependence among developed economies, international institutions and norms and widespread disgust with war as a practice.[15] These explanations appeal ultimately to either ideas or material conditions and the constraints and opportunities they create for actors. In practice, all explanations rely on both, although this is rarely recognized and their interaction remains unexplored. To further muddy the waters, most explanations for war's decline appear to be reinforcing, making them difficult to disaggregate and raising the possibility that some are expressions of others or manifestations of underlying common causes.

Let me illustrate this causal complexity with the most widely offered explanation for war's decline: public revulsion. The strongest claim for the relationship between public attitudes toward war and its practice is made by John Mueller.[16] He compares war to slavery and dueling, noting that both practices disappeared when public opinion turned decisively against them. War, he contends, is now obsolescent. This comforting thesis is appealing but unpersuasive. People have always opposed war and anti-war literature has a long history. The bible enjoins readers to

---

[13] Natural Resources Defense Council, Archive of Nuclear Data, www.nrdc.org/nuclear/nudb/datainx.asp.

[14] Sagan and Turco, *Where No Man Thought*.

[15] Mueller, *Remnants of War*, pp. 162–171; Väyrynen, "Introduction," for overviews.

[16] Mueller, *Retreat from Doomsday*.

beat their swords into plowshares, and, in Aristophanes' *Lysistrata*, Athenian and Spartan women agree to withhold their sexual favors unless their men make peace. Erasmus exposed war as a folly in his *Praise of Folly*, as did Voltaire in *Candide*. Quakers, formed in England in 1652, in the aftermath of the English civil war, revered human life because it was the vehicle for god's voice. They were among the first religious groups to work for peace. Anti-war sentiment and writings became more widespread and popular in the latter part of the nineteenth century and more so still after each world war. Distaste for war was high in 1914, and authorities in many countries suspected that any great-power war would be long, costly and destructive to winner and loser alike.[17] European public opinion was even more anti-war in 1939, even in Germany, the principal perpetrator of World War II.[18] Anti-war sentiment was sufficiently pronounced that it became necessary for the most aggressive leaders – Hitler and Mussolini included – to affirm peaceful intentions. Japan in turn justified its invasion of China as intended to establish peace or restore order.[19] As this book goes to press, the US, another country whose public is anti-war in the abstract, has been militarily engaged in Afghanistan for almost a decade and Iraq for seven years.

Mueller is not wrong in insisting that Western publics have become increasingly disenchanted with war, but his analogy to slavery and dueling is misleading. Once public opinion turned against these practices, their days were numbered despite fierce rearguard efforts by their defenders. When outlawed, they largely disappeared and have not returned, although pockets of slavery are reported to remain, not only in remote regions of the world but in some of its most prosperous cities.[20] War is different. American opinion has consistently been strongly anti-war, yet the majority supported intervention in Korea, Vietnam, Afghanistan and Iraq. Many proponents of these interventions described themselves as strongly anti-war but considered war necessary on the ground of national security. At their outset, the "rally round the flag" effect – a phenomenon first described by

---

[17] On the German side, see Mombauer, *Helmuth von Moltke*, pp. 210–213, citing relevant correspondence between Moltke and Falkenhayn.

[18] Kershaw, *The "Hitler Myth,"* pp. 139–147; Frei, "People's Community and War."

[19] Luard, *War in International Society*, pp. 330–331, 366–367.

[20] Sage and Kasten, *Enslaved*; Bales, *Disposable People* and *Understanding Global Slavery Today*.

John Mueller – consistently trumped anti-war sentiment for a majority of the American population.[21] The inescapable conclusion is that public revulsion with war has not prevented it in the past or the present. In democratic countries, leaders have routinely been able to mobilize support for military budgets and war by arousing the powerful emotions of fear and honor.

Take the case of the Iraq War. A February 2001 poll conducted by Gallup showed that 52 percent of the American people favored an invasion of Iraq and 42 percent were opposed. By January 2003, a poll sponsored by the *New York Times* and CBS revealed that this support had dropped to 31 percent, largely due to the opposition expressed by France and Germany. Following Secretary of State Colin Powell's speech at the United Nations on February 5, in which he claimed to have incontrovertible evidence that Saddam would soon possess weapons of mass destruction (WMDs), CNN and NBC polls showed a 6 percent increase in support; 37 percent of Americans now favored an invasion. More significantly, those opposed to war dropped from 66 percent the month before to 27 percent. In March 2003, just days before the invasion, a poll by *USA Today*, CNN and Gallup revealed that 60 percent were now prepared to support a war if the administration secured authorization from the UN Security Council. This number dropped to 54 percent if the Security Council refused to vote support, and to 47 percent if the administration refused to ask the UN for support. In April 2003, a month after the invasion, 72 percent supported the war. According to Gallup, public support for the war rose to an impressive 79 percent. The increase in support in the months before the invasion reflects the all-out public-relations campaign by the administration to link Saddam to the attacks of 9/11 and to convince people that he had, or was on the verge of possessing, WMDs.[22] There was no real debate as Congress and the media were loath to voice dissenting opinions given the strength of public support for the President and the willingness of the Vice-President to excoriate reporters and newspapers who questioned his policies.[23]

When no WMDs were discovered and occupying forces faced an insurgency, public opinion polls revealed a steady decline in support

---

[21] Mueller, *War, Presidents, and Public Opinion* and Mueller, *Public Opinion and the Gulf War*; Oneal and Bryan, "Rally 'Round the Flag Effect in US Foreign Policy Crises."
[22] Lebow, *Cultural Theory of International Relations*, pp. 461–462, 469–472.
[23] Mermin, *Debating War and Peace*; Schechter, "Selling the Iraq War."

for intervention in Iraq.[24] By August 2004, a *Washington Times* poll found that 67 percent of the public felt betrayed, believing that the war had been based on false assumptions.[25] By September 2006, a *New York Times* poll found that 51 percent of Americans believed that the US never should have entered Iraq, while 44 percent felt the administration had done the right thing.[26] In May 2007, according to a CNN poll, only 34 percent of the American people still favored the war in Iraq, while 65 percent were opposed.[27]

British prime minister Margaret Thatcher benefited from the same "rally round the flag" effect in the Falklands War, and Tony Blair somewhat less so in the Anglo-American invasion of Iraq.[28] Thucydides was the first historian to describe this dynamic in his account of the Peloponnesian War. Pericles' masterful speech turned around Athenian opinion, which had previously rejected Corcyra's plea for a defensive alliance.[29] In the debate preceding the disastrous Sicilian expedition, Thucydides portrays the power of a third motive – material interest – in which the paired speeches of Alcibiades and Nicias moved the assembly to vote credits for the war.[30] Has nothing changed in two-and-a-half millennia? Realists would say no. Human nature and the anarchy of the international system, they insist, make war a recurring phenomenon. The anarchy of the international system encourages the powerful "to do what they want," as the Athenians put it to the Melians, while the weak "suffer what they must."[31] I believe this pessimism unwarranted. Nor was it shared by Thucydides, whom realists consistently misread.[32] History offers grounds for cautious optimism. Unlike Athens and Sparta and Rome and Carthage, the superpowers avoided war and ended their Cold War peacefully. This outcome defied the expectations of many realists, as does the growing zone of peace among the developed industrial states. The reasons why the Cold War ended peacefully and why war as an institution is on the decline are less clear.

---

[24] Polls reported at Wikipedia, "Popular Opinion in the US on the War in Iraq," http://en.wikipedia.org/wiki/Popular_opinion_in_the_US_on_the_invasion_of_Iraq/.

[25] www.washingtontimes.com/upi-breaking/20040820-115103-7559r.htm.

[26] Wikipedia, "Popular Opinion in the US on the War in Iraq." [27] *Ibid.*

[28] Lai and Reiter, "Rally 'Round the Union Jack?"; Lewis, "Television, Public Opinion and the War in Iraq"; Kettell, *Dirty Politics?*

[29] Thucydides, *History of the Peloponnesian War*, I.32–44, for the speeches and assembly's decision.

[30] *Ibid.*, 6.9–24.   [31] *Ibid.*, 5.85–113.   [32] Lebow, *Tragic Vision of Politics*, ch. 3.

What is war?

Any study of war should begin by telling us what it is.[33] Superficially, this seems self-evident: when armies clash and people die. But this happens in civil wars and conflicts too. I exclude them from my study on the grounds that they generally arise in different circumstances and are characterized by different dynamics. There are, of course, important connections between inter- and intra-state war, as the same motives often guide their participants, and civil conflicts sometimes provoke interstate wars and *vice versa*.[34] International law distinguishes between civil war, waged between two parties of the same state, and interstate war, which it describes as an open and declared contest between two independent states that is waged by their governments. This definition is reasonable but not entirely suitable because it excludes conflicts where there is no official declaration of war (e.g. the Soviet–Japanese clash in Mongolia in 1939, the Korean War, American intervention in Indochina and Soviet intervention in Hungary, Czechoslovakia and Afghanistan). It also omits military confrontations between political units that have not been recognized as states by other states or their adversary (e.g. Boer War, Korean War). I consider both kinds of conflicts to be *de facto* wars.

Violence carried out by one group against another is a timeless practice. War is distinguished from violence by its political goals and the understandings participants have of its special character.[35] War was conducted on a large scale by ancient empires and over the centuries gradually made subject to certain rules. In the ancient world, rule-based warfare was most robust in classical Greece, where it was an accepted means of settling disputes over honor, standing and territory. Warring city-states would agree beforehand where to fight, agree to truces to reclaim wounded and dead combatants, and the victor – the side left in control of the battlefield – had the right to erect a trophy.[36] Aztec warfare was also highly stylized and intended to serve political and religious goals. Aztec political-military conventions interfered with their ability

---

[33] Vasquez, *War Puzzle*, pp. 21–28, for a good discussion of this problem.
[34] Petersen, *Understanding Ethnic Violence*, p. 52, makes an argument parallel to mine. He contends that civil violence is often a means used by groups in the hope of reordering the status hierarchy in an upward direction.
[35] Huntingford, "Animals Fight, But Do Not Make War."
[36] Van Wees, *Greek Warfare*; Lebow, *Cultural Theory of International Relations*, ch. 4.

to repel the Spanish invaders and may have been more responsible for their defeat than Spanish possession of horses and firearms.[37]

Rule-based warfare of this kind requires numerous intersubjective understandings.[38] By the nineteenth century, reinforcing feedback between understandings and rules had given rise to a highly differentiated European regional system in which states competed for standing, and those recognized as great powers assumed certain responsibilities for maintenance of the system. In the next hundred years, the system expanded to include non-Western and non-Christian political units and transformed itself into a global system. The definition of war and the rules governing it, initially European, are now effectively international. Modern war became an increasingly complex social practice. It was based on the concept of the state: a sovereign political unit with a near monopoly over the use of force on its territory. It required a system in which these political units not only functioned but understood they had an interest in maintaining. The system legitimated actors through their collective recognition by other actors – recognizing their sovereignty – and differentiated war from peace by means of legal definitions and associated practices.[39] War was linked to sovereignty because it was defined in terms of actions that encroached on sovereignty (e.g. invasion, economic blockade). Such transgressions also provided justifications for declaring war against another state. Conceived of in this way, war became a military contest fought for political goals, as Clausewitz famously recognized. Violence, he observed, is used to bend or break the will of an adversary, but its targets and modes of application are generally determined by rules or norms.[40] This conception of war is modern because before the seventeenth century we cannot really speak of states or effectively distinguish between intra- and inter-state violence. For these reasons, Hedley Bull argues that war "is organized violence carried on by political units against each other."[41] I add the proviso, common to many quantitative studies of war, that at least one of the participating political units must suffer at least 1,000 battle deaths. This is, of course, an arbitrary measure, but one that has become a convention in the discipline.[42]

---

[37] Hassig, *Aztec Warfare*.
[38] Winch, *Idea of a Social Science*, p. 52, on the relationship between intersubjective understandings and rules.
[39] Wright, *Study of War*, p. 698, on this point.   [40] Clausewitz, *On War*, Book 1.
[41] Bull, *Anarchical Society*, p. 184.
[42] Singer and Small, *Wages of War, 1816–1965*, pp. 37, 39, for the origins of this criterion.

The goals of warfare evolved over the centuries. We know little of prehistoric "war" but can reasonably assume that it arose from conflicts over women, watering holes, hunting grounds and territory considered valuable for religious or economic reasons. Early on, warfare became the principal means by which young men and their societies sought honor, prestige and standing. Homer's *Iliad* offers a sophisticated analysis of an aristocratic bronze age society in which war was a means of revenge and a vehicle for winning honor. For Greeks and Trojans alike, there was no distinction between king and state or private and public quarrels. With the development of the *polis*, and later, states, these categories emerged. Another important transition occurred as a result of nationalism and military conscription. The French Revolutionary and Napoleonic Wars, Clausewitz observed, had become the concern of peoples, not just their rulers. War became correspondingly more costly as its objectives became "national" and more far-reaching.[43]

These developments led some scholars to distinguish modern warfare from everything that preceded it. Levy, Walker and Edwards assert that the "wars for personal honor, vengeance, and enrichment of kings and nobles that characterized the Middle Ages ... were increasingly replaced by the use of force as an instrument of policy for the achievement of political objectives."[44] Such a claim unwittingly reflects the success of nineteenth-century German nationalist historians (e.g. Heeren, Ranke, Treitschke) in fostering a discourse on sovereignty intended to legitimize the power of the central government and the project of state building. Central to this discourse – and to contemporary realist and rationalist paradigms – is the depiction of foreign policy as strategically rational and intended to increase state power. While kings, nobles and empires are now history, they were responsible for foreign policy and war-making in Europe down to 1918 and more often drew their swords for reasons that bore little relationship to *Realpolitik*. Throughout the twentieth century and into the current one, honor, resentment, vengeance and sheer malice were – and remain – powerful motives in international affairs. States frequently go to war for reasons that have little, if anything, to do with security.[45]

---

[43] Clausewitz, *On War*, Book 6.

[44] Levy, Walker and Edwards, "Continuity and Change in the Evolution of Warfare"; Luard, *War and International Society*; Holsti, *Peace and War*, for variants of the claim that the goals of war have changed over the centuries.

[45] Suganami, "Explaining War"; Lebow, *Cultural Theory of International Relations*, for evidence.

The causes of war

Ever since Herodotus, historians have written about war. Many studies are embedded in large narratives of the rise and fall of empires and states. Livy (Titus Livius, c. 59 BCE–CE 17) and Edward Gibbon (1737–1794) produced monumental and influential histories of Rome in which war featured prominently. Thucydides was the first to address the origins of a war as a subject in its own right, although he situates his analysis in a larger narrative of the Peloponnesian War. To my knowledge, the first studies devoted exclusively to the generic origins of war were written in the aftermath of World War I. The causes of that conflict were particularly contentious and politically significant as all parties insisted they were fighting a defensive war. The Treaty of Versailles justified German reparations on the basis of that country's responsibility for the war, giving rise to an emotional German response, the publication by all the major powers of archival documents to support their claims of innocence and a burgeoning literature on the underlying and immediate causes of World War I.[46]

Since Thucydides, the origins of war have been framed in terms of their underlying and immediate causes. They are generally associated with necessary and enabling conditions. International relations has focused almost exclusively on underlying causes and has sought to develop general accounts of war. Some researchers contend that the causes they identity are sufficient in and of themselves to account for war. Others claim only to have discovered conditions or dynamics that make war likely but not inevitable. Studies of both kinds are invariably based on great-power wars and a handful of these at best. Theories of balance of power, power transition, alliances, economic imperialism, militarism, offensive dominance, military rigidity, inadvertent war and misperception rely overwhelmingly on World War I for their evidence. Generalizations based on single cases must remain propositions. Statistical studies of war rely on large data sets. They encounter equally insuperable problems, among them the difficulty, if not the impossibility, of meeting the two conditions critical to data sets: comparability and independence of cases. They cannot cope well, or at all, with causal complexity caused by multiple pathways to war, non-linear confluence and the possible independent role of the precipitants of war.[47]

---

[46] Herwig, "Clio Deceived"; Lebow, *Cultural Theory of International Relations*, pp. 376–381.
[47] Levy, "Causes of War"; Vasquez, *War Puzzle*, pp. 9, 48–50; Lebow, *Forbidden Fruit*, chs. 1, 3, 9.

I have no solution to these problems and for this and other reasons advance no propositions about when war is more likely to occur. I approach the problem of war differently. I interrogate the motives of initiators to determine why they resorted to force. I am less interested in their immediate goals (e.g. removing a military threat, conquest of territory, trade concessions) than I am in the reasons why they sought these goals. Kal Holsti, John Vasquez and Paul Senese all make the case for territorial disputes as key causes of war and control of territory as a key objective of their participants.[48] This finding, while interesting in its own right, tells us nothing about why territory was so contested. States can seek territory for reasons of security, economic interests or standing. Their motives for territorial expansion can change over the centuries, as Vasquez acknowledges. Territory, moreover, is only one of the ways in which these generic motives find expression. I am interested in motives at this deeper level, and following my argument in *A Cultural Theory of International Relations*, I contend that most, if not all, foreign-policy behavior can be reduced to three fundamental motives: fear, interest and honor. I believe that we can learn something important about the causes of war by understanding the underlying reasons why leaders go to war. This assumes, as I do, that most wars are set in motion by conscious decisions by leaders to use force, or at least to pursue initiatives they recognize have the potential to escalate into war.

To understand the causes of war we need to start with motives and the foreign-policy goals to which they lead. War offers a window into the minds of leaders and policymaking elites as decisions for war tend to be better documented than many other kinds of foreign policies. Analysis of the motives behind wars can provide important insights into general goals of foreign policy and how they have changed over the centuries. It can tell us how war was and is seen to advance or retard these goals and why this is so. Tracking the evolution of motives and their links to war might also allow us to make some educated guesses about the future likelihood of war. Such an approach finesses many of the problems associated with qualitative or quantitative efforts to find causes of war.

My analysis draws on a data set that I have assembled but, as I explain in Chapter 4, I do not use it to search for correlations. My data set is best understood as a poll of history based on indirect observation. It describes the motives associated with wars, not when wars arise. I assume these

---

[48] Holsti, *Peace and War*, pp. 46–63; Vasquez, *War Puzzle*; Senese and Vasquez, *Steps to War*. See Hensel, "Territory," for a literature review.

motives are equally in play when no war occurs, so they tell us nothing about the immediate causes of war. They do allow us to infer something about the frequency of war, the central question of this book. My approach takes a macro versus a micro perspective. I seek to understand the frequency and character of war across the centuries, not the reasons why individual wars arise. I posit a relationship between motive and risk-taking at variance with realist, power transition and rationalist theories of war. I do not attempt to establish this relationship through correlations but via case studies. Qualitative analysis of wars and their contexts are also the basis for my claim that general wars involving the great powers arise largely from miscalculated escalation. In contrast to the conventional wisdom, I argue that such wars are rarely intentional.

Consistency with evidence is a necessary but insufficient ground for provisional confidence in a theory or, in this instance, a set of related propositions. As a general rule, theories and propositions must be compared to other theories and propositions to determine how well, relatively speaking, they account for the observable variance. As I do not make causal claims of this kind, I do not engage in this kind of testing. I do not engage individual theories so much as I do competing paradigms. They are rooted in different motives and I attempt to determine the extent to which these motives are implicated in historical cases of war-initiation. I subject my propositions to the same test and find strong support for the spirit as the principal motive for war in the European system down to the present day.

My dissatisfaction with the existing literature on war, and with international-relations theory more generally, provided the incentive to write *A Cultural Theory of International Relations*. It develops a theory of international relations based on a parsimonious model of human motivation. Following Plato and Aristotle, I posit spirit, appetite and reason as fundamental drives, each with distinct goals. Each also generates different logics of cooperation, conflict and risk-taking. These motives further produce characteristic forms of hierarchy based on different principles of justice. Order at the individual, state, regional and international levels is sustained by these hierarchies; it weakens or breaks down when the discrepancy between behavior and the principles of justice on which they rest becomes obvious and intolerable.[49] Order and disorder at any level have implications for order and disorder at adjacent levels.

---

[49] Ray, "Democracy," for a recent, thoughtful assessment.

A fourth motive – fear – enters the picture when reason is unable to constrain appetite or spirit. Fear is a powerful emotion, not an innate drive. The unrestrained pursuit of appetite or spirit by some actors deprives others of their ability to satisfy these drives, and, more fundamentally, makes them concerned for their physical security. All four worlds I describe are ideal types. Real worlds are mixed in that all four motives are usually to some degree present. Real worlds are also lumpy in that the mix of motives differs from actor to actor and among the groupings they form. Multiple motives generally mix rather than blend, giving rise to a range of behaviors that appear inconsistent, even contradictory.

Existing theories of international relations are rooted in appetite (i.e. liberalism and Marxism) or fear (i.e. realism). In modern times, the spirit (*thumos*) has largely been ignored by philosophy and social science. I contend it is omnipresent and gives rise to the universal drive for self-esteem which finds expression in the quest for honor or standing. By excelling at activities valued by our peer group or society we win the approbation of those who matter and feel better about ourselves. Institutions and states have neither psyches nor emotions. The people who run these collectivities or identify with them do. They frequently project their psychological needs onto their political units and feel better about themselves when those units win victories or perform well. In classical Greece, the *polis* was the center of political life and a citizen's status was usually a reflection of that of his *polis*. Transference and esteem by vicarious association are just as evident in the age of nationalism where the state has become the relevant unit.

In *A Cultural Theory*, I use Homer's *Iliad* as a prototype to develop a paradigm of politics and international relations based on the spirit. I document its importance in domestic politics and critical foreign-policy decisions in case studies ranging from classical Greece to both world wars and the Anglo-American invasion of Iraq. I subsequently introduce the other motives and devise a set of cultural indicators to determine their relative distribution among the actors in question. I then predict the kinds of foreign-policy behavior this mix should generate, predictions that are on the whole validated by my case studies. In this volume, I draw out the implications of my theory for warfare and use the data set I have assembled to evaluate propositions derived from this understanding. The data set classifies states in terms of their power (leading great powers, great powers, declining great powers, rising powers, weaker states), identifies initiators of war, their motives (i.e. security, material well-being, standing, revenge and other) and outcomes (win, lose or draw). The data offer strong support for all six propositions and indicate the extent to which standing has been the principal motive for war since the modern state system came into being.

Overview of chapters

My book is divided into three parts. Part I reviews and critiques the literature on war and its causes. Chapter 2 engages explanations for war associated with the realist, power transition, Marxist and rationalist paradigms. Each paradigm has enriched our understanding of war, but each encounters serious problems. Part II offers a succinct recapitulation of my theory of international relations and derives from it six propositions concerning the kinds of states likely to initiate it and the kinds of states they are likely to attack. Chapter 3 offers the overview and propositions, and Chapter 4 describes the data set, which is reproduced in the Appendix. Part III explores the likelihood of war in the future. Chapter 5 investigates the changing relationship between fear, interest and war. Chapter 6 does the same for standing and revenge. I make the case for increasing disaggregation between these several motives and war, and as a result, predict a general decline in the frequency of war. This does not mean – especially in the next decade or two – that there will be no wars.

A theory about war must also be a theory about peace. It should tell us something about the conditions in which conflicts are resolved peacefully, or at least prevented from escalating into war. Paul Schroeder rightly observes that "it is often more difficult to detect the origins and growth of peace and even harder to explain them."[50] Peace is generally considered the opposite of war, although in Chapter 4 I argue it is more accurate to frame peace and war not as a simple binary but as anchors of opposite ends of a continuum. Theories within the liberal paradigm, most notably the Democratic Peace research program, speak to the question of peace; they do the reverse of theories of war by positing conditions in which war will *not* occur. I do not engage the controversy surrounding the Democratic Peace but in Part III offer arguments as to why war is becoming less likely across regime types.

---

[50] Schroeder, "Life and Death of a Long Peace."

What is novel about this book?

My approach and my findings challenge powerful components of the conventional wisdom about war and its causes. I analyze war-initiation in terms of motive and relative power of states. To my knowledge, this is the first attempt to do this. Contrary to realist expectations, I find security responsible for only nineteen of my ninety-four wars. A significant number of these wars pitted great powers against other great powers, but none of them were associated with power transitions. This does not mean that security is unimportant in international affairs; it had to be a primary concern of all states who were attacked. Material interests are also a weak motive for war, being responsible for only eight wars, and most of those in the eighteenth century. Moreover, security and material interest sometimes act in concert with one another and more often with other motives. In some wars they are secondary to these other motives. Standing, by contrast, is responsible for sixty-two wars as a primary or secondary motive. Revenge, also a manifestation of the spirit, is implicated in another eleven. There can be little doubt that the spirit is the principal cause of war across the centuries, and that it and its consequences have been almost totally ignored in the international-relations literature.

The salience of motives is a function of culture, not of any supposedly objective features of the international environment or the governance of states. The character and robustness of domestic, regional and international societies also determine the extent to which the several motives I analyze are implicated with war. Interest shows a sharp decline in this regard once mercantilism gave way to more sophisticated understandings of wealth. Security-motivated wars show no similar decline by century but come in clusters associated with bids for hegemony by great or dominant powers. I contend that the material and social conditions that channel these motives into warfare are associated with particular stages of history. The most recent clusters of security-related wars were associated with the run-up to and conduct of the two world wars of the twentieth century. They were in turn a product of the dislocations brought about by modernization in an environment where great-power competition and the drive for hegemony were conducted primarily by violent means. Now that this era has passed in Europe and is receding in much of the Pacific rim, and hegemony achieved by force is no longer considered a legitimate ambition, the security requirements and fears of great powers should be in decline.

There has been a sharp drop in wars of revenge since the eighteenth century, which I attribute to their close association with territorial conquest. All the wars of revenge in my data set represent efforts to regain territory lost in previous wars. As territorial conquest has been delegitimized and become more difficult and less rewarding for this and other reasons, it is likely that wars of revenge will become even less frequent. Against this optimistic forecast, we must recognize that wars of revenge can be triggered by other causes, as in the American invasion of Afghanistan.

As for wars of standing, they too can be expected to decline. During the postwar era, and even more so since the end of that conflict, war and standing have become increasingly disengaged in the sense that successful war-initiation no longer enhances standing. It may actually lead to loss of standing in the absence of UN approval of the military initiative in question. The Anglo-American intervention in Iraq – a war in which territorial conquest was not an issue – is a case in point. Changing values and norms encourage rational leaders to find other, peaceful ways of claiming standing. To the extent that this happens, the frequency of war involving either rising or great powers can be expected to diminish sharply.

Looking at motives for war in historical perspective, our attention should be drawn to three significant shifts in thinking. The first, noted above, concerns the nature of wealth and its consequences for interstate relations. Until Adam Smith and modern economics, the world's wealth was thought to be finite, making interstate relations resemble a zero-sum game in which an increase in wealth for one state was believed to come at the expense of others. Once political elites learned that total wealth could be augmented by the division of labor, use of mechanical sources of energy and economies of scale, international economic cooperation became feasible, and ultimately came to be seen as another means of generating wealth. Trade and investment, and the economic interdependence to which this led, did not prevent war, as many nineteenth- and early twentieth-century liberals hoped, but it did more or less put an end to wars of material aggrandizement.

The second shift in thinking began in the nineteenth century and accelerated during the twentieth. It is about the collective versus autarkic pursuit of security. Alliances, informal or formal, have always been part and practice of foreign policy, but they took on new meaning at the Congress of Vienna. The victors of the Napoleonic Wars sought to act collectively to maintain the postwar *status quo* and thereby prevent the resurgence of revolution and interstate war. This was a short-lived and ultimately unsuccessful experiment, due in large part to the unrealistic goals of Austria, Prussia and Russia, not only of restraining France, but of holding back democratization and the unwillingness of Britain to support this project.[51] Periodic congresses later in the nineteenth century were to a large degree effective in reducing great-power and regional tensions by means of agreements and suasion. Following World War I, the League of Nations was given the more ambitious task of preventing war by means of collective security.[52] For many reasons it was an abject failure, but the principle of collective security endured, and actually strengthened its hold in English-speaking countries. The United Nations, established in 1945, made it the principal mission of the Security Council. This institution's record has been mixed, as was that of the numerous regional alliances that came into being during the Cold War. The North Atlantic Treaty Organization (NATO) is by far the most successful, although there is no evidence that it ever prevented a Soviet attack on Western Europe. NATO and other international groupings have played a prominent and arguably successful role in keeping the peace or helping to terminate wars in the post-Cold War era. Collective security has become the norm and an important source of regional and international stability.

The third and most recent shift in thinking concerns the nature of standing in international affairs. Since the emergence of the modern international system, great powers have always sought to maintain control over standing, the means by which it is determined and who is allowed to compete for it. Throughout this period, military power and success in using it was the principal means of gaining standing and recognition as a great power. There are many ways of achieving status within states, and the more robust regional and international orders become the more multiple hierarchies will also emerge at the international level. States will feel more confident about seeking standing in diverse ways and devoting resources toward this end that might otherwise be reserved for security. Such behavior is likely to be rewarded. A BBC World Service poll conducted in early 2007 indicates a significant increase in standing of countries associated with alternate visions of the international system. When asked what countries exerted a positive

---

[51] Nicholson, *Congress of Vienna*; Gulick, *Europe's Classical Balance of Power*; Kissinger, *World Restored.*
[52] Northedge, *League of Nations*; Walters, *History of the League of Nations.*

influence in the world, Canada and Japan topped the list at 54 percent, followed by France (50 percent), Britain (45 percent), China (42 percent) and India (37 percent).[53]

Positive responses at home and abroad create a positive reinforcement cycle in which praise and respect from third parties build national esteem, play well politically and strengthen the link between such policies and national identity. Such a process has been underway for some time in Germany and Canada and to a lesser extent in Japan.[54] If an international orientation remains dominant in Japan, China plays a responsible role in Asia, India and Pakistan avoid another military conflict, the Middle East remains troubled but its problems do not contaminate other regions, the European Union prospers and strengthens its economic and political links with both Russia and China, fear is likely to decline as a foreign-policy motive and those of appetite and spirit correspondingly increase. States will have stronger incentives to seek standing on the basis of criteria associated with these motives and to spend less on the maintenance of powerful military forces. Claims for standing on the basis of military power will become even less persuasive. As standing confers influence, states will have additional incentives to shift their foreign policies to bring them into line with the dominant incentive structure. In such a world, states would view even more negatively the use of force in the absence of unqualified international support or, at the very least, authorization from the UN Security Council. From the vantage point of, say, the year 2030, we might look back on the Iraq war as one of the defining moments of the international relations of the twenty-first century because of the way it delegitimized the unilateral use of force and foregrounded and encouraged alternative, peaceful means of gaining standing.

These three shifts have two common features. Each developed slowly and progressed in fits and starts. Changes in beliefs took a long time to become sufficiently widespread to affect practice, and practice was at first halting and unsuccessful. Over time, however, patterns of behavior changed and the motives in question became increasingly disaggregated from war. These shifts in thinking did occur at the same time and certainly did not have immediate practical effects. The revolution in thinking about wealth begun in the late eighteenth century did not

---

[53] *The Age* (Melbourne), March 6, 2007, p. 7.
[54] On the Japanese debate, Rozman, "Japan's Quest for Great Power Identity"; Hughes, "Japan's Re-emergence as a 'Normal' Military Power"; Samuels, *Securing Japan*.

fully become the conventional wisdom until the late nineteenth century, and did not act as a check on war until at least a half-century later. Collective security, a product of the early nineteenth century, took almost 150 years to show meaningful political consequences. Shifts in thinking about standing is a twentieth-century phenomenon, and only began to affect political practice during the Cold War. As norms and practices have shifted more rapidly in the last fifty years, there is reason to hope that the delegitimization of standing through military conquest will become even more robust and further encourage the rise of alternative means of claiming standing.

The three shifts in thinking are to some degree related. The economic shift was largely independent of any putative lessons of international relations. It arose in response to studies of domestic political economy but was quickly seen to have important implications for foreign policy. Trade and investment are forms of international economic cooperation and encouraged hopes that this might be extended into the political sphere. Costly wars undoubtedly provided another incentive to experiment with collective security. Shifts in standing, like collective security, are largely a response to costly wars. But they are also facilitated by economic interdependence and collective security. They create closer, more cooperative relationships with other states at the official and unofficial levels, making the use of force against them increasingly costly and inappropriate. To the extent that this cooperative grouping constitutes the group which confers standing, or is important in this regard, associated states must find non-violent and even non-confrontational means of claiming standing. Of equal importance, cooperative relationships carry with them the expectation that the circle of states included in such relationships can be expanded. The use of force in circumstances where it will retard this process, or be seen to damage or undermine the security of the existing community, will be frowned upon and will damage the reputation of war-initiators. Both dynamics are currently at work in the international system.

As the shift in conceptions of standing is still in its formative stages, this author can only hope that a book that demonstrates how traditional conceptions of standing have been responsible for war can help accelerate this change and, with it, the search for and acceptance of alternative means of claiming and receiving standing.

2

Theories of war

There is a burgeoning literature in international relations on war and its causes. It is supplemented by important works in history, sociology, psychology and economics. Most of the major studies of war by international relations scholars approach it from a realist perspective. They assume security is the principal concern of states and its absence the principal cause of war. Realist theories elaborate conditions (e.g. security dilemma, polarity, power transition) thought to be responsible for acute conflicts and mechanisms (e.g. military preparedness, alliances, the balance of power) expected to determine when they lead to war. Scholars working in the liberal paradigm are more interested in peace than war and have theorized its underlying conditions. The Democratic Peace, the flagship liberal research program on this topic, stipulates that democracies do not fight one another, although its proponents disagree among themselves about why this is so. It is a narrow claim, as Democratic Peace theorists acknowledge that democracies are no less warlike than other regimes. V. I. Lenin authored a Marxist theory of war. It assumes that economic interest is the principal driver of foreign policy, and attributes World War I to competition for markets and raw materials. In the last decade, rational theories of war have gained prominence. Most embody realist principles and assume that leaders are substantively and instrumentally rational.

International relations scholars study war from diverse methodological perspectives. Some works are almost exclusively theoretical and offer no empirical evidence in support of their propositions. Scholars who employ empirical evidence use qualitative and quantitative data to develop and evaluate a wide range of theories and propositions. Scholars differ in the claims they make for their theories. Some attempt to explain war in general, while others limit their scope to great-power wars or their subset of system-transforming wars. Some assert that their theories adequately account for the kinds of wars they address. Others claim only to have discovered important conditions that make war likely but not inevitable and acknowledge the need to take into account other contributing factors.

In this chapter, I review the claims and methods of the most important of the theories of war. Some less prominent theories (e.g. diversionary theory of war, Freudian theories, Schumpeter's class-based account of World War I) I omit or refer to only *en passant* in later chapters. The Democratic Peace – which addresses the motives for peace, not for war – I will return to later in the book, when I take up the future prospects for peace. My evaluation is largely conceptual, although I question some historical interpretations that are foundational to some theories. In Chapter 4, I use my data set to assess their principal substantive claims.

Realism

Realism was once the dominant paradigm in international relations and still remains a major one.[1] Almost fifty years ago, Arnold Wolfers divided realists into two groups: those who attribute war to the "evil" arising from human nature; and those who consider war a "tragedy" arising from unavoidable systemic imperatives. In the first category, Wolfers places Thucydides, Machiavelli, Hans Morgenthau and Henry Kissinger.[2] For Morgenthau, the leading theorist of the early postwar era, all politics is conflictual because it is a manifestation of the *animus dominandi*, or lust for power. Theorists who characterize human motives as universal and immutable cannot account for variations in war and peace across epochs and cultures without invoking additional explanations. Nor can they explain why certain states are intent on challenging the *status quo* while others are keen to defend it, or why state preferences change, as Germany's did so dramatically over the course of the twentieth century.

Morgenthau introduces two intervening variables to account for such variation: the robustness of society and the motives of actors. The difference between domestic and international politics, he insists, is "one of degree and not of kind."[3] Quoting Gibbon, he describes eighteenth-century Europe as "one great republic" with common

---

[1] Jordan, Maliniak, Oakes *et al.*, "One Discipline or Many," reports on a survey that finds the three main paradigms – realism, liberalism and constructivism – are statistically even in the US with about 20 percent of scholars identifying with each. A plurality (25 percent) say that they don't identify with any paradigm.

[2] Wolfers, *Discord and Collaboration*.   [3] Morgenthau, *Politics Among Nations*, p. 21.

standards of "politeness and cultivation" and a common "system of arts, and laws, and manners." "Fear and shame" and "some common sense of honor and justice" induced leaders to moderate their ambitions.[4] The sense of community was ruptured by the French Revolution and only superficially restored in its aftermath. It broke down altogether in the twentieth century when the principal powers became divided by ideology as well as by interests. In the 1930s, by Morgenthau's count, four major powers – Germany, the Soviet Union, Japan and Italy – rejected the very premises of the international order. The Soviet Union continued to do so after 1945, reducing international politics in the early postwar era "to the primitive spectacle of two giants eyeing each other with watchful suspicion."[5] The ends pursued by the great powers as well as the means adopted to achieve them vary in the first instance as a function of their integration into a larger community based on shared values.

Morgenthau believes that state goals vary independently of the robustness of society. He describes three foreign-policy orientations: states seek to preserve the *status quo*, overturn it and display prestige. These orientations are not essential to states but change with leaders and circumstances.[6] They are not always self-evident, but assessments of them drive the balance of power, the central mechanism of Morgenthau's and many other realist theories. According to Morgenthau, war is least likely when the *status quo* powers have a clear military advantage and a demonstrable will to use it if necessary to defend the territorial *status quo* against all challengers. War is most likely when an imperialist power – his term for a state intent on challenging the *status quo* – or a coalition of such states, has a military advantage or when *status quo* powers lack the will to combine and oppose this threat. Early critics of Morgenthau object to the looseness of his concepts, especially the balance of power, which allows him to use it in multiple and seemingly contradictory ways.[7] Later critics raise a more fundamental substantive objection: Morgenthau and other realists who emphasize the balance of power appear to base their theories on a set of political and cultural assumptions most appropriate, and perhaps limited, to eighteenth-century Europe, often described the grand age of the balance of power.[8]

---

[4] *Ibid.*, pp. 159–166, 270–284; Morgenthau, *In Defense of the National Interest*, p. 60.
[5] Morgenthau, *Politics Among Nations*, p. 285.   [6] *Ibid.*, pp. 21–25, 58–60.
[7] Haas, "The Balance of Power"; Claude, *Power and International Relations*, pp. 25–37; Wight, "The Balance of Power."
[8] Watson, *Evolution of International Society*; Lebow, *Tragic Vision of Politics*; Little, *Balance of Power in International Relations*, pp. 100–124.

Realists who offer "tragic" explanations for war generally attribute it to the so-called anarchy of the international system. For "first generation" realists like Nicholas J. Spykman, Walter Lippmann, Edward Mead Earle, Frederick Schumann and E. H. Carr, the term "anarchy" was a shorthand for "the absence of government," "the law of the jungle," or "social order without hierarchy."[9] Even Morgenthau acknowledged that "cultural uniformity, technological unification, external pressure, and, above all, a hierarchic political organization," make states more stable and less subject to violent change than "the international order where these conditions are generally absent"[10]

John Herz developed the concept of the "security dilemma" to explain why states were driven to embrace violence as much by fear as by any putative lust for power. The quest for power, he argued, is frequently a response to threat, not its primary cause. States acquire power to avoid attack, domination or annihilation by others. These efforts to safeguard their security make "others more insecure and compel them to prepare for the worst. Since none can ever feel entirely secure in such a world of competing units, power competition ensues, and the vicious circle of security and power accumulation is on."[11] For Herz, the security dilemma has a "fatalistic inevitability," but he acknowledges that there is an important difference between tensions and war. Wise and courageous leaders might avoid being stampeded into war even in the tensest confrontations.[12] Like Morgenthau, his contemporary and quondam colleague, Herz emphasized the determining role of leaders. Neither specified the qualities associated with these leaders or the conditions under which they might be expected to exercise restraint.

Morgenthau and Herz situate their arguments at the system level but augment them with arguments at the state and leader levels. Kenneth Waltz developed a theory of international relations entirely at the system level. Following Herz, he reasoned that the anarchy of the international system generates insecurity and prompts states to arm themselves and prepare for war. Miscalculation is the most important cause of war and generally arises from lack of information. The international environment is partially opaque, making it difficult to estimate the capability and resolve

---

[9] Guzzini, "Concept of Power," p. 503.
[10] Morgenthau, *Politics Among Nations*, p. 21; Morgenthau, *Scientific Man vs. Power Politics*, p. 105.
[11] Herz, "Idealist Internationalism and the Security Dilemma," p. 157.
[12] Booth and Wheeler, *Security Dilemma*, p. 23.

of other actors. Miscalculation is most likely in multipolar systems where there are more actors, where alliances are more important and balance of military power and resolve accordingly more difficult to calculate.[13]

Waltz insists that he has produced a theory of international relations, not of foreign policy. He does not address variation within systems, only across them.[14] Hierarchy is the most stable and peace-prone system, followed by multi- and then bipolarity. Waltz's claims are amenable in principle to falsification, but not in the manner in which they have been formulated by Waltz. He insists that the determination of polarity is a simple matter: "We need only rank [the powers] roughly by capability."[15] Differences among realists indicate just how ambiguous, even arbitrary, such rankings are. Many realists routinely date bipolarity from 1945, but Morgenthau contends that the Soviet Union only became a superpower sometime in the 1950s when it acquired the industrial capacity for waging nuclear war.[16] Waltz, whose definition of power is similar to Morgenthau's, insists that the world became bipolar in the late 1940s.[17] In 1990, Waltz and Mearsheimer argued that bipolarity was coming to an end, or had already disappeared and given way to multipolarity.[18] By 1993, Waltz had reversed himself and insisted that the world remained bipolar despite the breakup of the Soviet Union.[19] Some realists insist that the world became "unipolar" when the United States emerged from the Cold War as the sole surviving superpower.[20] Other realists disagree and make the case for a multipolar world.[21] So much for Waltz's assertion that the question of polarity "is an empirical one," that "common sense can answer."[22]

Waltz's proposition about the probability of war in different systems could only be verified by comparisons across a large number of systems.

---

[13] Waltz, *Theory of International Politics.*
[14] *Ibid.*, pp. 71, 121, and Waltz, "International Relations Is Not Foreign Policy."
[15] Waltz, *Theory of International Politics*, pp. 129–131.
[16] Morgenthau, *Politics Among Nations*, 3rd edn., p. 114. White, "Nature of World Power in American History."
[17] Waltz, *Theory of International Politics*, pp. 180–181.
[18] Waltz, "Emerging Structure of International Politics"; Mearsheimer, "Back to the Future."
[19] Waltz, "Emerging Structure of International Politics."
[20] Krauthammer, "Unipolar Moment," and Krauthammer, "Unipolar Moment Revisited"; Wohlforth, "Stability of a Unipolar World"; Huntington, "Lonely Superpower"; Mastanduno, "Preserving the Unipolar Moment."
[21] Layne, "Unipolar Illusion"; Kupchan, "After Pax Americana."
[22] Waltz, *Theory of International Politics*, p. 131.

By even the most generous counting rules, recorded history has produced only a few hierarchical and bipolar systems. It is not clear what value Waltz's proposition would have even if it could be tested and confirmed, as statistical base rates tell us absolutely nothing about individual cases. By limiting his theory to the system level, Waltz makes it irrelevant to the real world. Some of Waltz's acolytes recognize this limitation and have tried to make neorealism relevant to foreign policy, as has Waltz himself.[23] They have introduced distinctions at the state and sub-state levels, undermining the original and principal theoretical justification of Waltz's enterprise.[24]

The most prominent effort to make neorealism relevant to foreign policy is John Mearsheimer's *The Tragedy of Great Power Politics*. It develops a deductive theory based on neorealist principles and uses it to make a series of predictions – see below – about the near future. Mearsheimer maintains that great powers have two strategic goals: to acquire as much power as possible to prevent the hegemony of other powers. Great powers, he insists, have always been willing to go to war for either goal. All of Mearsheimer's predictions about the post-Cold War world have been wrong.[25] The United States has not withdrawn from Europe, has not refused to commit its forces to maintain regional peace, has not attempted to curtail Chinese economic growth or acted as an offshore balancer. Neither Japan nor Germany have acquired nuclear weapons; there is no indication that relations among the great powers have become more tense, let alone war-prone; NATO has survived despite the end of the Cold War and disappearance of the Soviet Union; and there has been no "hard" or "soft" balancing against the United States, the sole surviving hegemon.[26]

System-level theories suffer from the problem faced by Morgenthau: if anarchy is a constant – rare epochs of hierarchy aside – the security dilemma is ever-present and cannot account for variation in the frequency or intensity of warfare. Unit- and system-level theories alike require additional, auxiliary explanations, theories or propositions. For

---

[23] Elman, "Horses for Courses"; Rose, "Neoclassical Realism and Theories of Foreign Policy"; Fearon, "Domestic Politics, Foreign Policy, and Theories of International Relations." Waltz, "Spread of Nuclear Weapons."

[24] Walt, *Origins of Alliances*; Mearsheimer, *Tragedy of Great Power Politics*; Kydd, "Sheep in Sheep's Clothing."

[25] Mearsheimer, "Back to the Future" and Mearsheimer, *Tragedy of the Great Powers*; Ikenberry, *America Unrivaled*, p. 3; Wohlforth, "US Strategy in a Unipolar World."

[26] Brooks and Wohlforth, "Hard Times for Soft Balancing."

realists of both "evil" and "tragic" orientations, the principal add-on concept is the balance of power. It is used descriptively to characterize the distribution of power in the system at any given time or the character of the system and prescriptively as a guide for foreign policy.[27] It is frequently used in confusing, even contradictory, ways because it refers to two distinct dynamics that are rarely broken out analytically. The balance of power is both the unintended consequence of great powers striving for hegemony and others combining to oppose them, and the complex of ideational and material conditions that at times allow great powers to regulate or ameliorate the consequences of the drive for hegemony.[28] The former is considered a cause of war by realists, while the latter might be considered to promote peace.

There are numerous balance of power theories and propositions. As more than one international relations scholar has lamented, there is no agreement in the discipline about what the balance of power is or what it accomplishes or is expected to accomplish.[29] By far the most common expectation is that the balance of power will prevent hegemonies from forming.[30] Hegemony is generally understood to be the capability of a great power to impose its preferences on the international system as a whole.[31] Even here there is disagreement. Some realists contend that the overwhelming power of one state (e.g. *pax Romana*, American hegemony) is conducive to peace.[32] Others insist that great concentrations of power in one or a few states makes war more likely by limiting the possibilities of blocking coalitions, thereby weakening or negating deterrence. They regard the ideal distribution of power as one in which a powerful uncommitted state, intent on upholding the *status quo*, is able to play the role of balancer (*pax Britannica*).[33] There is also a long-standing controversy about whether multipolar or bipolar systems are

---

[27] Morgenthau, *Politics Among Nations*; Kaplan, *System and Process in International Politics*; Claude, *Power and International Relations*; Little, *Balance of Power in International Relations*, pp. 2, 20, 94–96.

[28] Little, *Balance of Power in International Relations*, p. 92.

[29] Levy, "Causes of War"; Little, *Balance of Power in International Relations*.

[30] Wright, *Study of War*; Claude, *Power and International Relations*, pp. 51–56; Waltz, *Theory of International Politics*, p. 131; Mearsheimer, *Tragedy of the Great Powers*, p. 341. Also Levy, "What Do Great Powers Balance Against and When?"; Wohlforth, Little, Kaufman *et al.*, "Comedy of Errors."

[31] Doyle, *Empires*, p. 40.

[32] Organski, *World Politics*; Waltz, *Theory of International Politics*.

[33] Morgenthau, *Politics Among Nations*; Gulick, *Europe's Classical Balance of Power*; Claude, *Power and International Relations*.

more war-prone.[34] Balance of power theories predict inconsistent, if not diametrically opposed, outcomes from balance and imbalance. Richard Little observes that discussions of the balance of power devote surprisingly little attention to the even more problematic concept of "power" on which all formulations of the balance of power rest.[35]

Despite these problems, balance of power theories retain their appeal. Robert Jervis contends that the balance of power is not only the best-known, but arguably the most convincing explanation for much international behavior.[36] Empirical research nevertheless finds little or no relationship between power configurations and the incidence of war.[37] Collective action theorists describe balancing as a collective good that is difficult to bring about.[38] Realists find confirming evidence in the phenomenon of bandwagonning, where threatened states align themselves with the threatening power rather than allying with others against it. Some have explored the circumstances in which threatened states might prefer it to balancing.[39] In a recent and comprehensive study of the balance of power, Kaufman, Little and Wohlforth draw on evidence across cultures and epochs to argue that balanced and unbalanced distributions of power are about equal in frequency. Military expansion is "well-nigh universal behavior," and such aggrandizement is often tolerated by "myopic advantage-seeking" actors who pursue narrow short-term interests in preference to system maintenance.[40] Several highly regarded historical studies of the balance of power in Europe conclude that it was most effective in the eighteenth and nineteenth centuries, but attribute its success, as did Morgenthau, to the robustness of European transnational society and the skill of leaders.[41] Wight, Schroeder and Kissinger all argue that group pressures to adhere to accepted norms and

---

[34] Morgenthau, *Politics Among Nations*, 6th edn., pp. 378–379. 390–391; Kaplan, *System and Process in International Politics*, p. 34; Claude, *Power and International Relations*, p. 48; Deutsch and Singer, "Multipolar Systems and International Stability"; Rosecrance, "Bipolarity, Multipolarity, and the Future"; Waltz, *Theory of International Politics*, ch. 8.

[35] Little, *Balance of Power in International Relations*, p. 29.

[36] Jervis, *System Effects*, p. 131.

[37] Vasquez, *Power of Power Politics*; Sabrovsky, *Polarity and War*; Gochman, "Capability-Driven Disputes"; Mansfield, "Concentration of Capabilities and the Onset of War."

[38] Olson, *Logic of Collective Action*.

[39] Walt, *Origins of Alliances*; Christensen and Snyder, "Chain Gangs and Passed Bucks"; Schweller, "Bandwagoning for Profit."

[40] Kaufman, Little and Wohlforth, *Balance of Power in World History*, pp. 229–230.

[41] Gulick, *Europe's Classical Balance of Power*; Kissinger, *World Restored*; Schroeder, *Transformation of European Politics*.

practices were even more effective in restraining key state actors.[42] Morgenthau makes a similar claim in *Politics Among Nations*.[43] Narratives that look to culture to explain when and why the balance of power works only undercut its claims to universality.

Contemporary realists belong roughly to three schools of thought: offensive, defensive and classical. Offensive realism is associated with John Mearsheimer's *Tragedy of the Great Powers* and is based on a pessimistic and largely deterministic view of international relations. Many scholars in the field consider it simplistic and dangerous in its policy implications. I have already critiqued its key theoretical claims and empirical predictions. My data set offers no support for its understanding of the causes of war.

Defensive realism is a more widely accepted approach and is associated with the writings of Stephen Van Evera, Charles Glaser, Chaim Kaufman and Stephen Walt.[44] It assumes rational actors who make security their first priority because of the anarchy of the international system and the security dilemma it creates. Security comes to resemble a zero-sum game because improvement for any actor or alliance make other states and alliances more insecure. Stephen Van Evera, the original advocate of defensive realism, advances two principal propositions: war will be more common in periods when conquest is believed to be easy; and states whose leaders believe they have large offensive opportunities or defensive vulnerabilities will initiate more wars than other states. He further contends that actual imbalances that make conquest easy are rare, but erroneous perceptions of their existence are common and explain many wars. He offers World War I as a paradigmatic case.[45]

Whatever validity there is to defensive realism, World War I, on which the theory is based, turns out to be a disconfirming case. New evidence from German archives and accounts based on it dismiss fear of strategic disadvantage as a cause of German aggression in the July crisis. Chief-of-Staff Moltke had few concerns about German defensive capabilities and very little faith in his army's ability to execute the so-called Schlieffen Plan. Moltke and General Erich von Falkenhayn wanted war for reasons

---

[42] Wight, *Systems of States*, pp. 23, 149; Schroeder, "International Politics"; Kissinger, *World Restored*, p. 1.

[43] Morgenthau, *Politics Among Nations*, p. 195.

[44] Glaser, "Realists as Optimists"; Glaser and Kaufmann, "What Is the Offense–Defense Balance?"; Glaser and Walt, "International Relations"; Van Evera, *Causes of War*.

[45] Van Evera, *Causes of War*.

that had little to nothing to do with security and a lot to do with hatred of France and their belief that victory would deal a serious blow to social democracy. The Kaiser, the ultimate decisionmaker, was more concerned with upholding his and Germany's honor.[46] Defensive realists have not come up with convincing evidence that other great power wars were the result of perceptions of offensive or defensive imbalance. More importantly, as my data set will show, only a relatively small number of wars can be attributed to security as a motive.

Classical realism looks to Thucydides as its founding father and Machiavelli, Clausewitz, Herz and Morgenthau as representatives of this tradition. It is intended to serve as a normative guide and to highlight the connections between ethics and successful foreign policies. It stresses sensitivity to ethical dilemmas and the practical implications and the need to base influence, wherever possible, on shared interests and persuasion. Classical realism is realist because it recognizes the central role of power in politics of all kinds, but also its limitations and the ways in which it can be made self-defeating. It eschews formal propositions of the kind made by offensive and defensive realism because its proponents contend that decisionmaking is extremely sensitive to context and agency. Rather, classical realists describe scripts that are frequently acted out in international relations. The most important concerning war is the hubris of great powers; success encourages their leaders to overreach in the erroneous belief that they can successfully execute elaborate scenarios that require bending others to their will. Drawing on Greek tragedy, Thucydides portrays Athens and the Peloponnesian War in this light. Phillip II, Louis XIV, Napoleon, Wilhelminian and Nazi Germany followed variants of the same script, as arguably did the US in the post-Cold War world.[47] This insight of classical realism is not testable in a direct sense because it makes no predictions. However, it does suggest that a major cause of great power wars is the effort of dominant powers to extend their authority and achieve hegemony, and the related proposition that many of these wars will arise from miscalculated escalation or failure of the initiator to consider anything but a best-case scenario.

---

[46] Zuber, *Inventing the Schlieffen Plan*; Herwig, *The First World War*, pp. 18–23; Mombauer, *Helmuth von Moltke and the Origins of the First World War*; Lebow, *Cultural Theory of International Relations*, 352–365.

[47] Lebow, *Tragic Vision of Politics* and *Cultural Theory of International Relations*, pp. 459–480; Erskine and Lebow, *Tragedy and International Relations*.

Power transition

Like their balance of power counterparts, power transition theories are remarkably diverse and sometimes contradictory in their expectations. The rubric of power transition encompass power transition theories proper, theories of hegemonic war and long cycle theories into which they have been incorporated.[48] Long-cycle theories were first proposed by World War I veteran and economist Alec Macfie and are based on empirical correlations between repetitive economic phenomena and war. Macfie saw trading cycles as key; wars were most likely when economic recovery from a recession was well underway, a pattern he associated with twelve wars between 1850 and 1914.[49] More recently, Modelski and Thompson claim to have identified periodic cycles of hegemony, system management and global war that span the last five centuries. They attribute war to systemic succession crises that are brought about by changing distributions of power which in turn are the result of uneven growth rates.[50]

The most prominent power transition theory is that of Organski and Kugler, who distinguish their approach from realism on the ground that they portray the international system as more ordered than anarchical.[51] Order arises from the ability of a dominant power to impose its preferences on other actors. Over time, habits and patterns are established and states learn what to expect from one another. "Certain nations are recognized as leaders ... Trade is conducted along recognized channels ... Diplomatic relations also fall into recognized patterns ... There are rules of diplomacy; there are even rules of war."[52] Order advances the wealth, security and prestige of the dominant power, but typically at the expense of the other great powers. Dominance is seldom absolute and war is accordingly still possible. The most serious and hardest fought wars are those between dominant powers and dissatisfied

---

[48] Toynbee, *Study of War*; Väyrynen, "Economic Cycles"; Wallerstein, *The Politics of the World Economy*.

[49] Macfie, "Outbreak of War and the Trade Cycle."

[50] Modelski, "Long Cycle of Global Politics and the Nation-State"; Modelski, *Exploring Long Cycles*; Modelski, *Long Cycles in World Politics*; Thompson, "Cycles, Capabilities and War"; Thompson, "Uneven Economic Growth, Systemic Challenges, and Global War"; Thompson, "Polarity, the Long Cycle and Global Power Warfare"; Boswell and Sweat, "Hegemony, Long Waves and Major Wars"; Levy, "Long Cycles, Hegemonic Transitions and the Long Peace"; Rasler and Thompson, *Great Powers and Global Struggle*.

[51] Organski and Kugler, *War Ledger*, p. 358.   [52] *Ibid.*, pp. 315–316.

challengers. The latter are states who "have grown to full power after the existing international order was fully established and the benefits already allocated."[53] The dominant nation and its supporters are generally unwilling to grant the newcomers more than a small part of the advantages they derive from the *status quo*. Rising powers are accordingly dissatisfied and make war to impose orders more favorable to themselves.[54] War is most likely when a challenger enters into approximate parity with the dominant state in material capabilities.[55]

Organski and Kugler's theory of war is mechanical and deterministic. "The fundamental problem," they insist, "that sets the whole system sliding almost irretrievably toward war is the differences in rates of growth among the great powers and, of particular importance, the differences in rates between the dominant nation and the challenger that permit the latter to overtake the former in power. It is this leapfrogging that destabilizes the system."[56] They identify five wars of hegemonic transitions: Napoleonic, Franco-Prussian, Russo-Japanese and both world wars.

Robert Gilpin's *War and Change in World Politics* also stresses the relative balance of military power between leading states and would-be challengers. However, Gilpin focuses more on the declining than rising powers. Dominant states make cumulative commitments that come to exceed their capabilities. Imperial overstretch "creates challenges for the dominant states and opportunities for the rising states of the system."[57] The latter aspire to remake "the rules governing the international system, the spheres of influence, and most important of all, the international distribution of territory."[58] Dominant states regard preventive war as the most attractive means of eliminating the threat posed by challengers. Other possible responses are reducing commitments, cutting costs by further expansion, alliances, rapprochements and appeasing challengers.[59] For Gilpin, hegemonic wars pit dominant powers against challengers. Such wars reorder the system; they extend the dominant power's control or allow a successful challenger to impose its own order.[60] Hegemonic wars are fought *à outrance* and draw in most, if not all, great powers. As examples, Gilpin offers the Peloponnesian War, the Second Punic War, the Thirty Years War, the wars of Louis XIV, the French Revolutionary and Napoleonic Wars and World Wars I and II.[61]

---

[53] *Ibid.*   [54] *Ibid.*, pp. 364–367.   [55] *Ibid.*, pp. 19–20.   [56] *Ibid.*, p. 61.
[57] Gilpin, *War and Change in World Politics*, p. 186.   [58] *Ibid.*, p. 187.
[59] *Ibid.*, pp. 191–193.   [60] *Ibid.*, p. 198.   [61] *Ibid.*, p. 200.

Power transition theories advance three claims about war: rising powers go to war against dominant powers or are attacked by them before they are capable of initiating a successful military challenge; when hegemonic states and rising powers go to war, they do so to defend or revise the international order in their favor; war effectively resolves the conflicts of interest caused by power transitions. All three claims and the assumptions on which they rest are put forward with little to nothing in the way of empirical justification.[62]

Organski and Kugler identify five wars they maintain their theory should explain: the Napoleonic, the Franco-Prussian, Russo-Japanese and World Wars I and II. They exclude the Napoleonic War from their study on the ground that there are insufficient data on the power capabilities of the participants. They exclude the Franco-Prussian War and the Russo-Japanese War because, they contend, they were fought without allies.[63] This is factually incorrect as Prussia was backed by the North German Confederation and the South German States of Baden, Württemberg and Bavaria. They are left with two cases but provide no historical evidence to support their assertion that these are wars of power transition.

The Peloponnesian War is the only conflict for which Gilpin makes an unambiguous claim. Quoting Thucydides, he asserts that it was a preventive war initiated by Sparta.[64] He calls it a hegemonic war, defined as a conflict between or among great powers, arising from growing disequilibria in power and fought with few limitations. He maintains that hegemonic wars are always preemptive wars. There is a general perception that "a fundamental historical change is taking place and the gnawing fear of one or more of the great powers that time is somehow beginning to work against it and that one should settle matters through preemptive war while the advantage is still on one's side."[65] Gilpin gives seven additional examples: the Second Punic War, the Thirty Years War, the wars of Louis XIV, the French and Napoleonic Wars and World Wars I and II. This is an odd, even confusing, list: the Thirty Years War describes multiple wars among multiple European powers, Louis XIV was involved in several wars (and it is not clear to which Gilpin refers) and the French Revolutionary Wars ought reasonably to be broken down into the wars of the First through the Seventh Coalition.

---

[62] Lebow and Valentino, "Lost in Transition," for a more extensive critique.
[63] Organski and Kugler, War Ledger, pp. 157–158.
[64] Gilpin, War and Change in World Politics, p. 191.   [65] Ibid., p. 201.

Neither set of authors does more than assert a fit between cases and theories. For Organski and Kugler, World Wars I and II qualify because they occurred before the power of the coalition of challengers could overtake that of the coalition led by the dominant country.[66] They offer no evidence that the initiators of these conflicts understood the balance of capabilities and likely changes the same way as "objective observers" (i.e. the authors), or that they went to war for reasons having anything to do with the balance of capabilities. Gilpin's reading of the Peloponnesian War is highly questionable, and, that war aside, Gilpin does not discuss any of the wars he attributes to power transition.[67] He does not identify the combatants or the initiators or provide estimates of the balance of capabilities and expected changes in its direction. He makes no attempt to show that the initiators went to war because they feared future defeat if they remained at peace.

Most of literature on power transition that follows on Organski and Kugler and Gilpin attempts to devise measures of capability and other indicators of power but makes no effort to validate its claims by examining the motives, calculations and decisions of historical actors. An exception is Dale Copeland, who attempts to explain major wars, defined as those involving all the great powers. He attributes them to great power decline. Weak declining powers, he contends, rely on diplomacy to preserve themselves and their interests, but powerful states prefer war. In multipolar systems, they will only draw their swords if they are strong enough to take on all great powers who are not allies; defeating just a rising challenger would leave them vulnerable to other predators. In bipolar systems, the declining power need only defeat the other pole, and war is thus a more likely response to decline. Declining states resort to force only when they perceive their decline as steep and inevitable.[68] Copeland's variables are loosely defined, and his coding is sometimes at odds with his definition and the best available evidence. Decline, the critical dependent variable, is poorly operationalized. In every historical case, Copeland picks and validates a contemporary assessment (e.g. the Spartan war party, the German generals, US hardliners) that fits his theory and ignores all competing understandings. He unconvincingly portrays World Wars I and II as preventive wars started by Germany to stem its decline vis-à-vis Russia, and the Cold War as a conflict begun by the United States for the same reason.

[66] Organski and Kugler, *War Ledger*, p. 58.
[67] Lebow, *Tragic Vision of Politics*, pp. 55–114.   [68] Copeland, *Origins of Major Wars.*

A careful look at post-1648 wars offered in evidence by Gilpin, Organski and Kugler and Copeland indicates that *none* of these conflicts can persuasively be attributed to power transition. The two principal wars of Louis XIV were motivated primarily by the French king's insatiable quest for *gloire*. Louis had little concern for the power of neighboring states and insufficient awareness of the likelihood that they would combine against him.[69] The French Revolutionary Wars were not triggered by either side's concern for the balance of power. The French Assembly wanted to spread its revolution abroad while Austria and Prussia wanted to restore the old regime. In the War of the First Coalition (1792–1797), both sides erroneously expected to win a quick victory.[70] Napoleon's wars against the Rhenish states and Prussia (1806), and his invasion of Russia (1812), were pure wars of expansion, not of preemption or prevention. Neither our measures of power nor accepted historical interpretations of initiators' motives for the French Revolutionary and Napoleonic Wars is congruent with power transition theories.

World War I is frequently described as a preventive war by international relations theorists and some historians. The power transition variant of this claim rests on Germany's alleged fear of Russia and the corresponding need to implement the so-called Schlieffen Plan before Russian railway construction and mobilization reforms (the former financed by France) made it unworkable, leaving Germany vulnerable to invasion on two fronts. But as Figures 2.1 and 2.2 indicate, in terms of latent capability, Russia was substantially more powerful than Germany well before 1914; it had a roughly equivalent GDP and more than twice the population. Although Russia's railroad and mobilization programs might have made it better prepared for war in the immediate future, they did not affect the long-term balance of power between Germany and Russia. Taking power transition on its own terms, so-called objective measures confound its argument in this its key case.

New historical evidence casts additional doubt on the long-questionable claim that Germany went to war in 1914 out of concern for Russia's rising power. It is apparent that Germany's Chief-of-Staff, Helmuth von Moltke, wanted war for reasons that had little to do with strategic calculations. He hated France and wanted to punish it. He also

---

[69] Bluche, *Louis XIV*, p. 246; Blanning, *Pursuit of Glory*, pp. 538–540.
[70] Blanning, *Origins of the French Revolutionary Wars*, pp. 69–95.

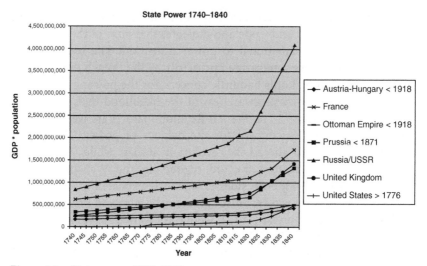

Figure 2.1   State power, 1740–1840

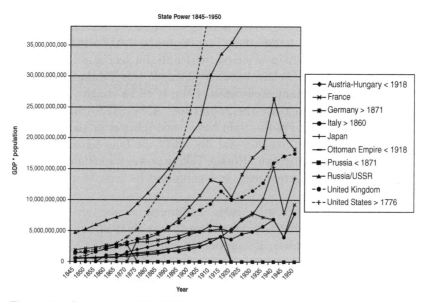

Figure 2.2   State power, 1845–1950

sought war as a means of upholding and strengthening the Junker aristocracy *vis-à-vis* the rising commercial classes and the growing appeal of materialism. German military exercises indicated that Moltke's offensive strategy was unlikely to defeat France but that a good defense could handily repel, if not crush, a combined French and Russian assault. Moltke withheld this information from the Chancellor and Kaiser and played up Germany's need to conduct an offensive before 1917 in the hope of stampeding them into war.[71] The Chancellor was influenced by Moltke, but the Kaiser – the real decisionmaker in Berlin – was inclined to draw his sword after Sarajevo for reasons of honor and self-validation.[72]

World War II is an equally problematic case for power transition. Hitler's war in the west and invasion of the Soviet Union were not driven by a fear of growing Russian or French power. Indeed, Hitler rejected the utility of conventional measures of military and economic power, emphasizing instead the determining influence of will, morale, leadership and racial purity. Hitler did – quite irrationally – fear encirclement of Germany by France, Britain and Russia, a situation he ultimately brought about by his military aggression. He saw Germany's advantage over these countries in the late 1930s as fleeting not because they were growing faster than Germany, but because none of them had fully mobilized the latent power they possessed and because he saw a passing opportunity to divide his enemies and defeat them piecemeal.[73] Beyond Hitler's recognition that he could not challenge the United States before becoming the undisputed master of Europe, there is little indication that longer-term estimates of the balance of power between Germany and its adversaries entered into his calculations.[74] This is also true for Mussolini, a rank opportunist. His goal was colonial expansion in the Mediterranean and Africa, and his attack on France was motivated by his belief that Hitler would win the war and that Italy had to join him to gain any spoils.[75] Japan possessed powerful military forces but nothing close to the power capabilities of either the Soviet Union or the United

---

[71] Zuber, *Inventing the Schlieffen Plan*; Lebow, *Cultural Theory of International Relations*, pp. 352–363.

[72] Herwig, *The First World War*, pp. 18–23; Lebow, *Cultural Theory of International Relations*, pp. 352–365, on this case and the primacy of the Kaiser.

[73] Weinberg, *The Foreign Policy of Hitler's Germany*, vol. 1, p. 358; Rich, *Hitler's War Aims*, vol. 1, pp. 3–10; Fest, *Hitler*, pp. 213–218.

[74] *Ibid.*

[75] Bosworth, *Mussolini*, p. 370; Lowe and Marzari, *Italian Foreign Policy*, pp. 133–160.

States. Its occupation of Manchuria and invasion of China was classic
imperialism and more influenced by domestic politics than strategic
calculations. Its attack on the United States and other colonial powers
in the Pacific was initiated in the unreasonable expectation that
Washington would seek a negotiated peace after sharp setbacks and
that in the absence of American support China would also come to
terms. To the extent that timing was critical, it was the tactical calculation
that within years the Western embargo on oil would make it impossible
for Japan to wage a naval war.[76]

For power transition theories, war serves the function of finalizing or
continuing one state's dominance over another, leaving the victorious state
in a better position to impose or maintain a favorable international order.
However, none of the wars cited by power transition theorists resulted in
the long-term reduction of the vanquished state's power. Organski
and Kugler identify five power transition wars: the Napoleonic, Franco-
Prussian, Russo-Japanese and World Wars I and II. France was defeated
in 1815 by a coalition of power. The victors stripped France of its
conquests but made no effort to dismember or weaken it; their primary
goal was to restore the monarchy and do so under conditions that
would help it gain legitimacy. France accordingly maintained its superiority in power over Britain and Prussia until 1870. Germany's superiority over France increased following the Franco-Prussian War, but
this had more to do with the increasing rate of growth of German power
than any reduction in France's rate of growth or its loss of Alsace-
Lorraine. Indeed, France's power continued to grow at roughly the
same or faster rate in the twenty-five years after the war as it did in
the twenty-five years before. Russia suffered a major defeat in the
Russo-Japanese war of 1904–1905, but its superiority over Japan actually increased after the war. Germany's power was only temporarily
reduced by World War I, despite its loss of considerable territory. Even
after Germany's crushing defeat and partition at the end of World War
II, the Federal Republic of Germany surpassed France and Britain in
total power by 1960.

The collapse of Austria-Hungary and the Ottoman Empire in the wake
of World War I are the principal exceptions. Austria was unambiguously
an initiator in World War I, and the Ottoman Empire entered in the
hope of gaining spoils. The war destroyed both empires. Since

---

[76] Nish, *Japan's Struggle with Internationalism*; Iriye, *Origins of the Second World War*;
Sun, *China and the Origins of the Pacific War*.

Austria-Hungary and the Ottoman Empire were the fifth- and seventh-ranked powers in Europe respectively, it also seems unlikely that their demise would have substantially increased the ability of the victorious allies to impose their preferences on the system as power transition theories expect.

War has not solved the power transition problem because most wars do not significantly reduce the basic sources of the vanquished state's power: its GDP and population. The bloodiest wars seldom kill more than 1–2 percent of a combatant country's population. Even more devastating population losses can be recovered quickly. Russia lost perhaps 25 million citizens in World War II, but its population rebounded and surpassed its pre-war levels by 1956. The only way by which war can reduce a state's long-term power is through permanent partition, dissolution, or conquest and occupation of territories containing a large proportion of its population and economic resources. A few states have pursued such aims (e.g. Napoleonic France, Wilhelminian and Nazi Germany), but have not achieved them, or did so only fleetingly.

Marxism

Like liberalism, Marxism is a theory of society with assumptions that can and have been extended to encompass the foreign policies of capitalist states, and, in the aftermath of the Bolshevik revolution, those of so-called socialist states. The most prominent Marxist analysis of war – Lenin, *On Imperialism* – was written during World War I and describes that conflict as the inevitable outgrowth of imperialism and the last gasp of mature capitalism.[77] Lenin's argument about imperialism draws as much on liberal economist John Hobson as it does on Marx.[78] He assumes that as profit rates decline at home capitalists invest abroad to make higher returns on their money by exploiting cheap labor and raw materials. The state, by now controlled by capitalist cartels, protects these investments and markets by establishing colonies. Colonial expansion postponed the crisis of capitalism but provoked a world war because by 1914 there were no new lands to conquer and the colonial powers had no recourse but to turn on one another. Marx and Engels were on the whole favorable to colonialism because it substituted capitalism for feudalism. Lenin avoided contradicting them by contending that capitalism

[77] Lenin, *On Imperialism*.
[78] Hobson, *Imperialism*; Seabrooke, "The Economic Taproot of US Imperialism."

changed from a competitive to a monopolistic form in the late nineteenth century.

On Imperialism is an intellectual *tour de force*, but clearly wrong in important respects.[79] European foreign investment did not go primarily to colonies, and overseas investment did not realize higher profits than investments at home.[80] By 1914, Britain and Germany, the most developed European countries, invested heavily in each other, other European countries, the United States and South America, and much less so in their respective colonies. The principal motive for colonies in the second half of the nineteenth century was political, not economic. Case studies indicate that colonial expansion was more often motivated by questions of standing and security, or a response to internal bureaucratic and domestic political conflicts.[81] Nor were imperial ambitions a principal motive for war in 1914. They waxed and waned with the perceived prospects of victory in World War I and were very much in the background of the decisions that led to the outbreak of that war.[82] World War I did not lead to socialist revolution and the end of capitalism. Revolution came in Russia, the least developed major power with the smallest working class, and had only short-lived secondary irruptions in Hungary and Bavaria.[83] Lenin's revolutionary project bypassed a necessary state of historical development, as did the communist takeover of China a generation later.

In recent years, the work of Italian Marxist Antonio Gramsci has loomed large in international relations theory. Gramsci wrote in the first decades of the twentieth century and was concerned with questions of uneven capitalist development and the failure of socialist revolution to

[79] Hamilton, *Marxism, Revisionism, and Leninism*, pp. 155–206; Brewer, *Marxist Theories of Imperialism*.

[80] Feis, *Europe*; Cairncross, *Home and Foreign Investment*; Edelstein, *Overseas Investment in the Age of High Imperialism*; Davis and Huttenback, *Mammon and the Pursuit of Empire*; Frieden, "International Investment and Colonial Control"; Kennedy, *Industrial Structure, Capital Markets, and the Origins of British Economic Decline*, pp. 152–153.

[81] The starting point of this debate is Robinson and Gallagher, "Imperialism of Free Trade"; and Robinson and Gallagher, *Africa and the Victorians*. See also Smith, *Pattern of Imperialism*; Mommsen and Osterhammel, *Imperialism and After*; Lebow, *Cultural Theory*, ch. 7.

[82] Hamilton and Herwig, *Origins of World War I*, offer a country-by-country overview and thoughtful general survey. Studies like Fischer, *Germany's Aims in the First World War*, which emphasize the role of imperialism and territorial expansion unfairly read back aims that developed in the course of the war into the minds of policymakers on the eve of the war.

[83] For Lenin's rejoinder, see *State and Revolution*.

THEORIES OF WAR 43

break out in the most developed capitalist states. His concept of hegemony, central to many contemporary Marxist analyses of international
relations, needs to be understood as an explanation for the uneven
development of capitalism. Marx assumes an unproblematic process of
primitive accumulation, one that severs any direct connection the mass
of producers have with the means of production – except for their own
labor – and transforms them into a mass of atomized individuals who
can be treated as commodities.[84] As capitalism spread from its English
core, Gramsci argued, it produced different kinds of social transformations because of the local constellations of political and economic forces
it encountered.

Gramsci's analysis relied on his understanding of southern Italy, a
region like Russia in the sense that it had not yet undergone extensive
capitalist development. The northern Italian bourgeoisie had not penetrated and transformed the south because of the resistance of local
landowners and the church, who had a vested interest in the *status
quo*. The southern peasantry remained tied to the land and enmeshed
in clientelist relations with landowners. They could not represent themselves because they lacked autonomous, independent, mass organizations. Political unification of Italy had been achieved through
trasformismo, an alliance of elites whose interests were in other ways
fundamentally opposed. In Gramsci's view, Lenin was right to carry out a
Jacobin coup in the name of the masses – the silent majority, so to speak.
Unless Italian communists did the same, he maintained, fascism would
crush the organized power of northern proletariat.[85]

Gramsci described how southern landowners maintained their hegemony by consent and coercion. They propagated a discourse that recon-
ciled peasants to the *status quo* and employed force against the minority
who resisted. Such a discourse blinded peasants to their class interests –
engendered "false consciousness" in Engel's terminology – but it was open
to challenge by subordinate collective actors.[86] Gramsci's conception of
hegemony recognized the power of agents and moved away from the
structural determinism of orthodox Marxism, one reason it has proven
attractive to the contemporary left. Starting with Robert Cox, neo-

---

[84] Marx, *Capital*, vol. 1, p. 875.
[85] Antonio Gramsci, "Revolution Against Capital," Milan edition of *Avanti!*, December 24,
1917; republished by *Il Grido del Popolo*, January 5, 1918.
[86] Gramsci, *Selections from the Prison Notebooks*, recognized civil society as contested
terrain, and was the first important Marxist theorist to move away from the mechanical
reduction of civil society to the political economy.

Gramscians have applied the concept of hegemony to the international system to understand the ways in which advanced capitalist states maintain themselves through a combination of discourse and coercion. In the tradition of Marxism, they envision their analyses as important contributions to the counter-hegemonic project.[87] Critics have objected to, among other things, the global application of a concept developed to explain geographically and historically specific features of capitalist social relations.[88]

Marxism is best understood as a creative attempt to understand the present and predict the future based on an early understanding of the character and likely evolution of capitalism. It suffers from many of the pitfalls associated with grand theories. It is rooted in an arbitrary *telos*, based on a single driver – class conflict – and incorporates a narrow notion of wealth – surplus value.[89] Its uncompromising determinism – Engels insisted that European history would have been the same if Napoleon had never been born – leaves little room for agency and logically undercuts its appeal as a transformative project. As Habermas notes, it ignores self-reflection, one of the defining characteristics of human beings, and, with it, their ability and commitment to alter their circumstances and thereby change the course of history.[90] Marx and his followers nevertheless deserve credit for taking their analysis of capitalism a step further than liberals. Like liberals, they consider the character of political units to be a central determinant of behavior in the international system. But, unlike liberals, Marx attempts to account for the character of those units in terms of a universal theory of historical development. While that theory may be flawed, it represents the only full-blown attempt to bridge multiple levels of analysis and show how the character of international relations in any epoch is a reflection of broader economic and political developments.

Reason and rationalist theories

Rationality is a core assumption of all existing theories of war. It provides the necessary links connecting systemic opportunities and

---

[87] Cox, "Gramsci, Hegemony and International Relations"; Gill and Law, "Global Hegemony and the Structural Power of Capital"; Murphy, "Understanding IR."

[88] Germain and Kenny, "Engaging Gramsci"; Burnham, "Neo-Gramscian Hegemony and the International Order."

[89] Hamilton, *Marxism, Revisionism, and Leninism*, for a thoughtful critique.

[90] Habermas, *Knowledge and Human Interests*, chs. 10–12; and Habermas, *Theory and Practice*, pp. 195–252.

constraints, formulations of the national interest and specific foreign policies. Traditional realist theorists (e.g. Morgenthau, Herz, Wolfers, Hoffmann), assume that leaders are, or have the potential to be, instrumentally rational. They can game the system, formulate the national interest, estimate the relative power of their own and other states, determine which of them support and oppose the territorial *status quo* and negotiate alliances with other actors who share their goals. Classical realists nevertheless recognize the inherent difficulty of these tasks and the potential for ideology, domestic political pressures and cognitive limitations to skew the judgments and choices of leaders. Morgenthau invoked all three to account for the blindness of British and French leaders in the 1930s to the threat posed by Hitler, as he did later to explain American intervention in Vietnam, which he considered sharply at odds with the national interest.[91] Morgenthau still maintained that his theory, and realism more generally, was preferable to other theories and approaches because it offered a better description of the actual behavior of states. His claim is undercut in part by his recognition that key twentieth-century policies were sharply at odds with his theory. More recently, Mearsheimer is guilty of the same kind of contradiction.

At a deeper level, realism can be faulted for its Kantian belief that reason alone can lead intelligent observers to a consensus about the national interest. In practice, all conceptions of national interest are political; they rest on subjective assumptions that reflect the ideology and interests of those who advance them. The triumph of one conception of the national interest over others is a political process, not a rational one. Failure to recognize these truths can lead realists to make absurd claims, as Mearsheimer and Walt do in their effort to explain the Iraq War. As they regard the war so contrary to American interests, they need some extraordinary explanation for it and find it in the alleged power of the Jewish lobby to bend American foreign policy to suit Israeli interests – and this despite the fact that Israeli leaders were not at all keen about the war.[92] The more telling point for our purposes is that, if realist theorists like Morgenthau, Mearsheimer and Walt describe major wars as non-rational anomalies – when viewed from the perspective of the national interest – then their theories are of little value in explaining and predicting war.

---

[91] Morgenthau, *Politics Among Nations*, 1st edn., pp. 43–44, 366–367, and 6th edn., pp. 9–10, 277–278. 372–375; Lebow, *Tragic Vision of Politics*, pp. 236–242; Scheuerman, *Hans Morgenthau*, pp. 165–195.
[92] Mearsheimer and Walt, *Israel Lobby and American Foreign Policy*.

Rather than confront this critical weakness, some realists stretch, bend and distort history to make anomalous events appear consistent with their theories and their predictions. Schweller, Copeland and Mearsheimer travel down this road. Schweller and Copeland offer reasons for considering Hitler's foreign policy rational and thus more evidence for their theories.[93] The indefensible nature of their reading of the 1930s aside, there is something morally reprehensible about theories that attempt to justify Hitler's aggressions as substantively rational.

Power transition is equally dependent on the cognitive abilities of leaders. They are expected to know which powers are rising and declining and to calculate their relative power *vis-à-vis* rivals. These assumptions are exposed as unrealistic by the research of the power transition theorists themselves. Since the publication of Organski and Kugler, other scholars have sought to test their claims by devising ever more sophisticated measures of power and the balance of power. More recent efforts to measure the degree of dissatisfaction of powers with the existing system also generate controversy.[94] Different measures lead to different assessments, and the same assessments have disputed consequences for actors. If scholars cannot agree among themselves about these fundamental issues of measurement and interpretation, how can policymakers be expected to do so?

Waltz's neorealism finesses this problem by being a theory of international relations, not of foreign policy, and by relying on system selection effects rather than reason-based adaptation by actors. He predicts a tendency toward isomorphism, with political units coming to resemble one another as states that maximize their war-fighting capabilities.[95] Alexander Wendt offers a weaker variant of this argument; he describes security needs as "objective interests," and insists, *pace* realists, that states must make them a priority. They cannot endure or change the world by ignoring them. "In the long run," he insists, "a persistent failure to bring subjective interests into line with objective ones will lead to an actor's demise."[96] This is a clever but unpersuasive move. There is no process of

[93] Schweller, *Deadly Imbalances*; Copeland, *Origins of Major War*, ch. 5; Mearsheimer, *Tragedy of Great Power Politics*, pp. 46, 181–182, 217–219.
[94] For some of this debate, see Tammen, Kugler, Lemke *et al.*, *Power Transitions*; Houweling and Siccama, "Power Transition as a Cause of War"; De Soysa, Oneal and Park, "Testing Power-Transition Theory Using Alternate Measures of Material Capabilities."
[95] Waltz, *Theory of International Politics*, p. 232.
[96] Wendt, *Social Theory of International Politics*, p. 234.

natural selection in international relations that culls the herd of actors who are weak, old or otherwise unable to compete. The number of states in the world increased from 57 in 1900 to 193 by the end of the century. In Europe, it grew, from 32 in 1945 to 47 today. Astute observers have noted that the international system is ordered in such a way to keep failed states alive, with consequences that are not always beneficial for their citizens.[97] And there is no evidence that states that lose their independence – permanently or temporarily – are any less efficient or competitive. Some well-functioning states like Estonia, Latvia and Lithuania, had the double misfortune of being small and located between rival great powers. Another common pattern is amalgamation, which often brings together well-functioning and competitively successful states, as it did in the unification of Germany and Italy, and may be doing so today in the European Union. Since 1945, the survival rate of small states has improved considerably, and some, like Singapore, the Cook Islands, Liechtenstein, Monaco and Malta, are flourishing.[98] For natural selection to work, Timothy McKeown reminds us, survival must be difficult.[99] The empirical evidence indicates that survival for states has become increasingly easy.

Darwinian selection in politics is unconvincing for a more profound reason. If a giraffe with a long neck can reach more leaves, it is more likely to survive and reproduce. Over time, the average neck length of the giraffe population has increased. Political skill is not inherited. Skillful leaders do not produce more offspring than their unsuccessful counterparts, nor are they followed in office by equally qualified successors.[100] Frederick the Great transformed Prussia from a backwater march into a great power. His descendants recklessly challenged Napoleonic France and in 1806 lost most of the territory he had gained. Hardenberg, Gneisenau and Scharnhorst reorganized the Prussian state and army, regaining their country's status as a great power. Bismarck built on this foundation, unified Germany and made it the dominant power in Europe. Wilhelm II and his advisors gambled recklessly and needlessly on victory in a European war, which led to Germany's defeat, partial dismemberment, costly reparations and restrictions on rearmament and

---

[97] Jackson and Rosenberg, "Why Africa's Weak States Persist"; Zacher, "Territorial Integrity Norm"; Sørensen, *Changes in Statehood*, chs. 8–9; Rotberg, *When States Fail.*
[98] Strang, "Anomaly and Commonplace in European Political Expansion."
[99] McKeown, "Limitations of 'Structural' Theories of Commercial Policy."
[100] Lebow, "The Long Peace."

the size of its armed forces. Gustav Stresemann made gradual but notable progress in reintegrating Germany into the European political community. Hitler led Germany into an even more destructive war that left the country smaller in size and divided into two ideologically opposed, quasi-independent, rump states. Over the course of the next half-century, the leaders of the Federal Republic of Germany pursued cautious policies that gained independence, respect and trust for their country and, ultimately, reunification. Germany's seesawing is more typical of international relations than the kind of linear development associated with evolution.

Marxism relies on the combination of reason and the unintended consequences of reason for its effects. Economic actors are assumed to be highly rational, especially capitalists who understand the advantage of large-scale production and low wages. In making their enterprises ever larger and more efficient, they create the need and opportunity for the working class to unite and carry out a socialist revolution. Capitalists are long- and shortsighted – as it suits Marxist needs. They are willing to educate and train workers, even paying indirectly for their military training, all with the goal of making them more productive in their factories and more effective on the battlefield. Marx and Gramsci also thought capitalists insightful enough to foster discourses that discourage subversive thoughts and encourage acceptance of their authority, and later Marxists describe planned obsolescence and accommodation with unions as equally clever ploys by capitalists to sustain their system. So capitalists are smart and reflective and invent various mechanisms to sustain their domination. But they are somehow prisoners of history because they are unable to grasp the longer-term consequences of their actions and the fact that world revolution is inevitable. Marxism makes capitalists thoughtful and capable of long-term planning when they need to explain the success of the system but unthinking and short-term in their horizons when they want to explain why it must fail. Marx's arguments, and Marxism in general, are riddled with contradictions.

Let us now turn to rational theories of war. I use this term to describe expected utility and game theoretic approaches that construct parsimonious and formalized theories of war. Like other rational choice theorists, they assume that actors are capable of "choosing the best means to gain a determined set of ends."[101] Rational theories of war make

---

[101] Morrow, *Game Theory for Political Scientists*, p. 17; Green and Shapiro, *Pathologies in Rational Choice Theory*, p. 17.

additional demands. They require actors to have transitive preferences, engage in Bayesian updating and resort to sophisticated forms of signaling to convey their preferences, commitments and resolve and to gain information about the capabilities and intentions of other actors. Leaders are also assumed to be free of any ideological commitments, political constraints and psychological pressures that might interfere with the application of pure reason to foreign-policy decisionmaking.

Rationalist theories differ in their understandings of war. Starting from the premise that war is a rational act, they look for conditions that would justify, or, at least, account for, it. An early example is Bruce Bueno de Mesquita's expected utility theory of war.[102] He asserts that states of all kinds, not just great powers, go to war when the expected benefits exceed the expected costs. Leaders who start wars expect to win, and do so in practice. He treats leaders as single actors able to veto a decision for war, but not always with sufficient authority to impose their preferences on others. They are rational, expected utility maximizers with different propensities for risk-taking and uncertain about the behavior of other states. He reasons that the probability of success in war is a function of a state's relative military capabilities; that military capability declines as the distance from the state that applies it increases; and that utilities are a function of the congruence of the policy objectives of states, reflected in their formal alliances. Given these assumptions, leaders calculate the benefits of victory against the costs of defeat, with victory and defeat weighted by their likely probability. These probabilities in turn are influenced by the loss of military capability as a linear function of distance and the likely consequences of third party intervention on either side. Here, alliances are used as surrogate measures of congruence of interest between and among states. Bueno de Mesquita tests his theory against data from the Correlates of War (COW) project and claims that it does a better job than power capability theories of predicting the onset of war from 1816 to 1980.

Bueno de Mesquita's model met with equal degrees of praise and criticism. Critics have questioned the realism of his assumptions about policymakers, binary outcomes of war and peace, treatment of conflict as a zero-sum game, use of alliances as measures of interests, failure to recognize and address the ambiguity surrounding efforts to determine the initiator of a war, failure to consider preemption as a possible response by the state about to be attacked, failure to take into account

[102] Bueno de Mesquita, *War Trap*.

Table 2.1 *Post-1945 wars*

War name	Dates	Military victory	Achieves war aims
First Kashmir Side A: India Side B: Pakistan	1947–1949	No	No

War of Israeli Independence
Side A: Coalition: Egypt (A1),
    Iraq (A2), Jordan (A3),
    Syria (A4)
Side B: Israel
	1948–1949	No	No

China–Tibet I Side A: China Side B: Tibet	1950	Yes	Yes
Korean Side A: Coalition: China (A1), North Korea (A2) Side B: US	1949–1953	No	No
Russo-Hungarian Side A: Hungary Side B: Russia (Soviet Union)	1956	Yes	Yes
Sinai/Suez Side A: Egypt Side B: Coalition: Israel (B1), France (B2), UK (B3)	1956	Yes	Yes
Vietnam Side A: North Vietnam Side B: US	1959–1975	No	No
Indo-Chinese Side A: China Side B: India	1962	Yes	Yes
Second Kashmir Side A: India Side B: Pakistan	1965	No	No
Six Day War Side A: Coalition: Egypt (A1), Iraq (A2), Syria (A3) Side B: Israel	1967	No	No
US–Cambodia	1971	No	No

Table 2.1 (*cont.*)

War name	Dates	Military victory	Achieves war aims
Israel–Egypt (War of Attrition) Side A: Egypt Side B: Israel	1969–1970	No	No
Football (El Salvador– Honduras) Side A: El Salvador Side B: Honduras	1969	Yes	Yes
India–Pakistan (Bangladesh) Side A: India Side B: Pakistan	1971	Yes	Yes
Yom Kippur Side A: Coalition: Egypt (A1), Syria (A2) Side B: Israel	1973	No	No
Cyprus Side A: Greece Side B: Turkey	1974	Yes	Yes
Vietnam–Cambodia Side A: Cambodia Side B: Vietnam	1977–1979	Yes	No
Ethiopia–Somalia (Ogaden) Side A: Coalition: Cuba (A1), Ethiopia (A2) Side B: Somalia	1977–1978	No	No
Uganda–Tanzania Side A: Tanzania Side B: Uganda	1978–1979	No	No
First Sino-Vietnamese Side A: China Side B: Vietnam	1979	No	No
Iran–Iraq Side A: Iran Side B: Iraq	1980–1988	No	No
Falklands/Malvinas War (UK–Argentina) Side A: Argentina Side B: UK	1982	No	No

Table 2.1 (*cont.*)

War name	Dates	Military victory	Achieves war aims
Israel–Syria (Lebanon) Side A: Israel Side B: Syria	1982	No	No
Second Sino-Vietnamese Side A: China Side B: Vietnam	1987	No	No
Iraq–Kuwait Side A: Iraq Side B: Kuwait/US	1990–1991	No	No

Democratic Republic of
  Congo–Rwanda/Uganda
Side A: Democratic Republic
  of Congo
Side B: Coalition: Rwanda (B1),
  Uganda (B2)
	1998–2003	Yes	No

Ethiopia–Eritrea Side A: Eritrea Side B: Ethiopia	1998–2000	No	No
Afghanistan (Taliban)–US (Northern Alliance) Side A: Afghanistan Side B: US	2001	Yes	No
Anglo-American Invasion of Iraq Side A: Iraq Side B: US	2003	Yes	No
Russian incursion into Georgia	2008	Yes	Yes

Note: the table was prepared by Benjamin Valentino and the author.

the expected costs of war, and failure to allow for any bargaining and strategic interaction between the would-be attacker and its target and their respective allies.[103]

[103] Zagare, "Review of *The War Trap*"; Majeski and Sylvan, "Simple Choices and Complex Calculations"; Khong, "War and International Theory"; Levy, "Causes of War."

Bueno de Mesquita and collaborators have attempted to rectify some of these problems in subsequent publications.[104] They still ignore the role of domestic and bureaucratic politics, ideology, learning and psychological processes, all of them contextual features that case studies indicate are critical determinants of decisions for war and peace. Surprisingly, nobody has faulted Bueno de Mesquita for his fundamental, empirical assumption: a strong positive correlation between the expectations of leaders and the outcomes of their policies. Such an assumption is critical to rational models, because, if we find that leaders routinely lose the wars they start, they must be making their decisions for war on some very different basis than supposed by Bueno de Mesquita and his colleagues.

Benjamin Valentino and I tested this proposition on the thirty-one interstate wars fought since 1945 involving a minimum of 1,000 casualties. We found that only eight initiators (26 percent) achieved their wartime goals. If we relax our criterion for success and make it simply the defeat of the other sides' armed forces, the number of successful initiators rises to only ten (32 percent).[105] To the extent there is a war trap, it is the opposite of the one posited by Bueno de Mesquita. In the postwar world – and earlier as well, my data set will show – leaders routinely lose the wars they start. This outcome cannot be attributed to incomplete information because in many, if not most, of these conflicts information was available to initiators beforehand indicating that war would not achieve its intended goals. Examples include the US crossing of the 38th Parallel in 1950, India's challenge to China in 1962 and China's invasion of Vietnam in 1979.[106] In other cases, where the information was ambiguous in its implications, initiators often did little to probe their adversaries' resolve or capability and left themselves without any realistic route of retreat. Examples include Argentina's invasion of the Falklands/Malvinas in 1982 and Iraq's invasion of Kuwait in 1990.[107]

Geoffrey Blainey raises a different objection to the kind of argument made by Bueno de Mesquita. Wars have two sides and the leaders of both generally have optimistic expectations about the outcome.[108] In this situation, as sociologist Georg Simmel noted back in 1904, some element of miscalculation must, of necessity, enter into the picture. War provides

---

[104] Bueno de Mesquita, "War Trap Revisited"; Bueno de Mesquita and Lalman, "Reason and War"; Morrow, "A Continuous Outcome Expected Utility Theory of War"; and Morrow, "On the Theoretical Basis of a Measure of National Risk Attitudes."
[105] Lebow, Cooperation, Conflict and Ethics, pp. 13–15.
[106] Lebow, Between Peace and War, ch. 6; Logevall, Choosing War.
[107] Lebow, Between Peace and War; Gordon and Trainor, Cobra II; Isakoff and Corn, Hubris.
[108] Blainey, Causes of War, pp. 112–115.

the most compelling means of determining who has superior capability and more faithful allies, but it is a very costly way of answering this question.[109] It can be costly enough to weaken both sides and make them relatively weaker in the war's aftermath than third parties who did not enter the conflict. Given these absolute and relative costs, rational actors could presumably find some other way of settling disputes. James Fearon reaches the same conclusion. Although states have different levels of power and opposing preferences, these differences do not provide rational grounds for war. Rationalist theories in this view fail to address, or address effectively, the central puzzle: "that war is costly and risky, so rational states should have incentives that all would prefer to the gamble of war." A good rationalist theory must demonstrate why states cannot find this preferable outcome. Fearon explores three causal logics that might account for this behavior. Rational leaders may be unable to find a mutually acceptable agreement because each side has incentives to misrepresent its capabilities and resolve. They may find such an agreement but be unable to commit to it because one or both sides do not trust the other to abide by its terms. Or, they may fail to find an agreement because certain issues are indivisible, either/or propositions. He reasons that the combination of the first two logics can bring about a deadlock and war in situations where a mutually acceptable bargain exists.[110]

Fearon's logic is unobjectionable, but its relevance to the real world is another matter. Beyond rationality, it implicitly assumes that the conflicts in question are the only ones of concern to leaders, or that they can be addressed independently of their perceived consequences for other foreign and domestic problems. Leaders invariably see connections between particular disputes and broader conflicts: John F. Kennedy framed his response to the discovery of Soviet missiles in Cuba in terms of its expected consequences for the Western position in Berlin; and Margaret Thatcher was concerned about the implications of her policy in the Falklands for the future of South Georgia, Belize and Hong Kong.[111] Both leaders were also concerned about the domestic consequences of any agreement: Kennedy feared that concessions could lead to his defeat in the next election, even his impeachment. The Argentine junta had the same fears when confronted with the extraordinary outpouring of popular support for their occupation of the Falklands, which

---

[109] Simmel, *Englischsprächige Veröffentlichungen*, p. 299.
[110] Fearon, "Rationalist Explanations for War."
[111] Lebow, "Miscalculation in the South Atlantic."

convinced them not to withdraw their forces as originally planned. Thatcher worried about losing office if she did not dislodge the Argentines from the Falklands.[112] Considerations of these kinds do not necessarily make war rational, but are necessary to understand why bargains are struck in some instances and not in others. So are other factors, such as the expected cost of war, which is a principal reason why Kennedy and Khrushchev were so desperate to reach an accommodation in the missile crisis.[113] German and Austrian decisionmaking in World War I, the case most extensively discussed by Fearon, was governed by considerations entirely outside his model. Failure to reach an agreement had little to do with misrepresentation of capabilities or intentions – those of Austria-Hungary were patently obvious to other actors – nor was it attributable to commitment problems. For Austrian leaders, war was the only outcome understood as honorable and they did everything possible to make an accommodation impossible.[114] Like all simplistic formulations in international relations, Fearon's theory offers little insight into as complex a phenomenon as war. It is not even useful as a benchmark against which to evaluate real-world behavior because it directs our attention to considerations independent of the context in which they take on meaning.

Game theorist Robert Powell also attributes war to information problems. "A purely informational problem exists when states fight solely because of asymmetric information. Were there complete information, there would be no fighting." For Powell, rapid and significant changes in power capabilities give rise to two-stage games in which peaceful interaction is not always the rational choice because there are situations in which preventive war makes sense for a state. When the costs of military preparations and readiness are taken into account, he asserts, "states may prefer fighting if the long-term cost of continually procuring the forces needed to perpetually deter an attack on the *status quo* is higher than the expected cost of trying to eliminate the threat."[115]

The most recent entry in the field is Charles Glaser, who has produced a rationalist theory of international relations. His theory requires states to possess substantive as well as instrumental rationality. "States are assumed to be able to identify and compare options, evaluating the prospects that

[112] Ibid.
[113] Bundy, Danger and Survival, pp. 403–413, 436–445; Garthoff, Reflections on the Cuban Missile Crisis, pp. 76–96; Lebow and Stein, We All Lost the Cold War, pp. 94–148, 348–368.
[114] Herwig, First World War, pp. 8–18; Lebow, Cultural Theory of International Relations, ch. 7.
[115] Powell, "War as a Commitment Problem."

they will succeed, as well as their costs and benefits." They must also "hold beliefs and understandings that are well matched to the evidence available about their international situation; without holding these beliefs a state would be unable to choose an optimal strategy." Toward this end, states must "invest an appropriate amount of effort into collecting and evaluating information that would inform them about their environment."[116] Glaser's theory builds on material and informational variables. The former determine a state's military capabilities, and the latter, what it knows about an adversary's motives and what it believes about its own. The interaction of these variables with a state's motives determines its choice of strategies. Following Arnold Wolfers, a traditional realist, Glaser recognizes only two types of motives: security and greed.[117] States motivated by security should be more accepting of the *status quo* and more inclined toward cooperative policies. However, if possession of more territory would make a state better able to defend itself and reduce an adversary's willingness to attack, it should be more inclined toward war.[118]

Rationalist theories of this kind are open to devastating criticisms. First and foremost, their assumptions are unrealistic. Political leaders do not often exhibit the kind of instrumental rationality required by these theories, especially when considering such highly charged emotional issues like peace and war. Nor can states effectively be "black boxed," arbitrarily making their leadership unitary and unconstrained by domestic politics and goals. Case studies show that preferences are not necessarily transitive and often change in the course of bargaining, that leaders have difficulty estimating risk, in distinguishing signals from noise, in understanding the meaning of what they recognize as signals, and do not update expectations in conformity with Bayesian models.[119] The concept of moves, central to most of these theories, is hard to map onto real-world crisis bargaining given the proclivity of leaders to interpret signals as noise and *vice versa*.[120]

Rationalist theorists respond to these criticisms in two ways. They dismiss them as beside the point because they make no pretense of describing real-world behavior. Charles Glaser declares himself agnostic

---

[116] Glaser, *Theory of Rational International Politics*, pp. 1–3; Elster, *Solomonic Judgments*, pp. 3–7.

[117] Wolfers, *Discord and Collaboration*.

[118] Glaser, *Theory of Rational International Politics*, pp. 4–5.

[119] Garthoff, *Détente and Confrontation*; Lebow and Stein, *We All Lost the Cold War*; Lebow, "Beyond Parsimony."

[120] Lebow, "Beyond Parsimony."

about whether states act rationally. If they behave irrationally, he concedes, his theory "will do less well at explaining past behavior." Glaser's nonchalance is difficult to fathom as a theory that bears little resemblance to reality is hardly worth the effort. Physical scientists would never grant such a theory scientific status, and some level this charge against string theory, which has become increasingly arcane and untestable by presently available means.[121] Even more than string theory, rationalist theories of war have become self-referential and defend themselves on the basis of their internal logic.

Another common response is to fall back on the argument of economist Milton J. Friedman, who famously asserted that there need be no correspondence between the assumptions of a theory and reality. *Pace* Friedman, Bueno de Mesquita insists that his theory should be assessed solely on the basis of its ability to explain and predict outcomes. Not surprisingly, unrealistic assumptions of the kind he builds his model on make it incapable of predicting real-world outcomes.[122]

Rationalist models might still be useful if they could identify and analyze dynamics that shape actual behavior; this was the intended goal of Morgenstern and von Neumann, the creators of game theory. Such models might provide a template against which to measure and understand actual behavior, a goal that is not infrequently proclaimed. They fail to serve either end. The equilibria they find depend entirely on the assumptions built into the models. Different assumptions and causal logics lead to different equilibria. Without attempting to evaluate these models and their assumptions against real behavior, we cannot know which – if any – capture the dynamics of actual crises. The same failing renders them useless as templates.

Rationalist models also have a naïve understanding of rationality: they assume it is independent of context and culture. Early critics of game theory were quick to point out that instrumental reasoning required actors to make trade-offs between their goals and the risks they appeared to entail.[123] These trade-offs are determined by the values of actors, not the logic of any game. It is arbitrary to rely on any algorithm like "minimax," the standard choice of many first-generation game theorists, to address these trade-offs. This problem has not been solved by later theorists, nor can it be by its very nature. We must look outside the game and beyond

[121] Woit, *Not Even Wrong*, pp. ix–xiii; Smolin, *Trouble with Physics*, pp. 1–17.
[122] Friedman, "Methodology of Positive Economics"; Moe, "On the Scientific Status of Rational Models," for a critique.
[123] Rapoport, *Strategy and Conscience*.

the preferences of actors to their motives and values. Prospect theory demonstrates that actors who frame their goals as loss-avoidance rather than gain-seeking will be more risk-prone.[124] This also appears to hold true for foreign policy decisionmakers.[125] Elsewhere I have offered a refinement of prospect theory based on the assumption that risk-taking varies as a function of the motives of actors. When motivated by spirit or fear, actors respond to risk differently than they do when motivated by interest. This pattern is also evident in foreign-policy choices.[126]

Rationalist theories require substantive assumptions about the motives of actors and their risk-taking propensities. Their authors tend to smuggle them into their models. For the most part, they rely on variants of realist theories; Glaser, to his credit, is explicit about his choice, although he offers no defense of why he has chosen one set of assumptions versus others. Rationalist theories, in effect, build on arbitrary assumptions and arbitrary decision rules to produce arbitrary theories that ignore political reality and show a poor fit with it.

Correlational studies of war

Correlational studies of war are primarily a postwar phenomenon. They were given a big boost by the Correlates of War (COW) project started in 1963 at the University of Michigan.[127] The original approach of COW was inductive: its originators sought to construct a data set that would allow a search for regularities. In recent decades, researchers have used COW and other data sets, including those compiled by Jack Levy and the Peace Research Institute Oslo, to test a series of propositions about the causes and consequences of war. Statistical studies have not led to any theories of war, although they have been used to test a wide range of propositions and other theories. They have generated some interesting empirical findings. Summarizing this literature, Daniel Geller reports that: "Geographic proximity/contiguity, static parity in capabilities and shifts toward parity, unbalanced external alliance ties, and the presence

---

[124] Kahneman and Tversky, "Prospect Theory"; Kahneman and Tversky, "Loss Aversion in Riskless Choice"; and Kahneman and Tversky, *Choices, Values, and Frames*.

[125] Levy, "Loss Aversion, Framing, and Bargaining"; Farnham, *Avoiding Losses/Taking Risks*; McDermott, Special Issue of *Political Psychology* on Prospect Theory; McDermott, *Risk-Taking in International Politics*; Welch, *Painful Choices*.

[126] Lebow, *Cultural Theory of International Relations*.

[127] Suzuki, Krause and Singer, "Correlates of War Project," for an historical overview.

of an enduring rivalry are factors substantially and positively associated with the occurrence of both militarized disputes and wars."[128]

To make any claims for external validity, statistical studies must meet two fundamental conditions: individual cases must be comparable and independent of one another. Existing data sets of war fall short on both counts. Even post-1648, wars have occurred in widely varying cultural, political and technological contexts, making comparisons meaningless in the absence of some serious efforts to take these differences into account. Great power war in the eighteenth century, waged by dynastic rulers using a mix of mercenary and conscript armies, differed greatly from warfare among industrialized states in the early twentieth century, many of whose leaders were beholden, formally or informally, to public opinion. Both contexts differ from the Cold War, with its potential to go nuclear and destroy the states and peoples involved. Some of these differences are more apparent in retrospect than they were to policy-makers at the time. So our understanding of context, as important as it is, must be approached through the understanding of relevant actors. Existing data sets rarely account for context, and never, to my knowledge, code relevant variables from the perspective of actors.[129]

Wars are rarely independent, as they often come in clusters. One war can trigger another, and one cluster can generate a set of lessons that are applied to future challenges, whether germane or not. Japan's invasion of China in 1931, Italy's attack on Abyssinia in 1935, Italian, German and Soviet intervention in the Spanish Civil War, the Soviet–Japanese clash in Mongolia in 1939 and the Russo-Finnish War of the same year were part of the run-up to and inseparable from World War II. That war in turn is really a general signifier for even more closely related wars: the German and Soviet invasions of Poland, Germany's war in the West, the Italian attack on France, German subjugation of Yugoslavia, Albania and Greece, the German invasion of the Soviet Union, the undeclared naval war in the Atlantic between the US and Germany, the Japanese attack on the Western powers in the Pacific, and official US entry into the war. Many of these components of World War II can be treated analytically as separate wars, the same way the various coalitions in the French and Napoleonic Wars are routinely described as separate, if related, wars.

---

[128] Geller, "Explaining War"; Vasquez, "Why Do Neighbors Fight?"
[129] Many of these points are made by Suganami, *On the Causes of War*, pp. 104–111. Vasquez, *War Puzzle*, pp. 58–60, also acknowledges fundamental differences in war across the ages.

Conversely, World War II and World War I, or at least their European components, can be lumped together as part of a thirty-year continental war. The precedent here is the Peloponnesian War (415–404 BCE), which Thucydides treats as a single conflict but contemporaries considered a successor war to the Archidamian War (431–421 BCE). The Thirty Years War and the French Revolutionary Wars, often used to describe a series of related wars, continue the tradition.

Any of these descriptions is acceptable, and all pose problems for data sets. If general wars are broken down into their individual components, they will be treated as independent cases, which they really are not. If they are coded as part of a single war, they hide the complexity and multiplicity of its several components. Both choices privilege efficient causes of different kinds. The first encourages us to look for general explanations for a war cluster, and the latter more idiosyncratic explanations for its individual components.

Wars are often related in a second sense: policymakers and their advisors confront contemporary challenges in terms of the lessons they have learned from past cases they consider comparable.[130] Appeasement was in part a response to the belief that deterrence and arms races had helped to provoke World War I, and the centrality of deterrence and arms buildups in the Cold War were a response to the belief that appeasement had been responsible for World War II.[131] American intervention in the Korean War cannot be understood in the absence of the alleged lessons of the failure to practice deterrence in the 1930s.[132] Successive American administrations have approached post-Cold War confrontations in terms of the lessons they learned, appropriate or not, from the Cold War. India and Pakistan in turn think about nuclear weapons and their implications for their conflict in terms of lessons they learned from the Cold War.[133]

There is a further problem to consider: the failure of any existing data sets to take into account the independent importance of immediate causes of war. Statistical studies of war assume that underlying causes are determining, and that, if they are present, something will happen to bring about a war. War usually requires a catalyst, and in 1914 it was provided by the assassinations of Archduke Franz Ferdinand and his wife Sophie at Sarajevo. I have argued elsewhere that not any catalyst would do, only one that met

---

[130] Khong, *Analogies at War.*   [131] Lebow, "Generational Learning and Foreign Policy."
[132] Neustadt, *Presidential Power*, pp. 120–145; Spanier, *The Truman–MacArthur Controversy*, pp. 104–113; Lebow, *Between Peace and War*, pp. 148–216.
[133] Paul, *Tradition of Non-Use*, pp. 124–142.

a series of conditions, among them creating a situation to which the Austrians felt honor-bound to respond: removing Franz Ferdinand, the major exponent in Austria of peace with Russia; allowing the German Kaiser and Chancellor to support Austria without accepting responsibility for war; and making it possible for German Chancellor Bethmann Hollweg to win the support of the socialists for war. Sarajevo was more of a cause in its own right than a catalyst and the result of another independent chain of causation.[134] Albert Hirschman has made a similar claim about the Russian Revolution.[135] There is no reason to think that Sarajevo or the Russian Revolution are unique. In the absence of an appropriate catalyst or confluence, events like wars and revolutions will not occur even if the appropriate underlying conditions are present. The only exception in the case of war are situations in which a state is intent on war and prepared to invent a pretext if one does not conveniently come along.[136] To address this problem, statistical studies would require two-stage data sets that take underlying and immediate causes into account.[137]

These problems may explain the character and quality of the findings of correlational studies. As noted at the outset of this section, the key findings are that geographic proximity, static parity in capabilities and shifts toward parity, unbalanced external alliance ties, and the presence of an enduring rivalry are all positively correlated with war. None of these findings are counter-intuitive and none could be said to pass the "grandmother test," something that any lay person might not reasonably propose after a few minutes of reflection. Nor do these propositions explain much of the variance, which is not surprising given the limitations of data sets and the complexity of war and its causes.

Almost six decades of reading history and five of writing detailed case studies of the crises, the origins of wars and the resolution of international conflicts have convinced me that major international developments almost invariably have multiple and reinforcing causes.[138] In a recent book, *Forbidden Fruit: Counterfactuals and International Relations*, I argue that such events are often the result of a non-linear confluence of causal chains with independent causes. World War I was produced by the confluence of three such chains that made leaders in

---

[134] Lebow, *Forbidden Fruit*, ch. 3. [135] Hirschman, *Exit, Voice, and Loyalty*, p. 343.
[136] Lebow, *Between Peace and War*, ch. 2, for an analysis of this situation.
[137] For an exchange on this question, see Thompson, "A Street Car Named Sarajevo"; Lebow, "A Data Set Named Desire."
[138] This point is also made by Vasquez, "Reexamining the Steps to War."

Vienna, Berlin and St. Petersburg significantly more willing to risk war in 1914 than they had been a year or two before. World War I was by no means unique in its causal complexity.[139] The kinds of data sets and statistical tests routinely used by quantitatively oriented international scholars to test theories of war cannot address this complexity.

The complex causation of many wars represents a serious challenge for theory-building. The most theories can do, I believe, is to identify pathways to war. Whether or not these pathways lead to war will almost always depend on factors outside any theory, most notably agency and chance in the form of events or confluences that make leaders more willing to go to war or risk it in pursuit of their political goals. In a recent study, Senese and Vasquez rather nicely describe one such pathway: that between rivals of roughly equal power that involves alliances, arms buildups and crises. They acknowledge that this pathway does not describe every war and does not inevitably lead to war, as the Cold War was resolved peacefully.[140]

Multiple pathways to war and the possible independence of catalysts necessary to start them also create serious problems for theory testing. How then could we evaluate the claims of competing theories and propositions about the causes of war? One strategy would be to turn to existing theories to describe different pathways to war. We could then seek to discover what sets these pathways in motion, that is, to push causation back another level. The next step would be to identify background conditions that might accelerate or impede these pathways to war, because all of them unfold in a wider political context. Finally, we would turn to the problem of immediate causes of war and try to ascertain the kinds of catalysts that might move any of these pathways toward war. To what extent are these catalysts common, infrequent or rare, and linked to or independent of our underlying causes? The complexity of any causal model developed by this method and the number of variables it generates creates another kind of problem. Statistical testing would require large data sets of comparable cases, a condition that cannot be met given the limited number of modern wars. An alternative strategy, which I lay out in *Forbidden Fruit*, works backwards from wars and their catalysts to underlying causes by means of counterfactual thought experiments and process tracing. This method too has drawbacks but is more suitable to studying causation in situations where the size of our data set is severely restricted.[141]

---

[139] Lebow, *Forbidden Fruit*.   [140] Senese and Vasquez, *Steps to War*.
[141] Lebow, *Forbidden Fruit*, chs. 3 and 9.

PART II

War in the past

## 3

Theory and propositions

Following the ancient Greeks, I contend that appetite, spirit and reason are fundamental drives, each seeking its own ends.[1] Existing paradigms of international relations are nested in appetite (Marxism, liberalism) or fear (realism). The spirit – what the Greeks often called *thumos* – had not until recently generated a paradigm of politics, although Machiavelli and Rousseau recognized its potential to do so. Using Homer's *Iliad* as my guide, I constructed an ideal-type honor society in *A Cultural Theory of International Relations* and used it as a template to analyze the role of the spirit in international relations in the ancient and modern worlds. In this chapter, I provide a brief overview of the characteristics and tensions of spirit-based worlds and their implications for warfare. In this connection, I derive six propositions about the origins of war which I then test against a data set.

I limit myself to four underlying motives: appetite, spirit, reason and fear. Modern authorities have offered different descriptions of the psyche and human needs. Freud reduces all fundamental drives to appetite, and understands reason only in its most instrumental sense. Another prominent formulation is Abraham Maslow's hierarchy of needs, developed from his study of great people and what accounted for their accomplishments.[2] More recently, psychologists have sought to subsume all human emotions to seven fundamental ones.[3] Maslow's hierarchy of needs is conceptually confusing and rooted in a distinctly nineteenth-century understanding of human nature.[4] Contemporary psychology's efforts to classify emotions assumes that its typology is universally applicable, which is highly questionable.[5] Even if defensible, this and other typologies include emotions like love, sadness and joy that can hardly be

---

[1] Lebow, *Cultural Theory of International Relations*.
[2] Maslow, *Motivation and Personality*; Maslow, *Toward a Psychology of Being*.
[3] Ekman, *Emotions Revealed*.
[4] Lebow, *Cultural Theory of International Relations*, pp. 132–133, for a critique.
[5] Konstan, *Emotions of the Ancient Greeks*, ch. 1.

considered central to foreign-policy decisionmaking. Other emotions, like anger, surprise, disgust and contempt, have more relevance but, I contend, can effectively be reduced to one or the other of my four motives.

The spirit

A spirit-based paradigm starts from the premise that people, individually and collectively, seek self-esteem. Self-esteem is a sense of self-worth that makes people feel good about themselves, happier about life and more confident in their ability to confront its challenges. It is achieved by excelling in activities valued by one's peers or society and gaining respect from those whose opinions matter. By winning the approbation of such people we feel good about ourselves. Self-esteem requires some sense of self but also recognition that self requires society because self-esteem is impossible in the absence of commonly shared values and accepted procedures for demonstrating excellence.

The spirit is fiercely protective of one's autonomy and honor, and for the Greeks the two are closely related. According to Plato, the spirit responds with anger to any restraint on its self-assertion in private or civic life. It wants to avenge all affronts to its honor, and those against its friends, and seeks immediate satisfaction when aroused.[6] Mature people are restrained by reason and recognize the wisdom of the ancient maxim, as Odysseus did in the *Odyssey*, that revenge is a dish best served cold.[7]

Self-esteem is a universal drive, although it is conceived of differently by different societies. For the Greeks, identity was defined by the sum of the social roles people performed, so esteem (how we are regarded by others) and self-esteem (how we regard ourselves) were understood to be more or less synonymous because the latter depended on the former. For modern Westerners, esteem and self-esteem are distinct terms and categories and are no longer synonymous. We also distinguish external honor – the only kind the Greeks recognized – from internal honor, a modern Western concept associated with behavior in accord with our values. We can act in ways that provoke the disapproval of others but still feel good about ourselves if that behavior reflects our values and beliefs and confers internal honor. We must nevertheless be careful about making hard and fast distinctions between Greeks and moderns because there is some evidence that internal honor was not entirely foreign to Athenians. Socrates accepts his death sentence, when it may have been

---

[6] Plato, *Republic*, 440c–441c.   [7] Homer, *Odyssey*, Books 18–22.

intended to make him go into exile, which is what his friends plead with him to do, because he insists on behaving in a manner consistent with his beliefs.[8]

People can satisfy some appetites by instinct, but must be taught how to express and satisfy the spirit through activities deemed appropriate by their society. They need appropriate role models to emulate. For Aristotle, emulation, like so much behavior, is motivated by pain and pleasure. We feel pain when we observe people, whom we consider much like ourselves, and who have qualities and positions to which we aspire. To escape this pain we act in ways that make it possible for us to possess these goods and feel pleasure when we obtain them.[9]

Societies have strong incentives to nurture and channel the spirit. It engenders self-control and sacrifice from which the community as a whole prospers. In warrior societies, the spirit finds expression in bravery and selflessness, from which the society as a whole profits. All societies must restrain, or deflect outwards, the anger aroused when the spirit is challenged or frustrated. The spirit is a human drive; organizations and states do not have psyches and cannot be treated as persons. They can nevertheless respond to the needs of the spirit the same way they do to the appetites of their citizens. People join or support collective enterprises in the expectation of material and emotional rewards. They build self-esteem the same way, through the accomplishments of the groups, sports teams, nations and religions with which they affiliate. Arguably, the most important function of nationalism in the modern world is to provide vicarious satisfaction to the spirit.

There are a bundle of concepts associated with the spirit that must be defined carefully. The first is self-esteem, which I have described as a universal human need on a par with appetite. For Plato and Aristotle, and classical Greek literature more generally, self-esteem or self-worth is an affect, and, like all emotions for the Greeks, is mediated by the intellect. We only feel good about ourselves when we recognize that we are esteemed by other actors whom we respect and admire for the right reasons.

Esteem and self-esteem – for me the more relevant concept – map onto different conceptions of identity. In the ancient world, I noted, identity was conceived of as social in nature.[10] People did not lack a concept of

---

[8] Plato, *Crito*.   [9] Aristotle, *Rhetoric*, 1388a29–1388b30.
[10] Yack, *Fetishism of Modernities*; Fitzgerald, *Metaphors of Identity*, p. 190; Lapid, "Culture's Ship."

self, but that self was relationally defined and can be described as the sum of their socially assigned roles.[11] Our word for person derives from *persona*, the Latin word for mask, and describes the outer face that one presents to the community.[12] In the modern world, individual identity is thought to have become increasingly important, and, with it, the concept of self-esteem has emerged. Durkheim observed that the replacement of the collectivity by the individual as the object of ritual attention is one of the hallmarks of transitions from traditional to modern societies. From Rousseau onwards, Enlightenment and Romantic ideologies emphasized the uniqueness and autonomy of the inner self.[13] Modernity created a vocabulary that recognizes tensions between inner selves and social roles but encourages us to cultivate and express our "inner selves" and original ways of being.[14]

Self-esteem is a subjective sense of one's honor and standing and can reflect or differ from the esteem accorded by others. Tension and conflict can arise, internally and socially, when the self-esteem of actors is considerably lower or higher than their external esteem. Esteem and self-esteem can also be described as respect and self-respect. The opposite of esteem is shame, an emotion that arises in response to the judgments that others make, or will make, about one. Both forms of esteem are stipulatively social. Aristotle describes shame as a "pain or disturbance in regard to bad things, whether present, past or future, which seem likely to involve us in discredit." Examples he provides include throwing away one's shield in battle, withholding payment from someone deserving of it, making a profit in a disgraceful way and having sexual relations with forbidden persons or at the wrong time or place.[15] Aristotle is clear that we shrink from knowledge of our behavior, not the acts themselves, as we are primarily concerned with how we appear in the eyes of those who matter most to us.[16] We must exercise due caution with the binaries of social and individual identities, and esteem and self-esteem, because, in addition to Plato, Greek tragedy (e.g. Sophocles' Ajax and Euripides'

[11] Durkheim, *Division of Labor in Society*, preface and pp. 219–222; Finley, *World of Odysseus*, p. 134.
[12] Hobbes, *Leviathan*, Part 1, pp. xvi, 112; Andrew, *Worlds Apart*, pp. 98–103.
[13] Hegel, *Phenomenology*, Bb, Cc; Norton, *Beautiful Soul*; Durkheim, *Elementary Forms of Religious Life* and *Division of Labor in Society*; Parsons, *Structure of Social Action*, pp. 378–390.
[14] Shotter, "Social Accountability and the Social Construction of 'You'"; Butler, *Excitable Speech*; Eakin, *How Our Lives Become Stories*; Gergen, *Invitation to Social Construction*.
[15] Aristotle, *Rhetoric*, 1383b15–1884a21.   [16] *Ibid.*, 1384a22–28.

Medea) reveals that self-esteem to some degree existed in fifth-century Athens. Even in the ancient world, these binaries may describe differences of degree than of kind.

Self-esteem is closely connected to honor (*timē*), a status for the Greeks that describes the outward recognition we gain from others in response to our excellence. Honor is a gift, and bestowed upon actors by other actors. It carries with it a set of responsibilities which must be fulfilled properly if honor is to be retained. By the fifth century, honor came to be associated with political rights and offices. It was a means of selecting people for office and of restraining them in their exercise of power. The spirit is best conceived of as an innate human drive, with self-esteem its goal, and honor and standing the means by which it is achieved.

Hierarchy is a rank ordering of statuses. In honor societies, honor determines the nature of the statuses and who fills them. Each status has privileges, but also an associated rule package. The higher the status, the greater the honor and privileges, but also the more demanding the role and elaborate its rules. Kings, formerly at the apex of the social hierarchy, were often expected to mediate between the human and divine worlds and derived authority and status from this responsibility. This holds true for societies as diverse as ancient Assyria, Song China and early modern Europe.[17] Status can be ascribed, as it was in the case of elected kings or German war chiefs. In traditional honor societies, the two are expected to coincide. The king or chief is expected to be the bravest warrior and lead his forces into battle. Other high-ranking individuals must assume high-risk, if subordinate, roles. Service and sacrifice – the means by which honor is won and maintained – have the potential to legitimize hierarchy. In return for honoring and serving those higher up the social ladder, people expect to be looked after in various ways. Protecting and providing for others is invariably one of the key responsibilities of those with high status and office. The Song dynasty carried this system to its logical extreme, integrating all males in the kingdom into a system of social status signified initially by seventeen, and then twenty, ranks. Obligations, including labor and military service, came with rank, as did various economic incentives. As in aristocratic Europe, the severity of punishments for the same crime varied by rank, but in reverse order.[18]

---

[17] Machinist, "Kingship and Divinity in Imperial Assyria"; Yates, "Song Empire." In Europe, the divine right of kings is reflected in key texts from Augustine to Bossuet.
[18] Yates, "Song Empire."

Great powers have had similar responsibilities in the modern era, which have been described by practitioners and theorists alike.[19] The United Nations Security Council is an outgrowth of this tradition. Its purpose, at least in the intent of those who drafted the United Nations Charter, is to coordinate the collective efforts of the community to maintain the peace. Traditional hierarchies justify themselves with reference to the principle of fairness; each actor contributes to the society and to the maintenance of its order to the best of its abilities and receives support depending on its needs. More modern hierarchies invoke the principle of equality. The United Nations attempts to incorporate both in two separate organs: the Security Council and the General Assembly.

Honor is also a mechanism for restraining the powerful and preventing the kind of crass, even brutal exploitation common to hierarchies in modern, interest-based worlds. Honor can maintain hierarchy because challenges to an actor's status, or failure to respect the privileges it confers, arouse anger that can only be appeased by punishing the offender and thereby "putting him in his place." Honor worlds have the potential to degenerate into hierarchies based on power and become vehicles for exploitation when actors at the apex fail to carry out their responsibilities or exercise self-restraint in pursuit of their own interests.

I define hierarchy as a rank order of statuses. Max Weber offers a different understanding of hierarchy: an arrangement of offices and the chain of command linking them together. Weber's formulation reminds us that status and office are not always coterminous, even in ideal-type worlds. In the *Iliad*, the conflict between Agamemnon and Achilles arises from the fact that Agamemnon holds the highest office, making Achilles his subordinate, while Achilles, the bravest and most admired warrior, deeply resents Agamemnon's abuse of his authority. In international relations, great powerdom is both a rank ordering of status and an office. As in the *Iliad*, conflict can become acute when the two diverge, and states – more accurately, the leaders and populations – believe they are denied office commensurate with the status they claim.

Standing and honor are another pair of related concepts. Standing refers to the position an actor occupies in a hierarchy. In an ideal-type spirit world, an actor's standing in a hierarchy is equivalent to its degree of honor. Those toward the apex of the status hierarchy earn the requisite

---

[19] Onuf, *Republican Legacy*; Kratochwil, *Rules, Norms, and Decisions*; Neumann, "Russia as a Great Power"; Bukovansky, *Legitimacy and Power Politics*, p. 70; Reus-Smit, *Moral Purpose of the State*, p. 137; Clark, *Legitimacy in International Society*, p. 100.

degree of honor by living up to the responsibilities associated with their rank or office, while those who attain honor by virtue of their accomplishments come to occupy appropriate offices. Even in ideal spirit worlds, there is almost always some discrepancy between honor and standing because those who gain honor do not necessarily win the competitions that confer honor. In the *Iliad*, Priam and Hector gain great honor because of their performance on and off the battlefield but lose their lives and city. In fifth-century Greece, Leonidas and his band of Spartan warriors won honor and immortality by dying at Thermopylae. Resigning office for the right reasons can also confer honor. Lucius Quinctius Cincinnatus was made dictator of Rome in 458 and again in 439 BCE. He resigned his absolute authority and returned to his humble life as a hardscrabble farmer as soon as he saved his city from the threat of the Volscians and Aequi. His humility and lack of ambition made him a legendary figure after whom a city in the wilderness of Ohio was named.[20] George Washington emulated Cincinnatus and retired to his plantation at the end of the Revolutionary War. Later, as first president of the new Republic, he refused a third term on principle and once again returned to Mount Vernon. His self-restraint and commitment to republican principles earned him numerous memorials and a perennial ranking as one of the top three presidents in history.

Honor and standing can diverge for less admirable reasons. Honor worlds are extremely competitive because standing, even more than wealth, is a relational concept. Hobbes compares it to glory, and observes that, "if all men have it, no man hath it."[21] The value placed on honor in spirit-based worlds and the intensity of the competition for it tempt actors to take shortcuts to gain honor. Once actors violate the rules and get away with it, others do the same to avoid being disadvantaged. If the rules governing honor are consistently violated, it becomes a meaningless concept. Competition for honor is transformed into competition for standing, which is more unconstrained and possibly more violent. This is a repetitive pattern in domestic politics and international relations.

The quest for honor generates a proliferation of statuses or ranks. These orderings can keep conflict in check when they are known and respected, and effectively define the relative status of actors. They intensify conflict when they are ambiguous or incapable of establishing precedence. This is most likely to happen when there are multiple ways (ascribed and achieved) of gaining honor and office. Even when this is

---

[20] Livy, *Early History of Rome*, III, 26–29.   [21] Hobbes, *De Cive*, 1.1.

not a problem, actors not infrequently disagree about who among them deserves a particular status or office. This kind of dispute has particularly threatening consequences in international relations because there are no authorities capable of adjudicating among competing claims.

External honor must be conferred by others and can only be gained through deeds regarded as honorable. It has no meaning until it is acknowledged, and is more valuable still when there is a respectful audience. The Greek word for fame (*kleos*) derives from the verb "to hear" (*kluein*). As Homer knew, fame not only requires heroic deeds, but bards to sing about those deeds and people willing to listen and be impressed, if not inspired to emulate them. For honor to be won and celebrated, there must be a consensus, and preferably one that transcends class or other distinctions, about the nature of honor, how it is won and lost and the distinctions and obligations it confers. This presupposes common values and traditions, even institutions. When society is robust – when its rules are relatively unambiguous and largely followed – the competition for honor and standing instantiates and strengthens the values of the society. As society becomes thinner, as it generally is at the regional and international levels, honor worlds become more difficult to create and sustain. In the absence of common values, there can be no consensus, no rules and no procedures for awarding and celebrating honor. Even in thin societies, honor can often be won within robust sub-cultures. Hamas and other groups that sponsor suicide bombing, publicize the names of successful bombers, sometimes pay stipends to their families and always encourage young people to lionize them.[22] Such activity strengthens the sub-culture and may even give it wider appeal or support.

Honor societies tend to be highly stratified and can be likened to step pyramids. Many, but by no means all, honor societies are sharply divided into two classes: those who are allowed to compete for honor and those who are not. In many traditional honor societies, the principal distinction is between aristocrats, who are expected to seek honor, and commoners, or the low-born, who cannot. This divide is often reinforced by distinctions in wealth, which allow many of the high-born to buy the military equipment, afford the leisure, sponsor the ceremonies and obtain the education and skills necessary to compete. As in ancient

---

[22] Levitt and Ross, *Hamas*, pp. 59–60, report monthly stipends of US$5,000–5,500 to prisoners of Israel and US$2,000–3,000 to widows or families of those who have given their lives.

Greece, birth and wealth are never fully synonymous, creating another source of social tension. Wealth is generally a necessary, but insufficient condition for gaining honor. Among the egalitarian Sioux, honor and status were achieved by holding various ceremonies, all of which involved providing feasts and gifts to those who attended. Horses and robes, the principal gifts, could only be gained through successful military expeditions against enemy tribes, or as gifts from others because of the high regard in which brave warriors were held.[23]

Recognition into the elite circle where one can compete for honor is the first, and often most difficult, step in honor worlds. The exclusiveness of many honor societies can become a major source of tension, when individuals, classes or political units demand and are refused entry into the circle in which it becomes possible to gain honor. What is honorable, the rules governing its attainment, and the indices used to measure it are all subject to challenge. Historically, challenges of this kind have been resisted, at least initially. Societies that have responded to them positively have evolved, and in some cases gradually moved away from, wholly or partly, their warrior base.

A final caveat is in order. Throughout the book, I use the term "recognition" to mean acceptance into the circle where it is possible to compete for honor. Recognition carries with it the possibility of fulfillment of the spirit, and it is not to be confused with the use the term has come to assume in moral philosophy. Hegel made the struggle for recognition (*Kampf um Anerkennung*) a central concept of his *Philosophy of Right*, which is now understood to offer an affirmative account of a just social order that can transcend the inequalities of master–slave relationships.[24] In a seminal essay published in 1992, Charles Taylor applied Hegel's concept to the demands for recognition of minorities and other marginalized groups. He argued that human recognition is a distinctive but largely neglected human good, and that we are profoundly affected by how we are recognized and *mis*recognized by others.[25] The political psychology of recognition has since been extended to international relations, where subordinate states are assumed to have poor self-images and low self-esteem. Axel Honneth stresses the importance of avoiding master–slave relationships among states.[26] Fernando Cornil argues that subaltern states enjoy the trappings

---

[23] Hassrick, *Sioux*, pp. 296–309.   [24] Hegel, *Phenomenology of Spirit*, III.A.178–196.
[25] Taylor, "Politics of Recognition."
[26] Honneth, *Struggle for Recognition*; Honneth and Fraser, *Recognition or Redistribution?*

of sovereignty but often internalize the negative images of them held by
the major powers.[27]

I acknowledge the relationship between status and esteem, but make a
different argument. In terms of at least foreign policy, it is powerful
states, not weak ones, who often feel most humiliated. My explanation
for this phenomenon draws on Aristotle's understanding of anger, which
is narrower than our modern Western conception. It is a response to an
oligōria, which can be translated as a slight, lessening or belittlement.
Such a slight can issue from an equal, but provokes even more anger
when it comes from an actor who lacks the standing to challenge or insult
us. Anger is a luxury that can only be felt by those in a position to seek
revenge. Slaves and subordinates cannot allow themselves to feel anger,
although they may develop many forms of resistance. It is also senseless
to feel anger toward those who cannot become aware of our anger.[28] In
the realm of international relations, leaders – and often peoples – of
powerful states are likely to feel anger of the Aristotelian kind when they
are denied entry into the system, refused recognition as a great power or
treated in a manner demeaning to their understanding of their status.
They will look for some way of asserting their claims and seeking
revenge. Subordinate states lack this power and their leaders and populations learn to live with their lower status and more limited autonomy.
Great powers will feel enraged if challenged by such states.[29] I believe we
can profit from reintroducing the Greek dichotomy between those who
were included in and excluded from the circle in which it was possible to
achieve honor and Aristotle's definition of anger.

Let us turn to the wider implications of honor as a motive for foreign
policy. First and foremost is its effect on the preferences of states and
their leaders. Realists and other international-relations scholars insist
that survival is the overriding goal of all states, just as domestic politics
explanations assert that it is for leaders.[30] This is not true of honor
societies, where honor has a higher value. Achilles spurns a long life in
favor of an honorable death that brings fame. For Homer and the Greeks,
fame allows people to transcend their mortality. Great deeds carry one's

[27] Cornil, "Listening to the Subaltern."
[28] Aristotle, *Rhetoric*, 387a31–33, 1378b10–11, 138024–29. Konstan, *Emotions of the
Ancient Greeks*, pp. 41–76.
[29] Aristotle, *Rhetoric*, 1379b10–12.
[30] Morgenthau, *Politics Among Nations*, 3rd edn., p. 10; Waltz, *Theory of International
Politics*, p. 92; Mearsheimer, *Tragedy of Great Power Politics*, p. 46; Wendt, *Social Theory
of International Politics*.

name and reputation across the generations where they continue to receive respect and influence other actors. In the real world, not just in Greek and medieval fiction, warriors, leaders, and sometimes entire peoples, have opted for honor over survival. We encounter this phenomenon not only in my case studies of ancient and medieval societies but also in nineteenth- and twentieth-century Europe and Japan.[31] Morgenthau and Waltz draw on Hobbes, and Waltz on Rousseau, to argue that survival is the prime directive of individuals and political units alike. Leo Strauss sees Hobbes as an important caesura with the classical tradition and among the first "bourgeois" thinkers because he makes fear of death and the desire for self-preservation the fundamental human end in lieu of aristocratic virtues.[32] A more defensible reading of Hobbes is that he aspired to replace vanity with material interests as a primary human motive because he recognized that it was more effectively controlled by a combination of reason and fear. For Hobbes, the spirit and its drive for standing and honor remained a universal, potent and largely disruptive force.

As Thucydides and Hobbes understand, the quest for honor and willingness to face death to gain or uphold it make honor-based societies extremely war-prone. Several aspects of honor contribute to this phenomenon. Honor has been associated with warrior societies, although not all warrior societies are honor societies, and not all warrior societies are aristocratic. In such societies, war is considered not only a normal activity but a necessary one because without it young men could not demonstrate their mettle and distinguish themselves. More fundamentally, war affirms the identity of warriors and their societies. I have argued elsewhere that Thucydides considered the threat Athenian power posed to Spartan identity, not their security, the fundamental reason why the Spartan assembly voted for war.[33] Erik Ringmar makes a persuasive case that it was the principal motive behind Sweden's intervention in the Thirty Years War, where standing was sought as a means of achieving a national identity.[34] In *A Cultural Theory of International Relations*, I document how such considerations were important for leaders and peoples from post-Westphalian Europe to the post-Cold War world.

[31] Lebow, *Cultural Theory of International Relations*.
[32] Strauss, *Political Philosophy of Hobbes*; Macpherson, *Political Theory of Possessive Individualism*; Hayes, "Hobbes' Bourgeois Moderation."
[33] Thucydides, *History of the Peloponnesian War*, Book 1; Lebow, *Tragic Vision of Politics*, ch. 4.
[34] Ringmar, *Identity, Interest and Action*.

In honor societies, status is an actor's most precious possession. Challenges to status or to the privileges it confers are unacceptable when they come from equals or inferiors. In regional and international societies, statuses are uncertain, there may be multiple contenders for them and there are usually no peaceful ways of adjudicating rival claims. Warfare often serves this end, and is a common cause of war in honor societies. It often finds expression in substantive issues such as control over disputed territory, but can also arise from symbolic disputes (e.g. who is to have primacy at certain festivals or processions, or whose ships must honor or be honored by others at sea).

For all three reasons, warfare in honor worlds tends to be frequent, but the ends of warfare and the means by which it is waged tend to be limited. Wars between political units in honor societies often resemble duels.[35] Combat is highly stylized, if still vicious, and governed by a series of rules that are generally followed by participants. Warfare among the Greeks, Aztecs, Plains Indians, and eighteenth-century European states offer variants on this theme. By making a place for violence in community-governed situations, it is partially contained and may be less damaging than it otherwise would be.[36] However, these limitations apply only to warfare between recognized members of the same society. War against outsiders, or against non-elite members of one's own society, often has a no-holds-barred quality. Greek warfare against tribesmen or against the Persians at Marathon, Salamis and Plataea, American warfare against native Americans and colonial wars in general illustrate this nasty truth.

Despite the endemic nature of warfare in warrior-based honor societies, cooperation is not only possible but routine. Cooperation is based on appeals to friendship, common descent and mutual obligation more than it is on mutual interest. The norms of the hierarchy dictate that actors of high status assist those of lower status who are dependent on them, while those of lower status are obliged to honor and serve their protectors or patrons. Friendship usually involves the exchange of gifts and favors and provides additional grounds for asking for and receiving aid. Cooperation in honor societies is most difficult among equals because no actor wants to accept the leadership of another and thereby acknowledge its higher standing. This situation makes cooperation difficult even in situations where there are compelling mutual security concerns.

---

[35] Clausewitz, *On War*, Book One, ch. 1, pp. 75–76.
[36] Hobsbawm, "Rules of Violence," makes this point.

As honor is more important than survival, the very notion of risk is framed differently. Warrior societies are risk-accepting with respect to both gain and loss. Honor cannot be attained without risk, so leaders and followers alike welcome the opportunity to risk limbs and lives to gain or defend it. Actors will also defend their autonomy at almost any cost because it is so closely linked to their honor, unless they can find some justification for disassociating it from honor that is convincing to their peers. Risk-taking will be extended to the defense of material possessions and territory to the extent that they have become entwined with honor and symbols of them.

To summarize, honor-based societies experience conflict about who is "recognized" and allowed to compete for standing; the rules governing *agon* or competition, the nature of the deeds that confer standing and the actors who assign honor, determine status and adjudicate competing claims. Tracking the relative intensity of conflict over these issues and the nature of the changes or accommodations to which they lead provide insight into the extent to which honor remains a primary value in a society and its ability to respond to internal and external challenges. It also permits informed speculation about its evolution.

Appetite

Appetite is the drive with which we are most familiar. Plato considered wealth to have become the dominant appetite in Athens, a development that has found an echo in all societies where some degree of affluence becomes possible. There are, of course, other appetites, including sex, food, drink, clothing and drugs, but contemporary economists and liberals either ignore them or assume their satisfaction depends on, or is at least facilitated by, wealth.

Material well-being is generally abetted by the well-being, even prosperity, of other actors. This is a hard-won insight.[37] Early efforts at wealth accumulation often involved violence, as it appeared easier and cheaper to take other peoples' possessions than to produce them oneself or generate the capital necessary for their purchase. Until recent times piracy was an honored profession and slavery, often the result of raiding expeditions, was considered an acceptable means of acquiring wealth. Riches gained through conquest became an important goal of empires and the norm against territorial conquest only developed in the twentieth

---

[37] Hont, *Jealousy of Trade.*

century. Even trading economies (e.g. the Carthaginians, Portuguese and British) historically viewed wealth as a zero-sum game and sought to exclude competitors from access to the raw materials and markets they controlled. Recognition dawned only slowly that generating surplus through production and trade made societies and their rulers richer than they could through conquest, that production and trade benefited from peace and that affluence was as much the result of cooperation as it was of conflict. In was not until the late eighteenth century that even economists began to understand that the free exchange of capital, goods, people and ideas is in the long-term common interest of all trading states.[38]

Modern appetite-based worlds rest on the principle of equality, of which Rousseau is the outstanding theorist.[39] By the third decade of the nineteenth century, Tocqueville noted, equality was well on its way toward becoming the only principle on which legitimate government could be based.[40] In such an order, everyone is supposed to be recognized as an ontological equal and to have the same opportunities for advancement in such orders. The hierarchies that result – based on wealth – are no less steep than their spirit-based counterparts, but are entirely informal. They come with no defined statuses or privileges and without attached rule packages. Status is not as evident as in traditional hierarchies so actors must actively seek to display their wealth in support of their claims for standing.[41] Not everyone seeks to be identified and ranked this way. In the absence of rule packages, there is also no requirement to share resources with others who are less well-off. Redistribution of wealth, to the extent this occurs, must be imposed by governments through progressive income and estate taxes and deductions for charitable donations. Proponents of egalitarian orders assert that they benefit everyone with skills and commitment because status is based on personal qualities. Adam Smith maintains that one of the great benefits of these orders was the ending of personal dependency, allowing people to sell their skills and labor on the open market. Personal freedom and unrestricted markets are alleged to make more efficient use of human potential. They are also defended on the ground that they generate

---

[38] Smith, *Wealth of Nations*, ch. 1; Ferguson, *Essay on the History of Civil Society.*
[39] Rousseau, *Contrat Social*, explicitly rejects contracts of submission and the clientelist hierarchies they instantiate. Every citizen, he insists, must be bound by the same laws and obligations.
[40] Tocqueville, *Democracy in America*, 1, Introduction, pp. 3–6.   [41] *Ibid.*, II.3.2, p. 540.

greater wealth, making those who end up at the bottom of the hierarchy substantially better off than they would be in traditional, clientelist orders.[42]

Plato describes appetite and spirit as two distinct drives or motives. He provides examples to show how they can come into conflict, as when someone is thirsty but drinking in the circumstances would be socially inappropriate. In this example, behavior allows a culturally informed observer to determine which motive is dominant. In other instances, this might not be apparent, as wealth and honor have been implicated with each other from the beginning of human history and are sometimes difficult to disentangle. In ancient Greece, as in many societies, wealth was a prerequisite for honor.[43] In Europe, titles were not infrequently sold or awarded on the basis of wealth and, in seventeenth-century France, conferred privileges that were a vehicle for increasing one's wealth. In much of Western Europe by the mid-nineteenth century, and earlier in some countries, aristocrats were primarily distinguished from the rich bourgeoisie by the age of their wealth. More confusing still is the seeming fusion of wealth and standing in our epoch. Rousseau describes *amour propre*, the passion to be regarded favorably by others, as the dominant passion of modernity. In contrast to savage man, who sought esteem directly, his "civilized" counterpart seeks it indirectly, through the attainment and display of material possessions.[44] According to Adam Smith, we better our condition "in order to be observed, to be attended to, to be taken notice of with sympathy, complacency, and approbation."[45] Modernity, at least in the West, has arguably transformed wealth into ever more an instrumental good because it has become the chief source of standing. Schumpeter believed entrepreneurs to be motivated by "the dream to found a private kingdom" in the form of an eponymous company that carries one's name and fame across the generations. Like Greek and Trojan heroes on the battlefield, financial success for entrepreneurs is "mainly valued as an index of success and as a symptom of victory."[46]

In an ideal-type appetite, world actors would behave differently than they would in a spirit-based world. Cooperation would be routine, indeed the norm, and built around common interests. It would endure as long as actors

---

[42] Smith, *Theory of Moral Sentiments*, I.iii.3.6; Berger, *Capitalism Revolution*.
[43] Aristotle, *Politics*, 1286b922, recognizes that riches have become a path to honor.
[44] Rousseau, *Discourse on the Origin and Foundation of Inequality Among Men*, pp. 147–160, 174–175.
[45] Smith, *Theory of Moral Sentiments*, I.iii.2.1.
[46] Schumpeter, *Theory of Economic Development*, p. 82.

shared interests and would end when they diverged. As interests change in importance or salience, alliances (formal and informal) would shift, and yesterday's partners could become today's opponents. Relations among units would resemble the kind of shifting coalitions the authors of *Federalist Papers* expected to develop in the Congress.[47] Conflict would be as common as cooperation, as actors would have opposing interests on numerous matters of importance. Their conflicts, however, would be non-violent and rule-governed because all actors would recognize their overriding interest in maintaining peaceful relations and the institutions, procedures and general level of trust that enabled peaceful relations. The outcome of disputes would depend very much on the relative power of actors, the structure and rules of the institutions in which their conflicts were adjudicated and their skill in framing arguments, bargaining with opponents and building coalitions. Actors might even be expected to develop a set of rules about changing the rules of the game.

Because interests – primarily economic interests – dictate policy preferences, conflicts within political units would mirror those between them. Domestic and transnational coalitions would form to advance common interests and provide mutual assistance. Risk-taking in interest-based worlds is described by prospect theory: actors are willing to assume more risk to avert loss than they are to make gains.

Liberalism is the quintessential paradigm of politics and international relations based on the motive of interest. Theories and propositions rooted in this paradigm, including those associated with the Democratic Peace research program, do a comprehensive job of laying out the assumptions of an interest-based world and the behavior to which it gives rise. Many liberals nevertheless make the mistake of confusing their ideal-type descriptions of an interest-based world with the real world, which is a mixed world in which interest is only one of multiple motives. Liberals further err in thinking that the world they describe – one composed of capitalist democracies – is the only efficient response to the modern industrial world. A compelling argument can be made that it is only one of several possible interest-based responses, and that its emergence was highly contingent.

Reason

We also lack a paradigm for reason, but with more reason, so to speak. Just and ordered worlds do not exist at any level of aggregation. Greek

---

[47] *Federalist Papers*, No. 10 by James Madison.

and modern philosophers have had to imagine them. For Plato, it is Kallipolis of the *Republic* or Magnesia of the *Laws*. For Aristotle, it is *homonoia*, a community whose members agreed about the nature of the good life and how it could be achieved. For Augustine, it is a culture in which human beings use their reason to control, even overcome, their passions, and act in accord with god's design.[48] For Marx, it is a society in which people contribute to the best of their abilities and receive what they need in return. For Rawls, it is a utopia that conforms to the principles of distributive justice. As most of these thinkers acknowledge, disagreements would still exist in reason-informed worlds, but would not threaten the peace because they would not be about fundamental issues of justice and would be adjudicated in an environment characterized by mutual respect and trust. Plato, Aristotle and Rawls understand their fictional worlds as ideals toward which we must aspire, individually and collectively, but which we are unlikely ever to achieve. Their worlds are intended to serve as templates that we can use to measure how existing worlds live up to our principles. As Plato might put it, even imperfect knowledge of a form can motivate citizens and cities to work toward its actualization. Partial progress can generate enough virtue to sustain reasonable order in individuals and societies. Thucydides offers Periclean Athens as an example – one that Plato unambiguously rejects – while Aristotle makes the case for polity, a mixture of oligarchy and democracy.

Order in reason-informed worlds arises from the willingness of actors to cooperate even when it may be contrary to their immediate self-interest. All actors recognize that cooperation sustains that *nomos* that allows all of them to advance their interests more effectively than they could in its absence. Conflict exists in reason-informed worlds, but it is tempered not only by recognition of the importance of order, but, as Aristotle notes in his description of an *homonoia*, by a fundamental agreement about underlying values that minimizes the nature of conflict and the cost of being on the losing end. To maintain this consensus, actors often favor compromise over outright victory in conflicts. Compromises that allow common projects is also a vehicle for building and sustaining the common identities that maintain the underlying value consensus. Rawls' difference principle incorporates a risk-averse propensity on the part of actors which he assumes is a universal human trait that will still operate behind the veil of ignorance even though all

[48] Augustine, *City of God*.

other social orientations have been shorn away.[49] He has rightly been criticized for this move, and it is more reasonable to assume that even in a reason-informed world risk propensity will depend on the characteristics of the society and actors in question.

Reason-informed worlds also have hierarchies. In Plato's *Republic*, it is based on the principle of fairness. Everyone, including women, occupies a position commensurate with their abilities and character. Aristotle's aristocracy, which he regarded in the abstract as the ideal form of government, is also hierarchical and combines principles of fairness and equality. It is hierarchical in that aristocrats are in a superior position to the *demos* because of their superior qualities but egalitarian in the ways they relate to one another and their understanding that honor and office should be assigned on the basis of merit.[50] Rawls recognizes a hierarchy based on wealth and attempts to offset the principle of equality with that of fairness. The veil of ignorance and the original position are supposed to lead actors to conclude that everyone should have the same opportunities to better themselves. The principle of difference dictates that the only inequalities (hierarchies of wealth) that are allowed are those that demonstrably permit the poorest members of society to become better off.[51] Plato and Aristotle recognize that their reason-informed worlds would be short-lived. Plato expects his republic to become corrupt after a few generations, while Aristotle expects aristocracies to degenerate, even to the point of revolution when a few actors monopolize the honors of state.[52]

For reason to constrain spirit and appetite, it must educate them. This seeming tautology is resolved by the active involvement of parents and guardians who impose on young people the kind of restraints they are incapable of imposing on themselves, and educating them by means of the examples of their own lives.[53] Role models are critical components of the individual and civic education necessary to bring about reason-informed worlds.[54] Unfortunately, as Socrates discovered, people are at least as likely to resent, even punish, others who lead just lives. Plato and Aristotle sought unsuccessfully, I would argue, to find some way out of this bind, and the difficulty of doing so was an important reason for their general pessimism. Plato resorted to the "noble lie" to create his fictional

[49] Rawls, *Theory of Justice*, pp. 8, 53, 57, 65.   [50] Aristotle, *Politics*, 1307a26–27.
[51] Rawls, *Theory of Justice*, p. 65.   [52] Aristotle, *Politics*, 1306b22–26.
[53] Aristotle, *Nicomachean Ethics*, 1101b14–1103b26.
[54] Plato, *Republic*, Book II, 377b to III, 399e.

city of Kallipolis; its founders agree among themselves to tell their descendants that their *nomos* was established by the gods. He does not tell us how the founders themselves gained enough wisdom and insight to devise these laws and willingly submit themselves to their constraints.

The understanding of reason shared by Thucydides, Plato and Aristotle differs in important ways from modern conceptions of reason. For the ancients, as we have seen, reason is an instrumental facility and a drive with goals of its own. A second important difference is its relation to affect. Plato and Aristotle believe that reason can only have beneficial effects in concert with the proper emotions.[55] Dialogue is valuable for Plato because of its ability to establish friendships. When we feel warmly toward others, we empathize with them and can learn to see ourselves through their eyes. This encourages us to see them as our ontological equals. Affect and reason combine to make us willing to listen to their arguments with an open ear, and, more importantly, to recognize that our understandings of justice, which we think of as universal, are in fact parochial. We come to understand a more fundamental reason for self-restraint: it makes it possible for others to satisfy their appetites and spirits. Self-restraint is instrumentally rational because it makes friendships, wins the loyalty of others and sustains the social order that makes it possible for other actors to satisfy their appetites and spirit. Self-restraint also brings important emotional rewards because spirit and appetite are best gratified in the context of close relations with other people.

For Thucydides, Plato and Aristotle, what holds true for individuals holds true for their cities. The most ordered and just cities are those with properly educated citizens. Guided by reason and love for their *polis*, citizens willingly perform tasks to which they are best suited and take appropriate satisfaction from their successful completion. The foundation of the city is the friendship (*philia*) that citizens develop with one another, and regional peace is built on friendship among cities (*poleis*).[56] At both levels, relationships are created and sustained through a dense network of social interactions and reciprocal obligations that build common identities along with mutual respect and affection.[57]

Despite the modern emphasis on reason as an instrumentality, we find echoes of Plato and Aristotle in the writings of some influential

---

[55] Aristotle, *Poetics*, 1448b5–7, 1450.
[56] Aristotle, *Nicomachean Ethics*, 1155a14, 26–28, 1159b25, 1161a23, 1161b12; Plato, *Republic*, 419a–421a.
[57] Thucydides, *History of the Peloponnesian War*, I.32–36.

eighteenth- and nineteenth-century thinkers. Adam Smith maintains that reason can teach prudence, discipline and honesty to self-interested people – a set of qualities he calls "propriety" – that lead them, among other things, to defer short-term gratification to make longer-term gains.[58] This is very similar to Aristotle's concept of *phronesis*, often translated as "practical reason" or "prudence." It arises from reflection upon the consequences of our behavior and that of others. It is concerned with particulars, but it can help us make better lives for ourselves by influencing what goals we seek and how we go about attempting to achieve them.[59] Hegel is even closer to Aristotle in arguing that reason must combine with affect, and the two together can teach people to act ethically and affirm their civic obligations. Insight grounded in reason (*Einsicht durch Gründe*) has the potential to liberate us, at least in part, from our appetites, give direction to our lives and help us realize our full potential as individuals.[60]

Fear

Real worlds at best approximate this ideal, and most do not even come close. Those that function reasonably well must, of necessity, contain enough reason to constrain appetite and spirit and direct them into productive channels. They must restrain actors, especially powerful ones, by some combination of reason, interest, fear and habit. Self-restraint is always difficult because it involves deprivation, something that is noticeably out of fashion in the modern world where instant gratification and self-indulgence have increasingly become the norm. Experimental evidence indicates that about one-third of Americans put their personal material interests above shared norms when there are no constraints on them other than conscience. This behavior can only effectively be constrained by high levels of normative consensus, resource dependence on other actors and dense links to these actors and a broader community.[61]

Spirit- and appetite-based worlds are inherently unstable. They are intensely competitive, which encourages actors to violate the rules by

[58] Smith, *Theory of Moral Sentiments*, I.1.5, VI.1.
[59] Aristotle, *Nicomachean Ethics*, 1139a29–30, 1139a29–1142a.
[60] Hegel, *Hegel's Philosophy of Right*, 132, 144, 147, 149–152.
[61] Zelditch, "Process of Legitimation"; Zelditch and Walker, "Normative Regulation of Power"; Johnson, Dowd and Ridgeway, "Legitimacy as a Social Process"; Tyler, "Psychological Perspectives on Legitimacy and Legitimation."

which honor or wealth is attained. When enough actors do this, those who continue to obey the rules are likely to be seriously handicapped. This provides a strong incentive for all but the most committed actors to defect from the rules. This dilemma is most acute in spirit-based worlds because of the relational nature of honor and standing, which makes it a zero-sum game unless there are multiple hierarchies of honor and standing. Appetite-based worlds need not be this way, but actors often frame the acquisition of wealth as a winner-takes-all competition and behave competitively even when cooperation would be mutually beneficial. Here, too, lack of self-restraint encourages others to follow suit in their pursuit of wealth. Disregard for rules accordingly takes two forms: non-performance of duties (including self-restraint) by high-status actors, and disregard of these status and associated privileges by actors of lesser standing. The two forms of non-compliance are likely to be self-reinforcing and have the effect of weakening hierarchies and order the orders they instantiate.

Aristotle defines fear as "a pain or disturbance due to imagining some destructive or painful evil in the future." It is caused by "whatever we feel has great power of destroying us, or of harming us in ways that tend to cause us great pain." It is the opposite of confidence and is associated with danger, which is the approach of something terrible. It is aroused by the expectation, rather than the reality, of such an event and encourages a deliberative response. It is often provoked by another actor's abuse of its power and is threatening to the social order, not just to individuals.[62]

Following Aristotle, I argue that the principal cause of the breakdown of orders is the unrestricted pursuit by actors – individuals, factions or political units – of their parochial goals. Their behavior leads other actors to fear for their ability to satisfy their spirit and or appetites, and perhaps for their survival. Fearful actors are likely to consider and implement a range of precautions which can run the gamut from bolting their doors at night to acquiring allies and more and better arms. Escalation of this kind is invariably paralleled by shifts in threat assessment. Actors who were initially regarded as friends, colleagues or allies and who evoked images rich in nuance and detail give way to simpler and more superficial stereotypes of adversaries or, worse still, of enemies.[63] This shift, and

---

[62] Aristotle, *Rhetoric*, 1382a21–33, 1382b28–35; Konstan, *Emotions of the Ancient Greeks*, pp. 129–155.

[63] Herrmann, *Perceptions and Behavior in Soviet Foreign Policy*; Tetlock, "Accountability and Complexity of Thought"; Levi and Tetlock, "Cognitive Analysis of Japan's 1941 Decision for War"; Levy, "Learning and Foreign Policy."

Table 3.1 *Motives, emotions, goals and means*

Motive	Goal	Instrument
Appetite	Pleasure	Wealth
Spirit	Esteem	Honor / standing
Fear	Security	Power

the corresponding decline in cognitive complexity, undermines any residual trust and encourages worst-case analyses of their motives, behavior and future initiatives. Mutually reinforcing changes in behavior and framing can start gradually but at some point can accelerate and bring about a phase transition. When they do, actors enter into fear-based worlds.

Fear is an emotion, not a fundamental human drive. In this sense it differs from appetite, spirit and reason. It arises from imbalance and the application of human imagination to its likely, or even possible, consequences. Fear triggers a desire for security which can be satisfied in many ways. In interstate relations, it is usually through the direct acquisition of military power (and the economic well-being that makes this power) or its indirect acquisition through alliances. It is also a catalyst, as it is at the domestic level, for institutional arrangements that provide security by limiting their capabilities and independence of actors who might do one harm. Table 3.1 compares fear to appetite, spirit and reason.

My take on fear-based worlds differs from most realists in two important respects. I do not attribute fear-dominated worlds to anarchy, but to a breakdown in *nomos* caused by the lack of constraint by elite actors. The logic of anarchy assumes that those who are weak are the most threatened in fear-based worlds. They are also the most likely to balance or bandwagon. The breakdown-of-*nomos* thesis suggests that it is elite actors who set the escalatory process in motion and are often the ones who feel most threatened. The history of the last two centuries provides numerous examples of this phenomenon at the domestic and international levels. The same kinds of breakdowns occur within states and the systems in which they interact, and are the result of the same dynamics. I believe Thucydides intends his account of the slide to civil war and barbarism in Corcyra to be read as a parallel in almost every respect to the process that spread war throughout Hellas. Both outcomes are described by the Greek word *stasis*, translated as either civil war, acute conflict or the breakdown of order.

Fear-based worlds differ from their appetite- and spirit-based counterparts in important ways. They are highly conflictual, and neither the ends nor the means of conflict are constrained by norms. Actors make security their first concern and attempt to become strong enough to deter or defeat any possible combination of likely adversaries. Arms races, reciprocal escalation, alliances and forward deployments intensify everyone's insecurity, as the security dilemma predicts. Precautions are interpreted as indicative of intentions, which provoke further defensive measures that can lead to acute conflict, and perhaps to outright warfare brought about by preemption, loss of control or a decision to support a threatened third party. Thucydides suggests that the Spartan declaration of war on Athens was the result of a process of this kind.[64] Such patterns of escalation are well-described in the international-relations literature.[65]

In traditional spirit-based worlds (those dominated by warrior elites), wars tend to be frequent but limited in their ends and means. In fear-based worlds, wars may be less frequent because they tend to be more unrestrained in their ends and means and, hence, are often – although not always – recognized as riskier and more costly. They are also more difficult to prevent by deterrence and alliances, the stock-and-trade realist tools of conflict management. One of the most revealing aspects of Thucydides' account of the Peloponnesian War is the absolute failure of all alliances and all forms of deterrence intended to prevent war. They almost invariably provoked the behavior they were intended to prevent.[66] General and immediate deterrence failed in fifth-century Greece for the same reasons they often do in modern times: they appeared to confirm worst-case fears of their targets, convincing them of the need to demonstrate more, not less, resolve, in the equally false expectation that it would deter their adversaries from further aggressive initiatives.[67] When target actors are focused on their own problems and

---

[64] Thucydides, *History of the Peloponnesian War*, I.131–89.
[65] Herz, "Idealist Internationalism and the Security Dilemma"; Herz, *Political Realism and Political Idealism*, p. 24; Herz, "Security Dilemma in International Relations"; Waltz, *Theory of International Politics*; Jervis, "Cooperation Under the Security Dilemma."
[66] Lebow, "Thucydides and Deterrence."
[67] Lebow, *Between Peace and War*, chs. 4–6; Lebow and Stein, "Deterrence"; Lebow and Stein, "Rational Deterrence Theory"; Lebow and Stein, *We All Lost the Cold War*, chs. 3 and 12; Hopf, *Peripheral Visions*; Chang, *Friends and Enemies*; Chen, *Mao's China and the Cold War*.

needs, and committed to their own strategic plans as the only means they see of addressing those problems, deterrence is likely to fail. Challengers are highly motivated to deny, distort, explain away or discredit obvious signs of adversarial resolve.[68] Both sets of conditions are less likely in appetite- and spirit-dominated worlds, and for this reason deterrence is least likely to succeed in precisely those circumstances where realists consider it most needed and appropriate.

Hierarchies sometimes exist in fear-based worlds. In Hobbes' "war of all against all," there are no hierarchies, only anarchy, although he leaves open the possibility of people going into league with others to protect themselves or take what they want from third parties.[69] Modern-day realists describe anarchy as the opposite of order, but nevertheless recognize the possibility of hierarchies. Under bipolarity, for example, many lesser powers attach themselves to one or the other of the hegemonic alliance systems in the expectation of protection or other benefits. Such a hierarchy can function along the lines of a traditional spirit-based hierarchy, as did the Spartan alliance or, arguably, NATO. Alternatively, it can be another fear-based order, as was the Athenian alliance or the Warsaw Pact. This helps to explain why the former endured after the end of the Cold War while the latter did not.

Fear-driven worlds are the opposite of honor and interest worlds in the sense that they are like lobster traps: easy to enter and difficult to leave. Once fear is aroused, it is hard to assuage. Worst-case analysis, endemic to fear-based worlds, encourages actors to see threat in even the most benign and well-meaning gestures. It creates a snowball effect, making fears of such worlds self-fulfilling. Actors who contemplate steps toward trust and accommodation rightfully worry that others will misunderstand their intent or exploit their concessions. Pure fear-based worlds are few and far between, but most political units for most of their history have had to worry to some degree about their security. For this reason, realists see fear-driven worlds as the default, and the state to which human societies inevitably return. History gives ample cause for pessimism, but also for optimism. If Thucydides' account of the Peloponnesian War reveals how lack of self-restraint and the fear it arouses can quickly lead actors into destructive realist worlds, his "Archeology" shows that escape is possible, as civilization arose from

---

[68] Lebow, *Between Peace and War*, chs. 4–6; Jervis, Lebow and Stein, *Psychology and Deterrence*, chs. 3 and 5; Lebow and Stein, *We All Lost the Cold War*, ch. 3.

[69] Hobbes, *Leviathan*, ch. 13, para. 8, and ch. 17, para. 13.

barbarism.[70] Recent history provides no shortage of examples of both processes. Competition for colonies in the late nineteenth century, sought primarily for reasons of standing, got out of hand, led to increasingly unrestrained competition in the Balkans and pushed the European powers toward World War I.[71] Beggar-thy-neighbor policies during the Great Depression reveal how quickly a partially liberal trading world can be destroyed.[72] Europe's phenomenal economic and political recovery after World War II, based in large part on the consolidation of democracy in Germany, Italy, and, later, Spain, Portugal and Greece, has transformed that continent in ways that would have been dismissed out of hand as idle dreams if offered as a prediction as late as the early 1950s.

Mixed worlds

The concept of an ideal type is implicit in Plato's forms as well as in Aristotle's constitutions, but was only developed by Max Weber at the beginning of the twentieth century. Weber had two somewhat different understandings of ideal types. He devised the concept initially to replace intuition as a means of understanding the behavior of societies with different values and worldviews. Ideal types of this kind have no external validity because they do not correspond to any historical reality. He offered his typology of authority as an example.[73] Weber later reconceptualized ideal types to give them a more empirical connection to the societies he studied. He described them as an analytical accentuation of aspects of one or more attributes of a phenomenon to create a mental construct that will never be encountered in practice but against which real-world approximations can be measured. Such ideal types were not intended as a basis for comparison, but a schema for understanding a specific culture or situation.[74]

All four of my worlds qualify as ideal types according to Weber's first definition. Worlds of spirit, appetite, reason and fear are analytical constructs, useful to understand the behavior of societies, but without direct correspondence in reality. This is most evident in the case of reason-informed worlds, which have remained a remote ideal ever

---

[70] Thucydides, *History of the Peloponnesian War*, 1.2–13. Lebow, *Tragic Vision of Politics*, ch. 3.
[71] The most forceful exponent of this thesis is Schroeder, "World War I as Galloping Gertie," and "Embedded Counterfactuals and World War I as an Unavoidable War." For a rejoinder, see Lebow, "Contingency, Catalysts and International System Change."
[72] Kindleberger, *The World in Depression*.   [73] Turner, "Introduction."
[74] Weber, *"Objectivity" in Social Science and Social Policy*, pp. 90–95.

since they were conceived by Socrates or Plato. In such a world, appetite and spirit have been constrained and shaped to desire only what produces true happiness and behavior that accords with justice.

Worlds of spirit, appetite and fear, but probably not reason, also fit Weber's later understanding of ideal types. They are abstractions of societies that exist, or have existed. All these worlds require some degree of reason, but it is instrumental reason. If actors constrain their appetite or spirit, it is for the same reason that Odysseus did when he discovered his house full of suitors importuning his wife, Penelope: he understood that by suppressing his rage now he would increase his chances of subsequent revenge. Reason as an end in itself operates at another level of abstraction. It constrains spirit and appetite, but does so in order to reshape and redirect them to enable a happier, ordered and more just life. All relatively stable systems depend on this process, but, in practice, reason's control over appetite and spirit never progresses to the point of bringing about anything close to a reason-driven world. I accordingly limit myself to three ideal-type worlds, and keep a reason-informed world in the background as a kind of ideal or Platonic form.

Realists do not think of their paradigm as an ideal type, but as a description of the real world of international relations. The validity of this claim depends very much on the formulation in question. Strong claims, like Waltz's assertion that "In international politics force serves, not only as the *ultimo ratio*, but indeed as the first and constant one," describe few, if any, actual worlds, and can only be considered ideal types.[75] Weaker claims bear a closer relationship to reality. Robert Gilpin contends that anarchy and the primacy of the state do not imply a world of constant warfare, only the recognition that "there is no higher authority to which a state can appeal for succor in times of trouble."[76] By relaxing their assumptions, realist, liberal and Marxist theories could make a better fit between their claims and real worlds. In doing so, they must give up making determinant claims and acknowledge that there is more going on in the world than can be described by their respective theories.

Weber was adamant about the need to distinguish ideal types from real worlds. The former give us a clear picture of what a "pure" world of its kind would be like, and a benchmark for measuring how closely it is approached by real worlds. By determining which features of real worlds conform most closely to one or more ideal-type worlds, we get a better

---

[75] Waltz, *Theory of International Politics*, p. 113.   [76] *Ibid.*, p. 17.

sense of what kind of worlds they are. The important point to keep in mind is that three motives, and usually fear as well, are present in every society. The relative emphasis put on them by societies and actors within those societies varies, as does the degree to which fear motivates their relations with other societies and actors. Motives are sometimes very difficult to separate out analytically, all the more so in the modern world where material possessions have become a marker of standing. Another complicating factor – again most apparent in the modern period – is the tendency of actors to respond to one motive but explain and justify their behavior with respect to another. Governmental officials routinely invoke security to justify policies motivated by spirit or interest because they believe it is easier to sell them to the public. As the spirit all but dropped out of the political and philosophical lexicon during the Enlightenment, although honor and "national honor" did not, behavior motivated by the spirit is the least likely to be acknowledged by contemporary actors. Despite these problems, it is often possible to make judgments about the actors' motives and how they are reflected in their foreign policies. In *Cultural Theory*, I discuss at some length the methods appropriate to such an enterprise. My supposition, validated by my case studies, is that multiple motives interact as mixtures, not solutions. They do not blend, but coexist, and often in ways that make the behavior of actors appear contradictory. As no simple explanation will reconcile such behavior, it offers *prima facie* support for the inference that mixed motives are at work.

War

If striving for honor or standing has been a dominant foreign-policy motive in the European system, and later in the international political one, the patterns of conflict, cooperation and risk-taking we observe should more closely resemble those I associate with spirit-based worlds. If standing, and not security or material interest, has motivated the war-initiation of great and rising powers, we ought to observe a distinctive pattern of war-initiation with respect to the states that make war, who they attack and the circumstances under which this occurs. This pattern should differ considerably from what we would expect in interest- or fear-driven worlds. To test the correspondence between a spirit-based world and the real worlds of European and international relations, I offer six propositions about the causes of warfare and the types of states it is likely to involve. These propositions are sharply at odds with the expectations of realist, power transition, Marxist and rationalist theories of war.

Proposition 1

The most aggressive states are rising powers seeking recognition as great powers and dominant great powers seeking hegemony.

This pattern reflects the importance of victory in war as the principal means historically of gaining international standing. Many great powers are not content with their status even when they are recognized as the leading great power. Driven by hubris, their leaders seek hegemony and start wars in the hope of achieving it. Examples include Spain under Philip II, France of Louis XIV and Napoleon, imperial and Nazi Germany and arguably the United States since the end of the Cold War. Rising powers seek recognition as great powers and are particularly aggressive for this reason.

Early modern Europe witnessed the consolidation of political units and the emergence of a number of medium-to-large-sized states. Spain, England, France and Russia were all built around core areas that, beginning in the late Middle Ages, exploited economic advantages to expand at the expense of neighboring territories. Small advantages, successfully exploited by clever and ambitious leaders, led to ever greater advantages between them and their neighbors. Marriage was another means of expansion, exploited most effectively by the Habsburgs, who at one point controlled Spain, much of the Holy Roman Empire, northern Italy and the Low Countries. The leaders of these states not only struggled with their own nobility and neighbors as part and parcel of their efforts at consolidation, but also struggled with one another in efforts to gain prestige. The two efforts were not unrelated, as prestige abroad facilitated consolidation at home, and *vice versa*.

Not surprisingly, the great powers were at war 95 percent of the time in the sixteenth and seventeenth centuries. This drops to 71 percent in the eighteenth century and to 29 percent in a modified nineteenth century (i.e. 1815–1914). The years between 1815 and 1914 were the first century-long span in which there were more years of peace than of war.[77] Nobles also sought honor through war. Rulers like Louis XIV faced pressures from below to make war. By 1691, at least 3,000 nobles were serving in Louis' elite corps, and more than 10 percent of all nobles did military service.[78] In his memoirs, Louis confessed that "I have officers whom I do not need. But I am sure they need me."[79]

---

[77] Wright, *Study of War*, pp. 121, 237, 242, 248, 638; Levy, *War in the Modern Great Power System*, pp. 139–141. See Hamilton, "European Wars: 1815–1914," for an overview.
[78] Blanning, *Pursuit of Glory*, p. 215.   [79] Treasure, *Making of Modern Europe*, p. 207.

In the course of the nineteenth and twentieth centuries, monarchies and dynastic rivalries increasingly gave way to democratic states with foreign policies allegedly governed by national interests. These states were no longer ruled by hereditary aristocrats but by elected officials, bureaucrats and lawyers who were responsible to wider constituencies, many of them motivated by economic interests. Historically, we associate the goals of honor and standing with the leaders of dynastic political units, but nationalism indicates that they are at least as important for modern democratic, industrial and post-industrial states. Drawing on psychological research, recent work on nationalism contends that people manifest strong desires for group membership and identification because they provide a "heightened level of self-worth."[80] My argument goes a step further to contend that people who identify with nationalities or nations to some degree seek vicarious fulfillment and enhanced self-esteem through their victories and suffer a corresponding loss of esteem, even humiliation, when they suffer setbacks.

For these reasons international relations reveals a striking continuity across the centuries. This continuity was also facilitated by continuing domination of war and diplomacy by aristocrats down to 1914. The quest for honor and standing, initially a preserve of the aristocracy, penetrated deeply into the middle classes, many of whose members took their cues from the aristocracy and sought to assimilate its values and practices. In *A Cultural Theory of International Relations*, I include case studies of imperialism and World War I to document how the need for self-esteem was deflected outward in the form of international competition and a willingness to use force in defense of the national "honor."[81]

Proposition 2

Rising powers and dominant powers rarely make war against each other. When they do, rising powers are allied with at least one great power.

Rising powers seeking status are seeking admission in a high-status group. They need to demonstrate their possession of the qualities that warrant their acceptance. This creates something of a conundrum, as the principal qualification is military success. Attacking and defeating

---

[80] Greenfield, *Nationalism*; Migdal, *Boundaries and Belonging*; Hall, *National Collective Identity*, p. 37, for the quote.

[81] Lebow, *Cultural Theory of International Relations*, ch. 7.

important members of the "club" would alienate one or more great powers and would be seriously counterproductive to states seeking admission. An attack that led to defeat or a stalemate could prove disproportionately costly to the rising power. Rising powers are most likely to make war against a great power when that power is temporarily vulnerable and preferably as part of a larger coalition. A case in point is Prussia, who, backed by Britain, attacked Saxony in 1756, provoking a war with Austria that escalated into the Seven Years War.

For their part, great powers have little incentive to attack rising powers. Rising powers are generally not strong enough to threaten their security or standing, and they are generally careful not to antagonize them. An important exception is the Franco-Prussian War, provoked by Prussia, a rising power, as a means of unifying Germany. Louis Napoleon's France opposed German unification, in part for security reasons; historically, France had sought to keep Germany divided among many small states and to treat those along the Rhine as semi-protectorates. However, this strategy and French opposition to German unification also reflected the long-standing French commitment, a sign of status and standing, to being the dominant power on the continent. Great powers generally prefer to deflect the aggression of rising powers against third parties and subsequently moderate it by recognizing successful rising powers as great powers. The great powers on the whole responded this way to Prussia and Russia in the eighteenth century, Germany after 1870, the United States at the end of the nineteenth century and Japan after 1905. This pattern is the reverse of that predicted by power transition theories. An important, but limited, exception to this rule are great powers who seriously misjudge the military capability of a rising power and mistakenly think they are attacking or provoking a weak third party. The best example is Russia's provocation of Japan in 1904 that triggered the Russo-Japanese War of 1904–1905. France's willingness to go to war in 1870 also involved a serious misjudgment of Prussian military might.[82]

Proposition 3

The preferred targets of dominant and rising powers are declining great powers and weaker third parties. They also prey on great powers

---

[82] Lebow, *Between Peace and War*, pp. 244–246; Wawro, *Franco-Prussian War*, pp. 52, 65–68.

who are perceived as temporarily weak, preferably in alliance with other great powers.

If great and rising powers do not generally attack one another, their obvious targets are weaker third parties. Wars against them represent a cheap and seemingly low-risk means of demonstrating military prowess and of gaining additional territory and their resources. Once great but now seriously declining powers are also attractive targets for rising powers as defeating them has been considered more honorable and impressive than victories over much weaker third parties. In the seventeenth century, Sweden became a great power by attacking the Holy Roman Empire and France by defeating Spain, both declining adversaries. In the eighteenth century, Russia became a great power by winning wars against Sweden and the Ottomans. The nineteenth century offers three examples: Prussia's successful challenge of Austria, the United States' victory over Spain and that of Japan over China. Given the frequency of wars of this kind initiated by upwardly mobile states over the last four centuries, defeat of a declining great power might be considered an essential prerequisite for gaining recognition as a great power.

Proposition 4

So-called hegemonic wars (i.e. those involving most, if not all, of the great powers) are almost all accidental and the result of unintended escalation.

Many realist and power transition theories assume that hegemonic wars reflect determined efforts by dominant powers to attain hegemony or by challengers to replace them as dominant powers. My theory suggests a different proposition: hegemonic wars are almost always accidental. This does not mean that dominant powers do not seek hegemony, only that most of them do not try to attain it by means of general war. Rather, they attack weak states and declining great powers in the expectation of fighting limited and localized wars. Sometimes, these wars escalate into wider conflicts – what some call hegemonic wars – when other states come to the aid of these third parties. The Wars of Spanish and Austrian Succession and World War I are cases in point. As rising powers are assumed not to attack leading powers, we should not expect them to begin hegemonic wars. The only exception should be an attack by a rising power on a weak or declining great power that provokes an unintended series of escalations that draw in most, if not all, of the great powers. The Seven Years War can be characterized this way.

Proposition 5

Unintended escalation and miscalculation of the balance of power have deeper causes than incomplete information.

Neorealism and many rationalist explanations for war implicitly assume that war is the result of imperfect information. I maintain that good information is often available beforehand and that attempts to fight localized wars are often unrealistic and likely, if not probable, to lead to wider wars with uncertain outcomes.

Such departures from rational decisionmaking generally have systematic causes. The first is related to the motive for war: standing and honor. Honor traditionally involves risk, and it is through facing risk courageously that one gains honor. Honor seekers, whether individuals or states, are far more risk-prone than other actors. As Plato noted, the spirit is easily angered by slights, which include failures to honor one appropriately. Anger will be most acute when those responsible for such slights lack standing. Honor seeking, especially when combined with anger, makes leaders dismissive of risks and of those who warn them of these risks. They are less likely than others to engage in a serious evaluation of the scenarios by which they seek to gain honor or standing or to punish those who have slighted them.

Proposition 6

Weak and declining powers not infrequently initiate wars against great powers.

Existing theories of war direct most of their attention to dominant and rising great powers. They ignore weak and declining powers, but I hypothesize that the latter are a significant cause of interstate war. They act primarily for reasons of revenge. They are particularly sensitive to their honor and standing as they have once been great powers. They are readily angered by predatory attacks on them, especially those that result in loss of territory and standing, and seek revenge. They almost inevitably lose these wars. Examples include Charles XII's attack on Russia in 1707 and Ottoman attacks on Russia in the nineteenth century.

Let us now turn to the data set against which they and competing explanations for war will be evaluated.

4

Data set and findings

I have constructed a data set composed of all wars since 1648 involving at least one or more great or rising powers. In this chapter, I describe the data set and justify its appropriateness to my propositions. I open with a discussion of key terms and coding rules. I then discuss my findings, which, I contend, offer considerable support for my propositions and call into question some of the foundational assumptions and claims of opposing theories.

Definitions

In the introduction, I noted that peace and war are commonly treated as dichotomous categories, although in practice they represent two ends of a continuum. In between these poles, we encounter various states of cooperation and violence. The term "Cold War" was coined to represent one such in-between state: a tense, armed peace with periodic military conflicts between superpower client states or between one superpower and another's ally (e.g. the Chinese–American component of the Korean War). Distinguishing war from peace is further complicated by the fact that they are legal categories, giving states the option of fighting wars without declaring them, as the Soviet Union and Japan did in Mongolia in 1939 and the US and China did in Korea in 1950. For purposes of my data set, I count as a war any interstate conflict that produced over 1,000 deaths independently of whether either of the protagonists considered themselves to be at war.

My propositions are about five kinds of actors: great powers, dominant powers, rising powers, declining great powers and weaker states. All five categories are widely used in the literature, but this does not make it any easier to devise good operational definitions of them.

Great power is the most problematic category. The term came into use in the eighteenth century, although certain powers were given special privileges by the treaties of Westphalia. It only received institutional recognition at the Congress of Vienna. It is a status conferred on powerful political states by other powerful states. Great powers chair international conferences, participate in more elite convocations and are expected to assume responsibilities commensurate with their status.[1]

Three problems confound the coding of this category. The first concerns the category itself. My data set covers 360 years, from 1648 to 2008. As great powerdom only became institutionalized in 1815, it is not technically correct to project it back to 1648. I nevertheless believe this move is defensible because in the 167 years between Westphalia and Vienna rulers and their advisors consistently made estimates of their own state's strength and that of others. They identified the most powerful actors and treated them differently. Powerful actors in turn demanded privileges and courtesies not granted to others. In all but name, great powers were great powers.

Second, is the difficulty of determining when a state becomes or ceases to be a great power. There is no formal process of application and recognition; a great power is a state recognized and treated as such by other great powers. This status only becomes apparent through inclusion in select organizations and gatherings, the ability to host conferences which great powers attend, and, more importantly, leadership of collective efforts to uphold the peace or other norms of the system. It is not always evident when and if consensus emerges among the great powers to treat another state as one of them, and at times there are differences among the great powers about who qualifies for admission into their elite circle. Recognition is complicated by the tendency of great powers, responding to their perceived national interests, to treat as great powers states who are not as powerful as other members of the "club" (e.g. Italy after unification, China after 1945) or continue this status as a matter of courtesy for states whose power has seriously declined (e.g. France post-1945). For most of the period in question, there was something of a consensus among contemporary observers, and more recently among historians, about who qualified as a great power. There are more differences of opinion about when some of these states ceased to be great powers.

The third problem is ideological. States that should have been great powers on the basis of their military strength and accomplishments were sometimes only belatedly recognized as such because they were

---

[1] Kratochwil, *Rules, Norms, and Decisions*; Reus-Smit, *Moral Purpose of the State*, p. 137; Clark, *Legitimacy in International Society*, p. 100.

non-Christian or non-European (e.g. the Ottoman Empire, Japan). For this reason, there are often differences between when such countries were recognized as great powers by their contemporaries and by present-day historians. In every case, I have gone with the estimates of the latter.

The category of *dominant power* describes a great power that is significantly more powerful than other great powers. It is a subjective category because it too is based on judgments by policymakers and observers who make their own assessments of power. Not surprisingly, the understandings of policymakers and observers of which state, if any, is a dominant power often bears only a passing resemblance to scholarly efforts to "objectivize" this category through the application of standard measures of power.

Valentino and I explore these discrepancies in our critique of power transition theory.[2] We created a ranking of latent state power by multiplying a country's GDP by its total population. Data for both GDP and population came from data compiled by Angus Maddison.[3] In the case of empires, the GDP and populations of contiguous territories were included. Missing data were filled by interpolation. Figure 4.1 plots the evolving distribution of power in Europe (plus the United States and Japan) from 1640 to 2000. Some might object that our procedure puts too much weight on population, thereby overestimating the power of very populous states like Russia while underestimating the power of smaller states like Britain. Indeed, with at least 70 percent more citizens than the next most populous state, Russia had by far the largest population in Europe throughout this period. Since at least 1648, GDP and population have been very closely correlated, at least among the great powers. This relationship is robust because prior to 1900 the economic productivity of the major powers, Britain aside, derived principally from agriculture.[4] Russia not only had the largest population in Europe, but the largest GDP from the mid-1700s to the mid-1800s. Russia's GDP never drops below the third highest in Europe (excluding the United States and Japan) during the entire period. Our raw measure of power, based on population and GDP, shows considerable stability in the European rankings of leading powers. Spain's dominance in the post-Westphalia period gave way to Russia in the early 1700s, and was not surpassed by the United States until 1895. The United States maintained its position as a leading power until China overtook it in the 1980s.

---

[2] Lebow and Valentino, "Lost in Transition."
[3] Maddison, *Monitoring the World Economy.*   [4] *Ibid.,* p. 39.

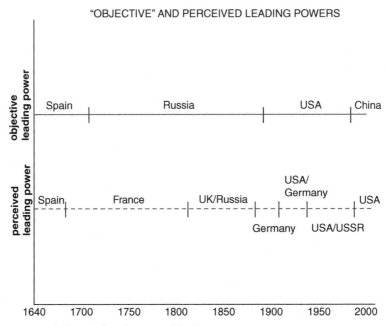

Figure 4.1 "Objective" and perceived leading powers

This ranking of leading powers bears at best a passing relationship to contemporary perceptions of leading powers represented by the lower line in Figure 4.1. By most accounts, France was perceived as the leading power from the early seventeenth century until the final defeat of Napoleon in 1815. For the remainder of the nineteenth century, Britain, and later Britain and Germany, were perceived as leading powers. By our measure, Russia remained the leading power for this entire period. The perception that the United States was the world's leading power did not take hold until the end of World War I, almost thirty years after it had become the most powerful state by our measure. It retained its lead until late in the twentieth century when it was surpassed by China in latent power.

What accounts for this discrepancy between power and perception? In the first instance, this imbalance is due to the efficiency of a state in extracting and using resources. Revolutionary France was particularly successful in this regard in comparison to Austria and Prussia. Britain was the most efficient state in the nineteenth century because of its political structure. Parliament was able to raise great sums of money at low interest rates on the open market to supplement what it raised through taxes. In the modern era, efficiency is also a function of technological capability. Throughout history, it is also attributable to agency.

Different leaders pursue different goals and devote widely varying percentages of their available income to building their armed forces and other activities that signal power or gain prestige. In pursuit of *gloire*, Louis XIV lavished extraordinary resources on his military, putting himself and his country deeply into debt. Prussia under the Hohenzollerns did the same. Frederick the Great spent over 75 percent of Prussia's income on his military, a figure way out of line with that spent by the great powers of his day.[5] In 2008, the United States, the modern-day Prussia, spent US $417 billion on defense. This amounted to 47 percent of the world total defense expenditures, although US GDP is only about 20 percent of world GDP.[6] Great powers that spend disproportionately on the military and use it to make conquests stand out among their peers and can attain dominant power status in the eyes of others even if it is not warranted by any measure of their overall material capabilities. For purposes of status and of balancing, perceptions of power appear more important than actual power or capabilities, just as perceptions of threat are more important than perceptions of power. I accordingly use the former to determine who qualifies as a dominant power.

Rising powers are states intent on gaining recognition as a great power and recognized as such by their contemporaries. Examples include Prussia and Russia in the eighteenth century, Italy in the nineteenth and the United States and Japan in the late nineteenth and early twentieth centuries. For most of the period under study, the international system was limited to Europe and its immediate environs and must be considered a regional system. Since World War II, distinct regional systems exist within the wider framework of the international system. For purposes of this study, I exclude from consideration powers not considered great internationally, although they may strive for regional dominance (e.g. Iran, Israel, Brazil). I code India after 1974 as a rising power by virtue of its nuclear capability, size, population and economy.

Historically, recognition as a great power has been gained by demonstrating military prowess. Until recently – more about this in Part III – rising powers could be identified by the percentage of disposable income they spent on their military. Sweden in the seventeenth century, Russia and Prussia in the eighteenth century and Japan in the nineteenth and twentieth centuries

---

[5] Lebow, *Cultural Theory of International Relations*, pp. 295–308.
[6] Hellmann, "Highlights of the Fiscal Year 2008 Pentagon Spending Request."

all spent disproportionately on their armed forces. European rulers in the eighteenth century typically spent between 20 and 40 percent of their income on their military establishments, although considerably more during wars. Peter the Great added forty new regiments to his army during the course of his reign, and throughout the Northern War allocated up to 80 percent of revenues for war or war-related industries.[7] In 1786, the last year of his reign, Frederick the Great spent 75 percent of his state's income on the army and directed another 5 percent to his war treasury.[8] Rising powers are often considered disruptive upstarts by great powers, which is another, more informal, way of identifying them. After Russia's victory over Sweden at Poltava in 1712, Peter the Great was commonly described as a dangerous barbarian; Leibniz referred to him as "the Turk of the north."[9] Frederick William I was considered a despot for imprisoning his son and executing his son's lover. With rare exceptions, great powers attempt to incorporate into the system those states who consistently demonstrate prowess on the battlefield. Japan was excluded in the nineteenth century but rapidly brought into the system after its defeat of Russia in 1905. The Soviet Union was not only excluded for ideological reasons, but a *cordon sanitaire* put in place to isolate it from the rest of Europe. This effort quickly failed and the Soviet Union was brought into the system and invited to join the League of Nations in 1934, but expelled in 1939 following its invasion of Finland.[10]

Declining powers are once great powers, perhaps once dominant great powers, who are understood to be losing power relative to other states. They may still retain the status of a great power, as Spain did throughout the eighteenth century and the Ottoman Empire in the nineteenth and early twentieth centuries. They are considered vulnerable not only because they are weak relative to other great powers but often because they are territorially overextended. Following its defeat by Russia in the Great Northern War (1700–1721), Sweden became a declining power in the eighteenth century, as did Poland-Lithuania until it ceased to exist after the last of its three partitions (1771, 1793 and 1795). Poland is atypical. It is usually difficult to ascertain when a great power becomes a declining power because there is no sharp and readily identifiable phase transition. The most important marker for most observers is defeat or poor performance in war. Given the goals of my research, it would be

---

[7] Hughes, *Peter the Great*, pp. 61–62. [8] Schulze, *Prussian Military State*.
[9] Hughes, *Peter the Great*, p. 86.
[10] Walters, *History of the League of Nations*, pp. 579–585, 801–810; Neilson, *Britain, Soviet Russia, and the Collapse of the Versailles Order*, pp. 50, 138–140.

Austria-Hungary: Rising Power, 1648–1714; Great Power, 1714–1918
Brandenburg-Prussia: Rising Power, 1648–1763; Great Power, 1763–1871
China: Rising Power, 1949–1990; Great Power, 1990–
England/Great Britain/UK: Rising Power, 1648–1688; Great Power, 1688–
France: Great Power, 1648–1659; Dominant Power, 1659–1815; Great Power, 1815–1940, 1945–
Germany: Great Power, 1871–1945; Rising Power, 1991–
India: Rising Power, 1974–
Italy: Rising Power, 1861–1943
Japan: Rising Power, 1868–1905; Great Power, 1905–1945; Rising Power, 1965–1990
Ottoman Empire: Great Power, 1648–1683; Declining Power, 1683–1918
Poland: Great Power, 1648–1733; Declining Power, 1733–1795
Russia: Rising Power, 1654–1721; Great Power, 1721–1917, 1991–
Sardinia-Piedmont: Rising Power, 1814–1861
Soviet Union: Rising Power, 1920–1941; Great Power, 1942–1991
Spain: Dominant Power, 1648–1658; Great Power, 1658–1713; Declining Power, 1713–1900
Sweden: Great Power, 1648–1711; Declining Power, 1711–1750
United Provinces: Great Power, 1648–1713; Declining Power, 1713–1792
United States: Rising Power, 1865–1917; Dominant Power, 1917–

Figure 4.2 Great, rising and declining powers: 1648–2000

tautological to use defeat as an indicator because attacks on such powers are what I am trying to explain. I accordingly rely on third-party estimates, but even this is not unproblematic because judgments of historians are made in retrospect and are inevitably influenced by their knowledge of how states fought in these wars. Some coding choices are more subjective than others. I have coded Austria-Hungary as a great power up until its collapse in 1918, although it could also be described as a declining power after its defeat by Prussia in 1866. Fortunately, these different codings make only a marginal difference to my findings: classification of Austria-Hungary as a declining power after 1866 results in only one less war initiated by a great power and one more by a declining power.

Weak powers are states who are widely recognized as militarily weak and easy prey for dominant, great and rising powers. They are most commonly small states with no natural defenses (e.g. the Palatinate in the seventeenth and eighteenth centuries). They can also be large and even populous states that are technologically backward (e.g. nineteenth-century Mexico and China) or developed states that have neglected their defense (Saxony in the eighteenth century).

Figure 4.2 identifies great, rising and declining powers from 1648 to the present. I have relied on multiple, well-regarded historical studies for these codings supplemented by my own judgment in cases where historians disagree.

Data set

In Chapter 2, I questioned the utility of studies of the origins of war that rely on correlational analyses. My data set would not perform any better, and I only use it descriptively. In this connection, it is useful to distinguish between the correlational and observational strategies. The latter is best described as a kind of indirect historical poll. Actors are surveyed to ascertain what they did and why they did it. Toward this end, I use secondary, and sometimes primary, sources to determine who was responsible for war and why they went to war. I observe the frequency and outcomes of these wars, data that I relate to the motives behind them, but not by means of correlation.

I evaluate my propositions against a data set of interstate wars fought between 1648 and 2008. The data set begins in 1648 because the Peace of Westphalia is the most widely recognized starting point of the modern state system. Before that, it is often difficult to distinguish between domestic and international conflicts. Warfare was a principal means by which rulers sought to establish control over territories they inherited or claimed and provoked resistance by those who would otherwise be subjugated. International violence could only be distinguished from its domestic counterpart after the emergence of "states" – sovereign political units with a *de facto* monopoly on the use of force within their borders – and some kind of international "system" to which they belonged. The latter conferred sovereignty on these units and made possible the institution of war.[11] In practice, Westphalia did not set up the modern state system, and we must be careful, as Dan Nexon properly cautions us, not to confuse the presence of a number of elements we associate with the sovereign territorial states with the actual existence of such a system.[12] By the eighteenth century, the system had more permanent players, rules and practices and some ability to manage conflicts short of war.[13]

---

[11] Tilly, "War Making and State Making as Organized Crime."

[12] Hinsley, *Power and the Pursuit of Peace*; Osiander, "Sovereignty, International Relations, and the Westphalian Myth"; Nexon, *Struggle for Power in Early Modern Europe*, pp. 265–288.

[13] Schroeder, "Life and Death of a Long Peace."

The Westphalian system was initially limited to Western powers and gradually extended to include non-Christian and non-European states. The nature of the units that made up the system changed dramatically over the course of 350 years. In 1648, almost all states were monarchies, many of them with few checks on their rulers. Since 1945, many have been democracies, although some more in form than in substance. This double transformation of membership and governance has unquestionably had profound implications for the behavior of political units, making comparisons in their behavior across the data set somewhat suspect. For the same reason, any patterns that span these centuries might be considered all the more impressive.

As I noted, my data set builds on an earlier one I constructed in 2007 for an article in which Benjamin Valentino and I evaluated the claims of power-transition theories.[14] As my part of the collaboration, I assembled a list of all interstate wars fought from 1648 to the present in which there were at least 1,000 combat deaths. To do this, I consulted widely used data sets (e.g. COW, Rasler and Thompson, Levy) and a number of prominent histories of the period in question. I included only wars in which at least one of the protagonists was a dominant, great or rising power. This gave a total of 94 wars (see Appendix) out of the approximately 150 interstate wars that have been fought since 1648.

Historian David Blainey doubts that any study of war aims will yield useful patterns. There is no evidence, he maintains, that "the desire for territory or markets or the desire to spread an ideology tended to dominate all other war aims. It is even difficult to argue that certain kinds of aims were dominant in one generation."[15] I do not contest this judgment, but hasten to point out that my propositions are about motives, not war aims. There is no necessary correlation between the two as war aims can be compatible with multiple motives and each of the motives I examine can find expression in a variety of war aims. Determining the motives of actors is nevertheless a challenging task and requires careful examination of relevant documents. Occasionally, they provide direct evidence about the motives of leaders and, more often, indirect evidence that allows me to infer them with some degree of confidence. An alternative, but complementary, strategy is to reason backwards from behavior to motives. Here, too, some degree of

---

[14] Lebow and Valentino, "Lost in Transition."
[15] Blainey, *Causes of War*, p. 149.

uncertainty is inevitable, especially when the behavior in question is compatible with multiple motives.

To determine the initiators of these conflicts, I consulted highly regarded secondary sources, all of which are cited in the bibliography. Coding initiators is usually, but not always, a straightforward matter. As Hidemi Suganami cautions, although wars usually result from a leadership decision to use force, culpability for them does not always lie with the state that took the last step. A declaration of war or the crossing of a border is usually the last step in a long process that involved provocations on both sides. The final step to war may have been forced in light of what preceded it. Suganami offers Japan's attack on Pearl Harbor as a case in point.[16] Historian Richard Evans goes further and considers such roles as "perpetrator," "victim" and "bystander" oversimplifications and "more an obstacle than aid to historical understanding."[17] Such an approach is reminiscent of Thucydides, whose layered text begins with a seeming determination of who was responsible for the war but is then undercut by an analysis of the causes of war that is increasingly difficult to reconcile with the concept of responsibility.[18]

My cases reveal different kinds of problems when it comes to coding. The First Coalition (1793–1797) of the French Revolutionary Wars has been dealt with extensively by historians, many of them with nationalist French or German agendas, each intent on blaming the other side and attributing to it far-reaching imperial aims. To code the case, we need to step back from these debates and look at the evidence more dispassionately. It tells a more complex story, of an Austria trying to prevent war, Prussia anxious to go to war to make territorial gains at the expense of France and a French National Assembly misled by Girondin warmongers to believe that one push east and the old regimes would collapse.[19]

The Franco-Prussian War also defies simple coding. France was goaded into declaring war by Bismarck's famous Ems Dispatch.[20] France was the technical initiator but Germany was the *de facto* initiator. In the 1815 War of the Seventh Coalition, I code the great-power coalition as the initiator, although it was Napoleon's return to power and the French army's preemptive march north into Belgium that provoked the

---

[16] Suganami, "Explaining War."   [17] Cited in *ibid.*
[18] Lebow, *Tragic Vision of Politics*, ch. 3.
[19] Blanning, *The Origins of the French Revolutionary Wars*, pp. 69–95.
[20] Pflanze, *Bismarck*, ch. 2; Wawro, *Franco-Prussian War*, pp. 18–20, 29–40.

renewal of war. The total number of initiators in the data set (1,078) is larger than the total number of wars because some conflicts, like the War of Austrian Succession (1740–1748), World War I (1914–1918) and World War II (1939–1945), have multiple initiators even when they are broken down into their components.

I am interested not only in who started wars but why they did so. Toward this end, I consulted appropriate secondary sources and occasionally primary sources as well. Some of my codings draw on case studies I published elsewhere; these include the wars of Louis XIV, Peter the Great, Frederick the Great and both world wars.[21] A data set is composed of a large number of cases, and individual cases must, of necessity, be summarized in the severely abbreviated form of codings. I restrict myself to five motives: security, interest, standing, revenge and a residual category of other. Security is fear-driven and the motive realists and many rationalists assume dominant and responsible for most wars. Concern for security can lead to preventive war, preemption or military action against third parties (e.g. unrestricted submarine warfare by Germany in 1918, the Soviet attack against Finland in 1939–1940) thought essential to win a primary conflict. To be as fair as I can to realist claims, I construe security broadly to include all kinds of war-initiation and code as security any war fought to preserve territory, independence or regimes (if they would be changed by a victorious adversary) or reputation (when it is considered important for reasons of security). The First through Third Coalitions against revolutionary France (1792 and 1798) I accordingly code as security-driven.

Interest is the principal liberal motive, and refers to policies intended to maximize wealth. Interest has long been a motive for war, and was the dominant or contributing incentive for some eighteenth-century wars. In our era, it was undoubtedly a major reason for Saddam Hussein's invasion of Kuwait in 1990. Sometimes, documentary evidence is available to substantiate the incentive interest provided for war. On other occasions, I rely on secondary sources, as I do with respect to security as a motive. Great care must be exercised in this regard because there is a tendency by historians, and even more so by international relations scholars, to interpret cases in terms of their intellectual orientations or preferred theories. To minimize this risk, I have consulted multiple sources for each case, and where there are divisions of opinion I have conducted my

[21] Lebow, *Cultural Theory of International Relations*, chs. 6–8; Lebow, *Forbidden Fruit*, ch. 3.

own investigation and sometimes assigned multiple codings for the same case. The origin of World War I offers an example. Initially, there was great controversy over which state or states were responsible, but there is now widespread agreement that Austria and Germany were the initiators, but there is no general agreement about the motives of their leaders. In deference to realists, I give security equal billing to standing as a motive, although in my judgment the latter was primary. I do the same for the American intervention in Afghanistan, which I would otherwise attribute to domestic politics and revenge. I believe the Bush administration was motivated primarily by their desire to invade Iraq and thought an invasion of Afghanistan would prepare the way politically for this goal.[22]

Standing describes relative ranking among states and, I contend, is the most important cause of war. It is an expression of the spirit, as is anger. Revenge is also an expression of anger, which, I noted earlier, *pace* Aristotle, is often aroused by slights to one's standing. Wars motivated by revenge are almost always efforts to regain territory lost to a predator in a previous war. In the eighteenth century, the Austrians went to war against Prussia, and the Ottomans against Austria and Russia for this reason. While revenge is an expression of the spirit, I code it as a distinct category because often, I believe, the conditions that trigger it are distinct from those that serve as catalysts for states hoping to enhance – rather than regain – their standing. Occasionally, the two combine, which is arguably the case in Louis XIV's Dutch war, Austria in 1914 and the American invasion of Iraq. As I am attempting to demonstrate the importance of standing as a motive, I have consistently attempted to privilege other motives whenever possible in my codings.

My residual category of "other" describes cases that cannot readily be subsumed under one of my other categories. Examples include wars where unwilling leaders have been drawn in by unauthorized military action of their subordinates, as in the 1938 attack on Changkufeng by the Japanese Kwantung Army. Other cases include wars motivated by domestic political concerns where regime survival was not at stake, as in the Prussian–Austrian war against Denmark in 1864. Prussia and Austria sought to improve their standing within the German community, but Bismarck also sought to divide and defeat the National–Liberal opposition in the Prussian legislature. I coded this case as both standing and other. I assign the coding of other to colonial

---

[22] Lebow, *Cultural Theory of International Relations*, pp. 459–480.

rebellions against great powers. Finally, there are Hitler's wars of aggression against Western Europe, the Balkan states and Russia. Some realists and others in thrall to the assumption of rationality have tried – unconvincingly, in my view – to account for these wars as rational responses to Germany's national or strategic interests.[23] I follow prominent biographers of Hitler (e.g. Bullock, Fest) and accounts of his foreign policy (e.g. Weinberg, Rich) who maintain that it defies rational explanation.

I am equally interested in the outcomes of wars. Did initiators win the wars they began? "Win" has two generally accepted meanings. The first is military victory, which involves a corresponding defeat of the other side. This outcome may be obvious in some situations but not in others. Who, for example, won the Chinese–American component of the Korean War or the 1969–1970 War of Attrition between Egypt and Israel? The second, more Clausewitzian, understanding of win is in reference to the goals for which the initiator resorted to force. On occasion, they can be achieved in the absence of victory. The Egyptians lost the 1973 October War against Israel but the costly nature of Israel's victory paved the way for a peace treaty with Egypt and a return of the Sinai Peninsula. The war accordingly helped Egyptian president Anwar el-Sadat to obtain his overall strategic goal.[24] On other occasions, victory fails to achieve the political goals for which the war was fought, as was the case with Israel's 1978 and 1982 invasions of Lebanon. There can also be a disconnect between the objectives of war and the underlying concerns that motivated it. In 2003, the US invaded Iraq and overthrew Saddam Hussein, achieving its proclaimed political goal. However, the Bush administration then faced an insurgency, growing military casualties and loss of support at home and abroad. In retrospect, military victory appears to have undermined, not advanced, the security or material interests of the US and its international standing. I believe future historians will regard the intervention as a serious political defeat. To avoid the problem of interpretation at multiple layers of analysis, I have chosen to use the most superficial definition of victory, the military one.

Military victory or defeat (or stalemate) frequently, but not always, correlates with the success or failure of a state's political goals. This is most likely when actors are motivated by interest or fear, and somewhat

---

[23] Schweller, *Deadly Imbalances*; Copeland, *Origins of Major Wars*, ch. 5; Mearsheimer, *Tragedy of Great Power Politics*, pp. 46, 181–182.
[24] Stein, "Calculation, Miscalculation, and Conventional Deterrence 1."

less so for leaders motivated by the spirit. As I noted in the previous chapter, honor can only be won by bravely facing risk, and, better yet, surmounting it. Facing up to a challenge without hesitation may be more important than winning, even when defeat can entail death of the actors in question or their state. Germany and Austria in 1914 offer a telling example. Emperor Franz Josef, chief of the general staff Franz Conrad von Hötzendorf and the war hawks in the army and foreign office considered the assassinations in Sarajevo of Archduke Franz Ferdinand and his wife Sophie a challenge by Serbia that could not be addressed diplomatically. They wanted war regardless of the consequences. The German Kaiser framed the conflict as a duel and his role that of "second" to Franz Josef. Honor had to be satisfied.[25]

Austrian and German prosecution of the war was also strongly influenced by considerations of honor. Conrad deployed the lion's share of his forces on the southern flank, and began an offensive against Serbia even though the principal threat to Austria-Hungary came from the expected Russian invasion of Galicia in the northeast.[26] As early as August 1916, Field Marshal Paul von Hindenburg acknowledged the strategic need to withdraw from Verdun and more generally to stop the war of attrition on the western front. He insisted on persevering because "the honor of Germany was at stake."[27] In November 1918, Prince Max of Baden's cabinet favored an armistice in the hope of protecting important national interests. Admiral Alfred von Tirpitz and General Erich Ludendorff were violently opposed and argued for a "last battle," to be fought on German soil to uphold the country's honor. They had no expectation of victory, quite the reverse. The allies required Germany to hand over its High Seas Fleet; instead, Admiral von Reuter had it scuttled at the British naval base in Scapa Flow. This affront to the British came at the same time the Germans were presented with a draft peace at Versailles, and the angered allies were unwilling to make many of the concessions the Germans desperately wanted.[28]

World War I is not an isolated case. From Louis XIV to George Bush, leaders have pursued honor or standing that was at the expense of important security and material interests. This is most likely to happen in two circumstances: when leaders are attempting to augment their honor or standing, or to preserve it in a war of revenge. Honor-driven

[25] Lebow, *Cultural Theory of International Relations*, pp. 338–365, for documentation.
[26] *Ibid.*, pp. 348–352.   [27] Neiberg, *Fighting the Great War*, p. 169.
[28] Lebow, *Cultural Theory of International Relations*, pp. 361–362.

leaders are angry leaders and, contrary to the expectations of prospect theory, are willing to take equally high risks in pursuit of gain or the avoidance of loss.[29]

Findings

My data set is reproduced in the Appendix. It is not a sample, as it includes all wars in the categories relevant to my propositions, so there is no need for tests for statistical significance. Some researchers interested in making predictions on the basis of their data nevertheless employ such tests. They treat their universe of cases as a sample of the universe of all possible cases. This is unnecessary in this instance because there was no state system before 1648, and, in this earlier period, as I noted previously, interstate wars are difficult to separate from intrastate violence. The present day is another cut-off point because I do not project my results forward. Rather, I argue that the international system is undergoing a transformation that is changing the distribution of motives for war and the association of these motives with war.

It would be equally fruitless to use statistical tests to establish the substantive importance of my findings. For such analysis to be meaningful, it requires appropriate benchmarks, and they do not exist. If I assert that standing is an important motive for war, in how many wars, or in what percentage of them, must it be implicated as a motive to validate or lend some degree of credence to my claim? Would 30 percent be significant, or ought it be 50 percent or more? As there is no accepted standard to which I can refer, I report my findings in the form of descriptive statistics, offer arguments for why I think these percentages are or are not substantively important and let readers draw their own conclusions. I do this for all claims I make except for those where comparisons are complicated by the asymmetrical distribution of the several kinds of states whose behavior I describe. Here, weighted comparisons are necessary.

On the whole, the data offer strong support for my propositions. They indicate patterns of war-initiation strikingly at odds with the expectations of realist, power transition and rational theories of war. They offer limited support at best for the balance of power theory.

[29] *Ibid.*, pp. 365–368, 537–539.

Proposition 1

The most aggressive states are rising powers seeking recognition as great powers and dominant great powers seeking hegemony.

There were 119 initiators of 94 wars, as some wars had multiple initiators or multiple components with different initiators. Dominant powers account for 24 initiations and rising powers for 27. Together they are responsible for 47 of my 94 wars (there were co-initiators of 4 wars), or 46 percent of the wars fought between 1648 and 2003. Great powers initiated 49 wars (52 percent), less than half of which were against a dominant or another great power. Great-power wars against dominant powers were most often in alliance with other great powers and part of a collective effort to keep a dominant power from achieving hegemony. The several coalitions against Napoleon in 1815 are cases in point. See Figure 4.3.

As there are many fewer dominant and rising powers than there are great powers in the system at any given time, we need a weighted measure to compare their respective aggressiveness. To do this, I calculated the total number of years for each of my four categories of initiators: dominant, great, rising and declining powers. France was a dominant power for 156 years, between 1659 and 1815, and the US for 91 years from 1918 to the present. This produces a total of 247 dominant power state-years, which represents 9 percent of the total state-years. Great-power state-years equal 1,259 (48 percent), and is the largest category as there were more states in this than other categories during this period and many of them stayed great powers

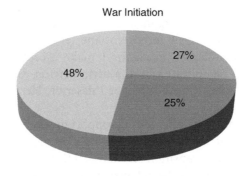

Figure 4.3   War initiation

for a long period of time. Great Britain (later the United Kingdom) was a great power from 1688 to the present, for 320 years, while Austria-Hungary was a great power for 204 years, from 1714 to 1918. Rising powers total 643 state-years (24 percent) and declining powers 498 (19 percent). In effect, dominant and rising powers, which account for only 33 percent of state-years, were collectively responsible for slightly less than half (46 percent) of all wars. By contrast, great powers initiated 38 percent of wars but represent almost half (48 percent) of state-years.

Equally revealing are the motives states have for starting wars. As some initiators had multiple motives, there are more motives (107) than wars (94). Standing, which I credit as the motives for 62 wars, or 58 percent of the total, is by far the most common motive. It is followed by security (19 cases, 18 percent), revenge (11 cases, 10 percent), interest (8 cases, 7 percent) and other (7 cases, 7 percent). The eighteenth century is commonly considered the great era of dynastic rivalry in which rulers went to war for honor and standing. However, there is only irregular variation in the percentage of wars caused by standing across the centuries. Eleven of 16 wars were motivated by standing in the eighteenth century, 21 of 24 in the nineteenth century and 17 of 31 in the twentieth. Standing is consistently a leading motive, something not true of other motives. Security is a decidedly more important motive for war in the twentieth century, where it is a dominant or contributing motive for 11 wars, and only a total of 9 in earlier centuries. Six of 9 wars motivated by interest took place in the seventeenth and eighteenth centuries when mercantilism was the accepted economic wisdom and leaders believed that the wealth of the world was finite.[30] The most unambiguous instance of interest as a motive for war was the Anglo-French takeover of Egypt in 1882, but even in this case standing was an important secondary motive.[31] Most wars of revenge took place in the eighteenth century. The category of other is relatively uniform and it is difficult to offer generalizations about its diverse causes, although, as I noted earlier, most, if not all, of them can ultimately be reduced to fear, interest or standing at the domestic level. See Figure 4.5b.

While standing is a consistent motive for war, it is not uniform in its manifestations. In the seventeenth and eighteenth centuries, it found expression within a context of dynastic rivalry: rulers sought to achieve *gloire* through conquest. Many of the rulers of this era personally led

---

[30] Hirschman, *Passions and the Interests*; Hont, *Jealousy of Trade*; Boyle, "Mystery of Modern Wealth."
[31] Al-Sayyid-Marsot, "British Occupation of Egypt from 1882"; Sanderson, *England, Europe and the Upper Nile*; Brown, *Fashoda Reconsidered*.

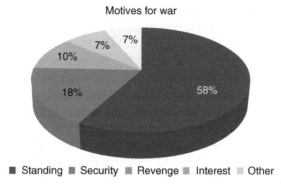

Figure 4.4   Motives for war

their armies into battle (e.g. Louis XIV, Frederick I and II, Peter the Great), greatly enhancing their claims to *gloire*. By the nineteenth century, this had changed; Napoleon was the last major ruler to appear regularly on the battlefield. The search for standing increasingly became a national concern, even in countries like Germany and Austria that could hardly be considered democratic. Foreign-policymaking elites were still overwhelmingly aristocratic in origin and perhaps more intensely committed to gaining or maintaining national honor now that traditional honor codes held less sway in interpersonal relations. Public opinion identified strongly with national states, also in countries where the intelligentsia and middle classes were kept at the peripheries of power and the status hierarchy. This phenomenon became more pronounced in the twentieth century and was a principal cause of World War I.[32]

Security has always been an important concern in international relations. My data nevertheless indicate that it is not a major cause of wars among the great powers. Only 19 of 94 wars appear to have been motivated by security in whole or in part. Seven of 18 initiators who appear to have acted out of concern for their security were also motivated by standing. A case in point is the 1898–1899 US declaration of war against Spain, which began with an attack on the Spanish colony of Cuba. President McKinley and many Senators were keen to establish America as a great power – which explains why they occupied and annexed Puerto Rico and the Philippines. For reasons of national security, they also considered it essential to intervene in the deadlocked civil war in Cuba because deterioration in health conditions on the island had been responsible for a Yellow Fever epidemic that spread to the American

[32] Lebow, *Cultural Theory of International Relations*, pp. 305–370.

Gulf states.[33] World War I also warrants double coding. I contend that standing was a principal motive for German and Austrian leaders, while more conventional interpretations stress security. As noted earlier, I have accordingly given security equal status. Another interesting case is the Soviet invasion of Afghanistan. For reasons of standing, Soviet leaders did not want to lose their political primacy in an adjacent client state. This concern was reinforced by fears that Islamic fundamentalism would spread into their own Muslim periphery.[34] Here, too, I credit both motives.

One war appears to have been motivated by security and material interests: the US and coalition attack on Iraq in 1990.[35] Most of the other nine war-initiations that I code as security-driven can confidently be attributed to this motive. They include the 1939 Soviet invasion of Finland and the Soviet attack in the same year on the Japanese Kwantung Army in Mongolia.[36] A few security-driven wars are open to alternative or multiple interpretations, among them the Japanese attack on the US and Western colonial powers in 1941. Because of the oil embargo organized by Washington, Japanese leaders became increasingly desperate and many considered they had no choice but to go to war before it was no longer possible.[37] This was nevertheless a dilemma of Japanese making: had the Japanese not invaded China as part of their drive to achieve hegemony in Asia, there would have been no embargo. Other cases are the Soviet invasion of Hungary and the US intervention in Indochina. As with Afghanistan, these interventions were considered essential to national security by Soviet and American policymakers respectively. In the Vietnamese and Afghan interventions, their understandings can be shown to be flawed, if not paranoid.[38]

The relative insignificance of security as a motive is to some degree an artifact of my data set. I examine war-initiation and, as we have seen, security only infrequently motivates initiators. It is undeniably a primary concern for states who are the targets of their attacks. To the extent that rising and dominant powers behave aggressively, security is correspondingly more important for other actors.

---

[33] Lebow, *Between Peace and War*, pp. 47–53.
[34] Garthoff, *Détente and Confrontation*, pp. 1023–1046.
[35] Lebow, *Cultural Theory of International Relations*, pp. 459–480.
[36] Jakobson, *Diplomacy of the Winter War*; Haslam, *Soviet Union and the Threat from the East*, pp. 112–134.
[37] Iriye, *Origins of the Second World War*, pp. 146–180.
[38] Logevall, *Choosing War*; Garthoff, *Détente and Confrontation*, pp. 1023–1046.

Proposition 2

Rising powers and dominant powers rarely make war against each other. When they do, rising powers are allied with at least one great power.

The data offer strong support for this proposition. Dominant powers initiated 24 wars and rising powers 27. They fought each other on only two occasions. In an extension of its 1635–1648 war against Spain, France attacked Spain again in 1648 and fought a decade-long war to supplant the Habsburgs – in control of Austria, Spain and the Low Countries – as the dominant power in Europe. England, a rising power, joined the struggle against Spain in 1648. The other case is the 1950 attack on US forces in Korea by the People's Republic of China. Beijing tried without success to deter an American invasion of North Korea and, when that failed, intervened to safeguard Manchuria and the Communist revolution.[39] Washington wanted to avoid war with China, but the Truman administration felt compelled to cross the 38th Parallel for domestic political reasons and was deliberately misled about the risks of war by field commander General Douglas MacArthur.[40]

Proposition 3

The preferred targets of dominant and rising powers are declining great powers and weaker third parties. They also prey on great powers who are perceived as temporarily weak, preferably in alliance with other great powers.

Weaker parties and declining once-great powers are understood to be relatively "soft" targets and low-cost means of demonstrating military prowess. They are secondarily a means of augmenting a state's strategic position or material capabilities through annexation or informal control. The data support this proposition. Of the 27 wars initiated by rising powers, 6 were against declining great powers and 7 against weak powers. Rising powers initiated 10 wars against great powers, almost all of them in alliance with great or dominant powers. A case in point was Prussia's attack on Austria in 1740 in alliance with France, Bavaria and Saxony, taking advantage not only of allies, but of Salic Law, under which Maria Theresa, a woman, had no claim to the Austrian throne. Frederick

---

[39] Chen, *China's Road to the Korean War*.

[40] Neustadt, *Presidential Power*, pp. 120–145; Spanier, *Truman–MacArthur Controversy*, pp. 104–113; Lebow, *Between Peace and War*, pp. 148–216.

succeeded in detaching the rich Austrian province of Silesia, awarded to Prussia by the Treaty of Aix-la-Chapelle in 1748. Rising powers often pursue a "jackal" strategy: they go after the weak or move in for a "kill" once a more powerful actor has been engaged and weakened by more powerful hunters.

Dominant powers initiated 23 wars, none of them against rising powers. They began 9 wars against great powers, 5 against declining powers and 10 weak powers. Louis XIV twice attacked the Spanish Netherlands (in 1672 and 1683), which was an outpost of Spain's European holdings and at the end of a long supply line, known as the "Spanish Road." In the War of Austrian Succession and the Seven Years War, France attacked a vulnerable Austria. The data indicate that dominant powers are the most disruptive actors. They start not only a large number of wars but particularly destructive wars that involve other great or dominant powers. They are responsible for every war since 1648 that drew in a majority of the great powers. See Figures 4.5a and 4.5b.

Proposition 4

So-called hegemonic wars (i.e. those involving most, if not all, of the great powers) are almost all accidental and the result of unintended escalation.

Hegemonic war is a plastic concept that is defined with reference to the power of the warring parties and to a war's outcome for the distribution of power in the system.[41] I avoid using the term for this reason but even more because it is inextricably connected to a set of theories about the causes of war (power transition and neorealism). Hegemonic war assumes particular causes rather than serving as a neutral category for testing competing explanations for war. I rely instead on the more inclusive concept of "systemic" war. It describes conflicts that draw in a majority of the existing great powers and the dominant power, if there is one at the time. At least one of these powers must be on the opposing side. My definition generates nine systemic wars. It excludes two of the wars sometimes described as part of hegemonic conflict between France and the Habsburgs (France's 1648 and 1654 wars against Spain) because they did not involve a majority of the great powers. It includes the

---

[41] Organski and Kugler, *War Ledger*; Gilpin, *War and Change in International Relations*.

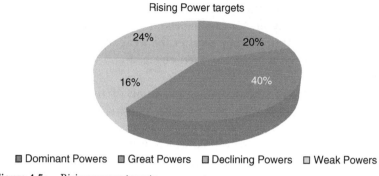

Figure 4.5a   Rising power targets

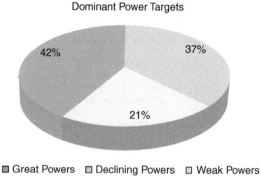

Figure 4.5b   Dominant power targets

Crimean War, not considered a hegemonic war because the two leading powers – Britain and France – were on the same side. It nevertheless involved a majority of the great powers, Austria and Prussia aside. As I do in the data set, I break these wars out into their major component parts. These systemic wars account for about 90 percent of the casualties caused by great powers wars over the last five centuries.[42]

In terms of duration and casualties, systemic wars are the most costly interstate wars. As Figure 4.6 indicates, they cannot be explained by so-called rational, strategic arguments. In almost every case, the initiators lost the wars they started. Figure 4.4 indicates that the number of

[42] Levy, *War in the Modern Great Power System*, ch. 4.

War	Initiator	Result	Cause
Franco-Dutch (1672–1679)	D	I loses	ME
Grand Alliance (1688–1697)	D	I loses	ME
Spanish Succession (1701–1714)	D	I loses	ME
Austrian Succession (1740–1748)	R	R wins	E
Seven Years (1756–1763)	R/D	I's lose	ME
French Revolutionary (1792–1815)	G/D	I's lose	multiple MFs
Crimean (1853–1856)	G	I loses	ME
World War I (1914–1918)	R/G	I's lose	ME/MF
World War II (1939–1945)	G	I's lose	MF

D = dominant power; R = rising power; G = great power; I = initiator; ME = miscalculated escalation; E = escalation; MF = military failure; PF = erroneous calculations of adversarial resolve and domestic support

Figure 4.6 Systemic wars

defeated initiators is even larger when we break out the French Revolutionary and Napoleonic Wars and World Wars I and II into their component conflicts. Every dominant and great power that initiated a systemic war was defeated. While this is true of the French Revolutionary and Napoleonic Wars as a whole, some clarification of their component wars is required. The First Coalition pitted France against Prussia and Austria. Both France and Prussia sought war, although France was the initiator. In Clausewitzian terms, France failed to achieve its objectives: the overthrow of the old regime in the east, but did extend its physical presence through military victories. The Fourth Coalition pitted Prussia, Austria and Russia against France, who was the initiator and victor of this round of fighting. In the Fifth Coalition, Austria and Britain fought France and Bavaria. This war also ended favorably for the French with victory at the Battle of Wagram in July 1809. Not content with control over most of the continent, Napoleon subsequently invaded Russia, which provoked another coalition, a French defeat and the first exile of Napoleon.

There are two principal reasons for this outcome. In 6 of 9 wars (in Figure 4.7) failure was due to miscalculated escalation. Initiators sought to win short, isolated wars against weaker powers. Their aggressions provoked the intervention of other powers and ultimately led to their defeat. This happened three times to Louis XIV. The Crimean War was brought about by Russia's failure to take seriously the threat of Anglo-French intervention on the side of the Ottoman Empire to preserve its control of Constantinople and the Straits. World War I was the result of Austria's unsuccessful attempt, with German backing, to wage an isolated war against Serbia. It provoked unwanted multiple escalations:

War	Initiator	Result	Cause
FRENCH REVOLUTIONARY			
First Coalition	G coalition	I wins	PF
Second Coalition	G coalition	I's lose	MF
Fourth Coalition	G coalition	I wins	MF
Fifth Coalition	G coalition	I's lose	MF
Invasion of Russia	D	I loses	MF
Seventh Coalition	D	I loses	MF
WORLD WAR I			
August 1914	G/D	I's lose	ME/MF
Unrestricted sub warfare	D	I loses	MF
WORLD WAR II			
Europe	G/R	I's lose	MF
Pacific	G	I loses	MF

[i] I code France as the initiator, and it failed to achieve its goals of toppling the Prussian and Austrian thrones. It did extend French influence to the east with the creation of the Batavian Republic and occupation of the Prussian Rhineland.

Figure 4.7 War breakouts

Russia supported Serbia, France supported Russia and Britain supported France. Subsequently, the Ottoman Empire, Bulgaria, Romania, Greece, Japan, the US and other nations entered the war bringing the total number of combatant states up to thirty-two. A. J. P. Taylor argued, unpersuasively in my opinion, that World War II was the result of miscalculated escalation; he contends that Anglo-French appeasement with regard to Czechoslovakia convinced Hitler that the Western powers would not come to the defense of Poland in 1939.[43] One war, the War of Austrian Succession, had a more complicated pattern of escalation that can be described as more willful than miscalculated.[44]

The second generic reason for failure is military: initiators were not powerful enough to defeat the states they attacked or the coalitions they aroused against them. In the War of the First Coalition, the French assumed that it would take only one push to topple the thrones of Austria and Prussia, while the Prussians made the mistake of believing that French armies would be in disarray without aristocratic officers and would readily be overwhelmed by the combined might of Austria and Prussia.[45] Napoleon made the same error in attacking Russia and, later,

---

[43] Taylor, *Origins of the Second World War.*
[44] Anderson, *War of the Austrian Succession*; Simms, *Three Victories and a Defeat*, pp. 247–273.
[45] Schroeder, *Transformation of European Politics*, pp. 100–276.

the United Kingdom of the Netherlands, during his hundred-day return to power from exile on Elba. The only success was Prussia's victory over Austria in the War of Austrian Succession. Frederick was foiled, and almost ruined, in his subsequent efforts at aggrandizement. Late in life, he acknowledged that the balance of power and the internal limitations of his state made it increasingly difficult to make additional territorial gains.[46]

Proposition 5

Unintended escalation and miscalculation of the balance of power have deeper causes than incomplete information.

Rationalist, realist and neorealist theories acknowledge the role of miscalculation in war-initiation. They nevertheless assume that would-be initiators make reasonable efforts to assess the military balance and to devise strategies to design around the military advantages of opponents. Rational actors can still miscalculate because the political-military environment is often difficult to read. Leaders cannot know the resolve and military capability of adversaries with certainty, or the likelihood that public opinion and allies will rally to their support of states that are attacked. War, as Clausewitz famously observed, is characterized by friction and chance.[47] Even in a world of incomplete information, rational leaders ought to have a better-than-even chance of getting it right if they gather pertinent information, assess its implications, and, preemption aside, start wars only when they consider the likelihood of success to be high. The empirical record tells a different story. All but one initiator of a war that escalated into a systemic war ended up a loser. In my critique of rational theories, I presented data on all interstate wars fought since 1945 indicating that this is a more general phenomenon. Some two-thirds of initiators lost the wars they began, and an even higher percentage failed to achieve the goals for which they went to war.

What explains this anomaly? Case studies indicate two principal causes for both kinds of decisional failures. The first is motivated bias. Leaders facing a combination of strategic and domestic threats they believe can only be surmounted by war, or a challenge to an adversary

---

[46] Anderson, *War of the Austrian Succession*, p. 61.
[47] Clausewitz, *On War*, pp. 119–122.

that raises the prospect of war, must reduce the anxiety associated with a decision to move forward. They generally do so by denying the risk associated with their policies. They solicit supporting information and encouragement from subordinates and intelligence agencies and become insensitive to information, even warnings, that their policies may, or are likely to, lead to disaster.[48] Janice Stein, Jack Snyder and I have documented this kind of motivated bias in a number of crisis decisions, including Germany, Austria and Russia in 1914, the US decision to cross the 38th Parallel in Korea in 1950, India's "Forward Policy" that provoked its 1961 border conflict with China, Khrushchev's decision in 1962 to secretly deploy missiles in Cuba, Israel's intelligence failure in October 1973, and Argentina's in its invasion of the Falklands/Malvinas in 1982.[49] Minimal or self-serving risk assessment is also typical of actors seeking honor or standing, which can only be won by assuming great risks.

Anger can have the same effect. It enters the picture when leaders believe they or their state has been slighted. Elsewhere, I document several decisions for war (e.g. Germany and Austria in 1914, the Anglo-American invasion of Iraq in 2003) where anger, associated with a concern for honor, combined to produce rash and ill-considered initiatives.[50] Historical accounts indicate evidence for this phenomenon in Louis XIV's wars against the Netherlands and the Rhineland-Palatinate, the Wars of the Second and Third Coalitions and the Crimean War. Extensive research into the individual cases in the data set might reveal just how often anger and the quest for honor or standing combine to bring about decisions to use force with only minimal evaluation of the risks. It would be interesting to determine the percentage of cases in which information is readily available, or actually on hand – as it was in several of the cases I studied – indicating that expectations of victory were unrealistic. Finally, we might inquire how often superficial risk estimates occur in the absence of either of these conditions or in wars not motivated by standing. Regardless of the possible causes of superficial risk assessment, the demonstrable fact that it is widespread helps explain some of the otherwise anomalous outcomes we observe. It also raises serious problems for rational theories of war.

---

[48] Janis and Mann, *Decision-Making*, pp. 57–58, 197–233.
[49] Lebow, *Between Peace and War*; Jervis, Lebow and Stein, *Psychology and Deterrence*; Lebow and Stein, *We All Lost the Cold War*.
[50] Lebow, *Cultural Theory of International Relations*, chs. 7 and 9.

Proposition 6

Weak and declining powers not infrequently initiate wars against great powers.

All studies of hegemonic war, and most studies of war-initiation, focus on the great powers. They ignore declining powers and weaker states. My data set indicates that both kinds of actors initiate wars against more powerful states. Declining powers started 14 wars and weak powers 4. Great powers were collectively the targets of 14 of these wars. Eleven of the 14 wars against great powers were wars of revenge in which declining or weak powers sought, without success, to regain territory taken from them in previous wars by great powers (or rising powers who had since become great). Not infrequently, the initiators lost additional territory as a result of these wars, as the Ottomans did in 1812 when they were forced to cede Bessarabia to Russia. Sweden suffered a worse fate when Charles XII attempted to punish the Baltic states in 1700. Russian support for his adversaries led him to launch an ill-prepared and disastrous invasion of Russia that resulted in Sweden's loss of regional hegemony. Wars initiated by weak and declining powers offer more evidence that angry leaders do not make careful estimates of risk. This phenomenon is all the more remarkable in the case of weak and declining powers, whose victory over more powerful states should be seen as problematic from the outset.

Conclusions

My data suggest that leaders of rising, great and dominant powers are rational in the sense that they generally choose declining and weak powers as their adversaries. This has traditionally been the cheapest way to demonstrate military prowess, augment state power and territory, and gain standing. Rational theories of war have failed to identify this pattern of aggression, although it has been remarkably consistent over the centuries.

Rational and offensive and defensive realist theories impute too much instrumental reason to actors. Leaders capable and willing to make the kinds of calculations rational theories require would also attempt to make serious estimates of the risks of war and, extraordinary situations aside, not resort to force unless the evidence indicated they had a high chance of achieving their political goals. In practice, initiators win slightly less than half of the wars they begin. They won 46, lost 45, drew 6 and 2 (Afghanistan and Iraq) are ongoing. Of the victories won by rising, great and dominant powers, 26 were against weak or declining powers. Even these wars can escalate into wider, unanticipated and undesired wars against great or dominant powers. In almost every case where such escalation occurred, leaders of the initiator were to varying degrees insensitive to the risks of escalation and ended up losing the war. Initiators lost all 9 of the systemic wars they provoked. Initiators of all kinds appear to do a relatively poor job of estimating the military balance. Evidence from case studies indicates a general tendency to overrate one's own military capability and to underestimate that of adversaries. Many initiators also expect their adversary to fight the kind of war they themselves are prepared to fight and win and are surprised when they resort to alternative strategies.

The behavior most strikingly at odds with rational theories of war, but consistent with classical realism, is the aggressiveness of dominant powers. Dominant states are generally not content with their status and authority. They seek more power through additional conquests, and by doing so hope to be able to impose their preferences on others. Habsburg Spain, France under Louis XIV and Napoleon, Wilhelminian and Nazi Germany and the United States in the post-Cold War era are cases in point. None of these states was seriously threatened by rising powers or coalitions of great powers. They went to war because they thought they were powerful enough to become more powerful still. For relatively little prospective gain, they took great risks. These powers consistently defied the expectations of prospect theory. Aggressive, dominant powers sought to control the European continent, if not the world. More troubling still for rational theories, their goals were clearly unrealistic. Brooks and Wohlforth rightly observe that one of the enduring tragedies of great-power politics "is precisely when decisionmakers believe they can ignore counterbalancing constraints that they are most likely to call them forth with overambitious foreign policies."[51]

There is no support for power transition theories. They are based on the premise that there is a dominant power with sufficient authority to order the international system in a manner that is beneficial to itself. This order is assumed to operate at the expense of other states, thus arousing their hostility. Rising powers go to war when they believe themselves strong enough to defeat dominant powers and restructure the system to their advantage.[52] Alternatively, dominant powers attack rising powers

[51] Brooks and Wohlforth, *World Out of Balance*, p. 26.
[52] Organski and Kugler, *War Ledger*.

to prevent them from becoming strong enough to consider challenges.[53] Since 1648, no European power has been in a position to order the system in this way.[54] My data indicate that rising powers and great powers rarely initiate wars against dominant powers. When they do, it is usually as part of a coalition with the goal of preventing an already dominant power from becoming even stronger and perhaps attaining the kind of hegemony that power transition stipulates as the norm. Dominant powers in turn only infrequently attack great powers, preferring instead to expand or demonstrate their prowess by attacking weaker parties.

The empirical evidence indicates a pattern of conflict the reverse of that predicted by leading power transition theories. Great power wars arise in the absence of hegemony, not because of it. These wars lead to power transitions and peace settlements that often impose new orders – but almost always as a result of a consensus among the leading powers. Postwar orders are never dictated by a single power and endure as long as a consensus holds among the major powers responsible for them.[55]

The realist concept of the security dilemma finds little support. Only nineteen wars were motivated by security. War, however, may not be the most appropriate test of the security dilemma. John Herz, who introduced the concept, maintained that states only launched preemptive wars *in extremis*.[56] Defensive realists attempt to define conditions, actual or perceptual, in which this occurs. The security dilemma may be responsible for insecurity, military buildups and the conflicts that result; I cannot use my data to evaluate this proposition. The data do suggest that the security dilemma can at most be responsible for only a few wars, as security was the motive for less than 20 percent of great-power wars. During the Cold War, the only so-called bipolar era in modern times, superpowers were as acutely sensitive to the loss and gain of allies and clients as they were in eras of bipolarity. Such behavior makes sense if we posit great power leaders as at least as much concerned with the effects on their standing as they are with any military or economic benefits or costs from bandwagonning or defection.

The logic of the security dilemma indicates that the most threatened states should be the weakest ones. More powerful states should feel less

---

[53] Gilpin, *War and Change in International Relations*.
[54] Kaufman, Little and Wohlforth, *Balance of Power in World History*.
[55] Lebow and Valentino, "Lost in Transition."
[56] Herz, *International Politics in the Nuclear Age*, p. 243; Reiter, "Exploding the Powder Keg Myth."

threatened, and dominant powers less threatened still. Kenneth Waltz relies on this last inference for his claim that bipolar systems are more stable and less war-prone than their multipolar counterparts.[57] Because the two poles are so powerful *vis-à-vis* everyone else, they are that much more secure and less affected by the addition or defection of third parties to or from their respective blocs. My data offer no support for this eminently logical conjecture, quite the reverse. Six of the 19 wars motivated by security took place during the Cold War, and all but one of them involved a superpower.

Balance of power theories assume that security is, or should be, the first concern of all states because of the anarchical nature of the international environment. Threats arise from the environment itself in the form of the security dilemma or from the ambitions of predatory states. Either phenomenon encourages states to augment their military capability and form alliances to deter would-be aggressors. Following Morgenthau, realists assume that war is least likely when the *status quo* powers have a clear military advantage and a demonstrable will to use force to maintain the *status quo*.[58] Conversely, war is most likely when an "imperialist" power, to use Morgenthau's language, or a coalition of them, have a military advantage or the *status quo* powers, for whatever reason, are unable to combine against them.

The data indicate mixed support at best for balance of power theories. Unfavorable balances of power fail to deter states seeking hegemony, but do prevent their victories. This claim must be advanced with some caution because my data set does not include "non-wars" that might have been deterred by an unfavorable balance of power, buttressed perhaps by effective practice of immediate deterrence. What does emerge from this data set and other studies is a striking pattern of miscalculated escalation by great and dominant powers and their failure to win any of the systemic wars for which they are responsible.[59] This outcome speaks well for balancing as a measure of last resort, but not of war prevention.

The aggressiveness of some declining and weak powers is at odds with both the security dilemma and balance of power theories. Weaker states should balance or bandwagon, not attack, more powerful neighbors. John Herz, however, would not be surprised by the aggressiveness of

---

[57] Waltz, *Theory of International Politics*, pp. 169–170.
[58] Morgenthau, *Politics Among Nations*, pp. 125, 155–159, 162–166.
[59] Lebow, *Between Peace and War*; Jervis, Lebow and Stein, *Psychology and Deterrence*; Kaufman, Little and Wohlforth, *Balance of Power in World History*, p. 238.

dominant powers, as he recognized that certain states were motivated by interests "that go beyond security proper."[60]

The evidence for standing as a motive for war is strong. Standing (n = 62) accounted for 58 percent of the total motives (n = 109), putting it far ahead of security (n = 20, 18 percent), other (n = 7, 6 percent), revenge (n = 11, 10 percent) and interest (n = 8, 7 percent). It is the leading motive in every century of the almost four centuries included in the data set. Revenge, like standing, is an expression of *thumos* or spirit. Together, standing and revenge account for 73 of 107 motives. They are responsible for 68 percent of all wars. These figures strike me as significant. The importance of standing as a motive of war may help explain the remarkable failure of so many initiators to make reasonable assessments of the military balance and the likelihood of escalation.

From the very beginning of civilization in Mesopotamia and the Mediterranean basin, individuals and political units have gained honor and standing through military prowess and secondarily through what Veblen calls conspicuous consumption.[61] For almost the entire period of the data set, powers became great because of their military and economic might. In the late nineteenth century, war began to lose some of its appeal. This process accelerated after both world wars. Various European and non-European rising powers have been attempting, with some success, to claim standing on the basis of other criteria.[62] In the postwar period, Germany, Japan and now China have sought standing primarily by non-military means. This development seems long overdue, as one of the defining characteristics of modernity is the opening of multiple pathways to honor and standing. To the extent that war is increasingly held in ill-repute, other means of claiming status will become more prominent and the frequency of war should decline.

[60] Herz, *International Politics in the Nuclear Age*, p. 234, note a.
[61] Veblen, *Theory of the Leisure Class*.
[62] Lebow, *Cultural Theory of International Relations*, pp. 480–504.

PART III

War in the future

5

Interest and security

Many wonders are there, but none is more *deinon* (wondrous, strange, powerful, awful) than man.

Sophocles[1]

In this chapter, I turn from war in the past to war in the future. I ask if the future will resemble the past. Will interstate war plague us in this century as it has in the past? Is it conceivable that interstate war could diminish and even disappear as peaceful means for resolving competition among states become more widely practiced?

There is a general tendency by social scientists to use their findings about the past to understand the future. Linear projection flies in the face of history: the future rarely resembles the past – in any domain – but especially politics and international relations. Sharp discontinuities dramatically transform the dynamics of social interactions. The limited, dynastic warfare that characterized eighteenth-century Europe was rendered obsolete by the French Revolution and its concept of the nation under arms. The peace of Europe was restored in 1815, and by the end of the century many thoughtful observers considered the likelihood of great-power war increasingly remote. World War I shattered this illusion and the optimism of European civilization. After several decades, the Cold War appeared to many policymakers and scholars as remarkably stable, and hardly anyone predicted its demise or the subsequent breakup of the Soviet Union. The post-Cold War world has evolved in ways that defy the expectations of liberals and realists alike.

Transformations of this kind are often the result of non-linear confluences in which largely independent chains of causation combine

---

[1] Sophocles, *Antigone*, line 332.

to produce dramatic, often tumultuous, shifts in behavior. There are good reasons for believing that World War I and the end of the Cold War were the result of such confluences.[2]

I deliberately eschew any attempt to predict the future of war on the basis of the past. This does not mean that the past is irrelevant in thinking about the future. Its observable patterns are appropriate starting points – not end points – for thoughts about the future. Careful examination of the past may also reveal changes in the conditions responsible for these patterns or regularities whose implications have not yet become manifest or are only beginning to affect behavior. With these ends in mind, I describe patterns in war-initiation from the seventeenth century to the present and focus on those I consider most important. I organize my analysis around the five motives I used to understand war-initiation and identify patterns and trends that emerge across the four centuries of my data set. I offer informed speculation about the extent to which these patterns are likely to endure and whether identifiable trends will become more pronounced. As the social revolution of the 1960s described earlier so effectively illustrates, the chains of causation that bring about non-linear confluences can take place in domains never thought relevant beforehand to the behavior in question. So any forecast based on observable patterns and trends must remain highly provisional, as we simply do not know in advance what other developments may come to exercise an important, if not decisive, influence on the perceived utility, frequency or character of war.

Patterns of warfare

Between Westphalia and the French Revolution, warfare was less frequent than in the past although often on a grander scale. Data sets that go back further than mine and attempt to include all wars indicate that early modern Europe was the most warlike era for which we have reliable historical evidence. There was a new war on average every three years. In the sixteenth and seventeenth centuries, the great powers were at war 95 percent of the time. The frequency of great power war-years drops to 71 percent in the eighteenth century, and to

---

[2] Lebow, *Forbidden Fruit*, chs. 3 and 4.

29 percent in a modified nineteenth century.[3] We must exercise some care with these figures because of the difficulty, noted in Chapter 4, of distinguishing interstate from intrastate war before 1648, and sometimes, afterwards as well.

Great power wars occurred on average once every fifteen years in the twentieth century, but once every four years in the sixteenth.[4] Twentieth-century wars were nevertheless far more destructive of life and property. Their lethality is attributable to several reinforcing developments, chief among them the involvement of entire peoples in war, far-reaching developments in military technology and organizational capability, and the greater acceptance of force as an instrument of state policy. Armies and navies were maintained at much higher peacetime levels, put under the direction of professionally trained officers who reported to a general staff and were assisted by technical elements who had the scientific, engineering and economic resources of the state behind them.[5]

From the late seventeenth to the early twentieth century, war appeared to many to be in the process of being tamed. Its ends and means became increasingly limited. As mentioned earlier, rulers no longer assassinated or poisoned their adversaries. They addressed one another and their representatives in respectful terms, even when their countries were at war.[6] The Italian and German wars in the first half of the sixteenth century encouraged the development of diplomatic missions and chanceries to assist rulers in the conduct of foreign policy. After 1648, Catholic and Protestant Europe were again in contact and their diplomats worked together to bring about peace accords at Utrecht (1713), Rastatt (1714), Carlowitz (1718) and Nystad (1721). International law developed rapidly as part of the broader effort to regulate and civilize the practice of war. Rules evolved to regulate the exchange of honors, the billeting of troops on foreign territory, the extraction of money and provisions from populations in war zones and the treatment of prisoners. The concept of neutral countries became widely accepted, although they still had to allow armies to pass through

---

[3] Wright, *Study of War*, vol. 1, pp. 121, 237, 242, 248, 638; Levy, *War in the Modern Great Power System*, pp. 139–144; Holsti, *Peace and War*; Hamilton, "The European Wars: 1815–1914."

[4] Levy, *War in the Modern Great Power System*.

[5] Clausewitz, *On War*; Millis, *Arms and Men*; Howard, *War in European History*.

[6] An important exception was Catherine the Great who gained the throne by colluding in the murder of her husband, Peter III.

their territories (*trasitus innoxius*). Those armies nevertheless had to provide restitution for any damage for which they were responsible. Prisoners of officer rank were routinely exchanged, but ordinary soldiers could still be sent to the gallows. That practice halted during the course of the eighteenth century when conscripts came to be regarded as people doing state service, not criminals.[7]

Warfare in the seventeenth and eighteenth centuries was limited in the first instance for technical and economic reasons. The introduction of the bayonet and more mobile and robust artillery rendered combat more deadly, making it more difficult and expensive to recruit mercenaries. States nevertheless found the means to finance and supply their ever larger armies. In 1552, Charles V's advisors estimated that they were supporting 148,000 men in Germany, the Low Countries, Lombardy, Naples, North Africa and Spain. In 1625, Philip IV of Spain could muster 300,000 regular troops and 500,000 militiamen. Louis XIV's army increased from 273,000 in 1693 to 395,000 in 1696. Even a small state like the emerging Dutch Republic could field 60,00 men by 1606. In 1756, the total number of Europeans under arms was about 1.3 million.

For economic and strategic reasons European armies preferred positional maneuvering skirmishes and sieges to pitched battles. The Duke of Marlborough, famous for his aggressiveness, fought only four major engagements in the course of his ten continental campaigns. One of them, the Battle of Malplaquet in 1709, was brought about by Marlborough's political need for a decisive victory. It was the largest engagement in Europe before Borodino in 1812 and involved 200,000 British, Dutch, French and Imperial forces. When the smoke cleared, there were 30,000 casualties.[8] We must exercise caution about attributing battle-avoidance to its destructiveness or cost as sieges were sometimes just as bloody and costly.

The great growth in standing armies was paralleled by a growth in population and the ability of some states to raise money for war. The French Revolution and Napoleon harnessed this potential to transform the character and scale of warfare, compelling their adversaries to follow

---

[7] Luard, *War in International Society*, pp. 160–161; Best, *Humanity in Warfare*, pp. 53–60; Anderson, *War and Society in Europe of the Old Regime*, p. 15.

[8] Chandler, *Art of Warfare in the Age of Marlborough*; Weigley, *Age of Battles*; Anderson, *War and Society in Europe of the Old Regime*, p. 17; Duffy, *Military Experience in the Age of Reason*, p. 17; Black, *European Warfare*, pp. 58–59; and Black, *Military Revolution?*, p. 7.

suit. Between 1792 and 1815 – the era of French revolutionary and Napoleonic warfare – there were 713 pitched battles.[9] Napoleon's army reached its maximum size of 600,000 on the eve of his invasion of Russia in 1812.[10] In 1814, the German states and Russia put about one million men in the field between them.[11] Clausewitz rightly observed that war had become:

> the concern of the people as a whole and took on an entirely different character, or rather closely approached its true character, its absolute perfection. There seemed no end to the resources mobilized; all limits disappeared in the vigor and enthusiasm shown by governments and their subjects. Various factors powerfully increased that vigor; the vastness of the available resources, the ample field of opportunity, and the depth of feeling generally aroused. The sole aim of war was to overthrow the opponent. Not until he was prostrate was it considered possible to pause and try to reconcile the opposing interests.[12]

With Napoleon safely out of the way, many politicians and generals convinced themselves that war among the great powers would once again become rare, or at least limited in its goals, and restrained in its scale and practice. Clausewitz thought this would only happen if "we again see a gradual separation taking place between government and people." He considered this highly unlikely for many reasons, chief among them the precedent set by the Napoleonic Wars. "Once barriers – which in a sense consist only in man's ignorance of what is possible – are torn down, they are not so easily set up again." "When major interests are at stake," Clausewitz warns readers, "mutual hostility will express itself in the same manner as it has in our own day."[13]

The nineteenth century offered evidence for both points of view. The number of wars sharply declined, making the years between 1815 and 1914 the first century-long span in which there were more years of peace than of war. The several great power wars – German unification (1864, 1866, 1870–1871) and Italian unification (1848, 1859) – were fought for limited objectives and were of limited duration. The exception was the three-year-long Crimean War (1853–1856). It nevertheless consisted of a series of short, if acute, engagements on land and at sea and a year-long siege of Sevastopol.

[9] Blanning, *Pursuit of Glory*, p. 643.   [10] Black, *European Warfare*, pp. 168–188.
[11] Clausewitz, *On War*, Book 8, ch. 3, pp. 502–503.   [12] *Ibid.*, p. 593.   [13] *Ibid.*, p. 593.

Public opinion appeared to be increasingly anti-war. The Napoleonic Wars spawned numerous peace societies on both sides of the Atlantic.[14] Following the lead of Richard Cobden and John Bright, liberals everywhere came to regard peace as the handmaiden to trade and industry. The two Hague Conferences of 1899 and 1907 took significant steps to limit the destructiveness of warfare.[15] A third, planned for 1917, and derailed by World War I, was to address the possible substitution of arbitration for war. The Hague Conferences, the Olympic Games, the first of which was held in 1896, enthusiasm for Volapük and Esperanto as international languages of peace, the growth of cross-border travel and the understanding it seemed to bring in its wake, all fanned the hope among progressive opinion that international relations might increasingly become law-governed. In 1849, American poet Ralph Waldo Emerson felt confident enough to proclaim that "War is on its last legs and a universal peace is as sure as is the prevalence of civilization over barbarism."[16] In 1899, Austrian Baroness Bertha von Sutter published an anti-war novel, *Die Waffen Nieder!* (Down with Arms) that quickly became an international best-seller and won her the Nobel Peace Prize in 1905. In 1910, Norman Angell, another best-selling author who would win a Nobel Prize, exposed as fallacious the belief that territorial conquest could augment national wealth.[17]

Evidence for Clausewitz's pessimism was provided by the American Civil War (1861–1865), which resembled its Napoleonic predecessor in its scope and destructiveness. The Franco-Prussian War, the third and final war of German unification, came close to escalating out of control after Louis Napoleon fled Paris.[18] The Russo-Turkish War (1877–1878), the Boer War (1899–1902) and the Russo-Japanese War (1904–1905) all proved more costly than either side had envisaged. The Russo-Japanese War also provided striking evidence to European observers of the ability of machine guns and barbed wire to repel infantry assaults with enormous loss. For the most part, the lessons of these conflicts, that seemed so evident in retrospect, were lost on Europe's military establishments. Field Marshal Helmuth von Moltke the elder, who engineered Germany's victory in the Franco-Prussian War, dismissed the American Civil War

[14] Ceadel, *Origins of War Prevention*; Cortright, *Peace*, pp. 25–40.
[15] Cortright, *Peace*, pp. 40–43.
[16] Emerson, "War," quoted in Mueller, *Retreat from Doomsday*, p. 26.
[17] Angell, *The Great Illusion*. Angell won his Nobel in 1933.
[18] Howard, *Franco-Prussian War*, pp. 371–431.

as "armed mobs chasing each other around the country, from whom nothing can be learned."[19] Committed to offensive operations for organizational, ideological and class reasons, and above all as a matter of honor, Europe's generals refused to reconsider their offensive strategies or their associated tactics. In 1914, their armies and countries paid dearly for their stubbornness. It was long the conventional wisdom that European general staffs were committed to offensive operations because they envisaged them as the only means of waging a victorious short war.[20] New evidence makes it apparent that by 1914 Germany's top generals had no illusions that war would be anything but costly and protracted and deliberately misled political leaders to believe that a quick, decisive victory against France was possible. German chief-of-staff, Helmuth von Moltke (the younger), also made certain that the German army had no war plan that would allow a war in the east just against Russia.[21] Moltke and Falkenhayn, I have argued elsewhere, were desperate to go to war out of hatred of France and in the belief that war would help preserve their class and its values.[22]

World War I was significantly more destructive than its Napoleonic predecessor. About 9.4 million combatants lost their lives and millions more were physically or psychologically maimed.[23] Over a million civilians died of starvation, ethnic cleansing or disease. The War and the postwar blockade of Germany and Austria by the victorious allies left Central Europe's population that much more vulnerable to the 1918–1919 influenza pandemic. World War I and its brutal aftermath had equally profound cultural and intellectual consequences. Europe's self-confidence was lost along with its leading role in the world, encouraging forms of literary, artistic and political expression that communicated defiance, doubt, confusion and alienation. The war understandably aroused great hopes of preventing any future outbreak of European hostilities. American President Woodrow Wilson, who had justified his country's entrance into the conflict as necessary to win "the war to end all wars," took the lead in structuring peace agreements that would reduce

---

[19] Quoted in Crawley and Bury, *New Cambridge Modern History*, vol. 10, p. 327.
[20] Ritter, *Schlieffen Plan*; Farrar, *Short-War Illusion*; Blainey, *Causes of War*, pp. 47–50; Snyder, *Ideology of the Offensive*, pp. 107–156.
[21] Mombauer, *Helmuth von Moltke*, p. 69, 103–104, 210–213; Afflerbach, *Falkenhayn*, pp. 259–260, 294–295, 300–307; Lebow, *Cultural Theory of International Relations*, pp. 357–359.
[22] Lebow, *Cultural Theory of International Relations*, ch. 7.
[23] Nicolson, *Longman Companion to the First World War*, p. 248.

the likelihood of future war. The centerpiece was to be a League of Nations, whose members would have the power to act collectively against any aggressor.[24]

Historian I. F. Clarke argues that World War I produced fundamental changes in Western attitudes toward war. In his judgment, "All that has been written about future wars since Hiroshima merely repeats and amplifies what was said between the two world wars."[25] In the 1920s and 1930s, there was widespread recognition that modern war had become, in the words of Winston Churchill, "the potential destroyer of the human race."[26] Sigmund Freud, another respected authority, worried that science had so mastered nature that it had provided states with the power "to exterminate one another to the last man."[27] In 1930, Albert Einstein offered his "two per cent" solution to war, arguing that, if only 2 percent of those called up refused to serve, "governments would be powerless, they would not dare send such a large number of people to jail."[28] Anti-war sentiment found expression in the 1921–1922 Washington Naval Conference, which resulted in three treaties and the Kellogg–Briand Pact to outlaw war, the latter signed by fifteen nations in August 1928.[29] Peace movements once again flourished in Britain, France and the United States until they ran up against Hitler and many, if not most, of their members recognized that his appetite for aggression could not be appeased by concessions.[30] Germany's defeat and loss of territory and its perceptions of the Treaty of Versailles as an unacceptable humiliation, aroused enormous resentment that would be fanned and mobilized by the German right and the National Socialists (Nazis) to deprive the postwar Weimar Republic of legitimacy.[31] As is well known, a rearming Nazi Germany, appeased by Britain and France, overturned key provisions of the Versailles settlement, and, allied with Italy, Japan and the Soviet Union, unleashed World War II in Europe.

World War II proved more destructive than World War I even though it was a war of movement. Estimates of dead range from 50 million

---

[24] Osgood, "Woodrow Wilson."   [25] Clarke, *Voices Prophesying War*, pp. 167–176.
[26] Churchill, *Amid These Storms*, p. 32.   [27] Freud, *Civilization and Its Discontents*, p. 81.
[28] Einstein, *Einstein on Peace*, pp. 117–118.
[29] Goldman, *Sunken Treaties*; Ferrell, *Peace in Their Time*.
[30] Lynch, *Beyond Appeasement*, pp. 93–125, 149–171; Cortright, *Peace*, pp. 67–92.
[31] Mommsen, *Rise and Fall of Weimar Democracy*; Weinberg, *Foreign Policy of Hitler's Germany*; Iriye, *Origins of the Second World War in Asia*; Lebow, *Cultural Theory of International Relations*, ch. 8.

upward, which includes soldiers and civilians.[32] The conduct of the war was brutal even measured by the standards of World War I. In the east, Germans starved, shot or worked to death enemy soldiers who surrendered. They shot commissars and Jews on sight and denuded of the countries they occupied food and other essential goods without any consideration of local needs.[33] The German air force conducted bombing campaigns against European cities, beginning with the destruction of Guernica in Spain and culminating in the assaults on London with V-1 flying bombs and V-2 rockets.[34] The German army killed or starved somewhere between 700,000 and 1.5 million Leningraders during 900 days of siege, air and artillery bombardment.[35] The Soviets in turn did not always allow German soldiers to surrender and sent those who did off to labor camps from which most never returned.[36] The Red Army used its own soldiers, usually punishment battalions, to clear minefields by marching formations through them.[37] All told, the Soviets lost over 26 million people during four years of war.[38]

The war in the Balkans resembled the war in the east but on a smaller scale. No quarter was given or asked by rival partisan forces or the Germans and communist partisans who opposed them. The fighting was accompanied by wide-scale murders of Serbs and Jews.[39] The allies committed their own atrocities, most of them in the form of aerial bombing, by day and night, of German cities; a single fire bomb attack on Dresden late in the war killed tens of thousands of people, almost all of them civilians.[40] Bomber crews were deliberately misled about their real targets – German cities, workers and civilized life – by a British government that recognized the violations of international law these attacks entailed.[41] Perhaps the most unrestrained warfare was in the Far East, where the Japanese carried out gratuitous violence against Asian civilians.[42] In Nanjing, Japanese soldiers went on a rampage and murdered

---

[32] Tucker, *Encyclopedia of World War I*, pp. 272–273; Tucker and Roberts, *Encyclopedia of World War II*, pp. 300–301.

[33] Dallin, *German Rule in Russia 1941–1945*; Bartov, *Eastern Front, 1941–45*, pp. 106–142; Krausnick, *Truppe des Weltanschauungskrieges*, Part I, chs. 1–3.

[34] Weinberg, *World at Arms*, pp. 574–576.   [35] Salisbury, *900 Days*, pp. 513–517.

[36] Merridale, *Ivan's War*, pp. 161, 241.   [37] Glantz, *Colossus Reborn*, p. 577.

[38] Volkogonov, *Triumph and Tragedy*, p. 418.

[39] Weinberg, *World at Arms*, pp. 523–527.

[40] De Bruhl, *Firestorm*; Hastings, *Bomber Command*, pp. 411–412; Bundy, *Danger and Survival*, pp. 63–68; Weinberg, *World at Arms*, p. 616.

[41] Boog, Krebs and Vogel, *Germany and the Second World War*, pp. 30–36.

[42] Dower, *Embracing Defeat*, pp. 41–49.

upward of 70,000 residents of the city.[43] American bombing raids against Japanese cities were equally destructive; the firebombing of Tokyo in June 1945 burned out 15.8 square miles of the city and killed an estimated 87,793 people.[44] The atom bombing of Hiroshima killed 145,000 people and signaled, as did the follow-on attack against Nagasaki, American willingness to use weapons of unparalleled destructive potential.[45] Like Russians and Germans, Japanese and Americans frequently refused to accept the surrender of enemy combatants.[46]

The Cold War had the potential to unleash an even more destructive war, one that would have transformed the hyperbole of Churchill and Freud into an ugly and irreversible reality. The Cold War only turned hot in peripheral regions and proxy wars. Direct encounters between the US and the Chinese in Korea, American intervention in Indochina, Soviet intervention in Afghanistan and various wars in the Middle East and Africa between superpower clients, were costly in life and on more than one occasion raised the prospect of a direct superpower encounter. The peaceful end of the Cold War came as a great surprise to everyone, and scholars disagree about why it happened, as they continue to debate its origins.[47]

The post-Cold War world has seen its share of wars, but none of them as destructive as any of the major wars of the Cold War. The 1980–1988 Iran–Iraq War, in which neither superpower was seriously involved, cost Iran an estimated 1 million casualties. Some Iranians were victims of Iraq's use of chemical weapons. Iraqi casualties are estimated at between 250,000 and 500,000. Thousands of civilians died on both sides from air raids and missiles.[48] The potential for catastrophic conflict nevertheless remains, as nuclear weapons have become more widespread. India and Pakistan have numerous weapons and missile delivery systems, as does Israel. Iran and North Korea appear actively committed to becoming

---

[43] Weinberg, *World at Arms*, p. 322; Fogel, *Nanjing Massacre in History and Historiography*; Wakabayashi, *What Really Happened in Nanking*, estimates 70,000 dead.

[44] Spector, *American War with Japan*, pp. 478–510; Selden, *Atomic Bomb*, p. xvi, quoting the Strategic Bombing Survey.

[45] Rhodes, *Making of the Atomic Bomb*, p. 734; Craven and Cate, *Army Air Forces in World War Two*, vol. 5, pp. 616–617.

[46] Dower, *War Without Mercy*, pp. 11–12, 63–71.

[47] Herrmann and Lebow, *Ending the Cold War*, for both sides of this debate.

[48] Cook and Walker, *Facts on File World Political Almanac*, p. 325; Chubin and Tripp, *Iran and Iraq at War*, p. 1, estimate 1.5 million.

nuclear states. An all-out nuclear exchange on the Indian sub-continent could kill more people than died in World War II.[49]

Reading the tea leaves

This brief review of warfare in the modern era reveals three contradictory trends: a decline in the overall frequency of war, an increase in its lethality and a steady growth of anti-war sentiment.[50] These trends are like tea leaves because optimists and pessimists read them differently and use them as the basis for diametrically opposed narratives. For optimists, they provide evidence that interstate war is an atavism and they look forward to the day when it disappears altogether, at least among the world's developed economies. In the eighteenth century Montesquieu wrote that "peace is the natural effect of trade."[51] Kant famously argued in 1798 that the "spirit of commerce" is "incompatible with war," a sentiment echoed by Jeremy Bentham and Manchester Liberals Richard Cobden and John Bright.[52] In 1848, John Stuart Mill wrote that "It is commerce which is rapidly rendering war obsolete."[53] Thorstein Veblen, Norman Angell and Joseph Schumpeter advanced similar arguments in the early twentieth century.[54]

More recently, Richard Rosecrance has argued that trading states have no incentive to go to war because it is always cheaper to gain raw materials and other kinds of goods through trade than through conquest.[55] The *Economist*, and the media more generally, gave wide play to the supposed finding that no two countries with McDonalds franchises have fought a war against each other. Thomas Friedman, a prominent propagandist of globalization, insists, as did the English radicals before him, that open economies promote democracy and peace.[56] Proponents

---

[49] On proliferation, see Hymans, *Psychology of Nuclear Proliferation*; Solingen, *Nuclear Logics*. On non-use, see Paul, *Tradition of Non-Use*.

[50] Tilly, *Coercion, Capital, and European States*, p. 185, also makes this point.

[51] Montesquieu, *Spirit of the Laws*, I, Book 20, ch. 1.

[52] Kant, *Perpetual Peace*, p. 39; Bentham, "A Plan for a Universal and Perpetual Peace"; Baum, "A Question for Inspiration in the Liberal Peace Paradigm," compares Bentham's peace to that of Kant.

[53] Mill, *Principles of Political Economy*, p. 582.

[54] Veblen, *Inquiry into the Nature of Peace*; Angell, *Great Illusion*; Schumpeter, *Imperialism and Social Classes*; Howard, *Lessons of History*; Rosecrance, *Rise of the Trading State*.

[55] Rosecrance, *Rise of the Trading State*, pp. 16, 24; Gartzke, "Capitalist Peace."

[56] Friedman, *Lexus and the Olive Tree*.

of the Democratic Peace research program contend that the most important postwar finding in international relations scholarship is the absence of wars between democracies.[57] Optimists also point to the "code of peace" or "global covenant," terms they use to describe the restraints, procedural and prudential norms and obligations that began to be put into place in the 1920s and greatly strengthened in the postwar era.[58] Among the most important of these norms is that of "territorial integrity."[59] Another is the taboo, or at least tradition of non-use, that has grown up around nuclear weapons.[60] John Mueller, author of a thoughtful book on the obsolescence of war, offers multiple, reinforcing reasons for his optimism. War, he insists, is on the decline, "not because it has ceased to be possible or fascinating, but because peoples and leaders in the developed world – where war was once endemic – have increasingly found war to be disgusting, ridiculous, and unwise."[61] Other historians and international relations scholars make similar arguments.[62]

In the nineteenth century, peace advocacy met considerable opposition from those who regarded war as uplifting, glorious, even beautiful, and peace as unmanly, decadent, materialist and corrupt. These attitudes were largely propagated by aristocrats, whose status and wealth were justified on the basis of military service and the courage and loyalty they displayed on and off the battlefield.[63] Many conservatives in France and Germany envisaged war as an efficacious means of extending the shelf life of traditional values and holding liberal materialism and socialism in check.[64] German historian and parliamentarian Heinrich von Treitschke became a prominent publicist for this point of view. He proclaimed that "War, with all its brutality and sternness, weaves a bond of love between man and man, linking them together to face death, and causing all class

---

[57] For opposing takes on this research program, see Levy, "Theory, Evidence, and Politics in the Evolution of International Relations Research Programs"; Lawrence, "Imperial Peace or Imperial Method?"

[58] Frost, "Tragedy, Ethics and International Relations"; Senghaas, "Zivilisierung und Gewalt"; Jones, *Code of Peace*; Jackson, *Global Covenant*; Väyrynen, "Introduction"; Holsti, "Decline of Interstate War"; Spruyt, "Normative Transformations in International Relations"; Hurrell, *On Global Order*.

[59] Zacher, "Territorial Integrity Norm"; Holsti, "Decline of Interstate War"; Spruyt, "Normative Transformations"; Fazal, *State Death*.

[60] Waltz, "Spread of Nuclear Weapons"; Tannenwald, *Nuclear Taboo*; Paul, *Tradition of Non-Use*.

[61] Mueller, *Retreat from Doomsday*; Mueller, *Remnants of War*.

[62] Black, *Why Wars Happen*; Kaysen, "Is War Obsolete?"; Van Creveld, "Waning of Major War"; Holsti, "Decline of Interstate War."

[63] Lebow, *Cultural Theory of International Relations*, ch. 6.   [64] *Ibid.*, ch. 7.

distinctions to disappear."[65] Many Social Darwinists also viewed war favorably, as they considered it the principal means by which progressive nations assert their superiority. Ernst Renan described war as "one of the conditions of progress."[66] According to statistician Karl Pearson, "The path of progress is strewn with the wreck of nations."[67] Herbert Spencer, by contrast, wrote that war had already served this function and was no longer necessary or beneficial to progress.[68]

World War I discredited pro-war discourses, although they were successfully revived by fascist movements in Italy and Germany and continued to thrive in Japan. It took a second world war to drive a stake through their heart. In today's world, even the most conservative and nationalist politicians rarely speak of war as anything other than costly and horrendous and a matter of last resort for defending national interests. The few exceptions prove the rule. At the height of the Cuban missile crisis, a panicked Fidel Castro sent a cable to Khrushchev urging him to launch a preemptive nuclear strike against the United States. Khrushchev was horrified and became that much more intent on reaching a quick accommodation with Kennedy.[69] Anti-war sentiment has nevertheless not succeeded in doing away with war as an institution. Although there were many fewer wars in the post-1945 era, there were still wars, and some of them initiated by countries (e.g. the United States, Great Britain, the Soviet Union) in which anti-war sentiment is particularly strong. So anti-war feeling is at best a necessary, but by no means sufficient, condition for peace. This is a relationship I will discuss in more detail in the conclusion.

Today, opposition to peace movements, and their expectations that warfare can be banished, comes from a very different source than it did a century ago. Conservative members of the academic and the national-security establishment maintain that war is an expression of human nature or the anarchy of the international environment. Periods of peace, no matter how long, they insist, have always ended in destructive wars. John Mearsheimer, among the more pessimistic of international relations scholars, argues that, if economic interdependence did not prevent World War I, "a highly interdependent world economy does

[65] Treitschke, *Politics*, vol. I, pp. 66–67, vol. II, pp. 395–396.
[66] Quoted in Mueller, *Retreat from Doomsday*, p. 45.
[67] Pearson, *National Life from the Standpoint of Science*, p. 64.
[68] Spencer, *Principles of Sociology*, p. 664.
[69] Lebow and Stein, *We All Lost the Cold War*, pp. 138–139, citing memoranda and recollections of relevant Soviet officials.

not make great power war more or less likely" today.[70] Some social scientists and historians detect a cycle of war-weariness following costly wars, with populations becoming forgetful about the costs of war after a generation or two and ready once again to enter the fray.[71] Historian David Blainey accuses optimists of confusing association with causation. The long period of peace between the Napoleonic War and World War I coincided with Europe's industrialization and the growing commercial and financial interdependence of its nation-states, but it was not the cause of that long peace. We may be observing the same mistaken attribution today, he contends, in efforts to explain the long peace among the great powers since 1945 in terms of nuclear weapons.[72]

Realists of all stripes are found in the pessimistic camp. They abhor war no less than their liberal counterparts but believe it is an ever-present threat and best kept at bay by sophisticated strategies of conflict management that include preparations to fight. Realists are fond of citing the Latin adage *Si vis pacem, para bellum* (If you wish for peace, prepare for war). They differ among themselves as to how much military force is needed for general and immediate deterrence and the circumstances in which force should be used. Many realists supported American intervention in Vietnam, but the two most prominent realist scholars of the era – Hans Morgenthau and John Herz – were early, outspoken opponents. The vast majority of American international relations scholars, realists as well, opposed the 2003 invasion of Iraq, but the few academics who supported it, among them Bush's National Security Advisor, were all self-proclaimed realists. Realists have criticized optimists – whom they label as "idealists" – for acting in ways that make war more rather than less likely. Morgenthau leveled this charge – quite unfairly – at the international lawyers and diplomats in the first decades of the twentieth century who attempted to outlaw war.[73] Morgenthau and E. H. Carr charged, with more reason, that appeasement, based on the false premise that Hitler could be tamed by satisfying Germany's "legitimate demands," only whetted his appetite and helped to bring about World

---

[70] Mearsheimer, *Tragedy of Great Power Politics*, p. 371.
[71] Richardson, *Statistics of Deadly Quarrels*; Toynbee, *Study of History*, vol. 9. See Blainey, *Causes of War*, pp. 5–9, for a critique.
[72] Blainey, *Causes of War*, pp. 29–30.
[73] Morgenthau, *Politics Among Nations*. On the so-called realist–idealist debate, see Lynch, *Beyond Appeasement*, pp. 93–124; Schmidt, "Anarchy, World Politics and the Birth of a Discipline"; Ashworth, "Did the Realist–Idealist Great Debate Ever Happen?"

War II.[74] Optimists, who are more likely to self-identify as liberals or constructivists, dismiss realist analogies between the present and the past as facile and misleading. Stephen Brooks points out that Mearsheimer's parallel to 1914 hinges on the positive economic value of territorial conquest, which is no longer the case.[75] Drucker, Rosenau and Lipschutz all maintain that the costs of mobilizing for war have become prohibitively high.[76]

Optimists warn that academic arguments about war and peace do not take place in a political vacuum and have the potential to make themselves self-fulfilling. Preparations for war make it more likely by promoting arms races, mistrust and worst-case analysis. They point to World War I, where alliance systems, arms races and war plans made great power war seem more likely, a belief that arguably helped to bring it about.[77] Empirical research on general and immediate deterrence has documented the ways in which these strategies are often more provocative than constraining, as they were in the run-up to 1914 and for much of the Cold War.[78] Optimists maintain that, by successfully socializing so many future journalists and policymakers to believe in the inevitability of conflict and the need for large arsenals and frequent displays of resolve, they promoted such behavior, not just in the United States, but globally.[79] Hans Morgenthau, the father of postwar realist theory, came to believe by the 1960s that American policymakers had over-learned the lesson of power and that it was a contributing cause of their ill-considered intervention in Vietnam.[80]

The contemporary American debate about the rise of China is another sobering example. It is framed in terms of power transition theory, which, we have seen, predicts that rising states are hell-bent on challenging reigning hegemons.[81] Predictions of Sino-American conflict or war

---

[74] Morgenthau, *Politics Among Nations*, pp. 43–45; Carr, *Twenty Years Crisis*.
[75] Brooks, *Producing Security*, p. 9.
[76] Drucker, "Global Economy and the Nation State"; Rosenau, "New Dimensions of Security"; Lipschutz, *After Authority*.
[77] Albertini, *Origins of the War of 1914*; Taylor, *Struggle for Mastery in Europe*; Ritter, *Schlieffen Plan*; Snyder, *Ideology of the Offensive*; Lebow, *Nuclear Crisis Management*.
[78] Lebow, *Between Peace and War*; Jervis, Lebow and Stein, *Psychology and Deterrence*; Hopf, *Peripheral Visions*.
[79] Lebow, "The Long Peace."
[80] Lebow, *Tragic Vision of Politics*, pp. 236–242; Scheuerman, *Hans Morgenthau*, pp. 165–195.
[81] Shirk, *China*, p. 4; Mearsheimer, *Tragedy of Great Power Politics*; Goldstein, *China's Grand Strategy*; Goldstein, "Great Expectations"; Goldstein, *Rising to the Challenge*; Mearsheimer, *The Tragedy of Great Power Politics*.

routinely invoke power-transition theory as the historical precedent.[82] Former Assistant Secretary of State Susan Shirk summed up this perspective with the claim: "History teaches us that rising powers are likely to provoke war."[83] In 2003, the United States–China Security Review Commission submitted its first annual report to the Congress, in which it warned against China's expansionist goals. Commissioner Arthur Waldron wrote that "China is not a *status quo* country" and the "wide-ranging purpose" of its foreign policy is to "exclude the US from Asia" and "threaten and coerce neighboring states."[84] This argument has been echoed in the realist academic literature.[85] There is no historical support for rising powers challenging dominant powers; it is a myth of international relations theory.[86] Nor is there any evidence – quite to the contrary – that China's foreign and defense policies can be interpreted in accord with power transition theory.[87] Power transition theory has nevertheless been deployed with some rhetorical success by neo-conservatives and realists alike to justify large military budgets, balancing against China and other confrontational foreign policies.[88]

Highly regarded China hands do not see it as a revisionist state. They point to China's relatively low military budget, its willingness to compromise to settle territorial disputes with neighbors, its effort to join and behave responsibly in international organizations and its preference for a peaceful resolution of its Taiwan problem.[89] They worry that efforts by the US to form an anti-China coalition in the Pacific rim might not only fail but push China, a country particularly sensitive to its standing, into behaving in ways that could make the US image

---

[82] Friedberg, "The Future of United States–China Relations"; Mearsheimer, *The Tragedy of Great Power Politics*.

[83] Shirk, *China*, p. 4.

[84] US–China Security Review Commission, *Report to Congress*. Quoted in Gries, *China's New Nationalism*, p. 11.

[85] Friedberg, "The Future of United States–China Relations"; Mearsheimer, *Tragedy of Great Power Politics*; Sutter, *China's Rise in Asia*; Swaine and Tellis, *Interpreting China's Grand Strategy*; Tellis, "A Grand Chessboard."

[86] Lebow and Valentino, "Lost in Transition."

[87] Chan, *China, the US, and Power Transition Theory*, pp. 82–83, 122–123; Yee, "Realist Analyses of China's Rise."

[88] Art, "The United States and the Rise of China."

[89] Fravel, "Regime Insecurity and International Cooperation"; Quingguo, "Peaceful Development"; Johnston, "Is China a Status Quo Power?"; Johnston, "China's International Relations"; Johnston, *Social States*; Kang, *China Rising*; Shambaugh, "China Engages Asia"; Deng, *China's Struggle for Status*.

of a threatening China self-fulfilling.[90] In contrast to their more alarmist colleagues, they give more credence to China's "peaceful rise" discourse.[91]

The fundamental intellectual distinction between optimists and pessimists concerns their understanding of the repetitive nature of social relations. Realists insist there are unchanging verities of international relations that cannot be transcended. Globalization in their view is not a panacea. Europe's economies were so tightly integrated on the eve of World War I that they did not reach this level again until the 1990s.[92] Nor can new weapons transform the character of the international relations although they can make war more deadly. Realists remind us that, ever since the use of the crossbow in medieval Europe, people have consistently and mistakenly predicted that the increased lethality of war would compel military restraint. Bayonets, rifles, machine guns, high explosives, aerial bombing and nuclear weapons all shocked the public and prompted such predictions. Victor Hugo warned that balloons had the potential to deliver devastating aerial attacks and urged that they be banned.[93]

Optimists believe in reflectivity and learning and with it the possibility for human beings to escape from what may have been until now timeless and tragic scripts. Mueller points to the success societies have had in outlawing slavery and dueling and the progress made in recent years toward race and gender equality.[94] The developed economies have also made great strides in devising multilateral and supranational institutions to limit, mitigate and overcome the consequences of periodic economic crises.[95] The European project has been hailed as a great achievement on both counts, as it helped to reconcile France and Germany, integrate member economies, do away with many national borders, foster democracy in southern Europe and promote development on the continent's peripheries. The European Union has many critics, but most agree that a major war in Western Europe is no more conceivable than one between

---

[90] Nye, "Case Against Containment"; Chan, China, the US, and the Power Transition Theory.

[91] Shambaugh, "China Engages Asia"; Chan, China, the US, and Power Transition Theory, pp. 82–83, 122–123; Gries, China's New Nationalism, pp. 135–150; Deng, China's Struggle for Status, pp. 8–10.

[92] Daudin, Morys and O'Rourke, Europe and Globalization.

[93] Cited in Väyrynen, "Introduction," p. 9.

[94] Mueller, Retreat from Doomsday, pp. 9–13.

[95] Keohane, International Institutions and State Power; Ruggie, Multilateralism"; Raymond, "International Norms"; Morgan, "Multilateral Institutions."

the United States and Canada. In 1957, Karl Deutsch developed the concept of a "pluralist security community," a region populated by sovereign states in which war had become all but unthinkable. He described North America (US and Canada) and Scandinavia as regions in which security communities had not only developed but were robust.[96] By the end of the Cold War, liberal international relations scholars were claiming that the entire North Atlantic Community, as Deutsch had envisaged, had become a pluralistic security community, as had New Zealand and Australia. Much of the Pacific rim may be moving in the same direction.[97] Using a data set of wars since 1495, Ole Holsti found that interstate war has consistently declined over the centuries and that "the world is significantly safer today than in any previous period."[98]

There is a certain irony to these debates. Pessimism about war often rests on a bed of optimism about human nature, while optimism about peace frequently invokes pessimism about that nature. The security dilemma, so central to realist understandings of international conflict, assumes that national leaders are rational actors capable of understanding and responding intelligently to the constraints and opportunities generated by the international environment. Indeed, instrumental reason coupled with concern for security is what leads them to act in ways that end up making their states and others less secure. Reason also provides the incentive to develop and deploy ever more deadly arsenals. Ironically, optimism about the ability of humans to reason is what generates deep pessimism about their ability to live in harmony with one another. There is nothing new about this orientation, which goes back to the ancient Greeks. The first *stasimon* of Sophocles' *Antigone* sings the "wonders of man and how he tames nature with his cunning and contrivances but when prompted by restlessness and evil is frightening to behold. The Greek word for wondrous, *deinon*, also means frightening."[99]

Optimists, by contrast, mobilize pessimism in the hope that it will serve as a catalyst for radical change. Some Marxists consider war inevitable and horrible but necessary to bring about socialist revolution. Arms controllers and environmentalists deploy a variant of this logic. They predict the worst possible outcomes if new weapons systems are not controlled and if humankind continues to degrade the environment.

[96] Deutsch, Burrell and Kann, *Political Community and the North Atlantic Area.*
[97] Lebow, "The Long Peace"; Adler and Barnett, eds., *Security Communities.*
[98] Holsti, "Decline of Interstate War."   [99] Sophocles, *Antigone,* lines 368–411.

Their pessimism is intended to appeal to the emotions and reason of public opinion and policymakers.[100] Like the realists whom they oppose, optimists envisage the combination of fear and reason as a powerful, positive incentive for change.

Interest

Our review of historical trends and scholarly responses to them reveal only ambiguous implications for the future of war. These differences rest on opposing sets of assumptions, and assumptions are rarely amenable to empirical evaluation. For these reasons, I take a different tack. Rather than offering yet another overall assessment of the likelihood of future wars, I break war-initiation down into its component motives and look at trends specific to these wars and the motives responsible for them. This allows a more fine-grained approach to the problem of war, and, I believe, a more meaningful one.

Interest is the weakest of my motives. There were only 9 wars, representing 7 percent of the total motives for my 93 wars, that could be attributed to interest. Six of these 9 wars took place in the seventeenth and eighteenth centuries, when mercantilism was the accepted economic wisdom and leaders believed that the wealth of the world was finite.[101] Adam Smith described the mercantilist fondness for specie as a major element in explaining the conflict-ridden character of early modern international relations. It made "commerce which ought naturally to be, among nations, as among individuals, a bond of union and friendship . . . the most fertile source of discord and animosity."[102] When economic thinking about the nature of wealth changed, and trade and investment came increasingly to be understood as mutually beneficial, interest declined as a motive for war.[103]

Although not a major cause of war, trade issues grew in importance in the eighteenth century as leaders came to recognize that national wealth, and, by extension, war-making potential, was increasingly dependent on trade. Trade regulations became weapons of political as well as commercial policy. Trade disputes were a source of enmity in Anglo-French,

---

[100] Brodie, *Absolute Weapon*; Jervis, *Meaning of the Nuclear Revolution*; Bundy, *Danger and Survival*; Mueller, *Retreat from Doomsday*; Lebow and Stein, *We All Lost the Cold War*, ch. 14; Paul, *Tradition of Non-Use*.

[101] Hirschman, *Passions and the Interests*; Hont, *Jealousy of Trade*; Boyle, "Mystery of Modern Wealth."

[102] Smith, *Wealth of Nations*, p. 460; Boyle, "Mystery of Modern Wealth."   [103] *Ibid*.

Anglo-Spanish and Anglo-Dutch relations in the eighteenth century.[104] The most unambiguous instances of interest as a motive for war are the first and second Anglo-Dutch Wars (1652–1654 and 1665–1667), the Anglo-Spanish War of 1739, the Opium Wars between Britain and China (1840–1842 and 1856–1860) and the Anglo-French takeover of Egypt in 1882. In the Anglo-Dutch Wars, English decisionmaking was nevertheless complex and influenced by dynastic and domestic politics as much as it was by commercial interests.[105] In the two nineteenth-century cases, standing was an important secondary concern.[106] Marxist interpretations of imperialism stress economic motives, but they have largely been discredited by historians. As noted in Chapter 2, the investments of colonizers largely went into the economies of other colonizers or third parties like Argentina and the United States. British, French and German leaders who espoused imperialism did so primarily for domestic political reasons or reasons of standing. Disraeli, Delcassé and Bismarck understood colonialism to represent a drain on their respective treasuries.[107]

In the twentieth century, there are no great power wars in which interest can convincingly be shown to have been a primary motive. Japanese expansion into Korea had an economic component to it, but it has been convincingly demonstrated that the principal motive was standing. There was a widely shared belief among the Japanese policymaking elite that empire was the *sine qua non* of great power status and that Japan should accordingly acquire colonies. Imperialism was also considered a useful vehicle for consolidating a modern state and was supported for this reason by a range of intellectuals and bureaucrats.[108] Material rewards played a surprisingly insignificant role in Japanese expansion but were used as a carrot to sell imperialism to the public. In 1894, when 8,000 Japanese troops were dispatched to Korea, foreign minister Mutsu Munemitsu admitted that he pressured the Korean government to make railway, mining, telegraph and other concessions

---

[104] Black, *European International Relations*, pp. 23–26.
[105] Wilson, *Profit and Power*, pp. 128–129; Seaward, *Cavalier Parliament and the Reconstruction of the Old Regime*, pp. 236–275; Jones, *Anglo-Dutch Wars of the Seventeenth Century*, pp. 46–47, 56–60, 77–78.
[106] Hurd, *Arrow War*; Wong, *Deadly Dreams*; Al-Sayyid-Marsot, "The British Occupation of Egypt from 1882"; Sanderson, *England, Europe and the Upper Nile*, pp. 381–405; Brown, *Fashoda Reconsidered*, pp. 23–24; Paine, *Imperial Rivals*, pp. 178–233.
[107] Lebow, *Cultural Theory of International Relations*, pp. 323–338.
[108] Iriye, "Japan's Drive to Great Power Status."

to justify the risk of war with China raised by Japanese intervention.[109] In 1910, Japan's trade with China was about five times greater than it was with its *de facto* colonies of Korea and Taiwan. Private investment also went to China, rather than to these colonies.[110]

Fritz Fischer attempted to make the economic case for Germany's invasion of Belgium and France in 1914. His primary evidence is the so-called "September Program," which called for far-reaching territorial annexations and economic concessions from both countries.[111] It undeniably reflects greed, but greed encouraged by a German government intent on maximizing its strategic advantage by strengthening heavy and other military industry and weakening France "to make her revival as a great power impossible for all time."[112] Bethmann Hollweg himself observed that *"l'appétit vient en mangeant"* (appetite comes from eating).[113] Germany's leaders did not go to war for the benefit of the industrialists, whose pursuit of profit they regarded as crass, but sought to enlist them for purposes of their own once war was underway. The September Program was prepared in the first flush of seeming victory in France. Fischer has his arrow of causation reversed.[114]

A more compelling case can be made for a twentieth-century war not in my data set: Iraq's 1990 invasion of Kuwait. It is not included because it did not involve a great or rising power. It is apparent that Saddam Hussein was infuriated by Kuwait's refusal to adhere to the agreed-upon cutback in production by OPEC oil producers in July, excuse Iraq from its US$1 billion debt obligation or lease it the strategically located island of Bubiyan, which controlled access to Iraq's only oil-exporting port. On July 16, Iraqi foreign minister Tariq Aziz sent an ultimatum to Kuwait demanding a cutback in oil production, forgiveness of Iraq's war debt,

---

[109] Yanabe Kentarō, *Nik-Kan gappei shōshi* (Tokyo, 1966), cited in Iriye, *Pacific Estrangement*, p. 44.

[110] Duus, "Japan's Informal Empire in China, 1895–1937."

[111] Fischer, *Germany's Aims in the First World War*, pp. 98–118, and his follow-on *War of Illusions*; Mayer, "Domestic Causes of the First World War"; Wehler, *Das deutsche Kaiserreich*; Geiss, *German Foreign Policy*.

[112] Theobald Bethmann Hollweg, "Provisional Notes on the Direction of Our Policy on the Conclusion of Peace," September 9, 1914. Quoted in Fischer, *Germany's Aims in the First World War*, p. 103.

[113] Riezler Diary, August 20, 1914. Quoted in Stern, "Bethmann Hollweg and the War."

[114] For critiques of the Fischer thesis and the broader argument that German foreign policy was intended to serve domestic political and economic goals, see Eley, *Reshaping the German Right*; Kaiser, "Germany and the Origins of the First World War"; Mommsen, "Domestic Factors in German Foreign Policy Before 1914"; Gordon, "Domestic Conflict and the Origins of the First World War"; Lebow, *Between Peace and War*, pp. 101–147.

lease of the island and US$12 billion in compensation for what Iraq had lost due to depressed oil prices. When mediation conducted by Egyptian president Hosni Mubarak did not quickly bring about a favorable settlement, Iraq massed armor on the Kuwait border and attacked early on the morning of August 2.[115] Iraq's demands indicate the extent to which economic issues not only provided a pretext for invasion but were a primary concern of Saddam at the time. In the follow-on Gulf War, in which a coalition led by the US expelled Iraq from Kuwait, interest qualifies as a secondary motive. The Bush senior administration was primarily concerned with maintaining political stability in the Middle East and preventing Iraq from become a dominant, aggressive power. However, their great power allies also wanted to keep Kuwait's oil out of Saddam's hands and flowing to Western markets.[116]

Great powers became empires through territorial conquest. Conquest was a claim for standing, but new territories often provided additional population and resources that could be used for further expansion. Empires are now history and territorial aggrandizement has become increasingly uncommon. More generally, my data indicate that wars motivated by interest are in sharp decline.

There are two principal reasons for this remarkable historical reversal. The first has to do with the cost versus the benefits of conquest. As recently as World War II, great powers could benefit economically by conquering territory.[117] The globalization of production among advanced states has greatly lowered the economic benefits of conquest, so much so, Stephen Brooks contends, that it is no longer profitable. Globalization has effectively shifted the incentives because the opportunity cost of being closed off from multinational corporations has increased dramatically in recent years. In the aftermath of territorial conquest, the inward flow of foreign direct investment into a conqueror would decline precipitously, creating serious economic constraints in most advanced economies. Innovation within conquered territories will also decline, another significant cost in a world whose economy is increasingly knowledge-based.[118]

There is a second reason for this historical reversal: the expected response of other actors. Brooks describes serious economic consequences,

[115] Stein, "Threat-Based Strategies of Conflict Management."
[116] Yetiv, *Explaining Foreign Policy*; Gause, *Iraq and the Gulf War*.
[117] Lieberman, *Does Conquest Pay?*, ch. 3.
[118] Brooks, *Producing Security*, pp. 9–10, 57–71, 162–206, 209–219.

but there is also a serious political-military downside to attempted conquest. In the nineteenth century, it was still possible to conquer territory and exploit it economically without necessarily arousing strong international opposition. American and Russian continental expansion provide striking examples of powers expanding their domains by conquest. Both subjugated less economically developed indigenous peoples. The US also made war against Mexico, a more developed political unit, and purchased territory from Spain, Russia and Mexico. Germany offers a counter-example. Its defeat of France prompted annexation of Alsace-Lorraine, an act of aggrandizement that made France a long-term enemy.[119] Following its defeat in World War I, Germany was forced to return Alsace-Lorraine to France, Eupen-Malmédy to Belgium and part of Schleswig-Holstein to Denmark. Parts of Silesia, Prussia and Pomerania went to the newly constituted states of Czechoslovakia and Poland.

The difference between the American and Russian experiences on the one hand and the German on the other has to do with nationalism and the relative power balance between the political units. Nationalism became widespread, if not intense, almost everywhere in Europe during the nineteenth century, making foreign occupation increasingly unacceptable to local populations. Ironically, the very same nationalism the Prussians aroused to oppose French occupation of their country after the twin defeats of Jena and Auerstädt in 1806 provided the impetus for a Polish uprising against Prussian occupation in 1806 and again in 1830–1831.[120] For the most part, Russians and Americans did not encounter this kind of opposition in the nineteenth century. The major exception was Mexican nationalism, which led to a rebellion against a French-imposed emperor and his execution in 1867. Mexico was, however, too weak to challenge the United States.

Nationalism spread almost everywhere in the twentieth century, and the cost of conquest and occupation rose as a result. We need only compare the successful Anglo-French occupation of Egypt in 1882 with the short-lived Anglo-French occupation of the Suez Canal Zone in 1956. The former intervention was directed against the Khedive, who had little local backing. The target for the latter was the popular regime of Gamal Abdel Nasser. Of equal importance, it aroused the opposition of the

---

[119] Pflanze, *Bismarck*, pp. 473–479.
[120] Schroeder, *Transformation of European Politics*, pp. 287–323; Simms, *Impact of Napoleon*, chs. 5–8; Nipperdey, *Germany from Napoleon to Bismarck*, pp. 323–324, 553.

Soviet Union and the United States, which compelled a withdrawal of Anglo-French forces and greatly strengthened Nasser's influence throughout the Arab world.[121]

Nationalism was recognized as a legitimate political force at the 1919 Paris Peace Conference. Points 9 through 13 of Woodrow Wilson's Fourteen Points called for a redistribution of territory on the basis of nationality and the principle was widely, if inconsistently, applied in establishing a postwar territorial order.[122] The Covenant of the League of Nations prohibited states from using force to alter territorial boundaries and signatories of the 1928 Kellogg–Briand Pact committed themselves to restrain from threatening or using force to change existing international boundaries. In 1931, Secretary of State Henry Stimson announced that the United States would not recognize any territorial changes arising from Japan's invasion of China, a position subsequently adopted by the League of Nations. German, Italian and Japanese expansion was ultimately defeated by an allied coalition and the independence of conquered countries restored, although with major territorial shifts in the case of Poland. Postwar territorial grabs – North Korea's invasion of South Korea, Argentina's of the Falklands/Malvinas and Iraq's of Iran and Kuwait – were repulsed or the occupied territories liberated by international coalitions, or single-handedly by Britain in the case of the Falklands. Kal Holsti argues that there is increasing consistency between this norm and international behavior justifying the claim "that conquest and territorial revision through armed forces have become delegitimized."[123]

Few twentieth-century conquests have stuck. Poland's invasion of the Soviet Union in 1919, intended to push the country's eastern frontier as far east as it was in 1772, was repulsed. The Soviet counter-offensive reached the gates of Warsaw, where it was halted and forced to retreat to the Soviet border.[124] The Western powers never accepted Soviet annexation of Estonia, Lithuania and Latvia in 1940, a product of the Stalin–Hitler Pact.[125] Those countries became independent again when the Soviet Union began to break up, as did almost all of the

[121] Gorst and Johnman, *Suez Crisis.*
[122] Boemeke, Feldman and Glaser, *Treaty of Versailles.* For the text of the Fourteen Points, see http://en.wikipedia.org/wiki/Fourteen_Points/.
[123] Holsti, "Decline of Interstate War," p. 144.
[124] Debo, *Survival and Consolidation,* pp. 191–212, 404, 406; Carley, "Politics of Anti-Bolshevism"; Borzecki, *Soviet–Polish Peace of 1921.*
[125] O'Connor, *History of the Baltic States,* pp. 113–145.

peripheral republics that were homelands of non-Russian peoples. The only territories conquered in the twentieth century that Russia still retains are Kaliningrad (the former German Königsberg) and Finnish Karelia, ceded after the Winter War of 1939–1940, although Ukraine remains in possession of eastern Ruthenia, formerly part of Czechoslovakia and annexed by the Soviet Union at the end of World War II.[126] There is a growing movement among Finns for Karelia's repatriation.[127] China's occupation of *de facto* independent Tibet in 1950–1951 is another problematic conquest; the Chinese have held on to Tibet and strengthened their position within it despite indigenous opposition that has widespread sympathy among Indian and Western publics. Israel's occupation of Arab territories during the Six Day War of 1967 could be justified under the laws of war as a temporary occupation arising from belligerency. Israeli occupation of Sinai lasted twelve years, from 1967 to 1979, and it is under increasing pressure to withdraw its settlements from the West Bank as part of an overall peace settlement with the Palestinians. The status of the still-occupied Golan Heights, part of Syria until 1967, is also unresolved. Israel has applied its common law to the territory but has explicitly avoided using the term annexation.[128]

Up to this point, interest-based wars have been linked to territorial expansion. But they need not have territorial expansion as their goal, just as territorial conquest, it should be noted, can be prompted by other motives. Historically, most wars motivated by interest have sought control over territory; the three Anglo-Dutch Wars of 1652–1654, 1665–1667 and 1672–1674 are notable exceptions. Commercial rivalry was an important factor in these wars, but so too were efforts in the first two conflicts by Charles II to enhance the power and prestige of the crown.[129] Recent decades have witnessed conflicts, although no wars, over control of natural resources. Britain and Iceland disputed fishing rights when Iceland extended its economic zone of control. Oil and seabed resources have been the principal source of contention, conflicts about oil in the South China Sea being the most hotly contested. China, Taiwan, Vietnam, the Philippines, Malaysia, Indonesia, Thailand and Kampuchea have overlapping claims to various

---

[126] Jakobson, *Diplomacy of the Winter War*, pp. 248–253. Van Dyke, *Soviet Invasion of Finland*, pp. 189–191.

[127] Wikipedia, "Winter War," 5.1, http://en.wikipedia.org/wiki/Winter_War#cite_note-50/.

[128] BBC, Regions and Territories: The Golan Heights http://news.bbc.co.uk/2/hi/middle_east/country_profiles/3393813.stm.

[129] Wilson, *Profit and Power*; Seaward, *Cavalier Parliament and the Reconstruction of the Old Regime*, pp. 259–265; Jones, *Anglo-Dutch Wars of the Seventeenth Century*, pp. 7–15.

island groups (Paracel, Spratly and Natuna) and offshore waters. These competing claims have given rise to military maneuvers, occupations and rhetorical bombast, but to date have resulted in only one non-combatant death. It is not inconceivable that they could be the cause or, more likely, the pretext for a military confrontation between disputants.[130] Similar tensions exist in the Middle East, where disputes over water rights are overlaid on long-standing political disputes between countries and between Palestinians and Israelis.[131]

Does interest-based war have a future? The gains of territorial aggression are increasingly marginal and the cost of attempted conquest and occupation increasingly high. Competition for natural resources, oil and water especially, has become more acute as these resources have become more critical. We can readily construct two opposing narratives. The first and, I hope, the more likely outcome is that competition for resources remains about the same as it is today, perhaps less intense if alternative sources of energy become more available and cost-effective. In this world, the likelihood of interest-motivated war would decline sharply. The second narrative assumes growing environmental pressures, if not catastrophe, caused by declining oil resources, global warming and rising seas. In this world, material interests and security would be increasingly difficult to differentiate, and wars in which control over natural resources were central objectives would become more likely. In this scenario, concern for security and the environment become ever more tightly coupled. The most important steps on the road to peace may accordingly be national, regional and international efforts to manage resources and halt global warming.[132]

Security

Territorial conquest has been sought for reasons of interest, security and standing. Initiators were motivated by security in 20 wars, which represents 18 percent of the total initiations. In 7 of these wars, initiators also appear to have been motivated by standing. Security as a motive is most

---

[130] Middlebury College, South China Sea website for the most up-to-date information and analyses, http://community.middlebury.edu/~scs/; Bateman and Schofield, *Outer Shelf Claims in the South China Sea.*

[131] Shapland, *Rivers of Discord.*

[132] Ullman, "Redefining Security"; Mathews, "Redefining Security"; Gleick, "Implications of Global Climate Changes for International Security"; Homer-Dixon, *Environment, Scarcity, and Violence,* pp. 133–176, whose examples are primarily interstate.

pronounced in the twentieth century, where it is implicated in 13 of 18 wars. What accounts for this distribution and what might its implications be for the future of war?

With the exception of the Spanish–American War and the American attack on Afghanistan, in which security was a co-equal motive with standing, the remaining security-motivated initiations were associated with the three global conflicts of the twentieth century: World Wars I and II and the Cold War. In each of them, I have argued, standing was also an important, if not primary, concern. Germany's declaration of unrestricted submarine warfare in April 1917 offers a more clear-cut case for security as a motive. Anxious to win its war against Britain and France and recognizing that they were losing a war of attrition, German leaders took a calculated gamble: that their U-boats could sink enough merchant ships to bring Britain to its knees before American entry in the war – almost certain to be provoked by U-boat warfare – could make any difference on the western front.[133] In effect, the German challenge of the US was an act of desperation by a great power fearful of otherwise losing what had become a long and costly war.

Two of the three World War II cases coded as security have similar origins in the sense that they involve military actions against third parties intended to enhance the initiator's strategic position in a primary conflict. The Russo-Finnish War of 1939–1940 was triggered by Soviet efforts to extend its defensive perimeter as far west as possible to help defend against an expected German *Drang nach Osten*. The Finnish frontier was only 32 kilometers from Leningrad, the second-largest city in the Soviet Union, and Finland had been ruled since 1937 by a conservative, pro-German government.[134] In the east, the Soviet Union faced a secondary threat from an aggressive Japan, and launched a crushing military offensive against the Kwantung Army, which had penetrated Mongolia. Decisive defeat of the Japanese bought Moscow respite in the east as the Japanese decided to direct their offensive operations against the Western colonial powers.[135]

In the third case, World War II, the Japanese attacks in December 1941 and early 1942 against the United States, British and Dutch colonial outposts in Asia is more complicated and difficult to code. Security enters the picture because the Japanese felt that their backs were against the wall because of the American-organized embargos of scrap and oil. The Navy

---

[133] Lebow, *Between Peace and War*, ch. 3.   [134] *Ibid.*
[135] Haslam, *Soviet Union and the Threat from the East*, pp. 112–134; Coox, *Nomonhan*.

General Staff warned in August 1940 that access to scrap and oil were "a matter of life and death" because they had only six months of oil reserves and were worried that the planned occupation of French Indochina could provoke an American economic embargo. Naval extremists nevertheless wanted to exploit Hitler's conquests in Europe to move south to grab Indochina and the Indonesian oil fields. Many of them had believed since the mid-1930s that war with the US was all but inevitable. Army leaders were confident of American neutrality. If we step back from these precipitating events to the 1930s, it is apparent that Japan was responsible for its own security dilemma. Its invasion of China, set in motion following the so-called Mukden Incident of September 1931, was part of a wider effort by Japanese militarists and their civilian supporters to establish Japanese domination in the Pacific rim from Siberia to Australia. Chinese resistance led to a widening, costly and unresolved war on the Chinese mainland, as Japanese forces penetrated ever deeper into the country on the false assumption that occupation of more territory would compel the Nationalists to come to terms. Japanese generals now reasoned that the occupation of Southeast Asia would cut the supply lines to Chongqing, so vital to the Nationalist regime, and convince them of the futility of further resistance. Instead, it provoked the scrap and oil embargo that put Japan and the Western powers on a collision course. Security is at best considered a secondary motive, one that only became prominent by reason of prior Japanese military aggression in Asia. That expansion in turn appears to have been driven by complex causes, which include nationalism, manifest as a drive for coequal standing with the Western power, a struggle for power between military and civilians and within the military itself.[136]

The four remaining cases are outgrowths of the Cold War. The American and Chinese interventions in Korea were both a response to security concerns. The Truman administration considered the North Korean invasion of the South a Moscow-inspired probe of American resolve and felt compelled to respond. The success of the Inchon invasion left North Korea relatively defenseless. Responding to domestic political pressures, and misled by MacArthur about China's ability to intervene, Truman ordered US forces to push north toward the Yalu River, the

---

[136] Crowley, *Japan's Quest for Autonomy*, pp. 301–378; Iriye, *Origins of the Second World War*, pp. 41–49, 89–94, 100–167; Sadao, "Japanese Navy and the United States"; Lebow, *Cultural Theory of International Relations*, pp. 409–417.

border with China.[137] Chinese leaders felt their security threatened by American subjugation of North Korea, envisaging it as a possible prelude to a further advance against their principal industrial base in Manchuria. Chinese leaders also had concerns about the survival of their newly established regime if they failed to demonstrate resolve in confronting the American challenge.[138] Soviet intervention in Hungary, American intervention in Indochina and Soviet intervention in Afghanistan were also prompted by concerns for resolve. In each instance, leaders worried that the other superpower and local adversaries would perceive them as irresolute and sponsor more serious challenges.[139]

Most of these cases fall into two distinct patterns. Germany's provocation of the US through unrestricted submarine warfare, the Soviet Union's attack on the Kwantung Army and on Finland, and the Japanese attack on Pearl Harbor and Western colonies in Asia were outgrowths of ongoing or expected primary conflicts. Some of these wars were preceded by "spinoff" crises, as was the case in the German–American, Soviet–Finland and Japanese–American confrontations. Spinoff crises arise when a state's preparations for fighting, or actual engagement, in a primary conflict provoke an otherwise undesired conflict with a third party. They are almost impossible to resolve because of the vital interests perceived to be at stake on both sides. The parties involved nevertheless make strenuous efforts to resolve these conflicts by diplomacy because neither seeks war and both expect it to be politically or militarily costly.[140] The principal exception in this sample of wars was the Soviet clash with the Kwantung Army. No real crisis preceded the Soviet attack, as Moscow wanted to maximize surprise, and, provided with good intelligence from its spy network in Tokyo, knew that negotiations were unlikely to succeed as the Kwantung Army was acting on its own authority.[141]

Each of these wars had idiosyncratic causes but all of them were associated with the two world wars; they were direct extensions of these conflicts or, in the case of the Soviet Union's military actions in

---

[137] Neustadt, *Presidential Power*, pp. 120–145; Spanier, *Truman–MacArthur Controversy*; Lebow, *Between Peace and War*, ch. 6; Foot, *Wrong War*.

[138] Whiting, *China Crosses the Yalu*; Simmons, *Strained Alliance*; Xu, *Cong Yalujiang dao Banmendian*; Zhang, *Mao's Military Romanticism*, pp. 3, 81.

[139] "Soviet Archival Documents on the Hungarian Revolution"; Taubman, *Khrushchev*, pp. 294–299; Kahin, *Intervention*; Logevall, *Choosing War*; Bradsher, *Afghan Communism and Soviet Intervention*, pp. 75–117; Wolf, "Stumbling Toward War."

[140] Lebow, *Between Peace and War*, ch. 3.   [141] Coox, *Nomonhan*, vol. 1, pp. 266–590.

Mongolia and Finland, the result of tensions leading up to World War II. None of these wars would have happened in the absence of the world wars and the context in which they arose. Both world wars have been described as part of a thirty-year European civil war, the most fundamental underlying cause of which was the challenge posed to traditional regimes by economic development and nationalism. This era of European development is now history, and the dangers of a continental war involving multiple great powers has greatly diminished, if not altogether disappeared. Other parts of the world have experienced similar turmoil, and it has also found expression in civil and foreign wars. For much of the Pacific rim, this era has also passed, and, here too, the likelihood of general war has receded dramatically. This important cause of security-motivated war has disappeared.

Other security-based wars were outgrowths of the Cold War. All four wars of this kind took the form of military interventions in contested territories. They arose from the same cause: sensitivity of the super-powers and China to loss of influence in client states. In two cases, this was a realistic concern: allowing Hungry to defect from the Communist bloc in 1956, or a relatively independent Czechoslovakia in 1968, would have made it very difficult for the Soviet Union to maintain its sphere of influence in Eastern Europe. In 1968, Soviet premier Leonid Brezhnev confided to Polish leader Władysław Gomułka that, in the absence of Eastern bloc solidarity, unrest might spill over into the Soviet Ukraine.[142] The US had its own domino theory, which was a principal reason for intervention in Vietnam. President Lyndon Johnson and his advisors worried that a communist takeover in Vietnam would make America look irresolute in the eyes of friend and foe alike and lead to the quick collapse, and possible communist takeover, of other governments in Southeast Asia.[143] In retrospect, American fear of falling dominos can be considered paranoid as none of these fears were realized in the aftermath of the American withdrawal from Vietnam. Local communist movements were not directed by Moscow, and the opening of Soviet archives during the era of *glasnost* makes it apparent that Soviet leaders never doubted American resolve.[144]

---

[142] *New York Times*, August 28, 1980, p. A4.
[143] Kahin, *Intervention*, pp. 9, 29, 40, 126, 173–176; Logevall, *Choosing War*, pp. 31, 247. For an alternative emphasis on the domestic political costs of withdrawal, see Gelb and Betts, *Irony of Vietnam*.
[144] Lebow and Stein, *We All Lost the Cold War*; Hopf, *Peripheral Visions*.

Exaggerated concern for relative power and resolve is by no means limited to the twentieth century. Thucydides describes something similar in his account of the origins of the Peloponnesian War. Pericles was unwilling to let pass the opportunity of augmenting Athenian power by taking Corcyra into alliance. The alliance embroiled the Athenians with the Corinthians and escalated into a war with Sparta and its allies. War could have been avoided if Athens had agreed to lift the siege of Potidaea and the economic blockade of Megara. Neither concession would have seriously threatened Athenian security and, on the positive side, held out the prospect of breaking up the Corinthian–Spartan alliance. Pericles was nevertheless adamant that Sparta's peace overtures be rejected because they would have made Athens appear irresolute and subordinate to Sparta.[145] Romans and Carthaginians came into conflict over Sicily, strategically located between Italy and North Africa, and again in Spain, another venue where the two expanding empires came into contact. Once again, questions of imperial expansion and standing were as important as strategic considerations in the calculations of the respective hegemons.[146]

The Americans considered resolve a prime requisite of security throughout the Cold War. Truman's gut reaction to Korea was that the communists were testing US resolve as Hitler had tested France and Britain. NSC-68 gave resolve coequal standing with military capability. Kennedy erroneously concluded that Khrushchev had deployed missiles in Cuba because he doubted his resolve. American intervention in Indochina, concern over an alleged "window of vulnerability" in the early 1980s and later worries about the political consequences of a Soviet advantage in theater weapons systems reveal a continuing fixation on the question of resolve. So too did the Cold War literature on deterrence – which stressed credibility as key – and portrayed commitments as a seamless web in which resolve (or its absence) in any one commitment had serious implications for all others.[147] "Few parts of the world are intrinsically worth the risk of serious war," Thomas Schelling wrote, "but defending them may preserve one's commitment to action in other parts of the world and at later times."[148]

---

[145] Thucydides, *History of the Peloponnesian War*, Book I; Lebow, *Tragic Vision of Politics*, pp. 86–89.

[146] Polybius, *Rise of the Roman Empire*, Books 1–2; Harris, *War and Imperialism in Republican Rome*, pp. 105–130.

[147] Lebow, *Between Peace and War*, pp. 82–97; Hopf, *Peripheral Visions*, pp. 1–7, for a discussion of this literature.

[148] Schelling, *Arms and Influence*, p. 125.

This kind of behavior stands in sharp contrast to Waltz's understanding of how bipolar systems function. He expects them to be less war-prone, in part because the addition or defection of a third party cannot materially affect either superpower's ability to provide for its security.[149] In practice, psychological pathologies associated with the security dilemma appear to make it just as acute in bipolar systems. Fifth-century Greece, pre-1914 Europe and the Cold War indicate that leaders engage in worst-case analysis and exaggerate the political consequences of defections just as they do each other's military advantages and intentions.

In all three eras, it is difficult to disentangle concerns for security from those about standing. In his narrative account of the origins of the Peloponnesian War, Thucydides makes it apparent that Spartiates felt more threatened by Athenian political, economic and cultural achievements than they did by its military might. The cornerstone of Spartan identity was military prowess and the hegemony it had won for this otherwise poor city-state. War against Athens was welcomed as a means of preserving hegemony.[150] The Cold War began as a confrontation over a power vacuum in central Europe whose victorious occupiers were driven by seemingly incompatible security and economic needs. After Stalin's death in 1953, it evolved into a conflict in which concern for relative standing in Europe and the so-called Third World became paramount. Soviet and American leaders and their advisors invariably used the language of security to justify their respective quest for advantages *vis-à-vis* their rivals in the varied domains in which they competed. In practice, the quest for superiority, and the prestige it conferred, became ends in themselves. Vast expenditure on unusable nuclear weapons and increasingly sophisticated delivery systems, military and economic aid to unreliable allies and space exploration made that conflict come to resemble a grand potlatch.[151]

A study of war must include those dogs that did not bark. Chief among these is the Cold War. It never went hot between the superpowers and many reasons have been offered for this outcome, including deterrence, memories of World War II and its costs and the ability of the superpowers to work out a *modus vivendi* to reduce and manage their

---

[149] Waltz, *Theory of International Politics*, pp. 168–170.
[150] Lebow, *Tragic Vision of Politics*, ch. 3.
[151] Lebow, *Cultural Theory of International Relations*, ch. 9, for documentation.

conflict.[152] Other scholars suggest that the Cold War was the result of an ideological struggle that began with the Russian Revolution in 1917 and continued until "new thinking" led Soviet leaders to abandon communism and search for accommodation with the West.[153]

Realists and liberals alike attribute the end of the war to the inability of the Soviet Union to compete with the West, and trace that in turn to its cumbersome and inefficient command economy and system of government. Realists contend that Gorbachev sought to negotiate the best terms he could while the Soviet Union still counted as a superpower.[154] Conservatives insist that Ronald Reagan's military buildup and Strategic Defense Initiative (Star Wars) hastened the Soviet Union's decline.[155] Liberals maintain that, in the Soviet Union, and even more in Eastern Europe, intellectuals and much of the population at large became thoroughly disenchanted with socialism and desperately wanted to share in the material affluence of the West. Still other analysts emphasize the restraining effect of nuclear weapons, which, while they did bring the Cold War to an end, kept crises from escalating out of hand and provided the umbrella of security that allowed Gorbachev to make the concessions necessary to transform East–West relations.[156] Finally, the end of the Cold War has been attributed to a non-linear confluence brought about by the interaction of multiple underlying conditions and triggering events.[157]

By the time Gorbachev became General Secretary, the Cold War had evolved into something very different than it was when it began in 1947.[158] It had become less volatile in response to efforts by the superpowers to reduce the risk of war through understandings about how their rivalry should be managed. "Rules of the road" were developed during

---

[152] Herrmann and Lebow, "What Was the Cold War? When and Why Did It Fail?," for an overview.

[153] English, *Russia and the Idea of the West*; English, "Power, Ideas, and New Evidence on the Cold War's End"; Lévesque, *The Enigma of 1989*; Evangelista, *Unarmed Forces*; Brown, *Gorbachev Factor*; Garthoff, *Great Transformation*; Lebow and Stein, *We All Lost the Cold War*.

[154] Wohlforth, "Realism and the End of the Cold War"; Davis and Wohlforth, "German Unification"; Zubok, "Why Did the Cold War End in 1989?"

[155] Matlock, *Autopsy of an Empire*.

[156] Oye, "Explaining the End of the Cold War"; Creveld, "The Waning of Major War"; Paul, *Tradition of Non-Use*.

[157] Breslauer and Lebow, "Leadership and the End of the Cold War"; Lebow and Stein, "Understanding the End of the Cold War as a Non-Linear Confluence."

[158] Herrmann and Lebow, "What Was the Cold War?"

the short-lived era of *détente* of the late 1960s and early 1970s.[159] Arms control and the West's recognition of the postwar territorial *status quo* in Europe also served as powerful sources of reassurance. The superpowers remained committed to their rivalry, and their pursuit of unilateral advantage undermined the promise of *détente*. The striking aspect of superpower goals in the 1970s and 1980s is how little they had to do with security and how much they reflected desires to gain the upper hand in a contest for standing – a subject I will address in more detail in the next chapter. This orientation did not change until Gorbachev became General Secretary in 1985. He and his advisors had concluded that such competition was costly, dangerous and inimical to their domestic reform agenda.

Gorbachev and his closest advisors understood the Cold War to have assumed a life of its own and both superpowers to have become its victims. The Cold War required enormous expenditures on weapons, which enhanced the power of the military-industrial complex and justified repression at home. Arms buildups and competition in the Third World also made war more rather than less likely. Gorbachev sought to escape from the economic and political restraints the Cold War imposed and to restructure the Soviet Union, politically and economically. "New Thinking" was a response to relative material decline and political stasis, and enabled by it. It encouraged and allowed Gorbachev to prioritize domestic over foreign policy and encouraged him to make concessions to the West to jumpstart the process of accommodation. Of equal importance, it provided a frame of reference that made feasible the kinds of concessions (e.g. a theater forces agreement in which the Soviet Union had to withdraw and destroy more weapons than the United States, unification of Germany within NATO) that previous Soviet governments would have considered anathema. Gorbachev and his principal advisors understood that efforts to make the Soviet Union secure through arms buildups, foreign entanglements, and, most disastrously, the military occupation of Afghanistan, had actually undermined Soviet security.

While Gorbachev was distancing himself from Lenin and his heritage, his strategy bore an uncanny resemblance to Lenin's approach to imperial Germany. Lenin had been willing to sign the grossly one-sided and exploitative Treaty of Brest-Litovsk because he gambled that subsequent events – he was hoping for a socialist revolution in Germany – would

---

[159] George, *Managing US–Soviet Rivalry*; George, Farley and Dallin, *US–Soviet Security Cooperation.*

negate the Treaty and advance Soviet interests in a more fundamental way.[160] Gorbachev's strategy rested on a similar premise: strategic and political concessions would be meaningless if they helped to end the Cold War and radically restructure the Soviet Union's relations with the West. Neither gamble worked out as planned. There was no successful revolution in Germany in 1918–1919, and Gorbachev's unwillingness to use force to keep communist governments in power in Eastern Europe led to the unanticipated breakup of the Warsaw Pact and the subsequent dissolution of the Soviet Union. Gorbachev's gamble was still the better one if evaluated in terms of the longer-term prospects for the people of the former Soviet Union.

One important lesson of the Cold War for our purposes is that leaders are not prisoners of strategic or political circumstances. They have the potential to transform long-standing adversarial relationships but must be motivated, as was Gorbachev, and Sadat before him, by domestic agendas that require resolution of these conflicts or, at least, significant progress in winding down the tensions associated with them.[161] To do this, leaders require political courage and alternative conceptions of security that justify restraint and extending the olive branch to themselves and relevant political constituencies.

The other, equally important lesson, is the extent to which security is a subjective discourse, not some "objective" feature of the international environment that can be inferred by the application of reason. Stalin, Khrushchev, Brezhnev and Gorbachev understood Soviet security quite differently. The evolution of Soviet thinking about security reflected changing ideas more than it did changing circumstances.[162] Protection of the Soviet homeland and its citizens may have been a primary concern for all these leaders but the means by which it was to be accomplished varied considerably. For Stalin, at one extreme, it dictated opposition to the Western powers, for Khrushchev it required a mix of conflict and cooperation, and, for Gorbachev, overwhelmingly cooperation. Each of these leaders framed security differently in part because of their other goals, which, depending on the leader and the year, included staying in power, expanding Soviet influence, economic and political reforms and

---

[160] Volkogonov, *Lenin*, pp. 183–194.   [161] Lebow, "Transitions and Transformations."
[162] English, *Russia and the Idea of the West*; English, "Power, Ideas, and New Evidence on the Cold War's End"; Lévesque, *The Enigma of 1989*; Evangelista, *Unarmed Forces*; Brown, *Gorbachev Factor*; Garthoff, *Great Transformation*; Lebow and Stein, *We All Lost the Cold War*.

improving the quality of life of Soviet citizens. Such shifts in thinking and conceptions of security are equally apparent in the People's Republic of China over the course of its sixty years of existence.

Provisional conclusions

Security-motivated wars and one critical non-war suggest two general conclusions, both of which have important implications for the future of war. The first pertains to the broader material and ideational context in which international relations takes place. It determines the distribution of motives responsible for wars. The second is the subjective understanding actors have of interest, security and standing. Together, I contend, they determine the frequency of war.

The material and ideational contexts of international relations have changed in dramatic ways in the course of the 350 years of the data set. I noted in the introduction that nation states, or units aspiring to this status, replaced dynastic states and empires as the dominant political form. Kingship and aristocracy gave way to democracy and modern forms of authoritarian rule. With these changes, there has been a corresponding evolution in the theory and practice of democracy since its modern emergence in European city states and England.[163] National identification on the whole became more important than religious and local loyalties in Europe and later, in many other parts of the world. National identification encouraged correspondingly higher expectations that the states to which loyalties were now directed would bring about greater material well-being and enhance self-esteem.[164] As we have observed, the practice of warfare also evolved. Some of its most important modern features, as Clausewitz was among the first to observe, were the direct response of nationalism.

Scholars have offered various periodizations of international relations based on the rise of nationalism, economic development and transformation of regimes. Most use major wars as convenient breaking points. The most common division is from Westphalia to the French Revolution and the wars that followed, from the Congress of Vienna to 1914, from 1914 to 1945, and from 1945 to the end of the Cold War. More elaborate

---

[163] Dunn, *Democracy*; Eley, *Forging Democracy*.

[164] Deutsch, *Nationalism and Social Communication*, was clear about this relationship. Lebow, *Cultural Theory of International Relations*, for a more comprehensive treatment.

typologies also exist; Paul Schroeder proposes seven divisions between 1763 (intense Austro-Prussian rivalry) and 1914.[165] Some international relations scholars see a major watershed with the development and use of nuclear weapons, arguing that post-1945 great power relations are qualitatively different.[166] All of these orderings are defensible, but none are really appropriate to my purposes as they are usually based on single dimensions. Any novel factor or major change influences the practice of international relations, but does so in a context shaped by other factors and developments. As most of these conditions (e.g. democracy, authoritarianism, nationalism, industrialization) evolved over time, they gave rise to complex patterns of interaction that are difficult, if not impossible, to periodize effectively. The best we can do, I believe, is to identify configurations of uncertain duration that have particularly important consequences for the frequency and character of war. Historians and international relations scholars have identified several such configurations, among them a cluster of reinforcing political, ideational and organizational conditions that appear to have made a European continental war more rather than less likely in the first decades of the twentieth century. These include nationalism, imperialism, Social Darwinism, industrialization and urbanization, mass politics, elites and regimes that felt threatened by political and economic change, commitments to offensive military doctrines and obsolescent decisionmaking institutions and procedures.[167]

International relations scholars who believe that war is on the wane point to another cluster of conditions that includes democratization, economic development and interdependence, anti-war sentiment, international institutions and even nuclear weapons. There are sharp differences of opinion concerning the relative weight of these factors. Pessimists interpret these developments differently, emphasizing the negative implications of nuclear weapons, globalization and even democratization.[168] All predictions to date rest on the perceived implications of one or more of these conditions. The continuing controversy about the origins of World War I indicates how difficult, if not impossible, it is,

---

[165] Schroeder, "Life and Death of a Long Peace."
[166] Brodie, *Absolute Weapon*; Jervis, *Meaning of the Nuclear Revolution*; Bundy, *First Fifty Years of the Bomb*.
[167] Hamilton and Herwig, *Origins of World War I*; Lebow, *Forbidden Fruit*, ch. 3, for reviews of this literature.
[168] On democratization, see Mansfield and Snyder, "Democratization and the Danger of War"; Mansfield and Snyder, *Electing to Fight*.

even in retrospect, to build a consensus about the key conditions in a cluster or the consequences of any of them for war and peace. Forecasts are more problematic still. Like their historical counterparts, they rest on assumptions and expectations that are untestable. There is no solution to this problem, which is why we must try to reduce uncertainty by augmenting our research with a second strategy: the understandings actors have of their motives and their implications for war and peace.

As we have seen, these understandings are fluid. In the case of interest, the perceived utility of war declined noticeably once mercantilism was discredited. States have continued to exploit conquered territories economically, but in none of the twentieth century wars in the data set was territory sought primarily for economic reasons. Conquest is increasingly difficult because of international opposition. The economic exploitation of conquered territories is also more problematic. Aggressors are likely to suffer from trade and investment embargos. Among the leading capitalist states, Stephen Brooks demonstrates, military development and production has become increasingly internationalized, making conquest more costly still.[169] To the extent that political authorities come to understand these costs and restraints, territorial aggression will decline; it has already, making interest-based wars even less likely.

Realists of all shades are united by the belief that security must be a primary concern of states and that it ultimately depends on military capabilities. However, security, like interest, is a social construction. Thinking about security is neither universal nor constant and has evolved considerably over the ages. The Cold War provides an excellent illustration. An exaggerated concern for resolve, seen as a central prerequisite for security, helped to sustain the Cold War long after the initial conflict over which it began – the territorial division of Europe – had been accepted by both sides. Gorbachev's understanding that the Cold War had become a conflict of prestige and standing that seriously endangered the security of both superpowers made possible the Soviet concessions that brought this conflict to an end.

The twentieth century was a particularly fertile era for "new thinking" about security. The concept of collective security, which I briefly described in the introduction, is perhaps the most prominent example. It found its first institutional embodiment in the Concert of Europe, but was extensively theorized in the post-World War I era after it became the

---

[169] Brooks, *Producing Security*.

core mission of the ill-fated League of Nations.[170] After World War II, it provided the central justification for the Security Council of the United Nations, where it is generally acknowledged to have made a modest contribution, and of numerous alliances, among them NATO, the Rio Pact, the US–Japan Mutual Security Treaty, SEATO, the Baghdad Pact and CENTO. NATO has been the most successful of these organizations, surviving and broadening its mission in the post-Cold War era.[171] Arms control became another pillar of security. The Hague Conference of 1899 banned certain kinds of projectiles and the launching of projectiles and bombs from balloons. The Washington Naval Treaty of 1922 limited the total tonnage of capital ships. Cold War arms control agreements between the superpowers functioned as vehicles of mutual assurance, and the 1987 Treaty on Intermediate-Range Nuclear Forces (INF) and the 1991 START Treaty helped to bring that conflict to a close.[172]

The twentieth century witnessed the emergence and gradual acceptance of the idea that security required more than just the absence of war. This principle too became embodied in the United Nations Charter, which charges its specialized agencies with promoting world health, child welfare, human rights and agricultural and other forms of development. In the academy, the distinction between negative peace (the absence of war) and positive peace (the restoration of relationships and a commitment to a just society where human beings can realize their potential) has been extensively theorized.[173] More recently, the long-standing conception of the state as a fortress that can effectively protect its citizens from external threats has seriously eroded. Scholars and policymakers alike have come to understand that the distinction between internal and international threats to security is largely artificial and that unilateral action and military measures are generally not the most efficacious means of coping with either. This is true of security threats as diverse as terrorism, drugs, immigration, disease and environmental degradation.[174]

[170] Schroeder, "19th Century International System"; Elrod, "Concert of Europe"; Northedge, League of Nations; Walters, History of the League of Nations; Jervis, "Security Regimes."
[171] Kupchan and Kupchan, "Concerts, Collective Security, and the Future of Europe"; Betts, "Systems for Peace or Causes of War?"; Downs, Collective Security Beyond the Cold War; Kay, NATO and the Future of European Security.
[172] Evangelista, Unarmed Forces; Evangelista, "Turning Points in Arms Control."
[173] Boulding, "Future Directions of Conflict and Peace Studies"; Galtung, Peace by Peaceful Means.
[174] Ullman, "Redefining Security"; Mathews, "Redefining Security"; Aydinli and Rosenau, Globalization, Security, and the Nation-State.

New understandings of security have significantly changed the ways in which some states think about and plan for security. Does this make interstate war less likely? The answer depends on the fit between these conceptions and the configuration of conditions, or material and ideational context, in which international relations take place. As we have seen, Hans Morgenthau and E. H. Carr argued that belief in the efficacy of international law and institutions in the 1920s and 1930s blinded progressive and peace-oriented opinion and leaders to the dangers posed by the Nazis and Fascists and contributed to the outbreak of World War II. Morgenthau and Carr greatly exaggerated the *naïveté* of prominent international lawyers, but were correct in their judgment that appeasement – something never advocated by these much-maligned "idealists" – was a grossly inappropriate strategy in the circumstances.[175] This does not mean that international law and institutions might not successfully serve the ends of peace in different circumstances or that hard-line deterrence strategies, arguably appropriate in the 1930s, were equally so in the 1960s, where they appear to have accelerated the arms race and provoked at least two acute crises. Strategies must be matched to circumstances, and any forecast about the future likelihood of peace and war will depend on a fortuitous overlay. I say "fortuitous" because so often in the past efforts to prevent war were based on the lessons of the previous war and thus were one conflict out of sync.[176] I will revisit this problem at the end of the next chapter.

Let me close on a cautiously optimistic note. The configurations of factors seemingly responsible for the two world wars of the twentieth century and the Cold War that followed were associated with a particular stage of history. They are unlikely to reappear again. Understandings of interest and security have also evolved, making wars fought for these motives less likely, at least among the great powers. For a more comprehensive analysis, we turn to our remaining three motives: standing, revenge and other.

---

[175] On this point, see Lynch, *Beyond Appeasement*, pp. 93–124; Schmidt, "Anarchy, World Politics and the Birth of a Discipline"; Ashworth, "Did the Realist–Idealist Great Debate Ever Happen?"

[176] Jervis, *Perception and Misperception*, pp. 117–124, 187, 262–270; Lebow, "Generational Learning and Foreign Policy."

6

Standing and revenge

I now address the motives of standing and revenge and my residual category of other. I review the frequency of these motives over the course of the centuries covered by the data set and the conditions that connect them to war. With regard to standing, the link to war is tight and consistent until the end of the nineteenth century when standing and war begin to diverge. This process accelerated during the twentieth century but was not uniform across regions. Today, we have reached the point where war-initiation is almost certain to reduce a state's external standing. The principal exception is intervention to uphold core community values with the authorization of the United Nations or appropriate regional organizations. I treat revenge as an independent motive, but like standing it is an expression of the spirit. It too has declined as a motive for war, in part for the same reason, but also because territorial conquest, its principal objective, is on the whole no longer acceptable or profitable.

The category of other is more complicated, as it includes all causes of war that cannot be assimilated to my four generic motives. Wars I code as other are most often an expression of domestic power struggles or efforts by weak regimes to buttress their popularity. There are obvious connections between internal and external problems and the circumstances that push leaders in the direction of more aggressive or accommodating foreign policies.[1] These circumstances are highly contextual, one of the many reasons it is difficult to forecast with any confidence.

Standing

As reported in Chapter 4, I found 107 motives for 94 wars. Standing was implicated in 62 of these wars, or 58 percent of the total, making it far and

---

[1] Lebow, *Between Peace and War*, ch. 4; Jervis, Lebow and Stein, *Psychology and Deterrence*, chs. 3–5 and 9; Lebow, "Transitions and Transformations."

away the leading motive. This holds true for every century of the data set. While standing is a consistent motive for war, it is not uniform in its manifestations.

In the seventeenth and eighteenth centuries, wars of standing took place within a European regional system dominated by kings and princes, most of whom regarded their states as dynastic patrimonies. Rulers frequently sought to achieve *gloire* through military victories and conquest. Louis XIV was absolutely explicit about his motives for the Dutch War (1672–1678): "I shall not attempt to justify myself," he wrote in his memoirs. "Ambition and [the pursuit of] *gloire* are always pardonable in a prince, and especially in a young prince so well treated by fortune as I was."[2] Protestants William of Orange and Frederick the Great also aspired to *gloire*. Many of the rulers of this era personally led their armies into battle (e.g. Louis XIV, Frederick I and II, Peter the Great), greatly enhancing their claims to *gloire*. Royal, dynastic and national honor and dignity dominate the diplomatic correspondence of the eighteenth century, although they appear less frequently in the correspondence of Catherine II of Russia (1762–1796), Frederick II of Prussia and Joseph II of Austria.[3] Eight eighteenth-century wars were associated with successions.[4] They provided opportunities for aggressive leaders to extend their dominion, as Prussia and France attempted to do when Maria Theresa succeeded to the throne of Austria or when Charles VII, Prince-Elector of Bavaria and Holy Roman Emperor, died in 1745. Leading states sometimes went to war in succession crises simply because their honor was involved. Louis XIV's bid for the throne of Spain on behalf of his grandson, which provoked a continental war, had everything to do with dynastic standing.[5] In 1733, France went to war because one of the candidates for the Polish throne was Louis XV's father-in-law.

Honor and standing were frequently pursued at the expense of state interests.[6] Louis XIV rejected the Dutch Republic's desperate peace offers following his initial campaign, although he had achieved his stated goals. Out of hubris and an insatiable search for *gloire*, he insisted on complete conquest of the Republic, turning the war into a long struggle and the intervention of other European states in a powerful anti-French

---

[2] Zeller, "French Diplomacy and Foreign Policy in the Their European Setting."
[3] Black, *From Louis XIV to Napoleon*, p. 79; Black, *European International Relations*, p. 17.
[4] Blainey, *Causes of War*, p. 68.   [5] *Ibid.*, p. 213.
[6] Swann, "Politics and the State in Eighteenth Century Europe."

coalition.[7] Against the advice of more sensible advisors (e.g. Vauban, Colbert, Hugue de Lionnes), Louis repeatedly began military ventures he could not bring to a successful conclusion and had to settle at Rijswijk and Utrecht for more modest gains in Europe and significant losses overseas. Charles XII of Sweden rejected a reasonable peace in 1714 after fourteen years of war on the grounds that "better times would not come till we get more respect in Europe than we now have."[8] In the Great Northern War (1699–1721), which ended in the total defeat of Sweden, Charles foolishly invaded Russia and led his army into an exposed position deep in what is now Ukraine, where it was crushed at Poltava. Charles could not restrain his spirit. He was seemingly driven by a burning desire to avenge the Danish-Russian-Saxon attacks on the Swedish empire and its German ally in 1700.[9]

The high cost of seventeenth and eighteenth century wars offers more evidence about motives. Louis XIV and the Habsburgs had to sell private assets to keep their armies in the field.[10] After the Great Northern War, France and Prussia were on the verge of financial collapse. The high costs and low success rate of war undercuts the claim that actors were motivated by material gain. Neither condition would, however, deter leaders intent on achieving *gloire*. The high cost of war might even make it more attractive, just as rich people seeking status today often flock to vastly over-priced hotels and restaurants in the hope of being seen by those they want to impress.

Jeremy Black, a leading authority on war in the seventeenth and eighteenth centuries, emphasizes the extent to which honor and opportunity drove war.[11] The quest for *gloire* contributed to the brutality of war and was responsible for consistently higher casualty rates among officers than among ordinary soldiers.[12] French officers were notorious for their efforts to win honor through their audacity. Marshal Charles Villars, the most successful commander on the French side in the War of the Spanish Succession (1701–1714), praised "the air of audacity so natural to the French," whose preferred method of battle "is to charge

---

[7] This has not prevented modern scholars from reading back *raison d'état* into Louis' foreign policy and, especially, his assault on the Netherlands. See Israel, *Dutch Republic*, pp. 131–132.
[8] Quoted in Hatton, *Charles XII of Sweden*, p. 375. [9] Holsti, *Peace and War*, pp. 68–69.
[10] Dickson, *Finance and Government under Maria Theresa*, vol. 2, pp. 272–299.
[11] Black, *European International Relations*, pp. 50–52, 54–55.
[12] Lynn, *Giant of the Grand Siècle*, pp. 464–465.

with the bayonet."[13] For much of the seventeenth century, the French army put less emphasis on victory than on its ability to maintain order while suffering casualties inflicted by the other side.[14] Such bravado was increasingly suicidal in an age when artillery and musket fire could destroy formations at a considerable distance, and a further indication of the overriding importance of *gloire*. For Louis XIV, war was all about bravery: "Good order makes us look assured, and it seems enough to look brave, because most often our enemies do not wait for us to approach near enough for us to have to show if we are in fact brave." The King personally led regiments into battle as late as 1692, making sure to give orders within musket range of the enemy.[15] Monarchs and aristocrats sought glory, and the prestige it conferred, as ends in themselves and as a means of maintaining or enhancing their authority. Black warns against reading the motive of *raison d'état* back into the eighteenth century as German historians of the nineteenth century did: "As with most conflicts of this period, there was scant sense of how any war would develop in diplomatic and military terms."[16]

In the nineteenth century, the search for standing became a national concern, even in countries like Germany and Austria that could hardly be considered democratic. Foreign policymaking elites were still overwhelmingly aristocratic in origin and even more intensely committed to the concept of national honor now that traditional honor codes held less sway in interpersonal relations. Public opinion identified strongly with national states and their "honor," and all the more so in countries where the intelligentsia and middle classes were kept at the peripheries of power and the status hierarchy. This phenomenon became more pronounced in the twentieth century and was a principal cause of World War I.[17]

Realists explain World War I with reference to opposing alliance systems, arms races, offensive dominance and conflict in the Balkans, all of which exacerbated fears of strategic disadvantage and general insecurity. They single out the rising power of Germany and its challenge to the existing order, although some emphasize Russia's growing power and its alleged destabilizing consequences instead. Marxist and Marxist-inspired analyses emphasize class divisions that encouraged aristocratic

---

[13] *Ibid.*, quote on p. 127; Lynn, *Giant of the Grand Siècle*, pp. 453–512, on French army tactics.

[14] *Ibid.*, pp. 128–129.

[15] Louis XIV, *Mémoires de Louis XIV pour l'instruction du dauphin*, vol. 2, pp. 112–113.

[16] Black, *European International Relations*, pp. 50–52, 54–55.

[17] Lebow, *Cultural Theory of International Relations*, ch. 7, for an elaboration.

regimes to pursue increasingly aggressive foreign policies. Intellectual historians draw our attention to the *Zeitgeist* and the ways in which Social Darwinism, acute nationalism and adulation of military heroes made conflict and war appear attractive and inevitable.[18]

I contend that imperial competition, offensive military strategies, most alliances and favorable views of war – widespread among continental elites – cannot be attributed to either appetite or fear. Imperialism and arms races were understood to be a drain on resources and strategically questionable, if not downright disadvantageous. Some leaders even recognized how ill-advised these policies were in material and strategic terms. Competition for colonies, like earlier forms of interstate competition, was driven by a desire to achieve national recognition and standing. Imperial competition was a core concern of some leaders, most notably the German Kaiser, but increasingly of politically relevant middle class voters who sought to buttress their self-esteem vicariously through the successes of their nation.[19]

My argument concerning the origins of World War I demands more extensive treatment than I can provide here, especially as it is at odds with so many long-standing interpretations. I refer interested readers to Chapter 7 of *A Cultural Theory*, which offers a lengthy case study that critiques realist accounts, develops my argument and offers evidence in support. Chapters 8 and 9 of that book contain case studies of the origins of World War II and the Anglo-American intervention in Iraq, two other wars motivated by standing that I discuss only briefly in this chapter.

Interstate competition became more acute because of the problems aristocratic regimes had in coping with modernity. Some of this difficulty involved challenges to the authority and privileges of the nobility by other classes, but, ironically, it also reflected the efforts of the upper middle class to emulate at least some of their values and practices. This phenomenon threatened to blur the distinction between new and old wealth, and, with it, the exclusive status of the latter. It led powerful members of the nobility to emphasize the importance of "high politics," the domain in which they still maintained unquestioned authority through their control of the armed forces and foreign ministries. The most threatened aristocratic regimes – Germany and Austria-Hungary – exercised less self-restraint in their foreign policies and increasingly violated the norms that governed interstate competition.[20]

---

[18] Hamilton and Herwig, *Origins of World War I*; Lebow, *Forbidden Fruit*, ch. 3, for overviews of these arguments.
[19] Lebow, *Cultural Theory of International Relations*, ch. 7.   [20] *Ibid.*

When we turn to the crisis leading up to World War I, it is evident that the Austrian war hawks responsible for the ultimatum to Serbia acted less from fear for their country's security and more from a desire to uphold its honor and their own. The Emperor was not at all optimistic about the prospects of victory but did not doubt that drawing the sword was the only honorable course of action. Kaiser Wilhelm's "blank check" was similarly motivated: he saw himself as acting as Franz Josef's second in a duel. French support for Russia reflected strategic calculations, but also concern for honor. In Britain, the cabinet was divided, and prime minister Herbert Asquith was able to muster a majority for war only by appealing to the need to "honor" Britain's commitment to defend the neutrality of Belgium. His foreign secretary, Edward Grey, also regarded the treaty to uphold Belgium's neutrality as a moral commitment, but was more concerned with the strategic implications of German occupation of the country.[21]

Standing is also deeply implicated in the origins of World War II, and, here too, I refer readers to my case study in *A Cultural Theory of International Relations*. In Germany, there was deep resentment toward the allies and the terms of the Treaty of Versailles. It is revealing that, for many Germans, the most hated feature of the Treaty was not the loss of territory, reparations or restrictions on the German military that it imposed, but the articles that required Germany to accept responsibility for the war and to hand over the Kaiser and other individuals for trial as war criminals. Compelled to sign the Treaty by the allies, the Weimar Republic never achieved legitimacy. Economic shocks further weakened the Republic. Right-wing opponents, Hitler among them, gained popular support by promising to restore Germany's position in Europe, and, with it, the self-esteem of the German people. Hitler's own motives for going to war were pathological because they went far beyond restoration of the *status quo ante bellum* to the conquest of Europe, if not the world.[22] Many of his foreign policy and defense initiatives – withdrawal from the League of Nations, rearmament of Germany, *Anschluss* with Austria and dismemberment of Czechoslovakia – were welcomed enthusiastically by most Germans and Austrians. His wars against Poland, Western Europe, Yugoslavia, Greece and the Soviet Union were decidedly less popular, but what support they did have derived in large part from the same

---

[21] *Ibid.*
[22] Weinberg, *Foreign Policy of Hitler's Germany*, vol. 1, p. 358; Rich, *Hitler's War Aims*, pp. 3–10; Bullock, *Hitler*, pp. 10–11, 622; Fest, *Hitler*, pp. 213–218.

motives.[23] The importance of honor to the officer corps secured Hitler the quiescence, if not the active support, of the German army, and its willingness to keep fighting long after officers of every rank realized the hopelessness, if not the evil character, of their cause.

The spirit was an equally important motive for Italy and Japan. Neither was attempting to live down the consequences of defeat and partial territorial dismemberment, but their aggressive, expansionist policies can be described in large part as efforts to gain standing in the international system. Both countries achieved great power status only belatedly. Italy emerged as a nation state in the latter half of the nineteenth century, and was considered the weakest of the great powers. It was the last European country to obtain a colonial empire, suffered a grievous defeat in Ethiopia in 1896 and arguably put in the worst military performance of any major combatant in World War I. Although on the winning side, Italy satisfied only some of its far-ranging territorial ambitions, and right-wing, anti-republican forces convinced many Italians that Britain and France had robbed them of their due. Their success in transforming Italy into a revisionist power was not merely the result of tactical skill, but of the predisposition of middle-class Italians to see themselves and their country as weak, lacking respect and vulnerable to the machinations of other powers. Territorial aspirations, disillusionment with a stagnant parliamentary system and a severe economic crisis made it possible for Mussolini to achieve power by a combination of legal and extra-legal means and gradually impose a dictatorship. His foreign policy, increasingly at odds with Italy's strategic and economic interests, was intended to consolidate and strengthen his regime by creating a modern-day Roman imperium that would enhance the self-esteem of Italians. Germany posed the principal threat to Italy, but Mussolini chose to ally with it against Britain and France because these latter two countries were the principal barriers to colonial expansion in the Mediterranean. Mussolini entered World War II erroneously believing that a German victory was all but inevitable, and that Italy could only satisfy its territorial ambitions by being on the winning side. While his decision for war was idiosyncratic and based on bad judgment, his invasion of France was supported by wide segments of the Italian elite, although less so by public opinion.[24]

---

[23] Kershaw, The "Hitler Myth," pp. 151–168.
[24] Aquarone, "Public Opinion in Italy Before the Outbreak of World War II"; Mack Smith, Mussolini, pp. 213–250.

The Japanese had even more compelling reasons for hostility to the *status quo* powers as they had been the object of European racism and economic exploitation and were only grudgingly accepted as a great power. In an earlier stage of their history, they had struggled to assert their equality with China, from whom, via Korea, Japan had received much of its culture. Japanese colonialism in China and Korea was in large part motivated by the desire for recognition and standing, from Asian as well as European audiences. This goal lay behind Japan's aggression against China in the 1930s. It was also motivated by the desire for economic autarchy, a goal pursued more for political than economic reasons as it was sought by the army as a means of making it more independent of the civilian leadership. That conflict in turn had much to do, as it did in Wilhelminian Germany, with problems of modernity and the extent to which many threatened aristocrats clung to pre-modern values and the middle class failed to develop the kind of world view Marx associated with the bourgeoisie. Japan's attack on the Western powers was an outgrowth of the war in China. Powerful figures in the Japanese military became convinced that they could win a limited war against the US and its allies in the western Pacific, compelling China in turn to accept Tokyo's terms for peace.[25] The Western embargo on oil and scrap, imposed as a result of Japan's aggression against China, strengthened the hand of Japanese hawks because it created a now-or-never mentality given their dependence on the West for oil and scrap. The attack on Pearl Harbor made no strategic sense given the military commitment Japan already had in China and the far greater military potential of the United States. Both the Japanese calculations about the American response, and their willingness to take extraordinary risks with their own security must be understood in terms of the spirit-driven values of a warrior class.[26]

Standing also played the leading role in the US decision to invade Iraq in 2003. The invasions of Afghanistan and Iraq were justified in the name of security by the Bush administration, which did everything in its power to link Iraq's ruler to the terrorists responsible for the attack of 9/11. Critics point to the arrogance and ideological fervor of leading members

---

[25] There is a nice parallel here to efforts by Philip II, who hoped to conquer England, or compel it to accept Spanish hegemony, in order to compel the Dutch to submit.

[26] Lebow, *Cultural Theory of International Relations*, ch. 8, for more argument and evidence.

of the Bush administration as underlying causes of these failures, and are certainly correct in doing so.[27] The Bush administration's hostility to Iraq and its concomitant desire to overthrow Saddam Hussein were evident from the moment it assumed office. The events of 9/11 provided the political cover for a long-planned invasion desired for reasons that had nothing to do with terrorism and much to do with anger and standing.

There were no compelling strategic or economic motives for invading Iraq. Despite frequently voiced claims by Noam Chomsky and others that the invasion was driven by the desire to control Middle Eastern oil, such an explanation is unpersuasive.[28] The US had traditionally allowed oil companies, interested only in the flow of reasonably priced oil, to make deals with all kinds of authoritarian regimes in the Middle East.[29] If the administration wanted access to Iraqi oil, all it had to do was end sanctions, as many people were urging on humanitarian grounds. Saddam would have been happy to sell oil to all comers as he was desperate for income and the price of oil would have dropped as Iraq's production re-entered the international market. Security is an equally indefensible motive. Saddam had been defeated in the Gulf War, although he was able to reassert his authority within Iraq. His air force and air defense network were in a shambles and "no-fly" zones had been imposed over the Shi'a and Kurdish regions of Iraq and enforced by NATO with frequent sorties. The UN maintained economic sanctions and interdicted any strategic materials that could assist in the development of WMDs. Saddam repeatedly limited inspections and expelled UN weapons inspectors, but there was never credible evidence indicating that he had recommenced his pre-war efforts to acquire a nuclear arsenal. A band of uncertainty nevertheless remained, and it was reasonable, even prudent, to compel Saddam to readmit UN inspection teams and give

---

[27] Hersh, *Chain of Command*; Daalder and Lindsay, *America Unbound*; Woodward, *Plan of Attack*; Fallows, "Blind into Baghdad"; Phillips, *Losing Iraq*; Suskind, *One Percent Doctrine*; Ricks, *Fiasco*; Isakoff and Corn, *Hubris*; Woodward, *State of Denial*; Gordon and Trainor, *Cobra II*; Galbraith, *End of Iraq*.

[28] Chomsky and Barsamian, *Imperial Ambitions*; "Imperial Ambition," Interview with Noam Chomsky by David Barsamian, *Monthly Review*, May 2003, www.monthlyreview. org/0503chomsky.htm; Chomsky, "Iraq: Yesterday, Today, and Tomorrow," Michael Albert interviews Noam Chomsky, December 27, 2006, www.chomsky.info/articles/ 20050704.htm; Callinicos, *New Mandarins of American Power*, pp. 93–98; Phillips, *American Dynasty*, pp. 248–259, 313–314; Harvey, *The New Imperialism*, pp. 1–25.

[29] Ingram, "Pairing Off Empires."

them unrestricted access. The US military buildup accomplished this goal and the UN inspectors found no evidence to support American claims that Iraq was attempting to acquire WMDs. Saddam could have reneged on his agreement once American forces stepped down, but he would have played into the Bush administration's hands by so doing. Such a double cross would have lent some credence to their claims that he was up to no good and would have made it easier for Washington to secure Security Council authorization to remove him from power.[30] In the absence of WMDs and a usable air force, and with a poorly equipped and trained army, Saddam was more a nuisance than a threat to his immediate neighbors. This was the position taken by Secretary of State Colin Powell, James Baker and Lawrence Eagleburger (George H. W. Bush's two secretaries of state), Republican Majority Leader Dick Armey, former National Security Advisor Brent Scowcroft and retired Marine Corps General Anthony Zinni.[31]

The Iraq invasion was intended to showcase US military might and political will, and to send a message of power and resolve to diverse Middle East audiences. As a warning to hostile states such as Iran and Syria, the invasion was meant to demonstrate the ease with which Washington could topple regimes and establish friendly governments. For the same reason, it was expected to make Saudi Arabia, Jordan and the Palestinians more pliant. In a more fundamental sense, the Iraq invasion was part and parcel of the strategy, vocally espoused by neo-cons and widely supported within the administration, to act decisively in a world in which no serious opposition was in sight, and, by so doing, lock in the United States as the world's sole hegemon.[32] Vice President Cheney felt disgraced by the American failure in Vietnam. He wanted a

[30] National Commission on Terrorist Attacks, *The 9/11 Commission Report*, pp. 61, 161, 334–335; *Iraq Survey Group Final Report*, Global Scan, www.globalsecurity.org/wmd/library/report/2004/isg-final-report/isg-final-report_vol3_cw_key-findings.htm; Cirincione, Mathews and Perkovich, *WMD in Iraq*, for the pre- and post-invasion non-discovery of WMDs.

[31] National Commission on Terrorist Attacks, *9/11 Commission Report*, pp. 334–335; Brent Scowcroft, "Don't Attack Saddam," *Wall Street Journal*, August 15, 2002, p. A12; Todd Purdum and Patrick E. Tyler, "Top Republicans Break with Bush on Iraq Strategy," *New York Times*, August 16, 2002, p. Al; James A. Baker II, "The Right Way to Change a Regime," *New York Times*, August 25, 2002, section 4, p. 9; Transcript of Lawrence Eagleburger, *Crossfire*, August 19, 2002; Walter Gibbs, "Scowcroft Urges Wide Role for the UN in Postwar Iraq," *New York Times*, April 9, 2003.

[32] Lebow, *Cultural Theory of International Relations*, pp. 459–480.

military victory that would erase that stain and also free the executive of the remaining shackles imposed on it in the war's aftermath.[33]

These cases suggest several conclusions about the spirit as a cause for war. First and foremost is the continuing importance of the spirit as a motive despite the transformation of regimes and the character of international relations over the course of the four centuries. Up to the French Revolutionary and Napoleonic Wars, the spirit was the principal cause of war because of the importance of honor and standing to kings and aristocrats, and war was the primary means of gaining honor and standing for states and individuals. Honor operated in a similar way at the state and individual levels: certain kinds of affronts and challenges required aristocrats, military officers especially, to seek satisfaction through duels.[34] States were considered persons and had to defend their honor by war. Upholding honor figured heavily in the French response to Bismarck's Ems Dispatch, which triggered the Franco-Prussian War, and, I have argued, in the Austrian and German responses to the assassinations at Sarajevo.

In the course of the last 100 years, the relationship between spirit and war has become more indirect and complex. In World War I, the concern of the Austrian Emperor, the German Kaiser and their chief military advisors for their personal honor and that of their state, was a powerful motive for war, but so too was the desire for honor by the middle classes. The latter was attributable to nationalism and the peculiar character of class relations in central Europe. It denied honor and standing to the middle classes, ironically intensifying their identification with the German and Austrian states, certain national minorities aside. This identification encouraged efforts by individuals to enhance their self-esteem through the accomplishments of their states. Unyielding leaders thus received broad political support, without which they might have been more restrained.

World War II was different in the sense that none of the leaders involved was motivated by honor. Hitler's goals were pathological and Mussolini was a crass opportunist. Only Japanese leaders could be said to be motivated in part by some concept of honor. The challenges to China

---

[33] Bob Woodward, "Vice President Praises Bush as Strong, Decisive Leader Who Has Helped Restore Office," *Washington Post*, January 20, 2005, p. AO7; Charlie Savage, "Dick Cheney's Mission to Expand – or 'Restore' – the Powers of the Presidency," *Boston Globe*, November 26, 2006; Jane Mayer, "The Hidden Power," *New Yorker*, March 12, 2006.

[34] Peltonen, *Duel in Early Modern England*, for an excellent review of the literature.

and the Soviet Union initiated by the Japanese military were an integral part of their strategy to extend and consolidate their power at home.[35] German, Italian and Japanese leaders nevertheless exploited the low self-esteem of their respective populations to gain power and pursue their foreign policy goals. Hitler's popularity soared in response to his "liberation" of the Saar and Rhineland, *Anschluss* with Austria, incorporation of Memel and the Sudetenland and establishment of protectorates over Bohemia and Moravia. However, in striking contrast to 1914, there was no great enthusiasm for war among the German people in 1939.[36]

The Anglo-American invasion of Iraq says something important about increasingly restrictive views of the circumstances in which one state can legitimately use force against another. In the fall of 2002 and in February 2003, the US was unable to gain Security Council approval for resolutions that would have allowed it to use "all necessary means" to compel Iraq to relinquish all WMDs. France, Germany and Russia, supported by other governments, considered military action premature.[37] The Bush administration's commitment to wage war in the absence of UN authorization led to a serious loss of support around the world. In a worldwide poll of its readers, *Time* magazine asked which country "poses the greatest threat to world peace in 2003." North Korea was identified as the greatest threat by 6.7 percent of the 700,000 respondents, Iraq by 6.3 percent, and the US by a whopping 86.9 percent.[38] The invasion of Iraq, the mistreatment of Iraqi prisoners, the killing of civilians as collateral damage, the holding of foreign nationals for years without charge at Guantanamo and the "extraordinary rendition" of prisoners to countries where they were tortured for information led to an even more precipitous drop in standing. In Britain, those with favorable opinions of the US dropped from 83 percent in 2000 to 56 percent in 2006. In other countries, the US underwent an even steeper decline.[39] In 2007, the BBC World Service found that 51 percent of respondents in

[35] Storry, *Double Patriots*, pp. 53, 77–86; Akira, "The Role of the Japanese Army"; Ogata, *Defiance in Manchuria*, pp. 137–194.

[36] Kershaw, *The "Hitler Myth*," pp. 139–147.

[37] Michael O'Hanlon, "How the Hardliners Lost," *Washington Post*, November 10, 2002, p. B7; Lebow, *Cultural Theory of International Relations*, pp. 461, 463–464.

[38] *Time Europe*, www.time.com/time/europe/gdml/peace2003.html; BBC News, 18 March 2003, http://news.bbc.co.uk/2/hi/americas/2862343.stm.

[39] The Pew Global Attitudes Project, "15-Nation Pew Global Attitudes Survey," release date, June 13, 2006.

twenty-seven countries regarded the US negatively, while only 48 percent had the same view of North Korea.[40] Since the Iraq War, the US has undergone a shift in its profile from a *status quo* to a revisionist power.[41]

The precipitous decline of the stature of the US in the eyes of the world can be taken as evidence that a shift is underway in the post-Cold War era about the nature of standing. For centuries, military power and victories over adversaries have conferred standing, if not honor. Iraq is only the latest indication that the use of force – even if successful – does not enhance standing unless it is used for purposes the international community thinks legitimate and is done with the sanction of the UN or appropriate international bodies. American prestige plummeted even before the insurgency began, that is, when it still appeared an unambiguous military victor. It is too early to conclude that standing on the one hand and the use of force on the other have completely diverged, but the tension between them has certainly become more acute. Intersubjective understandings about the legitimacy of foreign policy goals and the means appropriate to achieving them significantly shape the character of regional and international political systems. Changes in what is considered legitimate and appropriate accordingly have the potential to reshape the behavior of actors to the degree that standing matters to them, as we know it does for most individuals and states. As I have argued elsewhere, changes in behavior prompt changes in identities because we revise our understandings of ourselves to bring them into line with our behavior.[42] Changes in the identities of enough important actors can transform the character of the international system.[43] If such a transformation occurs, we may look back on the Iraq War, not so much as a turning point, but as an event that made us aware that such a process was underway.

To the extent that war no longer constitutes an effective claim for honor or standing, states must use other vehicles toward these ends. War has never been the only means of claiming standing or great power status. In the second half of the seventeenth century, display became increasingly important, although it did not diminish the appeal of war. Following the Spanish Habsburgs, whose leading position he sought for

---

[40] *The Age* (Melbourne), March 6, 2007, p. 7.
[41] This last point is also made by Clark, "How Hierarchical Can International Relations Be?"
[42] Bem, "Self-Perception Theory."
[43] Lebow, *Cultural Theory of International Relations*, pp. 480–504.

himself and France, Louis XIV spent an enormous amount of money on palaces, gardens, the arts and sciences. Other monarchs followed suit, as did many high-ranking members of the European nobility. In the nine-teenth century, public engineering works, inner-city reconstruction and beautification, colonies and fleets and winning international sporting competitions became increasingly important. In the second half of the twentieth century, status was associated with wealth, Olympic gold medals, Nobel prizes, nuclear weapons and space exploration. Until recently, display in all its forms was secondary to military success as a means of gaining standing and recognition as a great power. Historically, military success was usually followed by increased expenditures on dis-play. Most aspirants to great power status also sought to demonstrate their willingness to accept the system-maintenance responsibilities that came to be associated with great powers after the Congress of Vienna.

The founders of the Olympics hoped that the games might become a substitute for war. Instead, they became another venue for intense national competition and a source of international tension in their own right. The Nazis attempted to exploit the 1936 Berlin Olympics to show-case the Nazi Party and "Aryan" superiority. In the 1980 Moscow Olympics, the Americans organized a boycott in response to the Soviet invasion of Afghanistan and pressed sixty other countries into joining them. The Soviets and thirteen other Eastern bloc countries in turn boycotted the 1984 Los Angeles Olympics. At the 1972 Munich Olympics, Palestinian terrorists sought publicity for their cause by killing eleven Israeli athletes and coaches and a German policeman.

Other forms of competition have been more successful. Nobel prizes confer prestige not only to the scientists, doctors and authors who are their recipients but also on the countries from which they come. This was apparent as early as the 1920s when Germany and Switzerland both laid claims to Einstein after he was awarded a Nobel prize in physics. Prestige is one of many incentives states have for nurturing the sciences, medicine and the arts, all of which have important beneficial consequences for humanity in general. Development aid and assistance also represent a claim to status, although they are often motivated by other motives as well. The Scandinavian nations, Germany and some other members of the European Union and Japan are among the leading providers of foreign aid measured as a percentage of income. All of these states seek standing on the basis of their commitment to peace and contributions to the general welfare of humankind. Their claims have not fallen on deaf ears. A 2006 survey across twenty three countries revealed a strong preference for Europe to become more influential than the US.[44]

If states can gain prestige without becoming major military powers and lose it by spending too much on their military instrument, or using it in inappropriate ways, we need to disaggregate the concepts of power and prestige and examine them independently. Regional political systems, and, by extension, the international system, have become sites of contestation where a variety of actors, by no means all of them states, claim standing on the basis of diverse criteria. States invest considerable resources in publicizing and justifying the claims and in making efforts to impress others. The growing diversity in claims for recognition, and the possible decline in the traditional military-economic basis of standing, point to a growing tension between the informal criteria used by many governments and peoples to award standing and the more formal recognition conferred by international institutions like the Security Council and the G-8.

Success in gaining honor and standing by means unrelated to military muscle is likely to encourage other states to follow suit and invest more resources toward these ends. Should this development come to pass, it would direct competition for standing further away from war toward other domains.

Revenge

Revenge is an expression of anger, which, I argued in Chapter 4, is generally provoked by slights to one's standing. Revenge is an expression of the spirit, but I code it as a distinct category because its triggering conditions differ from those that provoke wars intended to enhance a state's or ruler's standing. Occasionally, motives of revenge and standing coexist and reinforce each other, as they appear to have done in Louis XIV's Dutch War and the Anglo-American invasion of Iraq.

Revenge was a leading motive in 11 wars (10 percent of the total). Almost all these wars had as their goal the reconquest of territory lost to an attacker in a previous war. They were initiated by declining or weak powers against recently risen great powers. Most often, the initiators lost additional territory as a result of these wars, as the Ottomans did in 1812 when they were forced to cede Bessarabia to Russia. Sweden suffered a

---

[44] "23 Nation Poll: Who Will Lead the World?," www.worldpublicopinion.org, June 14, 2006.

worse fate when Charles XII attempted to punish the Baltic states in 1700. Russian support for his adversaries led him to launch an ill-prepared and disastrous invasion of Russia that resulted in Sweden's loss of regional hegemony. Wars initiated by weak and declining powers offer more evidence that angry leaders do not make careful estimates of risk. This phenomenon is all the more remarkable in the case of weak and declining powers, whose victory over more powerful states should have been regarded as highly problematic from the outset.

Seven wars of revenge took place in the eighteenth century. Six of them were initiated by Sweden, Turkey and Poland against Russia, whose rise came at their expense. Only three twentieth century wars qualify as wars of revenge. It was an important consideration in Poland's attack on the Soviet Union in 1919, intended to overturn the results of prior partitions and regain the eastern frontiers of the old Polish empire.[45] It was an incentive for the Argentine junta to invade the Falklands/Malvinas and for the British to liberate them. Argentine settlers had been expelled from the Malvinas in 1831 and the British took control of the islands the following year. In the words of Argentina's leading newspaper, *La Prensa*, British occupation of the Malvinas constituted "an intolerable insult to Argentine independence and nationhood."[46] Public and governmental anger against the British was high, and rose to fury pitch when Thatcher's negotiations with the Argentine junta were understood as part of a duplicitous strategy to avoid resolving the dispute. From the British perspective, the unexpected invasion of the Falklands by a relatively weak country led by a reprehensible military junta was infuriating and unacceptable, especially to Britain's prime minister.[47]

Revenge was central to the 1973 attack on Israel by Egypt and Syria. Both countries sought to regain territory lost in 1967. Egyptian President Anwar el-Sadat also hoped to use the war to compel Israel to reach an accommodation, which he considered an essential enabling condition for domestic reforms or realignment of Egypt economically and politically with the West.[48] American intervention in Afghanistan in 2001 might also qualify in part as a war of revenge. The attacks of 9/11 wounded the US physically and psychologically as al-Qaeda killed a sizeable number of people, although many fewer than initial estimates. They destroyed a

[45] Debo, *Survival and Consolidation*, pp. 191–212, 404, 406; Carley, "Politics of Anti-Bolshevism."
[46] *La Prensa*, April 22, 1982.   [47] Lebow, "Miscalculation in the South Atlantic."
[48] Stein, "Calculation, Miscalculation, and Conventional Deterrence 1."

major landmark – the World Trade Center, an icon of American economic power – and damaged an even more hallowed building – the Pentagon – the center of American military might. The attacks were not conducted by another state, but by a rag-tag cabal of Middle Eastern terrorists, which made the offense more intolerable still. That such an unworthy adversary could so successfully attack the US aroused anger in the Aristotelian sense and a correspondingly strong desire for revenge. It also soon became apparent that terrorist attacks had succeeded because of refusal at the highest levels of government to take seriously the threat of terrorism and the remarkable incompetence on the part of the Federal Bureau of Investigation (FBI).[49] The administration successfully exploited American anger, deflecting it away from itself and toward Saddam.

The insult and resulting anger were made all the more acute by the failure of the Bush administration to kill Osama bin Laden or bring him to justice. Given public arousal in the immediate aftermath of the attacks – sentiment shared within the administration – the president was under pressure to strike out at someone, and Afghanistan was the obvious target. Treating al-Qaeda as a criminal group, best pursued by standard police measures, in collaboration with allies and other third parties, may have made more sense strategically, but may have been perceived as a more costly political option. Revenge in this case was a response to domestic opinion, not foreign policy considerations, so I have coded it as other. As noted earlier, the administration also desired a "war against terror" as a means of preparing the public and building up support for war against Iraq.

Anger may have entered the picture in a more personal way for the president when his advisors pushed for the overthrow of Saddam Hussein. The prospect of gaining revenge against the man who allegedly had tried to assassinate his father would have been particularly gratifying. At a September 2006 fundraiser in Texas, Bush described how Saddam tortured Iraqis, used gas against his Kurdish opponents and invaded Iran. And then came the clincher: "After all," he told his audience, "this is the guy that tried to kill my dad at one time."[50] Unnamed intelligence sources report that Cheney played upon Bush's concern to impress his parents by "cherry picking" intelligence that could be used to make the case that Saddam had tried to assassinate his father. If so, anger and the desire for revenge

---

[49] Dan Eggen, "Pre 9/11 Missteps by FBI Detailed," *Washington Post*, June 10, 2005, p. AO1.
[50] Quoted in Isakoff and Corn, *Hubris*, p. 115.

conceivably provided another incentive for Bush to consider an invasion of Iraq.[51] Could Bush's rage, like that of Achilles in the *Iliad*, have helped to drive the plot of this saga? In the absence of evidence, this must remain speculation.

The majority of revenge-motivated wars were initiated in response to prior defeats resulting in the loss of territory. These wars were initiated by rising powers seeking recognition as *de facto* great powers. The era has passed when territorial conquest was feasible and a means of gaining status. I argued in Chapter 5 that the cost of conquest has risen, as have the ability to hold on to conquered territories and extract resources from them. As conquest is less feasible and less rewarding in terms of its economic and psychological rewards, it has declined. The two most recent attempts at conquest have been unsuccessful: Argentina was expelled from the Falklands/Malvinas and Iraq from Kuwait. In the absence of wars of conquest, revenge loses its principal catalyst. However, as Afghanistan and Iraq indicate, Aristotelian anger can still provoke violent initiatives that qualify as wars of revenge whether or not leaders consciously frame them this way.

Other wars

I coded seven wars in this residual category. They include two wars provoked by groups or factions, not central governments themselves. These are the Polish–Turkish war of 1671, started by Cossacks living along the frontier, and the Japanese–Soviet confrontation of 1938, triggered by the Japanese Kwantung Army's unauthorized incursions into Mongolia. The Soviets launched a well-coordinated blitzkrieg-style counter-offensive in the vicinity of Lake Nomonhan, overwhelming the Kwantung Army and deterring its leaders from any further incursions into Mongolia.[52]

The most prominent anomalous case is Hitler's invasion of Poland in 1939 and his subsequent invasions of Western Europe, the Balkans and the Soviet Union. As I noted in Chapter 2, some scholars attribute rational motives to Hitler. Many proponents of deterrence describe

---

[51] Seymour Hersh, "A Case Not Closed," *New Yorker*, November 1, 1993, rev. version posted September 27, 2002, on the dubious nature of the alleged assassination attempt, www. newyorker.com/archive/content/articles/020930fr_archive02?020930fr_archive02/.

[52] Haslam, *Soviet Union and the Threat from the East*, pp. 112–134; Coox, *Nomonhan*, on the actual fighting.

Hitler as a risk-prone gain-seeker who could have been stopped if only France and Britain had stood firm. Other realists describe his expansion as fear-based: he quite reasonably attempted to humble the Soviet Union before it surpassed Germany in power.[53] Beyond Hitler's recognition that he could not challenge the United States before becoming the undisputed master of Europe, there is little indication that longer-term estimates of the balance of power between Germany and its adversaries entered into his calculations.[54] There is something unsettling, to say the least, about efforts to make Hitler's aggressions appear as rational responses to Germany's security dilemma. Hitler was intent on conquering Europe and then the world, and on exterminating Jews, Roma, homosexuals and most Slavs. These goals must be considered substantively and instrumentally irrational, if not downright insane.[55] Revenge certainly entered into the picture, especially in Hitler's attacks on Poland and France. Compelling evidence for the latter is Hitler's insistence that France's surrender take place in the same railway car at Compiègne where Marshal Foch compelled German generals to sign the armistice in November 1918. Afterwards, they dynamited the monuments the French had erected to commemorate the armistice.[56]

Alexander William Kinglake, a barrister and observer of nineteenth-century war, was convinced that Napoleon III had engineered the Crimean War to advance "the welfare and safety of a small knot of men then hanging together in Paris."[57] Quincy Wright, author of an influential 1942 study of the causes of war, maintained that war was frequently the result of the temptation "to indulge in foreign war as a diversion from domestic ills."[58] In the early 1950s, Harold Lasswell asserted that despotic regimes had an affinity for aggression that "comes from the internal stresses generated by arbitrary power."[59] Contemporary talking heads frequently allege that leaders engage in aggressive foreign policies for domestic political reasons. I find little evidence for this phenomenon. The most compelling nineteenth century example is the Franco-Prussian War, but the leader embracing war for domestic political purposes was Louis Napoleon of France, who initiated but did not provoke the war. Napoleon's desperate need to assuage French pride in order to retain

[53] Copeland, *Origins of Major Wars*.
[54] Weinberg, *Foreign Policy of Hitler's Germany*, vol. 1, p. 358; Rich, *Hitler's War Aims*, vol. 1, pp. 3–10; Fest, *Hitler*, pp. 213–218.
[55] *Ibid.*   [56] Shirer, *Berlin Diary*, pp. 414–415, 419, 462.
[57] Quoted in Blainey, *Causes of War*, p. 72.   [58] Wright, *Study of War*, pp. 278–281.
[59] Lasswell, *National Security and Individual Freedom*, p. 10.

power provided the opening for Bismarck's famous Ems Dispatch which the German leader knew would inflame French opinion and compel a declaration of war.[60] The twentieth century war that comes closest to fitting this description is the Argentine junta's invasion of the Falklands/Malvinas in 1982. The junta was hard-pressed at home because of its unpopular political and economic policies and clearly felt compelled not only to invade but to keep its invasion forces on the island despite its original intention to invade and withdraw on the same day, thereby sending a powerful signal to London. Argentine newspapers greeted the "recovery" of the Malvinas with banner headlines and all the political parties that opposed the junta now celebrated its seeming victory. The trade unions that had demonstrated against the junta the week before called upon their members to return to the Plaza de Mayo in support of its foreign policy. The junta was clearly motivated by issues of standing as well as domestic politics. Before its domestic position became so precarious, it had sought to regain the Malvinas by patient diplomacy, and, when that failed, by military pressure.[61]

In some wars, domestic politics must be considered an important secondary motive. In 1914, Austrian and German leaders, although pessimistic about the prospects of victory, believed that war would bring beneficial domestic payoffs. Austrian leaders expected victory to intimidate nationalist minorities and the German Kaiser and general staff expected it to give them the upper hand in their dealings with the Social Democrats.[62] Domestic political considerations may also have entered into the Bush administration's decision to invade Afghanistan. I have argued elsewhere that their principal incentive was to prepare the American people for an invasion of Iraq, a goal Cheney and Rumsfeld had harbored since they came to power.[63]

The remaining three cases are anomalous because of their initiators, not because of their motives. The 1857 war between Persia and Britain was initiated by a weak power against another weak power and provoked

---

[60] Wawro, *Franco-Prussian War*, pp. 18–19, 22–25; Pflanze, *Bismarck*, pp. 433–457.

[61] Lebow, "Miscalculation in the South Atlantic."

[62] Schroeder, "World War I as Galloping Gertie"; Rosenberg, *Imperial Germany*; Mayer, "Domestic Causes of the First World War"; Eley, *Reshaping the German Right*. Albertini, *Origins of the War of 1914*; Stevenson, *First World War and International Politics*; Williamson, *Austria-Hungary and the Coming of the First World War*; Fellner, "Austria-Hungary," pp. 9–25; Vermes, *István Tisza*; Herwig, *First World War*, pp. 8–18.

[63] Lebow, *Cultural Theory of International Relations*, ch. 9.

an unintended war with a great power. In the opening phase of the 1913 Balkan War, weak powers (the Balkan states) ganged up on a declining great power (the Ottoman Empire) that was engaged in another war. The Ottomans were drawn into the war's second phase as well, which pitted them and their prior Balkan adversaries against Bulgaria. In all three wars, the motives of the initiators can be characterized in terms of fear, interest or standing.

Future war

Our review of motives encourages optimism. Every motive has lost traction as a cause of war. This is most evident with interest. Interest-based wars were largely a product of the mercantilist era and remained a possibility as long as conquest could be made to pay. The last successful conquests were China's invasion of Tibet in 1950 and India's occupation of Goa in 1962, both justified as post-colonial liberations. By contrast, North Korea's invasion of South Korea in 1950, Uganda's invasion of Tanzania in 1978, Iraq's invasion of Iran in 1980 and of Kuwait in 1990 and Argentina's invasion of the Falklands in 1982 were all repulsed. Other postwar incursions, never intended as conquests, were on the whole no more successful.[64]

Conquest is not the only expression of material interest: states routinely come into conflict over natural resources, especially offshore oil. Environmental concerns also have the potential to create acute conflicts. To date, however, conflicts over fishing and disputed islands in oil-rich continental shelves have not progressed beyond minimal uses of force intended to signal resolve and improve a state's bargaining position.[65] More serious conflicts in the future cannot be ruled out even though they will become increasingly disruptive and costly to the extent that the parties involved are connected by high levels of trade and investment. Even when this is not the case, fighting may interfere with other trade and discourage third-party investors.

Wars of revenge also seem increasingly consigned to history. Most were unsuccessful and emotional responses to prior territorial aggrandizement by rising powers. Wars of revenge can also be triggered by terrorism. Austria-Hungary's decision in 1914 to go to war with Serbia was a direct response to the twin assassinations at Sarajevo, as was the

---

[64] See Table 7.1 for a list.
[65] On Southeast Asia, see Solingen, "Regional Conflict and Cooperation."

American invasion of Afghanistan in 2001. It was provoked by the actions of a non-state actor, al-Qaeda. The Bush administration had other motives as well for its intervention in Afghanistan: it considered it a prelude to an attack against Iraq. The Afghani government provided a welcome pretext for harboring and refusing to expel Osama bin Laden, who proudly assumed responsibility for the attacks against the US. There are striking similarities with 1914. Austria's prime minister and minister of war were looking for a pretext to attack Serbia. The assassinations shocked the German-speaking public of the Empire and the German Kaiser. Serbia was perceived as complicit because the Black Hand, the group responsible for the assassination, was centered in Belgrade and its leaders were military and civilian officials.[66] Another twentieth century war that fits this pattern is Israel's attack on Egypt in the Sinai in 1956. It is not in my data set because it did not involve a great or rising power. Israel was the target of *fedayeen* terrorist attacks and the Ben Gurion government used them as a pretext for invading Egypt in the aftermath of its arms deal with Czechoslovakia. Another contributing factor in this case was external support: Britain and France coordinated their assault on the Suez Canal with Israel's invasion of the Sinai.[67]

Terrorist incidents have become more common and, as in the past, there are often connections between terrorists and established governments, or at least renegade components of them. North Korea has been associated with terrorist acts in Asia.[68] There have been several terrorist attacks in India committed by Pakistani nationals. In November 2008, Islamic terrorists attacked tourist hotels and the train station in Mumbai, causing upward of 164 fatalities. The Indian government suspected Pakistani complicity but did not respond militarily because it was not looking for a pretext for war.[69] The threat of terrorism remains acute in many parts of the world, and there is always the possibility, which most experts consider remote, of a terrorist attack using weapons of mass

[66] Dedijer, *Road to Sarajevo*, pp. 366–400.

[67] Gorst and Johnman, *Suez Crisis*; Kyle, *Suez*.

[68] Council on Foreign Relations, Backgrounder, "State Sponsors: North Korea", www.cfr.org/publication/9364/state_sponsors.html.

[69] Somini Sengupta *et al.*, "India Seeks Extraditions in Mumbai Siege," *New York Times*, January 6, 2009; Richard A. Oppel, Jr., and Salman Masood, "Gunman in Mumbai Siege a Pakistani, Official Says," *New York Times*, January 8, 2009; Salman Masood, "Leaked Report Points to Larger Pakistani Role in Mumbai Attacks," *New York Times*, February 11, 2009; Hari Kumar, "Pakistani Charged in Mumbai Assault," *New York Times*, February 26, 2009.

destruction.[70] In these circumstances, we cannot rule out the possibility of a war of revenge, and all the more so if the weapons in question can be traced to a willing state supplier.

These several wars and incidents that did not lead to war suggest the provisional conclusion that a terrorist incident, no matter how deadly, is unlikely in and of itself to provoke a war. For terrorist acts to trigger wars, they probably need to meet three conditions: they must arouse public indignation and demands for retaliation; they must be traced to a seemingly complicit state against whom it is possible to retaliate militarily; and leaders must have other reasons for going after this state or its government. The first condition is not difficult to meet: public outrage and demands for revenge are easily aroused by acts of terrorism that kill many people, assassinate popular leaders or destroy national or religious icons. States are also frequently implicated in terrorist initiatives, Serbia, Egypt, Syria, Iran, Libya, Sudan, Pakistan and North Korea have all supported terrorism in the postwar era.[71] Complicity need not be proven if governments can convince public opinion that the state they have targeted for retaliation is responsible. Austria managed to do this in 1914 and the US in 2003, the latter with respect to both Afghanistan and Iraq. The third condition is less often present, which is why most terrorist incidents do not lead to war.

We cannot rule out future wars of revenge. Scenarios readily spring to mind. What if North Korea were to sell nuclear material to another country that it passes along to terrorists who explode a dirty bomb in an American city. Or consider a radical, desperate group in Pakistan who, with semi-official backing, carries out further atrocities in India, provoking a military response. There is also the prospect of an Israeli attack on Iran triggered by terrorist attacks with Iranian backing, especially against the background of seeming Iranian progress toward a nuclear capability. In all three scenarios, desires for revenge would reinforce arguments made on the ground of national security.

Finally, there is the problem of accidental war. It is almost invariably the result of loss of control but this can have political or institutional causes. In the former, disaffected officials sabotage policy or impose a policy of their own. Political loss of control characterized the Japanese Kwantung army's penetration into Mongolia and was responsible for a

---

[70] Archer, "'WMD' Terrorism"; Stern, *Ultimate Terrorists*, for a more alarmist account.
[71] US Department of State, "State Sponsors of Terrorism Overview," for the current list, www.state.gov/s/ct/rls/crt/2006/82736.htm.

brief, undeclared war with Russia.[72] Institutional loss of control is a more complex phenomenon. It occurs when individuals, acting on orders, or within the accepted confines of their authority, behave in ways that interfere with, undercut or are contrary to the objectives of national leaders. Institutional loss of control arises because policy decisions in large bureaucracies often have significantly unanticipated consequences. German mobilization plans in 1914 and civilian ignorance of their consequences are a well-known example. In the Cuban missile crisis, there were a series of incidents on both sides that threatened loss of control, the most dramatic being Fidel Castro's success in convincing local Soviet military authorities to fire at and bring down an American U-2 spy plane, killing its pilot. Fortunately, none of these incidents provoked further escalation and may even have helped to resolve the crisis by convincing Kennedy and Khrushchev that war was imminent.[73]

In the 1980s, a number of scholars began to worry about the possibility of accidental or inadvertent war due to the massive nuclear arsenals of both sides, their relatively high state of readiness, the ways in which their warning and alert systems were tightly coupled and could interact in ways poorly understood or not even envisaged by those in charge and national leaders.[74] This problem has diminished in the postwar era, as Russia and the United States keep their forces at much lower levels of readiness. We have little detailed information on Indian and Pakistani nuclear command and control and much reason to worry given the physical proximity of the two countries. It is not inconceivable that one side or the other could preempt in a crisis thinking the other was about to do so.[75] As I noted in the conclusion to the last chapter, the peace of the world rests as much on the commitments of leaders to avoid war and their willingness to take risks toward that end as it does with general trends that point to or away from the prospects of a peaceful world.

---

[72] Haslam, *Soviet Union and the Threat from the East*, pp. 112–134; Coox, *Nomonhan*.
[73] Lebow and Stein, *We All Lost the Cold War*, pp. 301–306.
[74] Bracken, *Command and Control of Nuclear Forces*; Blair, *Logic of Accidental Nuclear War*; Lebow, *Nuclear Crisis Management*; Sagan, *Limits of Safety*.
[75] Paul, "The Risk of Nuclear War Does Not Belong to History"; Paul, *Tradition of Non-Use*, pp. 124–142.

PART IV

Conclusion

7

Conclusion

Against war, it can be said that: it makes the victor stupid and the defeated malicious. In favour of war, it can be said that: through producing these two effects it barbarizes and therefore makes it more natural – it is the winter or hibernation time of culture; mankind emerges from it stronger for good and evil.

Nietzsche[1]

I have analyzed war in terms of four generic motives – security, interest, standing and revenge – and a residual category of other. Other aside, where there are too few cases to chart any trends, the frequency of wars driven by interest and revenge has undergone the greatest decline relative to the frequency of war in general. This is attributable in the first instance to decline in the appeal and success of territorial conquest, until now a primary war aim of interest-driven wars. Wars of revenge are less frequent for the same reason: historically, their principal objective was regaining territory lost in previous wars. Standing and security show an absolute, but not a relative, decline, which I attribute to a combination of material and ideational causes. In Chapters 5 and 6, I advanced this argument with respect to individual motives and used it as the foundation for forecasts about the likelihood of my four principal kinds of wars. In the present chapter, I explore the relationship between material and ideational conditions across categories and use this exercise to probe some of the deeper causes for the decline of war in the nineteenth and twentieth centuries.

Material conditions and ideas

In Chapter 5, I argued that interest-based wars were encouraged by the twin beliefs that the world's wealth was finite and that a state's wealth

---

[1] Nietzsche, *Human, All Too Human*, p. 239.

could be enhanced through conquest. Interest-based wars sharply declined as political elites understood that wealth could be increased by the division of labor and trade. Materialist considerations also entered the picture. Territory was the most common immediate objective of interest-based wars. As conquest became less acceptable and increasingly risky, the practice declined. An additional deterrent came into play in the postwar era: the growing difficulty of extracting wealth from conquered territories. This was still possible as late as World War II and its immediate aftermath. Hitler and Stalin made economic gains from their respective conquests, although Eastern Europe ultimately became a drain on the Soviet economy.[2]

Materialist considerations influenced not only the frequency of interest-based wars but their targets. The earliest interest-based wars in the data set were trade related but soon gave way to conflicts over territory. Today's most acute interest-based conflicts are over offshore fisheries and mineral and petroleum resources. Although they have provoked military maneuvers, even the ramming of ships and the occupation of disputed territory, all states concerned have been careful to avoid the kinds of encounters likely to lead to loss of life.[3] Claim and counter-claim and bloodless wars of maneuver have become the norm in regions whose states have increasingly interdependent economies. Ideational and materialist considerations have seemingly combined to bring this situation about. Political and economic interdependence significantly raises the costs of conflict and negatively affects the overall calculus of the possible gains to be made by using force to control disputed resources. Membership in communities and long-standing alliances stretch identities, making violence against fellow members increasingly repugnant. As we observed in the case of the three Iceland–Britain "cod wars," military incidents were followed by mutual efforts by both countries and their negotiators to befriend one another and thereby signal their continuing commitment to good interpersonal and interstate relations. In the Pacific rim, community is not as robust as its North Atlantic counterpart, but other considerations come into play. China, by far the most militarily powerful state, seeks to reestablish a variant of its traditional hegemony in Asia. This requires offering economic and security benefits to its neighbors in return for accepting its leadership role. Such aspirations, the Chinese understand, would be

[2] Painter, *The Cold War*, p. 191; Maier, *Dissolution*, pp. 59–72.
[3] Klare, *Resource Wars*; Bateman and Schofeld, *Outer Shelf Claims in the South China Sea*.

undercut by efforts to impose its will by force in disputes with its neighbors over territory or resources.

Territory has always provided resources and strategic depth. Control of harbors, choke points, river lines and mountain passes conferred additional strategic advantages. Many of these benefits were eroded or negated in the twentieth century by the development of mechanized warfare and air power. Even before the advent of modern warfare, security was never dictated by geography, as some leading nineteenth-century realists maintained.[4] Culture determined the acceptability, targets and goals of war and how it was waged.[5] Security, moreover, is a culturally based concept of modern origin, and one that has undergone considerable evolution in the course of the last three centuries.[6] This evolution reflects the transformation of so many actors from dynastic units to nation states and, with it, the substitution of national interests for dynastic ones. Material developments were also instrumental. Dynastic units generally relied on mercenaries and unwilling conscripts to fight their wars. National states could field larger and more dedicated conscript armies and more readily raise or borrow funds to equip and pay them. Battle largely replaced maneuver and siege as the medium of warfare. More recently, strategy has been influenced by changing public attitudes toward war. As war became more costly and less acceptable in the aftermath of World War II, Cold War strategy was focused on preventing war rather than fighting it and, whenever possible, sought to achieve political goals by the threat rather than the application of force.[7]

Leaders of democratic states have also become increasingly constrained with respect to conventional wars against lesser non-nuclear powers. To sustain political support at home, they must win such wars quickly and sustain minimal casualties. In the 1990 Gulf War, American forces took into account not only their own casualties but those they were likely to inflict on the other side. Chairman of the Joint Chief of Staff General Colin Powell was reluctant to finish off Saddam's

[4] Mahan, *Influence of Sea Power upon History*; Mackinder, "Geographical Pivot of History"; Mackinder, *Britain and the British Seas*; Haushofer, *Geopolitik des Pazifischen Ozeans*; Haushofer, Obst, Lautensach and Maull, *Bausteine zur Geopolitik*. See Guzzini, *Geopolitics Redux*, for a thoughtful analysis of geopolitics.
[5] Lebow, *Cultural Theory of International Relations*, for an elaboration.
[6] Stuart, *Creating the National Security State*, on the evolution of the concept in the US.
[7] Schelling, *Arms and Influence*; Bundy, *Danger and Survival*; Jervis, *Meaning of the Nuclear Revolution*.

retreating Republican Guard because of the one-sided slaughter this would have entailed.[8] Strategies that minimize casualties depend on the ability to fight wars from a distance and are only made possible by advances in battlefield intelligence, weaponry, delivery systems and their integration through sophisticated means of command and control.[9] These systems were developed in part for this purpose, indicating the close, interactive relationship between ideas and material capabilities.

Complex interactions of the kind described above are equally evident with regard to other causes of war. Standing is no longer the principal source of war because the conquest of foreign territory no longer confers status but undermines it. Standing has increasingly become associated with other kinds of achievements, among them wealth, cultural and scientific accomplishments, foreign aid and other actions on behalf of the international community at large. Standing nevertheless still rests on material foundations. It is difficult, if not impossible, for smaller, poorer states to compete in most of the domains in which standing is won. However, material resources cannot account for shifts in the nature of standing because resources that can be converted into cash like taxes are fungible. Shifts in patterns of expenditure reflect conscious choices by governments about the extent to which they aspire to inter-national standing and the domains in which they attempt to achieve it. The Soviet Union and the United States spent an extraordinary percen-tage of their wealth on their armed forces in comparison to other countries, and the US continues to do so long after the Cold War.

If material capabilities encourage and allow states to compete for standing, they might also be expected to restrain states, weak and powerful alike, from pursuing unattainable goals. Historically, such constraints have been weak or absent among leading great powers. Beginning with Spain, successive leading powers overextended and severely weakened themselves in unsuccessful quests for hegemony. The data indicate that leading powers were responsible for most systemic wars. None of the leaders involved deliberately set out to fight such a war, but pursued high-risk policies that provoked them by means of miscalculated escalation. To account for this pattern, we need to look at the values of leaders and policymaking elites. In Spain, France and

---

[8] Gordon and Trainor, *The General's War*, pp. 413–432.
[9] Rumsfeld, "Transforming the Military"; Gongora and von Riekhoff, *Toward a Revolution in Military Affairs*; Coker, *Waging War Without Warriors?*

Germany, the drive for regional or international hegemony greatly exceeded state resources under Charles V, Philip II, Louis XIV, Napoleon, Kaiser Wilhelm and Hitler. The same was true of Japan, a rising power in the first half of the twentieth century. The quest for standing combined with a domestic struggle for power between the armed forces and politicians and between moderates and extremists within the armed forces.[10]

Unlike its predecessors, the US has not attempted to conquer a region or the world but has sought to exercise hegemony by more subtle economic and political means.[11] It has nevertheless succumbed to leading-power hubris on multiple occasions, prompting it to intervene, directly or indirectly, to change governments in Asia and Latin America during and after the Cold War. Its imperial overstretch has been costly in lives and treasure but has not eroded the US position in the way it has that of previous leading powers because of its relative power and care in not waging wars against major powers.

Wars of revenge are also wars of ideas. The initiators of eleven of twelve wars of revenge were at a decided military disadvantage *vis-à-vis* their adversaries, but this did not prevent them going to war. Not surprisingly, they lost all but one of these wars and additional territory as a consequence. Their leaders were motivated by anger, and for the most part were insensitive to the kind of careful cost-calculus that war-initiation should entail. Some of them, like Charles XII of Sweden, were intent on revenge regardless of the outcome. Revenge-seeking in the twentieth century was more instrumentally rational, in that aggrieved states sought to isolate their opponents diplomatically or design around their military advantages. The German attack on France in 1940, motivated in large part by revenge, was preceded by a diplomatic arrangement with the Soviet Union and their mutual destruction of Poland, thereby removing any immediate threat in the east. The strategy of blitzkrieg, which achieved breakthroughs by concentrating armor and close-in air support, overcame France's superiority in men, tanks and planes.[12] Egypt and Syria's attack on Israel in 1973 – a war not in the data set – was in part a war of revenge designed to regain territory lost in 1967. Domestic political concerns were, of course, also important. Recognizing Israel's military superiority,

---

[10] Lebow, *Cultural Theory of International Relations*, chs. 6–8, for documentation.
[11] Ikenberry, *After Victory*; Lieber, *Eagle Rules?*
[12] Frieser and Greenwood, *The Blitzkrieg Legend*.

Egypt and Syria relied on surprise and hand-held Soviet missile launch-
ers to cope with Israeli armor.[13]

My review of motives leads to several conclusions. The first concerns
the difficulty of disaggregating material capabilities and ideas as causal
variables that can be subjected to independent testing. Both conditions
of wars are omnipresent and interdependent. They not only interact,
but each contributes to the way the other is framed and in turn shapes
behavior. These relationships become readily visible when we engage in
the kind of vertical analysis I call "leapfrogging." This consists of efforts
to use one set of causes to account for the other by moving back in time
from the outcome both attempt to explain.[14] Let me illustrate how this
works with respect to standing. Scholars who look to material conditions to do their heavy analytical lifting can argue that competition for
standing is only possible among political units that possess significant
capabilities and that the status hierarchy reflects the distribution of
these capabilities. This could evoke the rejoinder that the distribution
of capabilities is itself determined by the interplay of culture and
agency. Leaders committed to competition for standing are more likely
to build state structures to extract resources and transform them into
armies, fleets, palaces, public buildings or whatever else represents a
claim for status.

Proponents of material capabilities – and I include here arguments
based on the structure of regional or international systems – have a
ready rejoinder. In contrast to the Middle East, the Indian sub-
continent and China, Europe was never unified and its competing
political units accordingly had stronger incentives to build the infrastructure we have come to associate with the modern state. This in turn
made them more competitive *vis-à-vis* each other and internationally.
Against this argument, those who emphasize ideas can point to considerable variation of military capabilities within Europe as evidence
that this variation was as much a function of choice as it was of the
wealth of these political units. In the eighteenth century, at the height
of dynastic competition, spending on armed forces ranged from a low
of 20-plus percent to Prussia's high of almost 80 percent.[15] Culture also

---

[13] Safran, *From War to War*, pp. 317–382; Herzog, *Arab-Israeli Wars*, pp. 145–196; Oren,
Six Days of War, pp. 170–304.

[14] Lebow and Stein, "Understanding the End of the Cold War as a Non-Linear
Confluence," pp. 219–238.

[15] Schulze, "Prussian Military State"; Parker, *Military Revolution*, pp. 62–65; Lebow,
Cultural Theory of International Relations, ch. 6.

determines the fora in which political units assert their standing. As war came to be seen as too costly and destructive, states have been encouraged to compete in other domains. Materialists, of course, might respond that Japan, Germany, Canada and the Scandinavian countries have pioneered alternative means of claiming standing only because of their inability to compete militarily with the US.[16]

Each approach trumps the other and is trumped in turn. Such an exercise in one-upmanship is futile if its goal is to adjudicate disputing causal claims. It can be productive if used to illuminate the complex interrelationship between ideas and material capabilities. In this spirit, I use leapfrogging to probe some of the deeper causes for the historical decline of war and the growing belief among many scholars that it is obsolete. One of the powerful explanations for the decline of war is the growing disenchantment with war among the publics and elites of developed countries. For some, it is a cause in its own right for the decline in war. For others, it is an important manifestation of a deeper underlying cause. By examining the well-documented decline in public attitudes toward war, we can examine in more detail the relationship between ideas and material conditions. It indicates, among other things, just how difficult it is to separate out analytically competing explanations for war and the evidence they offer in support.

Why is war in such ill-repute?

Scholars who give precedence to material forces stress the destructive consequences of modern warfare and the commitment to war-avoidance to which it has given rise.[17] Others point to the growing difficulty of making conquests stick and of exploiting territories economically if and when they do.[18] Scholars who emphasize the power of ideas have proposed diverse explanations for why publics have become disenchanted with war. Some, like John Mueller, trace this shift in opinion to the nightmare of World War I, reinforced by the even more horrendous experience of World War II.[19] Liberals attribute changes in public attitudes to the emergence of trading states and the growing interdependence of developed economies.[20] Other liberals

---

[16] Waltz, "Structural Realism after the Cold War."
[17] Waltz, "Spread of Nuclear Weapons."   [18] Brooks, *Producing Security*.
[19] Mueller, *Retreat from Doomsday*.
[20] Rosecrance, *Rise of the Trading State*; Gartzke, "Capitalist Peace."

emphasize the emergence of democratic regimes and the so-called Democratic Peace. I have drawn attention to the important role of standing as a cause of war and how changing conceptions of standing have led to a decline in war.

These several explanations confront two analytical problems. The first is the difficulty of distinguishing effectively between material and ideational causes, as each can be subsumed to the other by means of leapfrogging. Many of the ideational explanations appear to rest on material conditions or changes. John Mueller's argument about public opinion is rooted in material capabilities because it attributes changing attitudes to war to a reaction to its human and material costs, which are in turn the result of industrialized warfare. A purely ideational explanation would emphasize the broader trend toward liberal-humanism, which might account, not only for negative attitudes toward war, but also for the prior emergence of revulsion with slavery and dueling. Such a narrative could in turn inspire a material account that attributes liberal-humanism to the wealth and education of the middle classes in the wake of the industrial revolution. This argument inspires the rejoinder that humanism cannot adequately be accounted for by material conditions as it was less pronounced in Germany, a more developed country than either France or Britain, and almost entirely absent in pre-1945 Japan.

Public disaffection with war might be attributed to other material conditions, most importantly in my view, the demographic shift associated with economic development. Beginning in Britain in the late eighteenth century, but gradually spreading east across Europe, there was a drop in the death rate followed approximately eighty years later by a roughly corresponding drop in the birth rate. This development produced a large increase in population but then a relative stabilization after the birth rate dropped. Many reasons have been suggested for these drops in death and birth rates, which also took place in Japan and other parts of the Pacific rim. One hypothesis is a shift in family strategy by upwardly mobile people. With more money in their pockets, couples had to choose between consumer goods and more children to feed and clothe. Restricted living quarters – a product of urbanization – and aspirations for upward mobility for one's children also encouraged having fewer of them. In cities, children became economic liabilities, not assets who could help till the fields and look after their parents in old age. This switch from a reptilian to a mammalian strategy of reproduction and child-rearing encouraged a reframing of the value of offspring. Parents become more emotionally attached to children who were more likely to survive the first five years of life and live longer if they reached adulthood. Many parents also become more emotionally invested in the success of their children, now increasingly a measure of status and self-esteem. For all of these reasons, life became more valuable, especially the life of young men in their prime with good prospects in front of them.

With economic development came secularization. Europeans became focused on this life rather than the next. First the intelligentsia, then people more generally, experienced doubts about the existence of god, heaven and hell. Many of those who maintained a belief in a deity or guiding spirit nevertheless rejected the idea of an afterlife. In Western Europe, on average, only 25–30 percent of the population now believe in an afterlife.[21] If this world is the only one that matters, the death of a son or a daughter in war is an irretrievable loss. The child will not ascend to heaven or be reunited with his family in an afterlife. Arguments about people turning against war because of its costs only address one side of a complex equation. We must also take into account the likelihood that people also turned against war because of their upward valuation of the importance of life.

The liberal trading states argument is strictly materialist in that it explains public attitudes to war in terms of economic rationality. This logic underlies the claims of Cobden and Bright and is more evident still in Schumpeter.[22] It is also pronounced in Thomas Friedman's panegyric on the glories of globalization.[23] The Democratic Peace is harder to unpack because it is a putative empirical finding that international relations scholars have subsequently sought to account for. Three kinds of arguments have been put forward. Institutional arguments, of which there are two variants, identify elections, separation of powers and the rule of law as sources of peace. Elections are deemed to be especially important because they allow citizens to remove officials from power, giving them incentives to avoid costly wars and the electoral punishment that comes in their wake.[24] Other scholars stress the transparency of democracy which is thought to

---

[21] Association of Religious Data Archives, www.thearda.com/internationalData/compare. asp; Pfaff, "Religious Divide," for higher figures on European beliefs in a deity and a breakdown by country.

[22] Schumpeter, *Imperialism and Social Classes*; MacMillan, *On Liberal Peace*, p. 103.

[23] Friedman, *Lexus and the Olive Tree*.

[24] See Mansfield and Snyder, *Electing to Fight*, for a critique.

restrain leaders and reassure foreign audiences by making commitments more credible and defection more costly and visible.[25] The normative explanation stresses the beneficial effects of political culture and more specifically how norms of consultation, compromise and reciprocity shape the resolution of conflicts within and between democracies.[26]

Other scholars emphasize the positive feelings of democratic publics for one another and their respective states. The trading states and Democratic Peace arguments hark back to Immanuel Kant, who recognized the importance of material conditions – citizens who must fight wars, he argued, are more likely to oppose them. He nevertheless gave primacy to ideas and the ways in which reason can lead human beings to a better understanding of their true interests.[27] Explanations for the Democratic Peace rooted in normative considerations are in the Kantian tradition. An early and prominent example is the work of Karl Deutsch, who was the first to theorize a sense of community among democratic peoples. He predicted the emergence of what he called "pluralistic security communities" among people who share common symbols and who have extensive social and economic contacts.[28]

My argument about standing is cultural, but cultural change almost always involves the interaction of ideas and material conditions. I contend that standing has been the most common cause of war historically and that war has declined in large part because it no longer confers standing. This shift in attitude was undoubtedly influenced by the destruction of the two world wars, and in this sense is a rational response to material conditions. I believe there is an independent and equally important ideational component. European revulsion with World War I may have had as much to do with its character as with its human and material costs. Postwar commentaries emphasize the utterly impersonal and industrial nature of that war and the extent to

[25] Fearon, "Domestic Political Audiences and the Escalation of International Disputes"; Smith, "International Crises and Domestic Politics"; Schultz, *Democracy and Coercive Diplomacy*; Lipson, *Reliable Partners*.
[26] Maoz and Russett, "Normative and Structural Causes of the Democratic Peace"; Dixon, "Democracy and the Peaceful Settlement of International Conflict"; Rousseau, *Democracy and War*.
[27] Kant, *Perpetual Peace*; Lawrence, "Imperial Peace or Imperial Method?"; Baum, "A Question for Inspiration in the Liberal Peace Paradigm."
[28] Deutsch, *Nationalism and Social Communication*; Deutsch et al., *Political Community and the North Atlantic Area*.

which human beings were replaceable parts whose survival at the front could be calculated with some precision.[29] It is worth considering the counterfactual that opposition to war would not have been nearly so pronounced if the war had been more like its Napoleonic predecessor, a war of maneuver that encouraged individual, recognizable acts of bravery that might have more than minor tactical consequences.[30] War deprived of its heroic and romantic associations, and considered instead an irrational source of slaughter, destruction and suffering, was no longer able to win honor for its combatants or standing for the states that sent them to their deaths. The wartime and postwar public's fascination with the supposed chivalry of aerial combat – almost entirely a fiction – and the use of knights and other iconic representations of chivalry on World War I memorials, suggest the need to impose this meaning on combat, even though it was sharply at odds with its reality.[31]

All materialist explanations represent a superficial cut at a more complex and layered reality. The strongest material argument concerns the cost of nuclear war, which was widely recognized by leaders of both superpowers, and, one hopes, are equally well appreciated by leaders of other nuclear powers. The only leader publicly dismissive of the costs of nuclear war was Mao Zedong, who maintained that China had such a large population that it could sustain nuclear attacks and still emerge as victor. Motivated perhaps by ignorance or bluff, Mao came in due course to develop more respect for nuclear weapons and their destructive capabilities.[32] Whether nuclear deterrence actually succeeded in preventing war is, of course, another matter. Soviet and American leaders were never so unhappy with the *status quo* that they contemplated war.[33] They had vivid memories of World War II and the destructiveness of conventional war. In the Cuban missile crisis, Secretary of Defense Robert McNamara remembered that President Kennedy worried more about a conventional than a

---

[29] Fussell, *Great War and Modern Memory*; Leed, *No Man's Land*; Wohl, *The Generation of 1914*.

[30] Clausewitz and Tolstoy, among others, give voice to this belief.

[31] Wilson, *Myriad Faces of War*, pp. 362–376, 608–617, 694–704; Goebel, *Great War and Medieval Memory*.

[32] Khrushchev, *Khrushchev Remembers*, pp. 467–470; Lewis and Litai, *China Builds the Bomb*, pp. 6–7, 36–37.

[33] Lebow and Stein, *We All Lost the Cold War*, chs. 13–14, on ambiguous role of deterrence and nuclear weapons on superpower relations during the Cold War.

nuclear war and that it was enough to engender caution.[34] There is also strong evidence that, while the reality of nuclear arsenals was unquestionably restraining, the strategy of nuclear deterrence, as practiced by both superpowers in the form of arms buildups, forward deployments and bellicose rhetoric, helped to provoke some of the confrontations it was intended to prevent.[35]

The nuclear explanation also has an important ideational foundation. After Hiroshima and Nagasaki, many, although not all, strategists and leaders recognized that they were dealing with a weapon of unprecedented destructive potential. The development of thermonuclear weapons in the early 1950s gave a further boost to those who argued that nuclear war was too threatening to contemplate. Fear of the consequences of nuclear war helped to produce what has been called the nuclear taboo.[36] In both superpowers there were nevertheless occasions when advisors or leaders contemplated the use of nuclear weapons. Truman spurned suggestions of a preventive nuclear attack on the Soviet Union and Eisenhower rejected their use in the Korean War. He turned down the recommendation of Admiral Radford and the Joint Chiefs of Staff that atomic bombs be used to rescue the French garrison at Dien Bien Phu.[37] In the Cuban missile crisis, the superpowers came closer to an inadvertent nuclear war than either of their leaders recognized at the time.[38] One possible counter-example is the Nixon administration in the 1970s, which was favorably inclined to a preemptive Soviet strike against Chinese nuclear facilities.[39] These episodes suggest that nuclear non-use was not inevitable but was rather the result of moral restraint. Over time, a norm of non-use developed, and became increasingly important to follow for states intent on maintaining their standing in the world community. To make non-use an accepted norm required key decisions by leaders to exercise restraint in circumstances where they or other leaders might have acted differently.

[34] Robert McNamara's comments, *Proceedings of the Hawk Key Conference*, pp. 81–83.
[35] Lebow and Stein, *We All Lost the Cold War*, for the strongest statement of this argument.
[36] Tannenwald, *Nuclear Taboo*; Paul, *Tradition of Non-Use*, pp. 4–13, prefers tradition of non-use to taboo because various powers still maintain plans for the possible first use of nuclear weapons.
[37] Tannenwald, *Nuclear Taboo*, pp. 115–134, 190–240; Paul, *Tradition of Non-Use*, pp. 38–63; Bundy, *Danger and Survival*, pp. 250–251, 266–270.
[38] Lebow and Stein, *We All Lost the Cold War*, pp. 294–296.
[39] Burr and Michelson, "Whether to 'Strangle the Baby in the Cradle'"; Gorbarev, "Soviet Policy Toward China"; Sagan, "More Will Be Worse."

Part of the horror nuclear weapons invoke undoubtedly reflects the level of casualties any nuclear exchange is expected to produce. Until the Kennedy administration, the only plan the Strategic Air Command (SAC) had for the use of nuclear weapons was an all-out attack against Russia and its Eastern European satellites and Chinese ally. "Wargasm," as it was jocularly known in SAC, was expected to kill upwards of 350 million people in the first week of war.[40] These numbers came down as the accuracy of delivery systems increased and the megatonnage of their warheads accordingly declined. However, the overall proliferation of weapons brought about the new threat of annihilation of the human race through a "nuclear winter." Even if this fear was exaggerated, the collateral damage associated with even a small-scale nuclear exchange – assuming such restraint was possible – would still have been high because of fallout and the location of so many high-value military targets among or close to civilian populations.[41] The nuclear taboo accordingly rests not only on the cost of nuclear war but also on discomfort with the indisputable fact that many, if not most, of its victims would be innocent civilians.

The second problem with these explanations for the decline in war is the difficulty of disentangling one explanation from the other. They overlap, are reinforcing and may describe different manifestations of more fundamental underlying conditions. The argument about public opinion and war, as noted above, is closely linked to the claim that the cost of war has made it increasingly unacceptable in developed countries. All developed countries are also trading states, and, China aside, they are also democracies. To make the case for changing public attitudes as a cause in its own right, we would have to show that there is significant variation in attitudes toward war across developed economies. Alternatively, we could argue that changing attitudes about war reflect a deeper set of attitudinal changes that are also responsible for the rise of trading states and democracies. This claim has intuitive appeal but is more difficult to establish. The trading state and Democratic Peace arguments have greater overlap because almost all trading states are democracies. To evaluate their respective merit we would need to live in a different world in which there were many trading states that were not democracies and *vice versa*.

---

[40] Shoup, "Document 25"; Ball, "Development of the SIOP, 1960–1983."

[41] Sagan and Turco, *Where No Man Thought*; United States Congress, Senate, Committee on Armed Services, *Nuclear Winter and Its Implications*.

The cost-of-war argument is equally difficult to separate from its competitors. Developed trading states are more vulnerable in war than their poorer, largely agricultural counterparts. Democracies tend to place a higher value on life than authoritarian regimes, which also raises the perceived costs of war. These are the same countries in which public opinion is the most anti-war. The US experience in Indochina and Israel's in the Middle East offer support for both propositions. The US won every battle but lost the war because the Vietnamese were willing to sustain many more casualties. More recent US interventions in Lebanon, Somalia, Afghanistan and Iraq offer additional evidence about American sensitivity to casualties. Israel's wars, especially the 1973 war, illustrate the same sensitivity to loss as does Israel's willingness to make significant concessions to secure the release of prisoners of war.[42]

My argument about war and standing overlaps with other explanations. I offer an ideational account for public disenchantment with war, but do not deny that this phenomenon to some degree reflects the cost and destructiveness of modern warfare. Democracy also enters the picture too, although not in the way it is mobilized by Democratic Peace adherents. Democracy encourages particular values and ways of thinking. As modern democracy was initially advocated by the commercial classes, it emphasizes appetite over the spirit. It delegitimizes discourses linking honor to foreign policy. With respect to war, the only motive fully developed democracies consider legitimate is self-defense, although publics may sometimes respond positively to military action to come to the aid of other democracies or bring them into being. Direct appeals to prestige, standing and honor are on the whole unacceptable or unconvincing, even though leaders and publics may be motivated by such concerns when self-esteem is connected with the success and standing of their state. I have argued elsewhere that such transference was a powerful source of Germany's aggressive foreign policy in the early twentieth century, a major cause of superpower competition during the Cold War and a source of support for the Bush administration's intervention in Afghanistan and Iraq.[43] My cases and data set suggest that democracy can restrain or encourage military adventures. I will say something about the conditions responsible for this phenomenon in the following section.

---

[42] Safran, *Israel*, pp. 506–532.
[43] Lebow, *Cultural Theory of International Relations*, ch. 9.

Is war still possible?

The several explanations for war's decline I have examined put considerable weight on elite as well as popular disenchantment with war, although they differ in the reasons they advance for this attitude. War has undoubtedly lost its romantic aura and has come to be seen as a scourge throughout much of the developed world, and beyond it as well. Thoughtful people have also come to see it as a crude instrument of foreign policy that most often fails to achieve its intended goals. At the same time, life has become more valuable for several reinforcing reasons, making the cost of war more dreadful still. These attitudinal shifts have made it more difficult to sell wars fought for any reason. They have not made war impossible. In the last decade, the US and the UK intervened in Afghanistan and Iraq, Israel briefly occupied the Gaza Strip and Russia made an incursion into Georgia. Three of these countries unambiguously qualify as democracies, and Russia might charitably be described as a transitional regime. The leaders responsible for all these military initiatives had strong support from their legislatures and publics. American leaders and Israeli leaders sold their interventions on the grounds of national security and their Russian counterparts did the same while also appealing to the plight of fellow-countrymen in the near abroad.[44] Success – the Israeli and Russian initiatives accomplished their immediate objects – probably makes it easier for leaders to invoke similar arguments in the future. Unsuccessful wars, especially those in which people come to believe that they were lied to by their leaders about the justification and purpose of war, will presumably have the reverse effect. This judgment must nevertheless be offered cautiously.

Within a generation of losing World War I, Germany started the European component of World War II. Hitler could go to war because he had become a dictator who had made the German army subservient and was largely unconstrained by public opinion. He also benefited from the *Dolchstoss* (stab in the back) thesis, propagated in the immediate aftermath of World War I by the German right. Germany, they maintained, had not lost the war but had been betrayed by the socialists, many of whom were Jews.[45] The political power of the right

---

[44] *Ibid.*; Gatosphere, "Russia-Georgia: Who Won the Information War," September 1, 2008, http://gatosphere.com/category/russia-georgia-who-won-the-information-war/.

[45] Dorpalen, *Hindenburg and the Weimar Republic*, pp. 51–52; Seiler, "'Dolchstoss' und 'Dolchstosslegende'."

and the vulnerability and cravenness of pro-Republic forces discouraged the German public from learning about, let alone coming to terms with, their leaders' responsibility for World War I. Hitler's attack on Poland in 1939 was justified on ground of security: the Nazis staged a convenient border incident on the eve of their planned invasion.[46] Germans widely regarded the attack on Poland as a war of revenge, as they did the subsequent invasion of France. Despite support for Hitler, and a general desire for revenge, there was little support for Hitler's wars. Most Germans desperately wanted to believe that peace could be maintained. When Germany invaded Poland in 1939, there was none of the enthusiasm for war that had been visible in 1914.[47]

More telling cases are Korea, Vietnam, the first Gulf War, Afghanistan and Iraq. Korea was an extremely unpopular war in the US, leading to a sharp drop in President Truman's public support and contributing to the Republican presidential victory in 1952.[48] The Korean experience did not deter Lyndon Johnson from intervening in Vietnam or the Nixon administration from expanding that war into Cambodia despite mounting opposition to the war at home.[49] Unlike Korea, which resulted in a costly stalemate, the Indochina intervention ended in an American defeat and subsequent legislation limiting the president's ability to send armed forces into action without prior congressional support.[50] Less than a generation later, President George Bush found it more difficult to mobilize congressional and popular support for military action to expel Iraq from Kuwait. The majority he needed among the public and in the Congress was made possible by the obvious nature of Iraq's aggression, United Nations' authorization of a war of liberation and the formation of an international coalition that received financial support from countries that did not participate in the fighting. The Gulf War of 1990–1991 was welcomed by a large segment of the American people as a vehicle for overcoming the trauma associated with the American defeat in Indochina. It provoked a display of yellow ribbons on cars, houses and trees, many of them with a "Support Our Troops" logo. Following

---

[46] Bullock, *Hitler*, p. 546, citing testimony from Documents in Evidence (before the International Military Tribunal at Nuremberg), 1, no. 751-PS.

[47] Kershaw, *The "Hitler Myth,"* pp. 139–147; Frei, "People's Community and War."

[48] Casey, *Selling the Korean War*, pp. 326–336.

[49] Foot, *The Wrong War*; Gelb and Betts, *Irony of Vietnam*; Kahin, *Intervention*.

[50] Fisher, *Presidential War Power*.

the earlier lead of Ronald Reagan, right-wing revisionists encouraged the myth that America would have won in Vietnam if public opinion had only supported their forces overseas.[51]

The Iraq War triggered a similar display of ribbons and other manifestations of patriotism, once again built around the home-grown *Dolchstoss* myth of "liberal" – by now a term of ill-repute – betrayal of American forces. The stab-in-the-back thesis became prominent in the Iraq conflict after it became evident that US occupiers were making no headway against the insurgents, could not provide security within major urban centers or create an army, police force or government without loyalties to specific religious factions. In the 2006 mid-term elections, President Bush tried and failed to make the case for "staying the course," and Bush supporters, many of them self-identified neo-cons, pushed their revisionist take on Vietnam to mobilize support and intimidate opponents of the war.[52] Public opinion nevertheless turned against the war and contributed to Barack Obama's presidential victory over John McCain, a Republican closely associated with the Bush administration's military intervention and much belated buildup of forces.

All of these wars were sold to the American people on the grounds of security. This is not the place to debate the legitimacy or truthfulness of this logic, only to note that such claims were hotly contested by critics of three of the five interventions (in Indochina, Afghanistan and Iraq). They succeeded in mobilizing considerable public opposition to these wars when the promise of quick success turned into frustrating, open-ended commitments. In Korea, the honesty of the Truman administration was not the issue – it was the costly stalemate after China entered the fighting.[53] At the outset, American public opinion supported its government in six post-1945 wars. This is the largest number of wars initiated by any state in the postwar era; India and China, which come next, initiated four wars each.

[51] "Mind Is a Difficult Thing to Change: Vietnam Interlude – After the Fall," April 28, 2005, http://neo-neocon.blogspot.com/2005/04/mind-is-difficult-thing-to-change.html, "Break-ing the Big Stick: Removing the Threat of War to Achieve Peace," May 31, 2007, http:// neoneocon.com/category/war/vietnam/; Robert Buzzanaco, "How I Learned to Stop Worrying and Love Vietnam and Iraq," *Counterpunch*, April 16–17, 2005, www.counter-punch.org/buzzanco04162005.html. For serious analyses, Lembcke, *The Spitting Image*; Hixon, *Historical Memory and Representations of the Vietnam War*.

[52] "US 'Will Stay the Course' in Iraq, Says Bush," US Department of Defense, American Forces Press Service, July 10, 2003.

[53] Casey, *Selling the Korean War*, pp. 326–336.

The history of American intervention suggests that, to succeed, presidents must sell interventions on compelling grounds of national security and win quick victories with few casualties. The First Gulf War met these conditions and established the precedent that the subsequent Bush administration tried and failed to emulate. It was unable to secure UN authorization for intervention, and could not put together an impressive multilateral coalition. Britain aside, other major powers opposed intervention, among them France and Germany, two of America's closest allies.[54] After invading Iraq and overthrowing Saddam's regime, the occupying forces failed to find any weapons of mass destruction, which had provided the public justification for American intervention. They were also unable to withdraw, as originally planned, because of a growing insurgency. Although Obama won the presidential election in 2008, in part because of his promise to end the war in Iraq, he made it clear upon taking office that American troops would have to remain in that country for some time, and ordered a buildup of forces in Afghanistan. These moves antagonized the left-wing of the Democratic Party but did not generate any widespread opposition.

Is America different from other democracies? If we examine the record of war-initiation since 1945, it is among the countries that turned most often to their military instruments. Of 31 wars fought during this period, Israel was involved in 6, the US and China in 5, Vietnam in 4 and India and Pakistan in 3 each (see Table 2.1). Israel and the US are tied in war-initiation. Israel initiated 4 wars, and fought in 2 others (1948 and 1973) in which it was attacked by Arab coalitions. The US initiated 4 of the 5 wars in which it fought.

These comparisons offer evidence that democracies are as war-like as any other regime.[55] With a conservative coding (that does not count Russia as a democracy), democracies initiated 12 of the 31 wars, and 10 of those were initiated by mature as opposed to developing or transitional democracies. When we take into account that for most of these years democracies represented about 27 percent of the world's government, they account for considerably more than their random share of wars.[56]

---

[54] Isakoff and Corn, *Hubris*; Gordon and Trainor, *Cobra II*; Lebow, *Cultural Theory of International Relations*, ch. 9; Rich, *Greatest Story Ever Sold*.

[55] Doyle, "Kant, Liberal Legacies, and Foreign Affairs"; Dixon, "Democracy and the Peaceful Settlement of International Conflict"; Ferejohn and Rosenbluth, "Warlike Democracies." See Huth and Allee, *Democratic Peace and Territorial Conflict in the Twenty Century*, for a review of this literature.

[56] Diamond, "A Report Card on Democracy," on the percentage of democracies.

The US, Israel and India are the democracies most responsible for war-initiation. Israel is a special case. Only one of the states contiguous with Israel acknowledges its existence, and that recognition only came after four wars. Israel is surrounded by hostile states and territory occupied by Palestinians. Israel was attacked in 1948, 1970 and 1973 by Egypt, or Egypt in coalition with other Arab states. Four of the wars initiated by Israel (1956, 1967, 1982 and 2008) were in response to Arab provocations. We can debate whether Israeli military action was ethical or effective, but it cannot be denied that the country faced, and continues to face, very real threats to its security, if not its survival. India is a transitional democracy and there is some evidence that states of this kind have been more war-like than mature democracies.[57] More relevant in the case of India is the pattern of violence associated with partitioned countries: multiple countries that came into existence with the breakup of colonial empires because one or more nationalities claim all or part of the territory. This made it necessary for colonial powers or the United Nations to divide the territory among claimants, or for division to result as the outcome of post-independence fighting. India initiated four wars, and all but one of them were with its post-colonial rival, Pakistan.

The more meaningful peer-group comparison for the United States is with the countries of Western Europe, Japan, the "Old Commonwealth" (Canada, Australia, New Zealand) and Latin America's democracies. Here, the US is clearly an outlier, as only two of these countries initiated wars (France and Britain against Egypt in 1956). Britain was also a partner of the US in the 1991 Gulf War and 2003 invasion of Iraq. The US differs from all these countries in several important ways. In *A Cultural Theory of International Relations*, I describe it as a *"parvenu"* power. These are states who are late entrants into the arena where they can compete for standing and do so with greater intensity than other states. They devote a higher percentage of their national income to military forces and pursue more aggressive foreign policies. Examples include Sweden under Gustavus Adolphus, Prussia and Russia in the eighteenth century and Japan and the US in the late nineteenth and twentieth centuries.[58]

[57] Mansfield and Snyder, *Electing to Fight*.
[58] Lebow, *Cultural Theory of International Relations*, pp. 295–297, 429–438, 477–480, 539–540, 545.

Unlike other *parvenu* powers, the constraints on the US were more internal than external: Congress, not other powers, kept American presidents from playing a more active role in European affairs in the 1920s and 1930s, and forced a withdrawal from Indochina in the 1970s. The American leaders and people were never spurned or humiliated by the other powers, but some American presidents and their advisors did feel humiliated by the internal restraints imposed upon them. Not infrequently, they sought to commit the country to activist policies through membership in international institutions that involved various long-term obligations (e.g. IMF, NATO), *fait accomplis* in the form of executive actions (e.g. the 1940 destroyer deal, intervention in the Korean War, sending Marines to Lebanon in 1958) and congressional resolutions secured on the basis of false or misleading information (the Gulf of Tonkin and Iraq War resolutions). Ironically, concern for credibility promoted the kinds of ill-considered and open-ended commitments like Vietnam and Iraq that later prompted public opposition and the congressional constraints that subsequent American presidents considered detrimental to their credibility. Instead of promoting a reassessment of national security strategy, these setbacks appear to have strengthened the commitment of at least some presidents and their advisors to break free of these constraints and assert leadership in the world, ushering in a new cycle of overextension, failure and renewed constraints.

The US is unique in other ways. It is far and away the most powerful economy in the world. At the end of World War II, it accounted for 46 percent of the world's gross domestic product (GDP) and today represents a still impressive 21 percent.[59] Prodigious wealth allows the US to spend an extraordinary percentage of its GDP on its armed forces in comparison to other countries. In the aftermath of the Cold War, most countries cut back on military spending, but US spending has increased. In 2003, the US spent US$417 billion on defense, 47 percent of the world total.[60] In 2008, it spent 41 percent of its national budget on the military and the cost of past wars, which accounted for almost 50 percent of world defense spending. In absolute terms, this was twice the total of Japan, Russia, the United Kingdom, Germany and China combined. Not surprisingly, it is the

---

[59] Deanne, "Waxing or Waning?," citing figures from the World Bank and the CIA.
[60] SIPRI, "The Major Spenders in 2003," www.sipri.se.

only state with a global military reach.[61] Democratic and Republican administrations alike have bet that extraordinary levels of military expenditure will sustain, if not increase, the standing and influence that traditionally comes with military dominance. It is intended to make the United States, in the words of former Secretary of State Madeleine Albright, "the indispensable nation," the only power capable of enforcing order.[62]

US defense expenditure also reflects the political power of the military-industrial complex. Defense spending encouraged dependence on the government by numerous companies and helped bring others into being. In 1991, at the end of the Cold War, twelve million people, roughly 10 percent of the US workforce, were directly or indirectly dependent upon defense dollars. The number has not changed significantly since. Having such a large impact on the economy gives defense contractors enormous political clout.[63] Those who land major weapons projects are also careful to sub-contract production across the country, not infrequently offering something to companies in every state. This too gives them enormous political leverage in the Congress, often enough to force reluctant administrations to buy weapons the military does not want.[64] Here, too, the US is unique. The Soviet Union once spent an even higher percentage of its GDP on its military, which was a major reason for its economic stagnation and subsequent demise.

Congress and presidents have consistently defended military spending as essential to national security. They are witting participants in a vicious cycle. Propaganda, sponsored by think tanks and so-called patriotic organizations, many with funding from defense contractors, creates foreign enemies for the public and greatly exaggerates the

---

[61] Global Issues, "World Military Spending," February 25, 2007, www.globalissues.org/ Geopolitics/ArmsTrade/Spending.asp#USMilitarySpending/; Christopher Hellman, "Highlights of the Fiscal Year 2008 Pentagon Spending Request," February 5, 2007, www.armscontrolcenter.org.

[62] Quoted in Alison Mitchell, "Clinton Urges NATO Expansion in 1999," New York Times, October 23, 1996, p. A20.

[63] Accordino, Captives of the Cold War Economy, p. 1; Lee, Public Budgeting Systems, p. 35.

[64] As I write, the current example is the F-22, which Obama finally killed in the Senate with the threat of a veto. Leslie Wayne, "Air Force Jet Wins Battle in Congress," New York Times, September 28, 2006; Editorial, "We Don't Need the F-22," New York Times, June 19, 2009; Associated Press, "White House Threatens Veto over F-22 Jet Fighters," June 24, 2009; Bryan Bender, "A Dog Fight Obama Seems Bound to Lose," Boston Globe, July 12, 2009, pp. A1, 10; Christopher Drew, "Bowing to Veto Threat, Senate Blocks Money for Warplanes," New York Times, July 22, 2009, p. A1.

threats they pose. This process began with the Soviet Union, shifted to China in the Cold War's aftermath and is currently focused as well on North Korea, Iran and Islamic fundamentalism. Arms buildups, forward deployments, bellicose rhetoric and military and diplomatic support for countries more directly in the firing line exacerbate tensions with these enemies, helping to make depictions of their hostility self-fulfilling. In the Cold War, behavior of this kind by both superpowers helped to provoke a series of war-threatening crises, culminating in the Cuban missile crisis.[65] In the post-Cold War period, the invasions of Afghanistan and Iraq have escalated tensions with the Islamic world, seemingly emboldened Iran and North Korea and have probably made the US an even more likely target of territorial attacks. It has certainly put American soldiers and civilians in harm's way throughout the Middle East. These conflicts not only make American fears self-fulfilling but provide justification for the kinds of arms buildups and forward deployments that helped to bring this situation about. It is a well-known adage that people with hammers look for nails. With such a large and capable military, there is a continuing temptation to try to influence outcomes around the world and to rely heavily on the nation's military capabilities to do this.

In comparison to its peer group of democracies, the US is the only country in which elements of an historical honor culture remain important. In Prussia and Wilhelminian Germany, the Junkers (east Elbian, land-owning aristocrats) constituted a distinct class whose hold on power was justified by their military service and legendary bravery. Their class values and representatives helped to shape Prussian and German foreign and military policy and contributed significantly to the outbreak of World War I.[66] The Junkers bled to death in World War I, although enough survived to provide proficient and compliant leadership of the *Wehrmacht* in Hitler's wars of aggression. Two world wars purged Germany and other European countries of such elites and thoroughly discredited their values. The Civil War did not do the same for the United States.[67] The South's honor culture continued to produce officers and enlisted personnel who gradually came to dominate the American military and are still over-represented within it.

---

[65] Lebow and Stein, *We All Lost the Cold War*, ch. 2.
[66] Afflerbach, *Falkenhayn*, p. 61; Mombauer, *Helmuth von Moltke*; Lebow, *Cultural Theory of International Relations*, ch. 7.
[67] Wyatt-Brown, *Southern Honor*; Wyatt-Brown, *Shaping of Southern Culture*.

Since the draft was abolished in 1973, the percentage of military enlistments from the South and West has risen. Between 1985 and 2001, recruits from the South increased from 34 to 42 percent. By contrast, recruits from the northeast dropped from 22 percent in 1977 to less than 14 percent in 2001. The regional distribution of newly commissioned officers is roughly similar; the South accounted for 42.5 percent of new army ROTC-commissioned officers in 2006 and 36.7 percent of West Point graduates in 2007.[68] Southern influence in the military is growing, making it an institution like the Prussian officer corps in the sense that it is cut off from the rest of society by virtue of its very different values. In the case of the American military, this is true not only of officers but of enlisted men and women.

Fortunately, American officers differ from their Prussian counterparts in that they have only indirect input into the policymaking process. As Leslie Gelb and Richard Betts demonstrated, it is civilian officials, not the military, who generally push for the use of force, although the military prefers to use it on a more massive scale once a decision for war is made. This finding held true in Iraq, where the military was appalled by the small size of the force Secretary of Defense Donald Rumsfeld wanted committed to the operation.[69] However, like its Junker counterpart, the US military is on the whole a compliant tool of political authorities in its willingness to sacrifice itself for, even become spokesmen for, the most questionable military adventures. Only one general resigned his commission when the military was pushed into invading Iraq; the others bit the bullet and prepared to attack with forces they thought inadequate for the task.[70]

Equally striking is the willingness of the military and their families to back wars like Afghanistan and Iraq despite the personal price they pay in fighting them. Public opinion polls consistently reveal that there is more support for ongoing wars and more support for interventionist foreign policies within the military than among civilians, and among southerners than people from other regions of the country.[71] These

---

[68] Michael Lind, "Bush's Martyrs," New Statesman, March 1, 2004, p. 20; Watkins and Sherk, Who Serves in the US Military?, p. 13, citing Department of Defense data.

[69] Gelb and Betts, Irony of Vietnam; Ricks, Fiasco, pp. 40–43, 66–84.

[70] Ricks, Fiasco, p. 67, Lieutenant-General Gregory Newbold is the only known pre-invasion departure from senior military ranks for opposition to the war.

[71] Valentino and Valentino, "An Army of the People?"

groups are also much more likely to identify with the Republican Party, which is more likely than the Democrats to support interventions and has a higher tolerance for casualties. Pro-war attitudes also reflect the honor culture from which many professional soldiers come or to which they are socialized.[72] This orientation makes it easier to sell wars to the public because the people who have to fight and die in them are the least likely to oppose them. It also makes it more difficult to oppose war because, under the guise of "Support Our Troops," dissenters who have never served in the military must bear the onus of appearing unpatriotic.

As I noted earlier, the US further differs from Europeans and Japanese in the strength of its religious faith. Gallup polls from 1947 to 1994 show that American belief "in god or a universal spirit" consistently hovers around the 95 percent level, in contrast to about 50 percent for Europeans and Japanese.[73] Gallup polls further reveal that between 81 and 93 percent of Americans believe in heaven, although, interestingly, only 54–85 percent believe in hell.[74] Belief in a deity and in heaven is far more prevalent within the military than outside and within the south than the rest of the country.[75] Both beliefs soften the consequences of death and make it more acceptable, especially if a military casualty is understood as god's will and family members hope, even expect, to be reunited in heaven with the departed loved one. The commitment to honor has the same effect by imparting important meaning to loss of life in combat and conferring status on their families within the community that shares these values.[76]

---

[72] See Holsti, "Of Chasms and Convergences," on Republican identification; and Gelpi, Feaver and Reifler, *Paying the Human Costs of War*, on greater willingness of Republicans to accept casualties. See Feaver and Gelpi, *Choosing Your Battles*, for contrary findings about close association with the military and a willingness to support war.

[73] Gallup polls, reported at www.religioustolerance.org/godpoll.htm. The Pew Forum on Religion and Public Life, "US Religious Landscape Survey," July 1, 2009, http://religions.pewforum.org/reports/, nevertheless shows an across-the-board decline in formal affiliation; Association of Religious Data Archives, www.thearda.com/internationalData/compare.asp. See Pfaff, "Religious Divide," for statistics that show less of a gap between the US and Europe.

[74] Gallup poll in 1994. Quoted in George Bishop, "What Americans Really Believe," *Free Inquiry*, Summer 1999, pp. 38–42. See also the Gallup poll referred to by *Charisma*, June 7, 2000, www.mcjonline.com/news/00/20000225e.htm.

[75] Holsti, "Of Chasms and Convergences."

[76] Lebow, *Cultural Theory of International Relations*, chs. 3 and 4, for the characteristics of honor societies and how they regard death.

These unusual features of American political, economic and social culture come together to produce what might be called the perfect national security storm. Wealth provides the material capability for the US to attempt to play a hegemonic role in the international system while its parvenu status and military-industrial complex provides the means and public support for such a policy. Southern honor subculture and the pervasiveness of religious belief ensure willing agents to execute wars and interventions and quietly accept the human cost they entail. It is not without reason that a significant percentage of the population in other democracies considers the US the greatest threat to peace.

The second major threat to world peace stems not from a country but from the residues of decolonization and the Cold War. The former gave rise to the phenomenon of partition. As noted earlier, partition is the breakup of former colonies into two countries because of ethnic disputes. The British Empire spawned the largest number of partitioned countries: the Republic of Ireland and Northern Ireland, Greek and Turkish Cyprus, Israel and Palestine, India and Pakistan, Pakistan and Bangladesh, and Malaysia and Singapore. Partition has generated some of the world's most intractable problems and accounts for almost one-third (10 of our 31) wars. It is also responsible for a significant percentage of the world's internal violence.[77]

Only one of the conflicts arising from partition has been resolved: the Malaysia–Singapore division allowed both countries to prosper and develop on the whole cordial relations. Progress has also been made in Ireland, but only after two civil wars and periodic irruptions of violence. Cyprus, the Middle East and the Indian sub-continent remain flashpoints. With the breakup of the Soviet Union, new partitions have taken place and dissatisfied ethnic groups have pursued separation by violent means from Russia (e.g. Chechnya) or from a successor state (e.g. South Ossetia from Georgia). The breakup of Yugoslavia, which might be considered a follow-on to the dissolution of the Soviet Union, spawned another series of violent conflicts. With luck, these conflicts have run their course, but, judging from the history of other partitioned countries, they retain the potential to become explosive in the future. There are nevertheless some grounds for optimism. The partitions associated with the breakup of the British Empire and the nationality conflicts exacerbated by the

[77] Henderson, Lebow and Stoessinger, *Divided Nations in a Divided World*.

dissolution of the Austro-Hungarian, Russian and Ottoman Empires were particularly violent and war-prone because they involved large territories (the Indian sub-continent), in important strategic or economic locations (Eastern Europe, the Middle East) and often drew in great powers on opposing sides (especially in the Middle East). The current crop of partitioned countries meets none of these conditions.

The Cold War gave us divided nations: the two Germanies, Koreas, Chinas and Vietnams.[78] These are countries with a long-standing sense of national unity which were politically divided as a result of the Cold War. Germany and Korea were the first to suffer this fate as Soviet and Western occupation zones became transformed into separate and competing political units. China's division dates from the Korean War and President Truman's 1950 decision to interpose the American Seventh Fleet in the Taiwan Straits to prevent the Chinese communists from unifying their country. Vietnam's temporary division was mandated by the 1954 Geneva Accords. Germany aside, each of these divisions provoked major wars. And, although swords remained sheathed in the case of Germany, its division was both a symptom and a cause of the Cold War. German reunification in 1990 was made possible by superpower accommodation and marked the end of the Cold War.

Korea and China remain divided. Sino-American rapprochement and the end of the Cold War have partially defused one of these conflicts. China remains committed to national unification as a matter of principle and has pledged to go to war if Taiwan should ever declare its independence. China's political elite believes that Taiwanese independence would disrupt their country's social stability, national unity and great power aspirations. Once again, there are grounds for cautious optimism. The Taiwanese independence movement seems to be waning rather than growing and the economic integration of the two states is increasing rapidly. In 2005, 70 percent of Taiwan's direct foreign investment was in China and 40 percent of its exports went across the Straits. Tourist exchanges have increased and over one million Taiwanese business people and their families have homes on the mainland. Time is on Beijing's side, and its government appears content to let matters run their natural course.[79] If China suffers an economic

---

[78] Ibid.
[79] Chan, *China, the US, and the Power-Transition Theory*, p. 92; Gries, *China's New Nationalism*, p. 11; Deng, *China's Struggle for Status*, pp. 257–258.

decline, or if Taiwan declares its independence, a clash could occur in the Straits, one that could draw in the US and put the two most powerful states in the world on a collision course.[80]

During the Cold War, Hans Morgenthau observed that preservation of the peace depended less on the balance of power and rather more on the moral qualities of leaders.[81] The same is true of the post-Cold War peace. In striking contrast to the Cold War, underlying conditions are on the whole favorable to peace, but many nationality conflicts, national rivalries and long-standing, unresolved conflicts remain. Keeping them from escalating into war, let alone ultimately resolving them, will require foresight, restraint and political courage by key actors in many states. Such courage is difficult when leaders believe, as many did in 1914, that a continental war was inevitable. In these circumstances, there is much less incentive for crisis resolution, and all the more so if the state in question has a military advantage which is expected to decline or disappear. Courage is easier in situations where leaders believe that avoiding war in a crisis has a good chance of forestalling it altogether, or at least in the long term with respect to the antagonist in question. Soviet and American leaders during the Cold War successfully managed a series of crises and by doing so made self-fulfilling their hope that war between them might be avoided. To the extent that this book might convince readers, and possibly even policymakers, that war is on the wane, it might increase incentives to avoid it in the short term.

Methodological postscript

David Hume acknowledged that cause was an illusion of the mind, a cognitive artifact that helps us make sense of our world. Causation rests on our observation of a "constant conjunction" between a putative cause and its effect. Cause is distinguished from effect by its temporal precedence.[82]

International relations theory, and social science more generally, has adopted the Humean understanding of causation.[83] It focuses our

[80] *Ibid.*   [81] Morgenthau, *Politics Among Nations*, pp. 285–286.
[82] Hume, *Treatise of Human Nature*, pp. 11, 27, 55, 60, 77, 84–86, 94–95, 104–108, 157, 161–173.
[83] Kurki, *Causation in International Relations*, pp. 88–146.

attention on what Aristotle called "efficient causes": change brought about by any agent or mover.[84] It structures social science in the form of "regularity determinism," which assumes that establishing regularities is the first step to making causal claims.[85] Unlike Hume, many contemporary researchers assume that causes are something more than linguistic constructs or useful metaphors.

Within the tradition of neo-positivism, it is essential to isolate, conceptually and empirically, competing theorized causes. With regard to the frequency of war, neither condition can be met. These are not technical problems that can somehow be solved by the application of reason, but something inherent in the very conceptualization of these explanations. The empirical problem is equally acute given the small size of any data set of post-1945, or even post 1815 wars and the impossibility of finding enough cases where one cause is present and others are not.

Leapfrogging suggests that thinking about causation in terms of efficient causes engages only the tip of the proverbial iceberg. Each hypothesized efficient cause, whether material or ideational, is itself an expression or product of causes at further temporal remove. To understand the historical decline in warfare, we need to explain its efficient causes(s), and this requires going back in time and often to different developments at different levels of analysis and their interaction. Leapfrogging also reveals the degree to which many competing explanations have common roots, but also different roots in diverse domains. These underlying causes interact with one another, sometimes in synergistic ways, and their effects are mediated by confluence and agency. A good explanation for the decline of warfare must accordingly identify and analyze these several levels of causes and some of what appear their most important connections.

This is a task to which regularity determinism is unsuited. At best, process tracing in cases and multiple cases in roughly similar contexts may allow us to suggest that such conditions or developments can "produce," "enable," "shape" or "constrain" other developments in non-deterministic ways. This is because they make these developments thinkable, acceptable, preferable and even likely, and other developments less so. These effects invariably depend on the presence of other conditions, whose causes may be entirely independent and whose

---

[84] Aristotle, *Physics*, II.3 and *Metaphysics*, V.2.
[85] Kurki, *Causation in International Relations*, p. 38.

effects may not be apparent beforehand. To look beneath the surface this way is to enter an open-ended, non-linear world.

To understand such worlds, we must turn to narratives that tell non-Humean stories. They should start with the trend, transformation or event we want to explain and identify possible efficient causes. We must choose the most promising of these and work our way back to identify what appear to be their most important causes and enabling conditions. Ideally, we want to find one or more underlying conditions to which these causal chains might be traced and the role, if any, that confluences play, always keeping in mind that agency is important because it is never fully a response to underlying conditions. In practice, it is more likely to lead to multiple underlying conditions, each of which has multiple underlying causes. Our quest may lead us, as it does with the declining frequency of war, to developments (e.g. longevity, secularization) that are at some remove from what is generally considered the political domain, and to others (e.g. the costs of two world wars) that are highly context-dependent. Such narratives can never be validated and can only rarely be falsified on the basis of evidence.[86]

Competing narratives will undoubtedly flourish, as they do now, but allow some degree of evaluation on the basis of their internal logic, their fit with empirical evidence, their comprehensiveness and their predictions. They may posit relationships that can be evaluated in other domains, with results that enhance or diminish confidence in them. My claim that war is declining because it no longer confers standing, directs our attention to changes in values which can be expected to produce competing discourses, debates and changes in other kinds of behavior. These are all subject to empirical investigation that can lead to deeper understandings of the extent to which and why such a value change appears to be underway at the present time. The same holds true for other explanations for the decline of war. Conceptually and empirically, our understanding, not only of war but also of social interactions more generally, will be enhanced by undertaking this kind of exercise for all our competing explanations. In a narrow sense, it might tell us something about the conditions associated with certain regularities, knowledge that could help guide neo-positivist research. It might also tell us something about the conditions under which these or other regularities no longer hold. By tacking

[86] Lebow, *Forbidden Fruit*, ch. 9; Lebow, "Constitutive Causality," for an elaboration.

back and forth between the standard search for regularities and a deeper search for the conditions that give rise to them or undermine them, we can develop a more dynamic and fruitful kind of social science in which change, not stability, is the norm and efficient cause is understood as the beginning, not an end point, of causal analysis.

Appendix

Data set

Name of war	Start	End	Initiator(s)	Other combatant(s)	Initiator: dominant power	Initiator: Great Power	Initiator: rising power	Initiator: declining power	Initiator: weak power	Explanation	Motive	Outcome
1 Franco-Spanish War	1648	1659	France	Spain	0	1	0	0	0	France supplants Habsburgs – in control of Austria, Spain and Low Countries – as the dominant power. Great power attacks dominant power.	Standing	Initiator wins
2 Anglo-Dutch I	1652	1654	England	Netherlands	0	0	1	0	0	England tries unsuccessfully to wrest commercial supremacy at sea from Holland. Rising power attacks great power.	Interest	Initiator loses
3 Russo-Polish War II	1654	1656	Russia	Poland-Lithuania	0	0	1	0	0	Russia makes territorial gains at Polish–Lithuanian expense. Rising power attacks great power.	Standing	Initiator wins
4 Anglo-Spanish	1654	1659	England	Spain	1	0	1	0	0	France attacks Spain. England allies with France seeking commercial benefits. Great power attacks dominant power. Rising power joins coalition against dominant power.	Standing, Interest	Initiator wins

	War						Description					Standing	Outcome
5	Northern War I	1655	1661	Poland, Netherlands, Crimean Khanate, Denmark, Holy Roman Empire	Sweden, Russia, Brandenburg	0	Began as a Swedish attack on Poland–Lithuania, already at war with Russia. Prussia and Denmark entered the war, and later Great Britain. The war brought about the collapse and reemergence of Polish power. Great power attacks great power. Two rising and one weak power are drawn in.	1	1	0	1	Standing	Initiators win
6	Russo-Polish War III	1658	1667	Russia	Poland-Lithuania	0	Really 1657–1667. Initiated independently by Cossacks, who drew Russia in. Rising power attacks declining power.	0	1	0	0	Standing	Initiator wins
7	Austro-Ottoman War	1663	1664	Ottoman Empire	Austria	0	Seesawing conflict over Hungary between Ottomans and Austrians. This round started by the Porte. Great power attacks great power.	1	0	0	0	Standing	Initiator loses
8	Sweden-Bremen War	1665	1666	Sweden	Bremen	0	Sweden defeats Bremen. Great power attacks weak power.	0	1	0	0	Standing	Initiator wins
9	Anglo-Dutch II	1665	1667	England	Netherlands	0	Charles II's unsuccessful attempt to influence succession in Holland. Rising power attacks great power.	0	0	1	0	Interest	Initiator loses

Name of war	Start	End	Initiator(s)	Other combatant(s)	Initiator: dominant power	Initiator: Great Power	Initiator: rising power	Initiator: declining power	Initiator: weak power	Explanation	Motive	Outcome
10 War of Devolution	1667	1668	France	Spain	1	0	0	0	0	Louis IX attempted to expand at expense of declining Spain. Checked by coalition of Holland, Great Britain, Sweden, German states. Dominant power attacks declining power. Miscalculated escalation.	Standing	Initiator loses
11 Polish-Turkish War II	1671	1676	Poland	Ottoman Empire	0	0	0	1	0	Border war started by Cossacks.	Other	Initiator loses
12 Anglo-Dutch III	1672	1674	England	Holland	0	0	1	0	0	Charles II felt compelled to assist Louis XIV in his invasion of Holland. Rising power joins coalition against great power.	Interest	Initiator loses
13 Franco-Dutch War	1672	1679	France, England, Münster, Cologne	Holland, Holy Roman Empire, Brandenburg	1	1	0	0	0	Louis IX seeking revenge against Holland. Dominant power attacks great power. Miscalculated escalation.	Revenge	Initiator loses
14 Austro-Ottoman War II (Great Turkish War)	1683	1699	Ottoman Empire	Austria (Holy Roman Empire), Venetian Republic, Poland	0	1	0	0	0	Ottoman offensive against Habsburgs. Defeated by European coalition. Habsburgs recapture Hungary. Great power attacks great power. Miscalculated escalation.	Standing	Initiator loses

						Standing	Initiator wins		Standing	Initiator loses
15	Franco-Spanish War (War of the Reunions)	1683	1684	France	Spain (fought in Spanish Netherlands; began in 1683)	1	0	0	0	0	Louis XIV invaded the Spanish Netherlands to exploit Habsburgs tied down before Vienna by the Turks. Regensburg truce forced Spain to give up Luxembourg. High point of French influence. Dominant power attacks great power.
16	League of Augsburg (War of the Grand Alliance)	1688	1697	Holy Roman Empire, England, Savoy, Spain, Sweden,	France, Irish Jacobites	1	0	0	1	0	Louis XIV invades the Palatinate. In the interim, the Turks had been defeated, Hungary occupied, William of Orange consolidated his power as leader of a coalition of Protestant states and moved toward alliance with Spain. Louis revoked Edict of Nantes. Succession issue in Palatinate provided the opening for attempt to extend further French power. Louis had antagonized almost all of Europe, provoking a wide coalition against him. Their goal was a return to the territorial *status quo* established by Treaties of Westphalia and Pyrenees. Leads to a world war. Big French losses in Low Countries, Italy and America, but Louis retains his gains in Germany. Dominant power attacks weak power. Miscalculated escalation.

Name of war	Start	End	Initiator(s)	Other combatant(s)	Initiator: dominant Great Power	Initiator: rising power	Initiator: declining power	Initiator: weak power	Explanation	Motive	Outcome
17 Russo-Turkish War	1695	1700	Russia, Austria	Ottoman Empire	0	1	0	0	Russia gains Azov, Vienna gains Hungary and Transylvania. Rising power attacks declining power.	Standing	Initiator wins
18 Great (Second) Northern War	1700	1721	Sweden, Ottoman Empire	Russia, Poland, Denmark, Saxony, Prussia	1	0	1	0	Primarily a contest between Charles XII of Sweden and Peter the Great. Swedish efforts to punish rebellious Baltic states led to war with Russia. Swedish victory at Narva not enough for Charles, continues into Russia and decisively defeated at Poltava in 1709. End of Swedish power in the Baltic. Russia gains Baltic port and becomes great power. Great power attacks weak powers and rising power.	Revenge	Initiator loses

												Standing	Initiator loses
19	War of Spanish Succession	1701	1714	Austria (Holy Roman Empire), Great Britain, Netherlands, Prussia, Portugal, Denmark, Norway	France, Spain	0	2	1	1	0	Louis XIV proclaimed his son king of England, Scotland and Ireland when ex-king James II died in 1701. In Spain, Louis rejected a compromise succession and attempted to incorporate Spain and the Spanish Netherlands in the French ambit. England, Dutch and Habsburgs declared war on France. Allied victories led to peace of Utrecht–Rastatt. Louis gained recognition of Philip V as king of Spain, but could not ascend to French throne. Habsburgs became major force in Europe, Great Britain became the major power in the western Mediterranean. Dominant power attacks declining power. Miscalculated escalation.	Standing	Initiator loses
20	War of the Quadruple Alliance	1718	1720	Austria (Holy Roman Empire), France, Great Britain, Netherlands, Savoy	Spain	0	0	0	1	0	Spain invades Sicily in attempt to regain authority in Italy, opposed by France and its allies. Declining power attacks weak power.	Standing	Initiator loses
21	Anglo-Spanish War	1727	1729	England, France	Spain	0	0	0	1	0	Failed Spanish attempt to recapture Gibraltar. Declining power attacks great power.	Standing	Initiator loses

Name of war	Start	End	Initiator(s)	Other combatant(s)	Initiator: dominant power	Initiator: Great Power	Initiator: rising power	Initiator: declining power	Initiator: weak power	Explanation	Motive	Outcome
22 War of Polish Succession	1733	1738	France, Spain	Poland, Russia, Austria	1	0	0	1	0	Effort by France to use Polish succession struggle to expand in Italy at Habsburg expense. Dominant power attacks weak power.	Standing	Initiator wins
23 Austro-Russian-Turkish War	1735	1739	Russia, Austria	Ottoman Empire	0	2	0	0	0	Russia attacks Ottomans in Crimea. Great power attacks declining power.	Standing	Initiator wins
24 War of the Austrian Succession	1740	1748	France, Prussia, Bavaria, Naples, Sicily, Sweden, Spain	Austria, Great Britain, Russia, Dutch Republic, Saxony, Kingdom of Sardinia, Hanover	1	0	1	1	0	Began as Prussian assault on Habsburgs to gain Silesia, and soon involved most European powers. Fought in Italy, Germany, Low Countries. Spread internationally; British–Spanish component known as War of Jenkins Ear. Also, Franco-British component fought at sea and in India and North America. Rising power attacks great power. Dominant power attacks great power.	Standing, Interest	Initiator (Prussia) wins, Initiator (France) draws

#	War	Start	End									Description		
25	Russo Swedish War	1741	1743	Russia	Sweden	0	0	0	1	0		War of the Hats. Sweden attacks Russia to regain territory but loses ports in Finland. Declining power attacks great power.	Revenge	Initiator loses
26	Seven Years War	1756	1763	Prussia, Great Britain, Electorate of Brunswick-Lüneburg (Hanover), Iroquois Confederacy, Portugal	Austria, France, Russia, Sweden, Saxony, Spain, Naples and Sicily, Sardinia-Piedmont	1	1	1	0	0	Prussia, allied with Great Britain, attacked Austria, who was supported by France, Russia, Sweden and Saxony. Southwest Germany, the Low Countries and Italy were the battle-ground for the armies of France and Austria. The Anglo-French component of the war was fought in India and North America as well. France lost its hegemony and position in North America. Great Britain became the world's leading naval power. Dominant power and allies attack a great power.	Standing	Initiator (Great Britain) wins, Initiator (Prussia) draws
27	Confederation of the Bar	1768	1772	Russia	Polish–Lithuanian Commonwealth	0	0	0	1	0	Attempt by Polish nobles to gain territory from Russia. Ended in defeat in exile. Declining power attacks great power.	Revenge	Initiator loses
28	Russo-Turkish War III	1768	1774	Russia	Ottoman Empire, Polish nobles	0	0	0	1	0	Sultan declares war on Russia and is defeated and faces rebellions. Russia gains port on the Black Sea. Declining power attacks great power.	Revenge	Initiator loses

	Name of war	Start	End	Initiator(s)	Other combatant(s)	Initiator: dominant power	Initiator: Great Power	Initiator: rising power	Initiator: declining power	Initiator: weak power	Explanation	Motive	Outcome
29	War of the American Revolution	1778	1784	Great Britain	France, Spain, Dutch Republic, US	1	0	0	0	0	France comes to aid of American colonies. Great Britain forced to recognize US independence. Dominant power attacks great power.	Standing, Revenge	Initiator wins
30	War of the Bavarian Succession	1778	1779	Austria	Prussia, Saxony	0	1	0	0	0	Frederick's last war, to prevent Austria from expanding its power in Germany. Austria checked, Saxony gains. Great power attacks great power.	Standing	Initiator wins
31	Russo–Turkish War IV	1787	1792	Russia, Austria	Ottoman Empire	0	1	0	0	0	Another futile attempt by the Ottomans to regain land from Russia. Declining power attacks great power.	Revenge	Initiator loses
32	Russo–Swedish War I	1788	1790	Russia, Denmark	Sweden	0	1	0	0	0	Swedish attempt to regain territory. Insignificant war with insignificant result. Declining power attacks weak power. Great power then attacks declining power.	Revenge	Initiator loses

No.	War	Start	End	Initiator	Other participants						Description	Motivation	Outcome
33	War of the First Coalition	1792	1797	France	Austria, Prussia, Great Britain, Spain, Portugal, Sardinia, Naples and Sicily, Ottoman Empire, Dutch Republic	0	1	0	0	0	Prussia was actively seeking war against France, while Austria hoped to preserve the peace. The French National Assembly, expecting to be attacked and convinced that a thrust east would bring revolution to Prussia and Austria, initiated a preemptive war.	Security	Initiator wins, although not in the Clausewitzian sense of achieving its war aims
34	Egyptian Campaign	1798	1801	France	Great Britain		1	0	0	0	Great Britain remained at war with France. Great Britain supported rebels on the Iberian Peninsula and waged a naval war in the Mediterranean and Atlantic. Great power attacks dominant power.	Standing	Initiator wins
35	War of the Second Coalition	1798	1802	France, Spain, Denmark-Norway	Austria, Great Britain, Russia, Portugal, Naples and Sicily, Ottoman Empire		1	0	1	0	Another attempt to eliminate revolutionary France. Napoleon won major victories against Austria. Great powers attack dominant power.	Security	Initiators lose
36	Napoleonic Wars	1803	1812	France	Austria, Great Britain, Russia, Prussia, Spain, Portugal, Sicily, Sardinia, Sweden,		1	1	0	0	Two-step continuation of earlier conflict. France invades Russia and is in turn attacked by a large coalition of weak and great powers when it retreats.	Standing, Security	Initiator (France) loses, Initiator (coalition) wins

Name of war	Start	End	Initiator(s)	Other combatant(s)	Initiator: dominant power	Initiator: Great Power	Initiator: rising power	Initiator: declining power	Initiator: weak power	Explanation	Motive	Outcome
				Hanover, United Netherlands								
37 Napoleonic Wars	1812	1812	France, Prussia (under compulsion)	Russia	1	0	0	0	0	France and allies invade Russia.	Standing	Initiator (France) loses
38 War of the Sixth Coalition	1812	1814	Austria, Great Britain, Russia, Prussia, Spain, Portugal, Sicily, Sardinia, Sweden, Hanover, United Netherlands	France	0	1	1	1	0	France is attacked by a coalition of powers upon its retreat from Russia.	Security	Initiators win

#	War	Start	End	Initiator	Target					Description	Motivation	Outcome
39	War of the Seventh Coalition	1815	1815	France	All the major powers above	1	0	0	0	The Concert of Europe declares Napoleon an outlaw and endorses military action against him. Napoleon invades Belgium in a bid to reestablish French power and solidify his rule.	Security, Standing	Initiator loses
40	Russo–Persian War	1801	1813	Russia	Persia	0	1	0	0	Russia and Persia clash over border territories. Great power attacks weak power.	Standing	Initiator loses
41	Russo–Turkish War V	1806	1812	Russia	Ottoman Empire	0	1	0	0	Egged on by France, Ottomans seek revenge and end up losing Bessarabia. Declining power attacks great power.	Revenge	Initiator loses
42	Russo Swedish War II (Finnish War)	1808	1809	Russia	Sweden	0	1	0	0	Sweden provides pretext for Russia to invade and annex Finland. Great power attacks declining power.	Standing	Initiator wins
43	War of 1812	1812	1814	US	Great Britain	0	1	0	0	British naval activities provoke American reaction. Leads to an inconclusive war. Great power attacks weak power.	Security	Draw
44	Franco-Spanish	1823	1823	Spain	France	1	0	0	0	Congress of Verona authorizes France to invade Spain to restore dynasty with Great Britain in opposition. Dominant power attacks declining power.	Security	Initiator wins

Name of war	Start	End	Initiator(s)	Other combatant(s)	Initiator: dominant power	Initiator: Great Power	Initiator: rising power	Initiator: declining power	Initiator: weak power	Explanation	Motive	Outcome
45 Russo-Turkish	1828	1829	Russia	Turkey	0	1	0	0	0	Offshoot of Greek war of independence. Russia invaded Balkans and gained Black Sea coast to mouth of Danube plus Armenia and Georgia. Great power attacks declining power.	Standing	Initiator wins
46 Mexican-American	1846	1848	US	Mexico	0	0	1	0	0	US colonial expansion at Mexico's expense. Rising power attacks weak power.	Standing	Initiator wins
47 Austro-Sardinian	1848	1848	Austria-Hungary	Sardinia-Piedmont	0	0	1	0	0	Italian rebellion against Austria supported by Sardinia. Rising power attacks great power.	Standing	Initiator wins
48 First Schleswig-Holstein	1848	1848	Prussia	Denmark	0	1	0	0	0	Prussia attacks Denmark. Great power attacks weak power.	Standing	Draw
49 Roman Republic (First War of Italian Independence)	1849	1849	Austria-Hungary	Sardinia-Piedmont, Sicily	0	0	1	0	0	War against Austria for Italian territory. Rising power attacks great power.	Standing	Initiator wins

#	War			Initiator(s)	Target						Description		
50	Crimean	1853	1856	France, Great Britain, Sardinia, Ottoman Empire	Russia	0	1	0	1	0	Coalition of powers to limit Russian penetration into Balkans. Great powers and declining power attack great power. Miscalculated escalation.	Standing	Initiator loses
51	Anglo-Persian	1856	1857	Persia	Great Britain	0	0	0	0	1	Persia makes unsuccessful bid for Herat in Afghanistan. Weak power attacks weak power, which leads to war with great power. Miscalculated escalation.	Other	Initiator loses
52	Italian Unification (Second War of Italian Independence)	1859	1861	France, Sardinia	Austria	0	1	1	0	0	France assists Sardinia in attempt to expel Austria from Italy. Rising and great power attack great power.	Standing	Initiators win
53	Franco-Mexican	1862	1867	France	Mexico	1	0	0	0	0	Unsuccessful colonial bid by Louis Napoleon. Dominant attacks weak power.	Standing	Initiator loses
54	Second Schleswig-Holstein (Danish War)	1864	1864	Prussia, Austria	Denmark	0	1	0	0	0	Prussia and Austria take Schleswig-Holstein from Denmark. Great powers attack weak power.	Standing, Other	Initiators win
55	Austrian-Prussian (Seven Weeks)	1866	1866	Prussia	Austria	0	1	0	1	0	Prussia gains primacy in Germany (*Kleindeutsch* solution). Great power attacks great power.	Standing	Initiator wins

Name of war	Start	End	Initiator(s)	Other combatant(s)	Initiator: dominant Great power	Initiator: Great Power	Initiator: rising power	Initiator: declining power	Initiator: weak power	Explanation	Motive	Outcome
56 Franco-Prussian	1870	1871	Prussia, German states	France	1	0	0	0	0	Prussia unifies Germany through defeat of France. Dominant power attacks great power.	Standing	Initiator loses
57 Russo-Turkish	1877	1878	Russia, Balkan states	Ottoman Empire	0	1	0	0	0	Russia attacks Ottoman Empire. Advance on Constantinople halted by British threat. Great power attacks declining power.	Standing	Initiator wins
58 Anglo-Egyptian	1882	1882	Great Britain, France	Ottoman Empire	0	1	0	0	0	Great Britain and France establish a condominium over Egypt. Great powers attack declining power.	Interest	Initiators win
59 Sino-French	1884	1901	France	China	0	1	0	0	0	Colonial aggrandizement. Great power attacks weak power.	Standing	Initiator wins
60 Franco-Thai	1893	1893	France	Thailand	0	1	0	0	0	Colonial aggrandizement. Great power attacks weak power.	Standing	Initiator wins
61 Sino-Japanese	1894	1895	Japan	China	0	0	1	0	0	Colonial aggrandizement. Great power attacks weak power.	Standing	Initiator wins
62 Spanish-American	1898	1901	US	Spain	0	0	1	0	0	US attack on Cuba, Puerto Rico, Philippines. Rising power attacks declining power.	Security, Standing	Initiator wins
63 Boxer Rebellion	1900	1900	European powers	China	0	1	0	0	0	Occupation of Chinese cities following anti-colonial uprising. Great powers attack weak power.	Standing	Initiators win

#	War			Initiators	Targets				Description		Outcome
64	Sino-Russian	1900	1900	Russia	China	0	1	0 0 0	Colonial aggrandizement of China. Rising power attacks declining power.	Standing	Initiator wins
65	Russo-Japanese	1904	1905	Russia	Japan	0	1	0 0 0	Dispute over Korea. Great power provokes rising power into attacking.	Standing	Initiator wins
66	Italo-Turkish	1911	1912	Italy	Ottoman Empire	0	0	1 0 0	Italian invasion of Tripoli triggers wider war. Rising power attacks declining power.	Standing	Initiator wins
67	First Balkan	1912	1913	Serbia, Bulgaria, Greece, Romania	Ottoman Empire	0	0	0 0 1	Albania becomes independent. Ottomans lose most remaining European territory. Weak powers attack declining power.	Other	Initiators win
68	World War I	1914	1914	Germany, Austria-Hungary, Ottoman Empire, Bulgaria	UK, France, Russia, Italy, Japan	1	1	1 0 0	Austrian declaration of war against Serbia leads to continental war. Great power backed by dominant power attacks weak power. Miscalculated escalation as intended local war in the Balkans turns into continental then world war.	Standing, Security	Initiators lose
69	World War I	1917	1917	Germany	US	1	0	0 0 0	Great power attacks great power.	Security	Initiator loses
70	Russo-Polish	1919	1920	Poland	Soviet Union	0	0	0 0 0	Polish attempt to reestablish eastern frontier of 1772.	Standing, Revenge	Initiator loses
71	Franco-Turkish	1919	1921	UK, France	Turkey	0	1	1 0 0	French occupation of Turkish territory ending in withdrawal. Great powers attacks weak power.	Standing	Initiator loses

Name of war	Start	End	Initiator(s)	Other combatant(s)	Initiator: dominant power	Initiator: Great Power	Initiator: rising power	Initiator: declining power	Initiator: weak power	Explanation	Motive	Outcome
72 Sino-Soviet	1929	1929	Soviet Union	China	0	0	1	0	0	Dispute over Manchurian railway. Rising power attacks weak power.	Interest	Initiator wins
73 Manchurian	1931	1933	Japan	China	0	1	0	0	0	Colonial aggression. Great power attacks weak power.	Standing	Initiator wins
74 Italo-Ethiopian	1935	1936	Italy	Ethiopia	0	0	1	0	0	Colonial aggression. Rising power attacks weak power.	Standing	Initiator wins
75 Sino-Japanese	1937	1945	Japan	China	0	1	0	0	0	Japanese invasion of China. Great power attacks weak power.	Standing	Initiator loses
76 Changkufeng	1938	1938	Japan	Soviet Union	0	1	0	0	0	Unsuccessful Japanese incursion into Mongolia. Great power attacks great power.	Other	Initiator loses
77 Nomonhan	1939	1939	Soviet Union	Japan in Mongolia	0	0	1	0	0	Soviet Union humbles Kwantung Army to protect Asian flank. Rising power attacks great power.	Security	Initiator wins
78 World War II (Europe)	1939	1939–41	Germany, Italy, Hungary	Most of Europe, Asia and the US	0	1	0	0	0	Germany and allies attempt to conquer Europe and North Africa. Great power attacks weak and great powers. Rising power attacks great power.	Other	Initiators lose

79	World War II (Pacific)	1941	1941	Japan	US, UK, France, Netherlands, Australia, Soviet Union	0	1	0	0	Japan attacks US and European colonial powers in Asia. Great power attacks great and weak powers.	Security, Standing	Initiator loses
80	Russo-Finnish	1939	1940	Soviet Union	Finland	0	0	1	0	Soviet Union attacks Finland to improve its position in expectation of war with Germany. Great power attacks weak power.	Security	Initiator wins
81	Franco-Thai	1940	1941	Thailand	France	0	0	0	1	Thais attempt to regain territory lost to France. Weak power attacks great power.	Revenge	Initiator wins
82	Korean	1950	1950	US plus coalition	North Korea	1	0	0	0	US intervenes to protect invaded client state. Dominant power attacks weak power.	Security	Draw
83	Korean	1950	1950	China	US and coalition	0	0	1	0	China attacks US forces in North Korea, forces retreat and ultimately fights a costly war of attrition.	Security	Draw
84	Russo-Hungarian	1956	1956	Soviet Union	Hungary	0	1	0	0	Intra-bloc intervention to prevent regime change. Great power attacks weak power.	Security	Initiators win
85	Sinai	1956	1956	Israel, UK, France	Egypt	0	1	0	0	UK and France attack Egypt. (As does Israel, but neither Egypt nor Israel is a great power, so this component is not included in the data set.)	Standing	Initiators lose (forced to withdraw)

Name of war	Start	End	Initiator(s)	Other combatant(s)	Initiator: dominant Great Power	Initiator: rising power	Initiator: declining power	Initiator: weak power	Explanation	Motive	Outcome
86 Vietnamese	1965	1973	US	North Vietnam, Viet Cong	1	0	0	0	US forces combat Viet Cong and North Vietnamese in South Vietnam and bombs North Vietnam. Dominant power attacks weak power.	Standing, Security	Initiator loses
87 Soviet-Afghan	1979	1980	Soviet Union	Afghanistan	1	0	0	0	Soviet Union invades Afghanistan. Great power attacks weak power.	Standing, Security	Initiator loses
88 Sino-Vietnamese	1979	1979	China	Vietnam	0	1	0	0	China attempts unsuccessfully to humble Vietnam. Rising power attacks weak power.	Standing	Initiator loses
89 Falklands/Malvinas	1982	1982	Argentina	UK	0	0	0	1	Argentina invades Falklands/Malvinas. Weak power attacks great power.	Standing	Initiator loses
90 Sino-Vietnamese	1987	1987	China	Vietnam	0	1	0	0	China conducts unsuccessful punitive invasion of Vietnam. Rising power attacks weak power.	Standing	Initiator loses
91 Gulf War	1990	1991	US plus coalition	Iraq	1	0	0	0	US and coalition defeat Iraq, compelling withdrawal from Kuwait. Dominant power attacks weak power.	Security, Interest	Initiator wins
92 US-Afghanistan (Taliban)	2001	2003	US	Afghanistan	1	0	0	0	US invades in support of local insurgents and overthrows Taliban. Dominant power attacks weak power.	Other, security	Ongoing

#	War	Start	End	Initiators	Target						Description	Standing	Outcome
93	Anglo-American invasion of Iraq	2003	2003	US, UK	Iraq	1	1	0	0	0	US invades and occupies Iraq and overthrows Saddam Hussein. Dominant and great power attack weak power.	Standing	Ongoing
94	Russian invasion of South Ossetia	2008	2008	Russia	Georgia	0	1	0	0	0	Russia "liberates" South Ossetia from Georgia.	Standing	Initiator wins
SUM 1648–2003 (94 total wars)				Sum of initiators	118	24	49	27	14	4			Is win 46
SUM 1648–1713				Sum	65	5	47	9	3	1			Is lose 40
SUM 1714–1815				Sum	35	9	13	4	9	0			Is draw 6
SUM 1816–1945				Sum	41	5	20	11	2	3			Ongoing 2
SUM 1946–2003				Sum	13	5	4	3	0	1			

BIBLIOGRAPHY

Accordino, John, *Captives of the Cold War Economy* (New York: Greenwood Publishing Group, 2000).

Adler, Emanuel and Michael Barnett, eds., *Security Communities* (Cambridge: Cambridge University Press, 1998).

Afflerbach, Holger, *Falkenhayn. Politisches Denken und Handeln in Kaiserreich* (Munich: Oldenbourg, 1994).

Agnew, Jean-Cristophe, *Worlds Apart: The Market and the Theater in Anglo-American Thought, 1550–1750* (Cambridge: Cambridge University Press, 1986).

Akira, Fujiwara, "The Role of the Japanese Army," in Dorothy Borg and Shumpei Okamoto, eds., *Pearl Harbor as History* (New York: Columbia University Press, 1973), pp. 189–196.

Al-Sayyid-Marsot, Alaf, "The British Occupation of Egypt from 1882," in Andrew Porter, ed., *The Oxford History of the British Empire: The Nineteenth Century* (Oxford: Oxford University Press, 1999), pp. 651–664.

Albertini, Luigi, *The Origins of the War of 1914*, trans. Isabella M. Massey, 3 vols. (Oxford: Oxford University Press, 1952–1957).

Albrecht-Carrié, René, *A Diplomatic History of Europe Since the Congress of Vienna* (New York: Harper & Row, 1958).

Anderson, M. S., *War and Society in Europe of the Old Regime* (London: Fontana Books, 1988).

The War of the Austrian Succession, 1740–1748 (London: Longman, 1995).

Angell, Norman, *The Great Illusion: A Study of the Relation of Military to National Advantage* (London: Heinemann, 1910).

Aquarone, Alberto, "Public Opinion in Italy Before the Outbreak of World War II," in Roland Sarti, ed., *The Ax Within. Italian Fascism in Action* (New York: New Viewpoints, 1974).

Archer, Toby, "'WMD' Terrorism: How Scared Should We Be?," Finnish Institution of International Affairs, UPI Briefing Paper 2, May 31, 2005.

Aristotle, *Metaphysics, Nicomachean Ethics, Physics, Poetics, Politics* and *Rhetoric*, in *The Complete Works of Aristotle: The Revised Oxford Translation*, ed. Jonathan Barnes (Oxford: Oxford University Press, 1984).

Aron, Raymond, *The Century of Total War* (Boston: Beacon, 1955).

   Peace and War: A Theory of International Relations (Garden City, NY: Doubleday, 1966).

Art, Robert J., "The United States and the Rise of China," in Robert S. Ross and Zhu Feng, eds., *China's Ascent: Power, Security, and the Future of International Politics* (Ithaca, NY: Cornell University Press, 2008), pp. 260–290.

Ashworth, Lucian M., "Did the Realist–Idealist Great Debate Ever Happen? A Revisionist History of International Relations," *International Relations* 16 (April 2002), pp. 33–52.

Augustine, *The City of God*, trans. Marcus Dods (New York: Modern Library, 1950).

Aydinli, Ersel and James N. Rosenau, eds., *Globalization, Security, and the Nation-State: Paradigms in Transition* (Albany, NY: State University of New York Press, 2005).

Bales, Kevin, *Disposable People: New Slavery in the Global Economy*, rev. edn. (Berkeley, CA: University of California Press 2004).

   ed., *Understanding Global Slavery Today: A Reader* (Berkeley, CA: University of California Press, 2005).

Ball, Desmond, "The Development of the SIOP, 1960–1983," in Desmond Ball and Jeffrey Richelson, eds., *Strategic Nuclear Targeting* (Ithaca, NY: Cornell University Press, 1986), pp. 57–83.

Ball, Desmond and Jeffrey Richelson, eds., *Strategic Nuclear Targeting* (Ithaca, NY: Cornell University Press, 1986).

Bartov, Omar, *The Eastern Front, 1941–45: German Troops and the Barbarization of Warfare* (New York: St. Martin's, 1985).

Bateman, Sam and Clive Schofield, *Outer Shelf Claims in the South China Sea: New Dimension to Old Disputes*, RSIS, Nanyang Technological University, July 1, 2009.

Baum, Tomas, "A Question for Inspiration in the Liberal Peace Paradigm: Back to Bentham?," *European Journal of International Relations*, 14, no. 3 (September 2008), pp. 431–453.

Bell, P. M. H., *The Origins of the Second World War in Europe* (London: Longman, 1986).

Bem, Daryl J., "Self-Perception Theory," in L. Berkowitz, ed., *Advances in Experimental Social Psychology* (New York: Academic Press, 1972), vol. 6, pp. 1–62.

Bentham, Jeremy, "A Plan for an Universal and Perpetual Peace," www.laits.utexas.edu/poltheory/bentham/pil/pil.e04.html.

Berger, Gordon, *Parties Out of Power in Japan, 1931–1941* (Princeton, NJ: Princeton University Press, 1977).

Berger, Peter, *The Capitalism Revolution: Fifty Propositions about Prosperity, Equality, and Liberty* (New York: Basic Books, 1986).

Best, Geoffrey, *Humanity in Warfare* (New York: Columbia University Press, 1980).

Betts, Richard K., "Systems for Peace or Causes of War? Collective Security, Arms Control and the New Europe," *International Security*, 17, no. 1 (Summer 1992), pp. 5–43.

Black, Anita, *Quotations in Black* (Westport, CT: Greenwood, 1981).

Black, Jeremy, *A Military Revolution? Military Change and European Society 1550–1800* (Basingstoke: Macmillan, 1991).

    European Warfare, 1660–1815 (New Haven, CT: Yale University Press, 1994).

    Why Wars Happen (New York: New York University Press, 1998).

    From Louis XIV to Napoleon: The Fate of a Great Power (London: Taylor & Francis, 1999).

    European International Relations, 1648–1815 (London: Palgrave, 2002).

Blainey, Geoffrey, *The Causes of War*, 3rd edn. (New York: Free Press, 1988).

Blair, Bruce G., *The Logic of Accidental Nuclear War* (Washington, DC: Brookings Institution, 1983).

Blanning, T. C. W., *The French Revolutionary Wars, 1787–1801: Occupation and Resistance in the Rhineland, 1992–1802* (New York: Oxford University Press, 1983).

    The Origins of the French Revolutionary Wars (London: Longmans, 1986).

    The Pursuit of Glory: Europe 1648–1815 (London: Penguin, 2007).

Bluche, François, *Louis XIV* (Oxford: Blackwell, 1990).

Boemeke, Manfred F., Gerald D. Feldman and Elisabeth Glaser, eds., *Treaty of Versailles: A Reassessment After 75 Years* (New York: Cambridge University Press, 2006).

Boog, Horst, Gerhard Krebs and Detlef Vogel, *Germany and the Second World War: VII: The Strategic Air War in Europe and the War in the West and East Asia, 1943–1944/5*, trans. Francisca Garvie *et al.* (New York: Oxford University Press, 2006).

Booth, Kenneth and Nicholas Wheeler, *The Security Dilemma* (New York: Palgrave, 2007).

Borzecki, Jerzy, *The Soviet-Polish Peace of 1921 and the Creation of Interwar Europe* (New Haven, CT: Yale University Press, 2008).

Boswell, Terry and Mike Sweat, "Hegemony, Long Waves and Major Wars," *International Studies Quarterly*, 35 (1991), pp. 123–149.

Bosworth, R. J. B., *Mussolini* (London: Arnold, 2002).

Boulding, Kenneth, "Future Directions of Conflict and Peace Studies," *Journal of Conflict Resolution*, 22, no. 2 (1987), pp. 342–354.

Boyle, Chris, "The Mystery of Modern Wealth: Mercantilism, Value, and the Social Foundations of Liberal International Order," *European Journal of International Relations*, 14, no. 3 (September 2008), pp. 405–430.

Bracken, Paul, *The Command and Control of Nuclear Forces* (New Haven, CT: Yale University Press, 1983).

Bradsher, Henry S., *Afghan Communism and Soviet Intervention* (Oxford: Oxford University Press, 1999).

Breslauer, George and Richard Ned Lebow, "Leadership and the End of the Cold War: A Counterfactual Thought Experiment," in Richard K. Herrmann and Richard Ned Lebow, eds., *Ending the Cold War* (New York: Palgrave, 2004), pp. 161–188.

Brewer, Anthony, *Marxist Theories of Imperialism: A Critical Survey* (London: Routledge and Kegan Paul, 1980).

Brodie, Bernard, *The Absolute Weapon* (New York: Harcourt, 1946).

Brooks, Stephen G., *Producing Security: Multinational Corporations, Globalization, and the Changing Calculus of Conflict* (Princeton, NJ: Princeton University Press, 2005).

Brooks, Stephen G. and William C. Wohlforth, "Hard Times for Soft Balancing," *International Security* 30 (Summer 2005), pp. 72–108.

World Out of Balance: International Relations and the Challenge of American Primacy (Princeton, NJ: Princeton University Press, 2008).

Brown, Anthony Cave, ed., *DROPSHOT: The American Plan for World War III against Russia in 1957* (New York: Dial Press, 1978).

Brown, Archie, *The Gorbachev Factor* (Oxford: Oxford University Press, 1996).

Brown, Roger Glenn, *Fashoda Reconsidered: The Impact of Domestic Politics on French Policy in Africa, 1893–1898* (Baltimore, MD: Johns Hopkins University Press, 1970).

Bueno de Mesquita, Bruce, *The War Trap* (New Haven, CT: Yale University Press, 1981).

"The War Trap Revisited: A Revised Expectation Utility Model," *American Political Science Review*, 77 (1985), pp. 157–176.

Bueno de Mesquita, Bruce and David Lalman, "Reason and War," *American Political Science Review*, 80 (1986), pp. 1113–1130.

Bukovansky, Mlada, *Legitimacy and Power Politics: The American and French Revolutions in International Political Culture* (Princeton, NJ: Princeton University Press, 2002).

Bull, Hedley, *The Anarchical Society* (New York: Columbia University Press, 1977).

Bullock, Alan, *Hitler: A Study in Tyranny*, rev. edn. (New York: Harper & Row, 1962).

Bundy, McGeorge, *Danger and Survival: Choices About the Bomb in the First Fifty Years* (New York: Random House, 1998).

Burnham, Peter, "Neo-Gramscian Hegemony and the International Order," *Capital and Class*, 54, no. 1 (1991), pp. 73–93.

Burr, William and Jeffrey T. Richelson, "Whether to 'Strangle the Baby in the Cradle': The United States and the Chinese Nuclear Program, 1960–1964," *International Security*, 25, no. 3 (Winter 2000/01), pp. 54–99.

Butler, Judith, *Excitable Speech: The Politics of the Performative* (New York: Routledge, 1997).

Butow, Robert J. C., *Japan's Decision to Surrender* (Stanford, CA: Stanford University Press, 1954).

  John Doe Associates: Backdoor Diplomacy for Peace (Stanford, CA: Stanford University Press, 1974).

Cairncross, A. K., *Home and Foreign Investment, 1870–1913* (Cambridge: Cambridge University Press, 1953).

Callinicos, Alex, *New Mandarins of American Power: The Bush Administration's Plans for the World* (London: Polity, 2003).

Carley, Michael J., "The Politics of Anti-Bolshevism: The French Government and the Russo-Polish War, December 1919 to May 1920," *Historical Journal*, 19 (1976), pp. 163–189.

Carr, E. H., *The Twenty Years Crisis, 1919–1939: An Introduction to the Study of International Relations* (London: Macmillan, 1939).

  Conditions of Peace (London: Macmillan, 1942).

Casey, Steven, *Selling the Korean War: Propaganda, Politics and Public Opinion, 1950–1953* (New York: Oxford University Press, 2008).

Ceadel, Martin, *The Origins of War Prevention: The British Peace Movements and International Relations, 1730–1854* (Oxford: Oxford University Press, 1996).

Chan, Steve, *China, the US, and the Power-Transition Theory: A Critique* (New York: Routledge, 2008).

Chandler, David, *The Art of Warfare in the Age of Marlborough* (London: Batsford, 1976).

Chang, Gordon H., *Friends and Enemies: The United States, China, and the Soviet Union, 1948–1972* (Stanford, CA: Stanford University Press, 1990).

Chen, Jian, *China's Road to the Korean War: The Making of the Sino-American Confrontation* (New York: Columbia University Press, 1994).

  Mao's China and the Cold War (Chapel Hill, NC: University of North Carolina Press, 2001).

Chomsky, Noam and David Barsamian, *Imperial Ambitions: Conversations in the Post-9/11 World* (New York: Metropolitan Books, 2005).

Christensen, Thomas J. and Jack L. Snyder, "Chain Gangs and Passed Bucks: Predicting Alliance Patterns in Multipolarity," *International Organization*, 44 (1990), pp. 137–68.

Chubin, Shahran and Charles Tripp, *Iran and Iraq at War* (Boulder, CO: Westview, 1998).

Churchill, Winston S., *Amid These Storms: Thoughts and Adventures* (New York: Scribner's, 1932).

Cirincione, Joseph, Jessica T. Mathews and George Perkovich, *WMD in Iraq: Evidence and Implications* (Washington, DC: Carnegie Endowment for International Peace, 2004).

Clark, Ian, *Legitimacy in International Society* (Oxford: Oxford University Press, 2005).
"How Hierarchical Can International Relations Be?," *International Relations*, 23, no. 3 (2009), pp. 464–480.

Clarke, I. F., *Voices Prophesying War, 1763–1914* (London: Oxford University Press, 1966).

Claude, Inis L., *Power and International Relations* (New York: Random House, 1962).

Clausewitz, Carl, *On War*, trans. M. Howard and P. Paret (Princeton, NJ: Princeton University Press, 1976).

Clodfelter, Michael, *Warfare and Armed Conflicts: A Statistical Encyclopedia of Causality, and Other Figures, 1994–2007* (Jefferson, NC: McFarland, 2008).

Coker, Christopher, *Waging War Without Warriors? The Changing Culture of Military Conflict* (New York: Lynne Rienner, 2002).
The Future of War: The Re-enchantment of War in the Twenty-First Century (London: Blackwell, 2004).

Cook, Chris and Whitney Walker, *The Facts on File World Political Almanac* (New York: Facts on File, 2001).

Coox, Alvin D., *Nomonhan: Japan against Russia*, 1939, 2 vols. (Stanford, CA: Stanford University Press, 1985).

Copeland, Dale C., *The Origins of Major Wars* (Ithaca, NY: Cornell University Press, 2000).

Cornil, Fernando, "Listening to the Subaltern: Postcolonial Studies and the Poetics of Neocolonial States," in Laura Chrisman and Benita Parry, eds., *Postcolonial Theory and Criticism* (Cambridge: D. S. Brewer, 2000), pp. 37–55.

Cortright, David, *Peace: A History of Movements and Ideas* (Cambridge: Cambridge University Press, 2008).

Cox, Robert, "Gramsci, Hegemony and International Relations: An Essay in Method," in Stephen Gill, ed., *Gramsci, Historical Materialism on International Relations* (Cambridge: Cambridge University Press, 1993), pp. 49–66.

Craven, Wesley Frank and Frank Lea Cate, *The Army Air Forces in World War Two* (Washington, DC: Office of Air Force History, 1983), vol. 5.

Crawley, Charles William (editor-in-chief) and John Patrick Tuer Bury (volume editor), *New Cambridge Modern History*, vol. 10: *The Zenith of European Power: 1830–1870* (Cambridge: Cambridge University Press, 1957).

Crowley, James B., *Japan's Quest for Autonomy: National Security and Foreign Policy, 1930–38* (Princeton, NJ: Princeton University Press, 1966).

Daalder, Ivo H. and James M. Lindsay, *America Unbound: The Bush Revolution in Foreign Policy*, rev. edn. (Hoboken, NJ: Wiley, 2005).

Dallin, Alexander, *German Rule in Russia 1941–1945: A Study in Occupation Policies* (London: Macmillan, 1957).

Daudin, Guillaume, Matthias Morys and Kevin H. O'Rourke, *Europe and Globalization, 1870–1914* (Paris: Observatoire Français des Conjonctures Economiques, 2008).

Davis, James and William C. Wohlforth, "German Unification," in Richard K. Herrmann and Richard Ned Lebow, eds., *Ending the Cold War* (New York: Palgrave, 2004), pp. 131–160.

Davis, L. E. and R. A. Huttenback, *Mammon and the Pursuit of Empire* (Cambridge: Cambridge University Press, 1987).

De Bruhl, Marshall, *Firestorm: Allied Air Power and the Destruction of Dresden* (New York: Random House, 2006).

De Soysa, Indra, John R. Oneal and Yong-Hee Park, "Testing Power-Transition Theory Using Alternate Measures of Material Capabilities," *Journal of Conflict Resolution* 41 (1997), pp. 1–30.

Deanne, Julius, "Waxing or Waning?," *Harvard International Review*, 26, no. 4 (Winter 2005), http://hir.harvard.edu/symposia/63/.

Debo, Richard K., *Survival and Consolidation: The Foreign Policy of Soviet Russia, 1918–1921* (Montreal: McGill-Queen's University Press, 1992).

Dechesne, M., J. Greenberg, J. Arndt and J. Schimel, "Terror Management and Sports: Fan Affiliation: The Effects of Mortality Salience on Fan Identification and Optimism," *European Journal of Social Psychology*, 30 (2000), pp. 813–835.

Dedijer, Vladimir, *The Road to Sarajevo* (New York: Simon & Schuster, 1966).

Deng, Yong, *China's Struggle for Status: The Realignment of International Relations* (Cambridge: Cambridge University Press, 2008).

Deutsch, Karl W., *Nationalism and Social Communication* (Boston: MIT Press, 1953).

Deutsch, Karl W. and J. David Singer, "Multipolar Systems and International Stability," *World Politics*, 16 (1964), pp. 390–406.

Deutsch, Karl W., Sidney A. Burrell and Robert A. Kann, *Political Community and the North Atlantic Area: International Organization in the Light of Historical Experience* (Princeton, NJ: Princeton University Press, 1957).

Diamond, Larry, "A Report Card on Democracy," *Hoover Digest*, no. 3 (2000), www.hoover.org/publications/digest/3491911.html.

Dickson, Peter George, *Finance and Government under Maria Theresa, 1740–1780* (Oxford: Oxford University Press, 1987).

Dixon, William J., "Democracy and the Peaceful Settlement of International Conflict," *American Political Science Review*, 88 (March 1994), pp. 1–17.

Dorpalen, Andreas, *Hindenburg and the Weimar Republic* (Princeton, NJ: Princeton University Press, 1964).

Dower, John, *War Without Mercy: Race and Power in the Pacific War* (New York: Pantheon, 1986).

    Embracing Defeat: Japan in the Wake of World War II (New York: Norton, 1999).

Downs, George, ed., *Collective Security Beyond the Cold War* (Ann Arbor, MI: University of Michigan Press, 1994).

Doyle, Michael, "Kant, Liberal Legacies, and Foreign Affairs, Part I," *Philosophy and Public Affairs*, 12 (Summer 1983), pp. 205–235. Part II, *ibid.*, pp. 323–353.

Empires (Ithaca, NY: Cornell University Press, 1986).

Drucker, Peter F., "The Global Economy and the Nation State," *Foreign Affairs*, 76 (1997), pp. 159–171.

Duffy, Christopher, *The Military Experience in the Age of Reason* (London: Routledge & Kegan Paul, 1987).

Dunn, John, *Democracy: A History* (Boston: Atlantic Monthly Press, 2006).

Durkheim, Emile, *The Division of Labor in Society*, trans. W. D. Halls (New York: Macmillan, 1984).

The Elementary Forms of the Religious Life, trans. Carol Cosman (Oxford: Oxford University Press, 2001).

Duus, Peter, "Japan's Informal Empire in China, 1895–1937: An Overview," in Peter Duus, Ramon H. Myers and Mark R. Peattie, *Japanese Informal Empire in Asia* (Princeton, NJ: Princeton University Press, 1989), pp. xi–xxix.

Eakin, Paul John, *How Our Lives Become Stories: Making Selves* (Ithaca, NY: Cornell University Press, 1999).

Edelstein, Michael, *Overseas Investments in the Age of High Imperialism: The United Kingdom, 1850–1924* (New York: Columbia University Press, 1982).

Einstein, Albert, *Einstein on Peace* (New York: Simon & Schuster, 1960).

Ekman, Paul, *Emotions Revealed: Recognizing Faces and Feelings to Improve Communication and Emotional Life* (New York: Henry Holt, 2003).

Eley, Geoff, *Reshaping the German Right: Radical Nationalism and Political Change After Bismarck* (New Haven, CT: Yale University Press, 1980).

Forging Democracy: The History of the Left in Europe, 1850–2000 (Oxford: Oxford University Press, 2002).

Elman, Colin and Miriam Fendius Elman, "Horses for Courses: Why Not Neorealist Theories of Foreign Policy?," *Security Studies*, 1, no. 6 (1996), pp. 7–53.

Elrod, Richard, "The Concert of Europe: A Fresh Look at an International System," *World Politics*, 28, no. 2 (January 1976), pp. 159–174.

Elster, Jon, *Solomonic Judgments: Studies in the Limits of Rationality* (Cambridge: Cambridge University Press, 1989).

Emerson, Ralph Waldo, "War," in *Miscellanies* (Cambridge: Riverside Press, 1904), pp. 150–176.

English, Robert D., *Russia and the Idea of the West: Gorbachev, Intellectuals, and the End of the Cold War* (New York: Columbia University Press, 2000).

"Power, Ideas, and New Evidence on the Cold War's End: A Reply to Brooks and Wohlforth," *International Security*, 26, no. 4 (2002), pp. 93–111.

Erskine, Toni and Richard Ned Lebow, eds., *Tragedy and International Relations* (London: Palgrave, 2010).

Evangelista, Matthew, *Unarmed Forces: The Transnational Movement to End the Cold War* (Ithaca, NY: Cornell University Press, 1999).

"Turning Points in Arms Control," in Richard K. Herrmann and Richard Ned Lebow, eds., *Ending the Cold War* (New York: Palgrave, 2004), pp. 83–106.

Fallows, James, "Blind into Baghdad," *Atlantic Monthly* (January/February 2004).

Farhang, Rajaee, *The Iran–Iraq War: The Politics of Aggression* (Gainesville, FL: University Press of Florida, 1997).

Farnham, Barbara, ed., *Avoiding Losses/Taking Risks: Prospect Theory and International Conflict* (Ann Arbor, MI: University of Michigan Press, 1995).

Farrar, Lancelot L., Jr., *The Short-War Illusion: German Policy, Strategy and Domestic Affairs, August–December 1914* (Santa Barbara, CA: ABC-Clio, 1973).

Fazal, Tanisha M., *State Death: The Politics and Geography of Conquest, Occupation, and Annexation* (Princeton, NJ: Princeton University Press, 2007).

Fearon, James D., "Domestic Political Audiences and the Escalation of International Disputes," *American Political Science Review*, 88, no. 3 (1994), pp. 577–592.

"Rationalist Explanations for War," *International Organization*, 49, no. 3 (1995), pp. 379–414.

Feaver, Peter D. and Christopher Gelpi, *Choosing Your Battles: American Civil–Military Relations and the Use of Force* (Princeton, NJ: Princeton University Press 2004).

Feis, Herbert, *Europe, the World's Banker, 1870–1914* (New Haven, CT: Yale University Press, 1930).

Fellner, Fritz, "Austria-Hungary," in Keith Wilson, ed., *Decisions for War, 1914* (New York: St. Martin's Press, 1995), pp. 9–25.

Ferejohn, John and Frances McCall Rosenbluth, "Warlike Democracies," *Journal of Conflict Resolution*, 52, no. 1 (2008), pp. 3–38.

Ferguson, Adam, *An Essay on the History of Civil Society*, 2nd edn. (Edinburgh: A. Kincaid and J. Bell, 1768).

Ferrell, Robert H., *Peace in Their Time: The Origins of the Kellogg–Briand Pact* (New Haven, CT: Yale University Press, 1952).

Fest, Joachim, *Hitler*, trans. Richard Winslow and Clara Winslow (New York: Harcourt, Brace, Jovanovich, 1974).

Finley, Moses I., *The World of Odysseus* (New York: Viking, 1978).

Fischer, Fritz, *Germany's Aims in the First World War* (New York: Norton, 1967).

War of Illusions: German Policies from 1911 to 1914, trans. Marian Jackson (New York: W. W. Norton, [1969] 1975).

Fisher, Louis, *Presidential War Power*, 2nd edn. (Lawrence, KS: University of Kansas Press, 2004).

Fitzgerald, T. K., *Metaphors of Identity* (Albany, NY: State University of New York Press, 1993).

Fogel, Joshua A., *The Nanjing Massacre in History and Historiography* (Berkeley, CA: University of California Press, 2000).

Fogel, Robert William, *The Escape from Hunger and Premature Death* (Cambridge: Cambridge University Press, 2004).

Foot, Rosemary, *The Wrong War: American Policy and the Dimensions of the Korean Conflict, 1950–1953* (Ithaca, NY: Cornell University Press, 1985).

Fravel, M. Taylor, "Regime Insecurity and International Cooperation: Explaining China's Compromises in Territorial Disputes," *International Security*, 30, no. 2 (2005), pp. 46–83.

Freeman, Mark A., "Liking Self and Social Structure: A Psychological Perspective on Sri Lanka," *Journal of Cross-Cultural Psychology*, 12 (1981), pp. 291–308.

Frei, Norbert, "People's Community and War: Hitler's Popular Support," in Hans Mommsen, ed., *The Third Reich Between Vision and Reality: New Perspectives on German History, 1918–1945* (Oxford: Berg, 2001), pp. 59–78.

Freud, Sigmund, *Civilization and Its Discontents*, trans. Joan Rivière (Garden City, NY: Doubleday, 1958).

Friedberg, Aaron L., "The Future of United States–China Relations: Is Conflict Inevitable?," *International Security*, 30, no. 2 (Fall 2005), pp. 7–45.

Frieden, Jeffrey, "International Investment and Colonial Control," *International Organization*, 48 (1994), pp. 558–593.

Friedman, Milton J., "The Methodology of Positive Economics," in Milton J. Friedman, *Essays in Positive Economics* (Chicago: University of Chicago Press, 1953), pp. 3–43.

Friedman, Thomas L., *The Lexus and the Olive Tree*, rev. edn. (New York: Farrar, Strauss and Giroux, 2000).

Frieser, Karl-Heinz and John T. Greenwood, *The Blitzkrieg Legend: The 1940 Campaign in the West* (Annapolis, MD: Naval Institute Press, 2005).

Frost, Mervyn, "Tragedy, Ethics and International Relations," *International Relations*, 17, no. 4 (December 2003), pp. 477–496.

Fussell, Paul, *The Great War and Modern Memory* (New York: Oxford University Press, 1975).

Galbraith, Peter W., *The End of Iraq: How American Incompetence Created a War Without End* (New York: Simon & Schuster, 2006).

Galtung, Johann, *Peace by Peaceful Means: Peace and Conflict, Development and Civilisation* (Oslo: Peace Research Institute, 1996).

Garthoff, Raymond L., *Reflections on the Cuban Missile Crisis*, 2nd edn. (Washington, DC: Brookings Institution, 1989).

   Détente and Confrontation: American–Soviet Relations from Nixon to Reagan, rev. edn. (Washington, DC: Brookings Institution, 1994).

   The Great Transformation: American–Soviet Relations and the End of the Cold War (Washington, DC: Brookings Institution, 1994).

Gartzke, Erik, "The Capitalist Peace," *American Journal of Political Science*, 51 (January 2007), pp. 166–191.

Gause, Gregory F., *Iraq and the Gulf War: Decision-Making in Baghdad* (New York: Columbia University Press, 2001).

Geiss, Imanuel, *German Foreign Policy, 1871–1914* (London: Kegan Paul, 1976).

Gelb, Leslie with Richard K. Betts, *The Irony of Vietnam: The System Worked* (Washington, DC: Brookings Institution, 1978).

Geller, Daniel S., "Explaining War: Empirical Patterns and Theoretical Mechanisms," in Manus Midlarsky, ed., *Handbook of War Studies, II* (Ann Arbor, MI: University of Michigan Press, 2001), pp. 407–479.

Gelpi, Christopher, Peter Feaver and Jason Reifler, *Paying the Human Costs of War* (Princeton, NJ: Princeton University Press, 2009).

George, Alexander L., *Managing US–Soviet Rivalry: Problems of Crisis Prevention* (Boulder, CO: Westview, 1983).

George, Alexander L., Philip J. Farley and Alexander Dallin, *US–Soviet Security Cooperation: Achievements, Failures, Lessons* (New York: Oxford University Press, 1988).

Gergen, Kenneth J., *An Invitation to Social Construction* (London: Sage, 1999).

Germain, Randall D. and Michael Kenny, "Engaging Gramsci: International Relations Theory and the New Gramscians," *Review of International Studies*, 24, no. 1 (1998), pp. 3–21.

Gill, Stephen, *Gramsci, Historical Materialism on International Relations* (Cambridge: Cambridge University Press, 1993), pp. 49–66.

Gill, S. and D. Law, "Global Hegemony and the Structural Power of Capital," *Global Governance*, 33, no. 4 (2004), pp. 475–499.

Gilpin, Robert, *War and Change in International Relations* (Cambridge: Cambridge University Press, 1981).

Glantz, David M., *The Siege of Leningrad, 1941–44: 900 Days of Terror* (London: Collins, 2004).
  Colossus Reborn: The Red Army at War, 1941–1943 (Lawrence, KS: University of Kansas Press, 2005).

Glaser, Charles L., "Realists as Optimists: Cooperation as Self-Help," *International Security*, 19 (Winter 1994–1995), pp. 50–90.
  Theory of Rational International Politics (Princeton, NJ: Princeton University Press, 2009).

Glaser, Charles L. and Chaim Kaufmann, "What Is the Offense–Defense Balance?," *International Security*, 22 (Spring 1998), pp. 44–82.

Glaser, Charles L. and Stephen Walt, "International Relations: One World, Many Theories," *Foreign Policy*, 110 (Spring 1998), pp. 29–45.

Gleditsch, Kristian, "A Revised List of Wars Between and Within Independent States, 1816–2002," *International Interactions*, 30 (2004), pp. 232–262.

Gleick, P. H., "The Implications of Global Climate Changes for International Security," *Climate Change*, 15 (October 1989), pp. 303–325.

Gobarev, Victor M., "Soviet Policy Toward China: Developing Nuclear Weapons 1949–1969," *Journal of Slavic Military Studies*, 12, no. 4 (December 1999), pp. 37–39.

Gochman, Charles S., "Capability-Driven Disputes," in Charles S. Gochman and Allan Ned Sabrosky, eds., *Prisoners of War? Nation-States in the Modern Era* (Lexington, KY: Lexington Books, 1990).

Goebel, Stefan, *The Great War and Medieval Memory: War, Remembrance and Medievalism in Britain and Germany, 1914–1940* (Cambridge: Cambridge University Press, 2007).

Goldman, Emily O., *Sunken Treaties: Naval Arms Control between the Wars* (University Park, PA: Pennsylvania State University Press, 1994).

Goldstein, Avery, "Great Expectations: Interpreting China's Arrival," *International Security*, 23, no. 3 (Winter 1997/1998), pp. 36–73.

Rising to the Challenge: China's Grand Strategy and International Security (Stanford, CA: Stanford University Press, 2005).

"Power Transitions, Institutions, and China's Rise in East Asia: Theoretical Expectations and Evidence," *Journal of Strategic Studies*, 30, nos. 4–5 (2007), pp. 639–682.

Gongora, Thierry and Harald von Riekhoff, eds., *Toward a Revolution in Military Affairs? Defense and Security at the Dawn of the Twenty-First Century* (Westport, CT: Greenwood, 2000).

Gordon, Michael R., "Domestic Conflict and the Origins of the First World War: The British and German Cases," *Journal of Modern History*, 46 (June 1974), pp. 191–226.

Gordon, Michael R. and Bernard E. Trainor, *The General's War: The Inside Story of the Conflict in the Gulf* (Boston: Little, Brown, 1995).

Cobra II: The Inside Story of the Invasion and Occupation of Iraq (New York: Pantheon, 2006).

Gorst, Anthony and Lewis Johnman, *The Suez Crisis* (London: Routledge, 1997).

Gramsci, Antonio, *Selections from the Prison Notebooks of Antonio Gramsci*, ed. and trans. Quentin Hoare and G. Nowell Smith (London: Lawrence & Wishart, 1971).

Quaderni del Carcere, ed. V. Geratana, 4 vols. (Turin: Einaudi, 1975).

Scritti di economia politica (Rome: Bollati Boringhieri, 1994).

Green, Donald P. and Ian Shapiro, *Game Theory for Political Scientists: A Critique of Applications in Political Science* (New Haven, CT: Yale University Press, 1994).

Pathologies of Rational Choice Theory: A Critique of Applications in Political Science (New Haven, CT: Yale University Press, 1994).

Greenfeld, Liah, *Nationalism: Five Roads to Modernity* (Cambridge, MA: Harvard University Press, 1992).

Gries, Peter H., *China's New Nationalism: Pride, Politics and Diplomacy* (Berkeley, CA: University of California Press, 2004).

Grigg, David B., *Population Growth and Agrarian Change* (Cambridge: Cambridge University Press, 1980).

Gulick, Edward Vose, *Europe's Classical Balance of Power* (New York: W. W. Norton, 1955).

Guzzini, Stefano, "The Concept of Power: A Constructivist Analysis," *Millennium*, 33, no. 3 (2005), pp. 495–522.

Geopolitics Redux, forthcoming.

Haas, Ernest B., "The Balance of Power: Prescription, Concept, or Propaganda," *World Politics*, 5 (1953), pp. 442–477.

Habermas, Jürgen, *Knowledge and Human Interests*, trans. J. Shapiro (London: Polity Press, 1987 [1968]).

Theory and Practice, trans. John Viertel (Boston: Beacon, 1973).

Hall, Ray, *Europe's Population: Towards the Next Century* (New York: Routledge, 1995).

Hall, Rodney Bruce, *National Collective Identity: Social Constructs and International Systems* (New York: Columbia University Press, 1999).

Hamilton, Alexander, James Madison and John Jay, *The Federalist Papers* (Baltimore, MD: Johns Hopkins University Press, 1981).

Hamilton, Richard F. *Marxism, Revisionism, and Leninism: Explication, Assessment and Commentary* (Westport, CT: Praeger, 2000).

Hamilton, Richard F. and Holger H. Herwig, eds., *The Origins of World War I* (Cambridge: Cambridge University Press, 2003).

Harris, William V., *War and Imperialism in Ancient Rome, 327–70 BC* (Oxford: Oxford University Press, 1979).

Harvey, David, *The New Imperialism* (Oxford: Oxford University Press, 2003).

Harwell, Mark A., *Nuclear Winter: The Human and Environmental Consequences of Nuclear War* (New York: Springer-Verlag, 1984).

Haslam, Jonathan, *The Soviet Union and the Threat from the East, 1933–41: Moscow, Tokyo and the Prelude to the Pacific War* (Pittsburgh, PA: University of Pittsburgh Press, 1992).

Hassig, *Aztec Warfare: Imperial Expansion and Political Control* (Norman, OK: University of Oklahoma Press, 1988).

Hassrick, Royal B., *The Sioux* (Norman, OK: University of Oklahoma Press, 1964).

Hastings, Max, *Bomber Command* (New York: Dial Press, 1979).

Hatton, Ragnild M., *Charles XII of Sweden* (London: Weidenfeld & Nicolson, 1968).

Haushofer, Karl, *Geopolitik des Pazifischen Ozeans. Studien über die Wechselbeziehungen zwischen Geographie und Geschichte* (Berlin: Kurth Vowinckel, 1924).

Haushofer, Karl, Erich Obst, Hermann Lautensach and Otto Maull, *Bausteine zur Geopolitik* (Berlin: Kurt Vowinckel, 1928).

Hayes, Carlton J. H., *A Generation of Materialism, 1871–1900* (New York: Harper & Row, 1941).

Hayes, Peter, "Hobbes' Bourgeois Moderation," *Polity*, 31, no. 1 (Autumn 1998), pp. 53–74.

Hegel, G. W. F., *Hegel's Philosophy of Right*, trans. T. M. Knox (Oxford: Oxford University Press, 1969).

Phenomenology of Spirit, trans. A. V. Miller (Oxford: Clarendon Press, 1977).

Hellman, Christopher, "Highlights of the Fiscal Year 2008 Pentagon Spending Request," February 5, 2007, available at www.armscontrolcenter.org.

Henderson, Gregory, Richard Ned Lebow and John G. Stoessinger, eds., *Divided Nations in a Divided World* (New York: David Mckay, 1974).

Hensel, Paul R., "Territory: Theory and Evidence on Geography and Conflict," in John A. Vasquez, ed., *What Do We Know About War?* (Lanham, MD: Rowman & Littlefield, 2000), pp. 57–84.

Herrmann, Richard K., *Perceptions and Behavior in Soviet Foreign Policy* (Pittsburgh, PA: University of Pittsburgh Press, 1985).

Herrmann, Richard K. and Richard Ned Lebow, eds., *Ending the Cold War* (New York: Palgrave, 2004).

"What Was the Cold War? When and Why Did It Fail?," in Richard K. Herrmann and Richard Ned Lebow, eds., *Ending the Cold War* (New York: Palgrave, 2004), pp. 1–30.

Hersh, Seymour M., *Chain of Command: The Road from 9/11 to Abu Ghraib* (New York: Harper, 2004).

Herwig, Holger H., "Clio Deceived: Patriotic Self-Censorship in Germany After the Great War," *International Security*, 12 (Fall 1987), pp. 5–44.

The First World War: Germany and Austria-Hungary, 1914–1918 (London: Arnold, 1998).

"Germany," in Richard F. Hamilton and Holger H. Herwig, eds., *The Origins of World War I* (Cambridge: Cambridge University Press, 2003), pp. 150–187.

Herz, John H., "Idealist Internationalism and the Security Dilemma," *World Politics*, 12 (1950), pp. 157–180.

Political Realism and Political Idealism: A Study in Theories and Realities (Chicago: University of Chicago Press, 1951).

International Politics in the Nuclear Age (New York: Columbia University Press, 1959).

"The Security Dilemma in International Relations: Background and Present Problems," *International Relations* (2003), pp. 411–416.

Herzog, Chaim, *The Arab-Israeli Wars: War and Peace in the Middle East from the War of Independence through Lebanon* (New York: Random House, 1982).

Hinsley, F. H., *Power and the Pursuit of Peace; Theory and Practice in the History of Relations Between States* (Cambridge: Cambridge University Press, 1963).

Hirschman, Albert O., *Exit, Voice, and Loyalty: Responses to Decline in Firms, Organizations, and States* (Cambridge, MA: Harvard University Press, 1970).

The Passions and the Interests: Political Arguments for Capitalism Before Its Triumph (Princeton, NJ: Princeton University Press, 1977).

Hixon, Walter L. *Historical Memory and Representations of the Vietnam War* (New York: Garland, 2000).

Hobbes, Thomas, *De Cive*, in Bernard Gert, ed., *Man and Citizen* (Indianapolis, IN: Hackett, 1991 [1651]).

Leviathan, ed. Richard Tuck (Cambridge: Cambridge University Press, 1996).

Hobsbawn, Eric J., "Rules of Violence," in Eric J. Hobsbawm, *Revolutionary: Contemporary Essays* (New York: Pantheon, 1973), pp. 209–215.

Hobson, John A., *Imperialism: A Study* (London: Allen & Unwin, 1938).

Hoffmann, Stanley, *The State of War: Essays on the Theory and Practice of International Politics* (New York: Praeger, 1965).

Holsti, Kalevi J., *Peace and War: Armed Conflicts and International Order, 1648–1989* (Cambridge: Cambridge University Press, 1991).

"The Decline of Interstate War: Pondering Systemic Explanations," in Raimo Väyrynen, ed., *The Waning of Major War: Theories and Debates* (London: Routledge, 2005), pp. 135–160.

Holsti, Ole R., "Of Chasms and Convergences: Attitudes and Beliefs of Civilians and Military Elites at the Start of a New Millennium," in Peter D. Feaver and Richard H. Kohn, eds., *Soldiers and Civilians: The Civil–Military Gap and American National Security* (Cambridge, MA: MIT Press, 2001), pp. 15–99.

Homer-Dixon, Thomas F., *Environment, Scarcity, and Violence* (Princeton, NJ: Princeton University Press, 1999).

Honneth, Axel, *The Struggle for Recognition* (Cambridge, MA: MIT Press, 1996).

Honneth, Axel and Nancy Fraser, *Recognition or Redistribution? A Political-Philosophical Exchange* (New York: Verso Press, 2003).

Hont, Istvan, *Jealousy of Trade: International Competition and the Nation-State in Historical Perspective* (Cambridge, MA: Harvard University Press, 2005).

Hopf, Ted, *Peripheral Visions: Deterrence Theory and American Foreign Policy in the Third World, 1965–1990* (Ann Arbor, MI: University of Michigan Press, 1994).

Houweling, Henk and Jan G. Siccama, "Power Transition as a Cause of War," *Journal of Conflict Resolution*, 32, no. 1 (1998), pp. 87–102.

Howard, Michael, *The Franco-Prussian War: The German Invasion of France, 1870–1871* (London: Rupert Hart-Davis, 1961).

War in European History (Oxford: Oxford University Press, 1976).

War and the Liberal Conscience (New Brunswick, NJ: Rutgers University Press, 1978).

Lessons of History (New Haven, CT: Yale University Press, 1991).

Hughes, Christopher W., "Japan's Re-emergence as a 'Normal' Military Power," Adelphi Paper 368–9 (London: International Institute of Strategic Studies, 2004).

Hughes, Lindsey, *Peter the Great: A Biography* (New Haven, CT: Yale University Press, 2002).

Hume, David, *A Treatise of Human Nature, 2nd edn.* (Oxford: Oxford University Press, 1978).

Huntingford, F. A., "Animals Fight, But Do Not Make War," in Jo Groebel and Robert H. Hinde, eds., *Aggression and War: Their Biological and Social Bases* (Cambridge: Cambridge University Press, 1989), pp. 25–34.

Huntington, Samuel P., "The Lonely Superpower," *Foreign Affairs*, 78 (1999), pp. 35–49.

Hurd, Douglas, *The Arrow War: An Anglo-Chinese Confusion, 1856–60* (New York: Macmillan, 1960).

Hurrell, Andrew, *On Global Order: Power, Values, and the Constitution on International Society* (Oxford: Oxford University Press, 2008).

Huth, Paul K. and Todd L. Allee, *The Democratic Peace and Territorial Conflict in the Twenty Century* (Cambridge: Cambridge University Press, 2002).

Hymans, Jacques E. C., *The Psychology of Nuclear Proliferation: Identity, Emotions and Foreign Policy* (New York: Cambridge University Press, 2006).

Ikenberry, G. John, *After Victory: Institutions, Strategic Restraint, and the Rebuilding of Order After Major Wars* (Princeton, NJ: Princeton University Press, 2001).

America Unrivaled: The Future of the Balance of Power (Ithaca, NY: Cornell University Press, 2002).

Ingram, Edward, "Pairing Off Empires: The United States and Great Britain in the Middle East," in Tore T. Petersen, ed., *Controlling the Uncontrollable? The Great Powers in the Middle East* (Trondheim: Tapir Books, 2006), pp. 1–32.

Ingram, Norman, *The Politics of Dissent: Pacifism in France 1919–1939* (Oxford: Oxford University Press, 1991).

Iriye, Akira, *Pacific Estrangement* (Cambridge, MA: Harvard University Press, 1972).

The Origins of the Second World War in Asia and the Pacific (London: Longman, 1987).

"Japan's Drive to Great Power Status," in Manius B. Jansen, ed., *The Emergence of Meiji Japan* (Cambridge: Cambridge University Press, 1995), pp. 268–330.

Isakoff, Michael and David Corn, *Hubris: The Inside Story of Spin, Scandal and the Selling of the Iraq War* (New York: Crown, 2006).

Israel, Jonathan, *The Dutch Republic: Its Rise, Greatness and Fall, 1477–1806* (Oxford: Oxford University Press, 1995).

Jackson, Frank and Carol Rosenberg, "Why Africa's Weak States Persist: The Juridical and the Empirical in Statehood," *World Politics*, 35 (1982), pp. 1–24.

Jackson, Robert, *Global Covenant: Human Conduct in a World of States* (Oxford: Oxford University Press, 2000).

Jakobson, Max, *The Diplomacy of the Winter War: An Account of the Russo-Finnish War, 1939-1940* (Cambridge, MA: Harvard University Press, 1961).

Janis, Irving L. and Leon Mann, *Decision-Making: A Psychological Model of Conflict, Choice, and Commitment* (New York: Free Press, 1977).

Jervis, Robert, *Perception and Misperception in International Relations* (Princeton: Princeton University Press, 1976).

  "Cooperation under the Security Dilemma," *World Politics*, 40, no. 1 (1978), pp. 167–214.

  "Security Regimes," *International Organization*, 36, no. 2 (Spring 1982), pp. 173–194.

  The Meaning of the Nuclear Revolution (Ithaca, NY: Cornell University Press, 1989).

  System Effects: Complexity in Political and Social Life (Princeton, NJ: Princeton University Press, 1997).

Jervis, Robert, Richard Ned Lebow and Janice Gross Stein, *Psychology and Deterrence* (Baltimore, MD: Johns Hopkins University Press, 1984).

Jia Quingguo, "Peaceful Development: China's Policy of Reassurance," *Australian Journal of International Affairs*, 59, no. 4 (2005), pp. 493–507.

Johnson, Cathryn, Timothy J. Dowd and Cecilia L. Ridgeway, "Legitimacy as a Social Process," *Annual Reviews of Sociology*, 35 (August 2006), pp. 53–78.

Johnston, Alastair Ian, "Is China a Status Quo Power?," *International Security*, 27, no. 4 (2003), pp. 5–56.

  Social States: China and International Institutions, 1980-2000 (Princeton, NJ: Princeton University Press, 2008).

Johnston, Ian, "China's International Relations: Political and Security Dimensions," in Samuel S. Kim, ed., *The International Relations of Northeast Asia* (Lanham, MD: Rowman & Littlefield, 2004), pp. 65–101.

Jones, Dorothy V., *Code of Peace: Ethics and Security in the World of Warlord States* (Chicago: University of Chicago Press, 1989).

Jones, James R., *The Anglo-Dutch Wars of the Seventeenth Century* (London: Longman, 1996).

Jordan, Richard, Daniel Maliniak, Amy Oakes, Susan Peterson and Mitchel J. Tierney, "One Discipline or Many? TRIP Survey of International Relations Faculty in Ten Countries," unpublished paper, February 2009.

Kahin, George McTurnan, *Intervention: How America Became Involved in Vietnam* (New York: Knopf, 1986).

Kahneman, Daniel and Amos Tversky, "Prospect Theory: An Analysis of Decision Making under Risk," *Econometrica*, 47, no. 2 (March 1979), pp. 263–292.

  "Loss Aversion in Riskless Choice: A Reference Dependent Model," *Quarterly Journal of Economics*, 106 (1991), pp. 1039–1061.

  eds., *Choices, Values, and Frames* (New York: Cambridge University Press, 2000).

Kaiser, David E., "Germany and the Origins of the First World War," *Journal of Modern History*, 55 (September 1983), pp. 442–474.

Kaldor, Mary, *New and Old Wars: Organized Violence in a Global Era* (Stanford, CA: Stanford University Press, 2001).

Kang, David C., *China Rising: Peace, Power, and Order in East Asia* (New York: Columbia University Press, 2007).

Kant, Immanuel, *Perpetual Peace*, trans. Ted Humphrey (Indianapolis, IN: Hackett, 2003).

Kaplan, Fred, *The Wizards of Armageddon* (New York: Simon & Schuster, 1983).

Kaplan, Morton A., *System and Process in International Politics* (New York: Wiley, 1957).

Kaufman, Stuart J., "The Fragmentation and Consolidation of International Systems," *International Organization*, 51, no. 2 (1997), pp. 173–208.

Kaufman, Stuart, Richard Little and William Wohlforth, eds., *The Balance of Power in World History* (New York: Palgrave, 2007).

Kay, Sean, *NATO and the Future of European Security* (Lanham, MD: Rowman & Littlefield, 1998).

Kaysen, Carl, "Is War Obsolete?," *International Security*, 14, no. 4 (1990), pp. 42–64.

Keeley, Lawrence H., *War Before Civilization* (New York: Oxford University Press, 1966).

Kennedy, Paul, *The Rise and Fall of the Great Powers: Economic Change and Military Conflict from 1500 to 2000* (New York: Random House, 1987).

Kennedy, W. P., *Industrial Structure, Capital Markets, and the Origins of British Economic Decline* (Cambridge: Cambridge University Press, 1987).

Keohane, Robert, *International Institutions and State Power: Essays in International Relations Theory* (Boulder, CO: Westview, 1989).

Kershaw, Ian, *The "Hitler Myth": Image and Reality in the Third Reich* (Oxford: Oxford University Press, 1987).

Kettell, Steven, *Dirty Politics? British Democracy, New Labour, and the Invasion of Iraq* (London: Zed Books, 2006).

Khong, Yuen Foong, "War and International Theory: A Commentary on the State of the Art," *Review of International Studies*, 10 (1984), pp. 41–63.

Analogies at War: Korea, Munich, Dien Bien Phu, and the Vietnam Decisions of 1965 (Princeton, NJ: Princeton University Press, 1992).

Khrushchev, Nikita, *Khrushchev Remembers*, trans. Strobe Talbott (Boston: Little, Brown, 1970).

Kim, Woosang, "Alliance Transition and Great Power War," *American Journal of Political Science*, 35, no. 4 (1991), p. 883.

"Power Transition and Great Power War from Westphalia to Waterloo," *World Politics*, 45, no. 1 (1992), pp. 153–172.

Kim, Woosang and James D. Morrow, "When Do Power Shifts Lead to War?," *American Journal of Political Science*, 36, no. 4 (November 1992), pp. 896–922.

Kindleberger, Charles P., *The World in Depression, 1929–1939* (London: Allen Lane, 1973).

Kissinger, Henry A., *A World Restored: Metternich, Castlereagh and the Problems of Peace, 1812–22* (Boston: Houghton Mifflin, 1957).

Klare, Michael, *Resource Wars: The New Landscape of Global Conflict* (New York: Macmillan, 2002).

Konstan, David, *The Emotions of the Ancient Greeks: Studies in Aristotle and Classical Literature* (Toronto: University of Toronto Press, 2006).

Kratochwil, Friedrich V., *Rules, Norms, and Decisions: On the Conditions of Practical and Legal Reasoning in International Relations and Domestic Affairs* (Cambridge: Cambridge University Press, 1989).

Krausnick, Helmut, *Die Truppe des Weltanschauungskrieges: Die Einsatzgruppen der Sicherheitspolizei und des SD, 1938–1942* (Stuttgart: Deutsche Verlags-Anstalt, 1981).

Krauthammer, Charles, "The Unipolar Moment," *Foreign Affairs*, 70 (1990/1991), pp. 23–33.

"The Unipolar Moment Revisited," *National Interest*, 70 (Winter 2002), pp. 5–18.

Kupchan, Charles A., "After Pax Americana: Benign Power, Regional Integration, and the Sources of Stable Multipolarity," *International Security*, 23 (1998), pp. 40–79.

Kupchan, Charles A. and Clifford A. Kupchan, "Concerts, Collective Security, and the Future of Europe," *International Security*, 16, no. 1 (Summer 1991), pp. 114–161.

Kurki, Milja, *Causation in International Relations: Reclaiming Causal Analysis* (Cambridge: Cambridge University Press, 2008).

Kydd, Andrew, "Sheep in Sheep's Clothing: Why Security Seekers Do Not Fight Each Other," *Security Studies*, 7 (Autumn 1997), pp. 114–155.

Kyle, Keith, *Suez: Britain's End of Empire in the Middle East* (London: Tauris, 2002).

Lai, Brian and Dan Reiter, "Rally 'Round the Union Jack? Public Opinion and the Use of Force in the United Kingdom, 1948–2001," *International Studies Quarterly*, 49, no. 2 (2005), pp. 255–272.

Lapid, Yosef, "Culture's Ship: Returns and Departures in International Relations Theory," in Yosef Lapid and Friedrich Kratochwil, *The Return of Culture and Identity in IR Theory* (Boulder, CO: Lynne Rienner, 1996), pp. 3–20.

Lasswell, Harold, *National Security and Individual Freedom* (New York: McGraw-Hill, 1950).

Lawrence, Andrew, "Imperial Peace or Imperial Method? Skeptical Inquiries into Ambiguous Evidence for the 'Democratic Peace,'" in Richard Ned Lebow and Mark Lichbach, eds., *Theory and Evidence in Comparative Politics and International Relations* (New York: Palgrave-Macmillan, 2007), pp. 188–228.

Layne, Christopher, "The Unipolar Illusion: Why New Great Powers Will Arise," *International Security*, 17 (1993), pp. 5–51.

The Peace of Illusions: American Grand Strategy from 1940 to the Present (Ithaca, NY: Cornell University Press, 2006).

Lebow, Richard Ned, *Between Peace and War: The Nature of International Crisis* (Baltimore, MD: Johns Hopkins University Press, 1981).

"Miscalculation in the South Atlantic: The Origins of the Falkland War," in Robert Jervis, Richard Ned Lebow and Janice Gross Stein, *Psychology and Deterrence* (Baltimore, MD: Johns Hopkins University Press, 1984), pp. 89–124.

"Generational Learning and Foreign Policy," *International Journal*, 40 (Autumn 1985), pp. 556–585.

Nuclear Crisis Management (Ithaca, NY: Cornell University Press, 1987).

"The Long Peace, the End of the Cold War, and the Failure of Realism," *International Organization*, 48 (1994), pp. 249–277.

"Transitions and Transformations: Building International Cooperation," *Security Studies*, 6 (Spring 1997), pp. 154–179.

"Beyond Parsimony: Rethinking Theories of Coercive Bargaining," *European Journal of International Relations*, 4 (1998), pp. 31–66.

"Contingency, Catalysts and International System Change," *Political Science Quarterly*, 115, no. 4 (Winter 2000), pp. 591–616.

"Review Article: The Beginning and Ending of War," *International Historical Review*, 23 (2001), pp. 368–373.

"A Data Set Named Desire: A Reply to William P. Thompson," *International Studies Quarterly*, 47 (June 2003), pp. 475–478.

The Tragic Vision of Politics: Ethics, Interests and Orders (Cambridge: Cambridge University Press, 2003).

Coercion, Cooperation and Ethics (New York: Routledge, 2006).

A Cultural Theory of International Relations (Cambridge: Cambridge University Press, 2008).

"Constitutive Causality: Imagined Spaces and Political Practices," *Millennium*, 38, no. 2 (December 2009), pp. 1–29.

Forbidden Fruit: Counterfactuals and International Relations (Princeton, NJ: Princeton University Press, 2010).

Lebow, Richard Ned and Thomas Risse-Kappen, *International Relations and the End of the Cold War* (New York: Columbia University Press, 1995).

Lebow, Richard Ned and Janice Gross Stein, "Rational Deterrence Theory: I Think Therefore I Deter," *World Politics*, 41 (January 1989), pp. 208–224.

"Deterrence: The Elusive Dependent Variable," *World Politics*, 42 (April 1990), pp. 336–369.

We All Lost the Cold War (Princeton, NJ: Princeton University Press, 1994).

"Understanding the End of the Cold War as a Non-Linear Confluence," in Richard K. Herrmann and Richard Ned Lebow, eds., *Ending the Cold War* (New York: Palgrave, 2004), pp. 189–218.

Lebow, Richard Ned and Benjamin A. Valentino, "Lost in Transition: A Critical Analysis of Power Transition Theory," *International Relations*, 23, no. 3 (2009), pp. 389–410.

Lee, Robert D. *et al.*, *Public Budgeting Systems* (New York: Jones & Bartlett, 2004).

Leed, Eric J., *No Man's Land: Combat and Identity in World War I* (Cambridge: Cambridge University Press, 1975).

Lembcke, Jerry, *The Spitting Image: Myth, Memory, and the Legacy of Vietnam* (New York: New York University Press, 1998).

Lemke, Douglas and William Reed, "Power Is Not Satisfaction: A Comment on De Soysa, Oneal and Park," *Journal of Conflict Resolution*, 42, no. 4 (1998), pp. 511–516.

Lemke, Douglas and Suzanne Werner, "Power Parity, Commitment to Change, and War," *International Studies Quarterly*, 40, no. 2 (1996), pp. 235–260.

Lendon, J. E., *Ghosts and Soldiers: A History of Battle in Classical Antiquity* (New Haven, CT: Yale University Press, 2005).

Lenin, V. I., *State and Revolution* (Moscow: Progress Publishers, 1917).

On Imperialism (Moscow: Progress Publishers, 1973).

Lévesque, J., *The Enigma of 1989: The USSR and the Liberation of Eastern Europe*, trans. K. Martin (Berkeley, CA: University of California Press, 1997).

Levi, Ariel and Philip E. Tetlock, "A Cognitive Analysis of Japan's 1941 Decision for War," *Journal of Conflict Resolution*, 24, no. 2 (June 1980), pp. 195–211.

Levitt, Michael and Dennis Ross, *Hamas: Politics, Charity, and Terrorism in Service of Jihad* (New Haven, CT: Yale University Press, 2006).

Levy, Jack S., *War in the Modern Great Power System, 1495–1975* (Lexington, KY: University Press of Kentucky, 1983).

"The Causes of War: A Review of Theories and Evidence," in Philip E. Tetlock, Jo L. Husbands, Robert Jervis, Paul C. Stern and Charles Tilly, eds., *Behavior, Society and Nuclear War* (New York: Oxford University Press, 1989), vol. 1, pp. 209–333.

"Long Cycles, Hegemonic Transitions and the Long Peace," in Charles W. Kegley, ed., *The Long Postwar Peace* (New York: Harper-Collins, 1991), pp. 147–176.

"Learning and Foreign Policy: Sweeping a Conceptual Minefield," *International Organization*, 48, no. 2 (Spring 1994), pp. 279–312.

"Loss Aversion, Framing, and Bargaining: The Implications of Prospect Theory for International Conflict," *International Political Science Review / Revue internationale de science politique*, 17, no. 2 (1996), pp. 179–195.

"What Do Great Powers Balance Against and When?," in T. V. Paul, J. J. Wirtz and M. Fortmann, eds., *Balance of Power: Theory and Practice in the 21st Century* (Stanford, CA: Stanford University Press, 2004).

"Theory, Evidence, and Politics in the Evolution of International Relations Research Programs," in Richard Ned Lebow and Mark Lichbach, eds., *Theory and Evidence in Comparative Politics and International Relations* (New York: Palgrave-Macmillan, 2007), pp. 177–198.

"Power Transition Theory and the Rise of China," in Robert S. Ross and Zhu Feng, eds., *China's Ascent: Power, Security, and the Future of International Politics* (Ithaca, NY: Cornell University Press, 2008), pp. 11–33.

Levy, Jack S., Thomas C. Walker and Martin S. Edwards, "Continuity and Change in the Evolution of Warfare," in Zeev Maoz and Azar Gat, eds., *War in a Changing World* (Ann Arbor, MI: University of Michigan Press, 2001), pp. 15–48.

Lewis, John Wilson and Xue Litai, *China Builds the Bomb* (Stanford, CA: Stanford University Press, 1988).

Lewis, Justin, "Television, Public Opinion and the War in Iraq: The Case of Britain," *International Journal of Public Opinion Research*, 16, no. 3 (2004), pp. 295–310.

Lieber, Robert, ed., *Eagle Rules? Foreign Policy and American Primacy in the Twenty-First Century* (Englewood Cliffs, NJ: Prentice-Hall, 2002).

Lieberman, Peter, *Does Conquest Pay? The Exploitation of Occupied Industrial Societies* (Princeton, NJ: Princeton University Press, 1996).

Lipschutz, R. D., *After Authority: War, Peace, and Global Politics in the 21st Century* (Albany, NY: State University of New York Press, 2000).

Lipson, Charles, *Reliable Partners: How Democracies Have Made a Separate Peace* (Princeton, NJ: Princeton University Press, 2003).

Little, Richard, *The Balance of Power in International Relations: Metaphors, Myths and Models* (Cambridge: Cambridge University Press, 2007).

Livy, *The Early History of Rome, Books I–V of The History of Rome from its Foundations*, trans. Aubrey de Sélincourt (London: Penguin, 1960).

Logevall, Fredrik, *Choosing War: The Lost Chance for Peace and the Escalation of War in Vietnam* (Berkeley, CA: University of California Press, 1999).

Louis XIV, *Mémoires for the Instruction of the Dauphin*, trans. Paul Sonnino (New York: Free Press, 1970).

Lowe, C. J. and F. Marzari, *Italian Foreign Policy, 1870–1940* (London: Routledge & Kegan Paul, 1975).

Luard, Evan, *War in International Society: A Study in International Sociology* (New Haven, CT: Yale University Press, 1986).

Lynch, Cecilia, *Beyond Appeasement: Interpreting Interwar Peace Movement in World Politics* (Ithaca, NY: Cornell University Press, 1999).

Lynn, John A., *Giant of the Grand Siècle: The French Army, 1670-1715* (Cambridge: Cambridge University Press, 1997).

Battle: A History of Combat and Culture (Boulder, CO: Westview, 2003).

Macfie, Alec L., "Outbreak of War and the Trade Cycle," *Economic History*, 3 (February 1938), pp. 89-97.

Machinist, Peter, "Kingship and Divinity in Imperial Assyria," in Gary Beckman and Theodore J. Lewis, eds., *Text, Artifact, and Image: Revealing Ancient Israelite Religion* (Providence, RI: Brown Judaic Studies, 2006), pp. 152-188.

Mack Smith, Denis, *Mussolini* (New York: Knopf, 1982).

Mackinder, Harold J., "The Geographical Pivot of History," *Geographical Journal*, 23 (1904), pp. 421-444.

Britain and the British Seas (Oxford: Oxford University Press, 1907).

MacMillan, John, *On Liberal Peace: Democracy, War and International Order* (London: Tauris, 1998).

"Immanuel Kant and the Democratic Peace," in Beate Jahn, ed., *Classical Theory in International Relations* (Cambridge: Cambridge University Press, 2006), pp. 52-73.

Macpherson, C. B., *The Political Theory of Possessive Individualism: Hobbes to Locke* (Oxford: Oxford University Press, 1962).

Maddison, Angus, *Monitoring the World Economy: 1820-1992* (Washington, DC: Organization for Economic Co-operation and Development, 1995).

Mahan, Alfred Thayer, *The Influence of Sea Power upon History, 1600-1783* (Boston: Little, Brown, 1890).

Maier, C. S., *Dissolution: The Crisis of Communism and the End of East Germany* (Princeton, NJ: Princeton University Press, 1997).

Majeski, Stephen J. and Donald J. Sylvan, "Simple Choices and Complex Calculations: A Critique of the War Trap," *Journal of Conflict Resolution*, 28 (1984), pp. 597-618.

Mansfield, Edward D., "Concentration of Capabilities and the Onset of War," *Journal of Conflict Resolution*, 36 (1992), pp. 3-24.

Mansfield, Edward D. and Jack Snyder, "Democratization and the Danger of War," *International Security*, 20 (1995), pp. 5-38.

Electing to Fight: Why Emerging Democracies Go to War (Cambridge, MA: MIT Press, 2005).

Maoz, Zeev and Bruce Russett, "Normative and Structural Causes of the Democratic Peace," *American Political Science Review*, 87, no. 3 (1993), pp. 624-638.

Marx, Karl, *Capital*, 3 vols. (Moscow: Progress Publishers, 1966).

Maslow, Abraham H., *Motivation and Personality* (New York: Harper & Row, 1954).

Toward a Psychology of Being (Princeton, NJ: Van Nostrand, 1962).

Massie, Robert K., *Peter the Great: His Life and World* (New York: Knopf, 1980).

Mastanduno, Michael, "Preserving the Unipolar Moment: Realist Theories and US Grand Strategy after the Cold War," *International Security*, 21 (1997), pp. 44–98.

Mathews, Jenifer T., "Redefining Security," *Foreign Affairs*, 68, no. 2 (Spring 1989), pp. 162–177.

Matlock, Jack F., Jr., *Autopsy of an Empire: The American Ambassador's Account of the Collapse of the Soviet Union* (New York: Random House, 1995).

Mayer, Arno, "Domestic Causes of the First World War," in Leonard Krieger and Fritz Stern, eds., *The Responsibility of Power: Historical Essays in Honor of Hajo Holborn* (Garden City, NY: Doubleday, 1967), pp. 286–293.

McDermott, Rose, *Risk-Taking in International Politics: Prospect Theory to American Foreign Policy* (Ann Arbor, MI: University of Michigan, 1998).

   ed., Special Issue of *Political Psychology* on Prospect Theory, 25 (April 2004), pp. 147–312.

McKeown, Timothy, "The Limitations of 'Structural' Theories of Commercial Policy," *International Organization*, 40 (1986), pp. 43–64.

McNamara, Robert S., *Argument Without End: In Search of Answers to the Vietnam Tragedy* (New York: Public Affairs, 1999).

   Fog of War: Lessons from the Life of Robert S. McNamara, ed. James G. Blight and Janet M. Lang (Lanham, MD: Rowman & Littlefield, 2005).

Mearsheimer, John, "Back to the Future: Instability in Europe after the Cold War," *International Security*, 15, no. 1 (Summer 1990), pp. 1–56.

   The Tragedy of Great Power Politics (New York: Norton, 2001).

Mearsheimer, John and Stephen Walt, *The Israel Lobby and American Foreign Policy* (New York: Farrar, Straus and Giroux, 2008).

Mermin, Jonathan, *Debating War and Peace: Media Coverage of US Intervention in the Post-Vietnam Era* (Princeton, NJ: Princeton University Press, 1999).

Merridale, Catherine, *Ivan's War: The Red Army 1939-1945* (London: Faber & Faber, 2005).

Migdal, Joel S., ed., *Boundaries and Belonging: States and Societies in the Struggle to Shape Identities and Local Practices* (Cambridge: Cambridge University Press, 2004).

Mill, John Stuart, *Principles of Political Economy* (London: Longmans, 1909).

Millis, Walter, *Arms and Men* (New York: Oxford University Press, 1956).

Modelski, George, "The Long Cycle of Global Politics and the Nation-State," *Comparative Studies in Society and History*, 10 (1978), pp. 314–335.

   Exploring Long Cycles (Boulder, CO: Lynne Rienner, 1987).

   Long Cycles in World Politics (Seattle: University of Washington Press, 1987).

Moe, Terry M., "On the Scientific Status of Rational Models," *American Journal of Political Science*, 23 (February 1979), pp. 215–243.

Mombauer, Annika, *Helmuth von Moltke and the Origins of the First World War* (Cambridge: Cambridge University Press, 2001).

Mommsen, Hans, *The Rise and Fall of Weimar Democracy*, trans. Elborg Forster and Larry Jones (Chapel Hill, NC: University of North Carolina Press, 1996).

Mommsen, Wolfgang J., "Domestic Factors in German Foreign Policy Before 1914," *Central European History*, 6, no. 1 (March 1972), pp. 4–18.

Mommsen, Wolfgang and Jurgen Osterhammel, eds., *Imperialism and After: Continuities and Discontinuities* (London: Allen & Unwin, 1986).

Montesquieu, Charles-Louis de, *The Spirit of the Laws*, trans. Anne M. Cohler, Bbaisa Carolyn Miller and Harold Samuel Stone (Cambridge: Cambridge University Press, 1989).

Morgan, Patrick M., "Multilateral Institutions as Restraints on Major War," in Raimo Väyrynen, ed., *The Waning of Major War: Theories and Debates* (London: Routledge, 2005), pp. 160–184.

Morgenthau, Hans J., *Scientific Man vs. Power Politics* (Chicago: University of Chicago Press, 1946).

  Politics Among Nations (New York: Knopf, 1948).

  In Defense of the National Interest (New York: Knopf, 1951).

  Politics Among Nations, rev. by Kenneth Thompson (New York: Knopf, 1985).

Morrow, James, "A Continuous-Outcome Expected Utility Theory of War," *Journal of Conflict Resolution*, 29 (1985), pp. 473–502.

  "On the Theoretical Basis of a Measure of National Risk Attitudes," *International Studies Quarterly*, 31 (1987), pp. 423–438.

  Game Theory for Political Scientists (Princeton, NJ: Princeton University Press, 1994).

Mueller, John, *War, Presidents, and Public Opinion* (New York: Wiley, 1973).

  Retreat from Doomsday: The Obsolescence of Major War (New York: Basic Books, 1989).

  Public Opinion and the Gulf War (Chicago, Chicago University. Press, 1994).

  "Accounting for the Waning of Major War," in Raimo Väyrynen, ed., *The Waning of Major War: Theories and Debates* (London: Routledge, 2005), pp. 64–79.

  The Remnants of War (Ithaca, NY: Cornell University Press, 2007).

Murphy, Craig N., "Understanding IR: Understanding Gramsci," *Review of International Studies*, 24 (1998), pp. 417–425.

National Commission on Terrorist Attacks, *The 9/11 Commission Report: Final Report of the National Commission on Terrorist Attacks upon the United States* (New York: Norton, 2004).

Neiberg, Michael S., *Fighting the Great War: A Global History* (Cambridge: Harvard University Press, 2005).

Neilson, Keith, *Britain, Soviet Russia, and the Collapse of the Versailles Order, 1919–1939* (Cambridge: Cambridge University Press, 2006).

Nelson, Keith and Spencer Olin, Jr., *Why War? Ideology, Theory and History* (Berkeley, CA: University of California Press, 1979).

Neumann, Iver B., "Russia as a Great Power, 1815–2007," *Journal of International Relations and Development*, 11 (2008), p. 128.

Neustadt, Richard E., *Presidential Power: The Politics of Leadership* (New York: Wiley, 1960).

Nexon, Daniel H., *The Struggle for Power in Early Modern Europe* (Princeton, NJ: Princeton University Press, 2009).

Nicolson, Colin, *The Longman Companion to the First World War* (London: Longman 2001).

Nicolson, Harold, *The Congress of Vienna: A Study in Allied Unity: 1812–1822* (New York: Viking, 1946).

Nieberg, Michael S., *Fighting the Great War: A Global History* (Cambridge, MA: Harvard University Press, 2005).

Nietzsche, Friedrich, *Human, All Too Human (1), A Book for Free Spirits*, vol. 3, trans. Gary Handwerk (Stanford, CA: Stanford University Press, 2000).

Nipperdey, Thomas, *Germany from Napoleon to Bismarck, 1800–1866*, trans. Daniel Nolan (Princeton, NJ: Princeton University Press, 1983).

Nish, Ian, *Japan's Struggle with Internationalism* (London: Athlone, 1992).

Northedge, F. S., *The League of Nations: Its Life and Times, 1920–1946* (Oxford: Oxford University Press, 1948).

Norton, Robert E., *The Beautiful Soul: Aesthetic Morality in the Eighteenth Century* (Ithaca, NY: Cornell University Press, 1995).

Nye, Joseph S., Jr., "The Case Against Containment: Treat China Like an Enemy and That's What It Will Be," *Global Beat China Handbook*, June 22, 1998.

O'Connor, Kevin, *The History of the Baltic States* (Westport, CT: Greenwood, 2003).

Ogata, Sadako, *Defiance in Manchuria* (Berkeley, CA: University of California Press, 1964).

Oldmeadow, Julian and Susan T. Fiske, "System-Justifying Ideologies Moderate Status = Competence Stereotypes: Roles for Belief in a Just World and Social Dominance Orientation," *European Journal of Social Psychology*, 37 (2007), pp. 1135–1148.

Olson, Mancur, Jr., *The Logic of Collective Action: Public Goods and the Theory of Groups* (Cambridge, MA: Harvard University Press, 1965).

Oneal, John R. and Anna Lillian Bryan, "The Rally 'Round the Flag Effect in US Foreign Policy Crises, 1950–1985," *Political Behavior*, 17, no. 4 (1995), pp. 379–401.

Oneal, John R., Indra de Soysa and Yong-Hee Park, "But Power and Wealth Are Satisfying: A Reply to Lemke and Reed," *Journal of Conflict Resolution*, 42, no. 4 (1998), pp. 517–520.

Onuf, Nicholas G., *World of Our Making* (Columbia, SC: University of South Carolina Press, 1989).

The Republican Legacy (New York: Cambridge University Press, 1998).

Oren, Michael B., *Six Days of War: June 1967 and the Making of the Modern Middle East* (Oxford: Oxford University Press, 2002).

Organski, A. F. K., *World Politics* (New York: Knopf, 1958).

Organski, A. F. K. and Jacek Kugler, *The War Ledger* (Chicago: University of Chicago Press, 1980).

Osgood, Robert, "Woodrow Wilson, Collective Security, and the Lessons of History," *Confluence*, 5, no. 4 (Winter 1957), pp. 341–354.

Osiander, Andreas, "Sovereignty, International Relations, and the Westphalian Myth," *International Organization*, 55, no. 2 (2002), pp. 251–287.

Oye, Kenneth A., "Explaining the End of the Cold War: Morphological and Behavioral Adaptations to the Nuclear Peace," in Richard Ned Lebow and Thomas Risse-Kappen, *International Relations and the End of the Cold War* (New York: Columbia University Press, 1995), pp. 57–84.

Paine, S. C. M., *Imperial Rivals: China, Russia, and Their Disputed Frontier* (Armonk, NY: Sharpe, 1996).

  The Sino-Japanese War of 1894–1895: Perceptions, Power, and Primacy (Cambridge: Cambridge University Press, 2003).

Painter, David S., *The Cold War: An International History* (London: Routledge, 1999).

Parker, Geoffrey, *The Military Revolution: Military Innovation and the Rise of the West 1500–1800*, 3rd edn. (Cambridge: Cambridge University Press, 2000).

Parsons, Talcott, *The Structure of Social Action* (New York: McGraw Hill, 1937).

Paul, T. V., "The Risk of Nuclear War Does Not Belong to History," in Raimo Väyrynen, ed., *The Waning of Major War: Theories and Debates* (London: Routledge, 2005), pp. 113–132.

  The Tradition of Non-Use of Nuclear Weapons (Stanford, CA: Stanford University Press, 2009).

Pearson, Karl, *National Life from the Standpoint of Science* (London: A. C. Black, 1905).

Peltonen, Markku, *The Duel in Early Modern England: Civility, Politeness and Honour* (Cambridge: Cambridge University Press, 2003).

Petersen, Roger D., *Understanding Ethnic Violence: Fear, Hatred, and Resentment in Twentieth-Century Eastern Europe* (Cambridge: Cambridge University Press, 2002).

Pfaff, Steven, "The Religious Divide: Why Religion Seems to Be Thriving in the United States and Waning in Europe," in Jeffrey Kopstein and Sven Steinmo, eds., *Growing Apart? America and Europe in the Twenty-First Century* (New York: Cambridge University Press, 2007), pp. 24–52.

Pflanze, Otto, *Bismarck and the Development of Germany: The Period of Unification, 1815–1871* (New York: Macmillan, 1961).

Phillips, David L., *Losing Iraq: Inside the Postwar Reconstruction Fiasco* (Boulder, CO: Westview, 2005).

Phillips, H. and David Killingray, *The Spanish Influenza Pandemic of 1918–19* (New York: Routledge, 2003), p. 7.

Phillips, Kevin, *American Dynasty: Aristocracy, Fortune, and the Politics of Deceit in the House of Bush* (New York: Viking, 2004).

Plato, *Crito*, in Plato, *The Collected Dialogues*, ed. Edith Hamilton and Huntington Cairns (Princeton, NJ: Princeton University Press, 1961).

    Republic, ed. and trans. I. A. Richards (Cambridge: Cambridge University Press, 1996).

Polybius, *The Rise of the Roman Empire*, trans. Ian Scott-Kilvery (London: Penguin, 1979).

Powell, Robert, *In the Shadow of Power: States and Strategies in International Politics* (Princeton, NJ: Princeton University Press, 1999).

    "War as a Commitment Problem," *International Organization*, 60 (2006), pp. 169–203.

Rapoport, Anatol, *Strategy and Conscience* (New York: Harper & Row, 1964).

Rasler, Karen A. and William R. Thompson, *The Great Powers and Global Struggle, 1490–1980* (Lexington, KY: University of Kentucky Press, 1994).

Rawls, John, *A Theory of Justice*, rev. edn. (Cambridge, MA: Harvard University Press, 1999).

Ray, James Lee, "Democracy: On the Level(s), Does Democracy Correlate with Peace?," in John A. Vasquez, ed., *What Do We Know About War?* (Lanham, MD: Rowman & Littlefield, 2000), pp. 299–318.

Raymond, Gregory A., "International Norms: Normative Orders and Peace," in John A. Vasquez, ed., *What Do We Know About War?* (Lanham, MD: Rowman & Littlefield, 2000), pp. 281–297.

Reiter, Dan, "Exploding the Powder Keg Myth: Preemptive Wars Almost Never Happen," *International Security*, 20 (Fall 1995), pp. 5–34.

Reus-Smit, Christian, *The Moral Purpose of the State: Culture, Social Identity, and Institutional Rationality in International Relations* (Princeton, NJ: Princeton University Press, 1999).

Rhodes, Richard, *The Making of the Atomic Bomb* (New York: Simon & Schuster, 1986).

Rich, Frank, *The Greatest Story Ever Sold* (New York: Penguin, 2006).

Rich, Norman, *Hitler's War Aims*, 2 vols. (New York: Norton, 1973–1974).

Richardson, Lewis F., *The Statistics of Deadly Quarrels*, ed. Quincy Wright and C. C. Lienau (Pittsburgh, PA: Boxwood Press, 1960).

Richelson, Jeffrey, "Population Targeting and US Strategic Doctrine," in Desmond Ball and Jeffrey Richelson, eds. *Strategic Nuclear Targeting* (Ithaca, NY: Cornell University Press, 1986), pp. 234–249.

Ricks, Thomas E., *Fiasco: The American Military Adventure in Iraq* (New York: Penguin, 2006).

Ringmar, Erik, *Identity, Interest and Action: A Cultural Explanation of Sweden's Intervention in the Thirty Years War* (Cambridge: Cambridge University Press, 1996).

Ritter, Gerhard, *The Schlieffen Plan*, trans. Andrew Wilson and Eva Wilson (New York: Praeger, 1958).

Roberts, Penfield, *The Quest for Security, 1715–1740* (New York: Harper & Row, 1947).

Robinson, Ronald and John Gallagher, "The Imperialism of Free Trade," *Economic History Review*, 6 (1953), pp. 1–15.

Robinson, Ronald and John Gallagher with Alice Denny, *Africa and the Victorians: The Climax of Imperialism in the Dark Continent* (New York: St. Martin's, 1961).

Rose, Gideon, "Neoclassical Realism and Theories of Foreign Policy," *World Politics*, 51, no. 1 (1998), pp. 144–172.

Rosecrance, Richard, "Bipolarity, Multipolarity, and the Future," *Journal of Conflict Resolution*, 10 (1966), pp. 314–327.

   The Rise of the Trading State: Commerce and Conquest in the Modern World (New York: Basic Books, 1986).

Rosenau, James R., "New Dimensions of Security: The Interaction of Globalizing and Localizing Dynamics," *Security Dialogue*, 25, no. 3 (1994), pp. 255–281.

Rosenberg, Arthur, *Imperial Germany: The Birth of the German Republic, 1871–1918*, trans. Ian Morrow (Boston: Beacon Press, 1964 [1928]).

Ross, Robert S. and Zhu Feng, *China's Ascent: Power, Security and the Future of International Politics* (Ithaca, NY: Cornell University Press, 2008).

   "The Rise of China: Theoretical and Policy Perspectives," in Robert S. Ross and Zhu Feng, *China's Ascent: Power, Security and the Future of International Politics* (Ithaca, NY: Cornell University Press, 2008), pp. 293–316.

Rotberg, Robert I., ed., *When States Fail: Causes and Consequences* (Princeton, NJ: Princeton University Press, 2004).

Rousseau, David L., *Democracy and War: Institutions, Norms, and the Evolution of International Conflict* (Stanford, CA: Stanford University Press, 2005).

Rousseau, Jean-Jacques, *Du Contrat Social* (Paris: Editions Garnier Frères, 1962).

   Discourse on the Origin and Foundations of Inequality (Second Discourse), in Roger D. Masters, ed., trans. Roger D. Masters and Judith R. Masters, *The First and Second Discourses* (New York: St. Martin's, 1964), pp. 77–229.

Rozman, Gilbert, "Japan's Quest for Great Power Identity," *Orbis* (Winter 2002), pp. 73–91.

Rubin, Mark and Miles Hewstone, "Social Identity Theory's Self-Esteem Hypothesis: A Review and Some Suggestions for Clarification," *Personality and Social Psychology Review*, 2 (1998), pp. 40–62.

Ruggie, John G., "Multilateralism: The Anatomy of an Institution," in John G. Ruggie, ed., *Multilateralism Matters: The Theory and Practice of an International Form* (New York: Columbia University Press, 1993).

Rummell, Rudolph J., "Libertarianism and International Violence," *Journal of Conflict Resolution*, 27 (1983), pp. 27–71.

Rumsfeld, Donald H., "Transforming the Military," *Foreign Affairs*, 81, no. 3 (May/June 2002), pp. 20–32.

Russett, Bruce R., *Grasping the Democratic Peace: Principles for a Post-Cold War World* (Princeton, NJ: Princeton University Press, 1993).

Russett, Bruce R., and John Oneal, *Triangulating Peace: Democracy, Interdependence, and International Organizations* (New York: Norton, 2001).

Sabrovky, Allan Ned, ed., *Polarity and War: The Changing Structure of International Conflict* (Boulder, CO: Westview, 1985).

Sadao, Asada, "The Japanese Navy and the United States," in Dorothy Borg and Shumpei Okamoto, eds., *Pearl Harbor as History* (New York: Columbia University Press, 1973), pp. 225–260.

Safire, William, "Useful Idiots of the West," *New York Times*, April 12, 1987.

Safran, Nadav, *From War to War: The Arab-Israeli Confrontation, 1848–1967* (New York: Pegasus, 1969).

Israel: The Embattled Ally (Cambridge, MA: Harvard University Press, 1978).

Sagan, Carl and Richard Turco, *Where No Man Thought: Nuclear Winter and the End of the Arms Race* (New York: Random House, 1990).

Sagan, Scott D., *Limits of Safety: Organizations, Accidents, and Nuclear Weapons* (Princeton, NJ: Princeton University Press, 1983).

"More Will Be Worse," in Scott D. Sagan and Kenneth N. Waltz, *The Spread of Nuclear Weapons: A Debate Renewed* (New York: Norton, 2003), pp. 46–87.

Sagan, Scott D. and Kenneth N. Waltz, *The Spread of Nuclear Weapons: A Debate Renewed* (New York: Norton, 2003).

Sage, Jesse and Liora Kasten, eds., *Enslaved: True Stories of Modern Day Slavery* (London: Palgrave Macmillan, 2008).

Salisbury, Harrison, *The 900 Days: The Siege of Leningrad* (New York: Harper & Row, 1969).

Samuels, Richard J., *Securing Japan: Tokyo's Grand Strategy and the Future of East Asia* (Ithaca, NY: Cornell University Press, 2007).

Sanderson, G. N., *England, Europe and the Upper Nile* (Edinburgh: Edinburgh University Press, 1965).

Schechter, Danny, "Selling the Iraq War: The Media Management Strategies We Never Saw," in Yahya Kamalipour and Nancy Snow, eds., *War, Media, and Propaganda: A Global Perspective* (Boulder, CO: Rowman & Littlefield, 2004), pp. 25–32.

Schelling, Thomas, *Arms and Influence* (New Haven, CT: Yale University Press, 1966).

Scheuerman, William E., *Hans Morgenthau: Realism and Beyond* (Cambridge: Polity, 2009).

Schmidt, Brian C., "Anarchy, World Politics and the Birth of a Discipline: American International Relations, Pluralist Theory and the Myth of Interwar Idealism," *International Relations*, 16 (April 2002), pp. 9–32.

Schroeder, Paul W., "World War I as Galloping Gertie: A Reply to Joachim Remak," *Journal of Modern History*, 44 (September 1972), pp. 319–345.

"The 19th Century International System: Changes in Structure," *World Politics*, 39, no. 1 (October 1986), pp. 1–26.

The Transformation of European Politics, 1763–1848 (Oxford: Oxford University Press, 1994).

"International Politics, Peace and War, 1815–1914," in T. C. W. Blanning, ed., *The Nineteenth Century* (Oxford: Oxford University Press, 2000), pp. 158–209.

"The Life and Death of a Long Peace, 1763–1914," in Raimo Väyrynen, ed., *The Waning of Major War: Theories and Debates* (London: Routledge, 2005), pp. 33–62.

Schultz, Kenneth, *Democracy and Coercive Diplomacy* (Cambridge: Cambridge University Press, 2001).

Schulze, Hagen, "The Prussian Military State, 1763–1806," in Philip G. Dwyer, ed., *The Rise of Prussia, 1700–1830* (London: Longmans, 2000), pp. 201–219.

Schumpeter, Joseph A., *Imperialism and Social Classes*, trans. Heinz Norden (New York: Kelley, 1951).

Capitalism, Socialism, and Democracy (New York: Harper & Row, 1963).

The Theory of Economic Development (New Brunswick, NJ: Transaction, 1983).

Schweller, Randall L., "Bandwagoning for Profit: Bringing the Revisionist State Back In," *International Security*, 19 (1994), pp. 72–107.

Deadly Imbalances: Tripolarity and Hitler's Strategy of World Conquest (New York: Columbia University Press, 1998).

Scott, H. M., *The Birth of a Great Power System, 1740–1815* (London: Pearson Longman, 2006).

Seabrooke, Leonard, "The Economic Taproot of US Imperialism: The Bush Rentier Shift," *International Politics*, 41 (2004), pp. 293–318.

Seaward, Paul, *The Cavalier Parliament and the Reconstruction of the Old Regime, 1661–67* (Cambridge: Cambridge University Press, 1989).

Seigel, Jerrold E., *The Idea of the Self: Idea and Experience in Western Europe Since the Seventeenth Century* (Cambridge: Cambridge University Press, 2005).

Seiler, Bernd, "'Dolchstoss' und 'Dolchstosslegende'," *Zeitschrift für Deutsche Sprache*, 22 (1966), pp. 1–20.

Selden, Mark and Kuoko Selden, *The Atomic Bomb: Voices from Hiroshima and Nagasaki* (New York: M. E. Sharpe, 1989).

Senese, Paul and John A. Vasquez, *Steps to War: An Empirical Study* (Princeton, NJ: Princeton University Press, 2008).

Senghaas, Dieter, "Zivilisierung und Gewalt Wie den Frieden gewinnen?," in W. R. Vogt, ed., *Frieden als Zivilisierungsprojekt – Neue Herausfoderungen an die Friedens- un Konfliktforschuung* (Baden-Baden: Nomos, 1995), pp. 37–55.

Shambaugh, David, "China Engages Asia: Reshaping the Regional Order," *International Security*, 29 (Winter 2004/2005), pp. 64–99.

Shapland, Greg, *Rivers of Discord* (New York: St. Martin's, 1997).

Shirer, William L., *Berlin Diary: The Journal of a Correspondent, 1934–1941* (New York: Knopf, 1942).

Shirk, Susan, *China: Fragile Superpower* (New York: Oxford University Press, 2007).

Shotter, John, "Social Accountability and the Social Construction of 'You'," in John Shotter and Kenneth. J. Gergen, eds., *Texts of Identity* (London: Sage, 1989), pp. 133–151.

Shoup, David, Document 25: Note by the Secretaries to the Joint Chiefs of Staff on Review of the NSTL/SIOP-62 and Related Policy Guidance, JCS 2056/220, "The Creation of SIOP-62: More Evidence on the Origins of Overkill," 11 February 1961, www.gwu.edu/~nsarchiv/NSAEBB/NSAEBB130/SIOP-25.pdf.

Simmel, Georg, *Englischsprachige Veröffentlichungen, 1893–1910* (Frankfurt: Suhrkamp, 2008).

Simmons, Robert B., *The Strained Alliance: Peking, Pyongyang, Moscow, and the Politics of the Korean Civil War* (New York: Free Press, 1975).

Simms, Brendan, *The Impact of Napoleon: Prussian High Politics, Foreign Policy and the Crisis of the Executive, 1797–1806* (Cambridge: Cambridge University Press, 1997).

   Three Victories and a Defeat: The Rise and Fall of the First British Empire, 1714–1788 (London: Penguin, 2007).

Singer, J. David and Melvin Small, *The Wages of War, 1816–1965* (New York: Wiley, 1972).

Small, Melvin and David J. Singer, "The War-Proneness of Democratic Regimes, 1816–1965," *Jerusalem Journal of International Relations*, 1 (1976), pp. 50–69.

Smith, Adam, *The Theory of Moral Sentiments* (Cambridge: Cambridge University Press, 2002 [1759]).

   The Wealth of Nations (New York: Modern Library, 1937).

Smith, Alastair, "International Crises and Domestic Politics," *American Political Science Review*, 92, no. 3 (1998), pp. 623–638.

Smith, Tony, *The Pattern of Imperialism: The United States, Great Britain, and the Late-Industrializing World Since 1815* (Cambridge: Cambridge University Press, 1981).

Smolin, Lee, *The Trouble with Physics* (New York: Penguin Books, 2007).

Snyder, Jack L., *The Ideology of the Offensive: Military Decision Making and the Disasters of 1914* (Ithaca, NY: Cornell University Press, 1984).

Solingen, Etel, "Regional Conflict and Cooperation: The Case of Southeast Asia,"
    Case Study, Columbia International Affairs Online, September 2001.
    Nuclear Logics: Contrasting Paths in East Asia and the Middle East (Princeton,
    NJ: Princeton University Press, 2007).
Sophocles, "Antigone," in D. Slavitt and P. Bovie, eds., *Sophocles*, 2, trans.
    K. Cherry (Philadelphia: University of Pennsylvania Press, 1999).
Sørensen, Georg, *Changes in Statehood: The Transformation of International
    Relations* (London: Palgrave, 2001).
"Soviet Archival Documents on the Hungarian Revolution, 24 October–4
    November 1956," trans. Johann Granville, in *Cold War International
    History Project Bulletin*, no. 5 (Spring 1995), pp. 22–23, 29–34.
Spanier, John, *The Truman–MacArthur Controversy and the Korean War*, rev.
    edn. (New York: Norton, 1965).
Spector, Ronald H., *The American War with Japan: Eagle Against the Sun* (New
    York: Free Press, 1985).
Spencer, Herbert, *Principles of Sociology* (New York: D. Appleton, 1906).
Spruyt, Hendrik, "Normative Transformations in International Relations
    and the Waning of Major War," in Raimo Väyrynen, ed., *The Waning
    of Major War: Theories and Debates* (London: Routledge, 2005),
    pp. 185–226.
Stein, Janice Gross, "Calculation, Miscalculation, and Conventional Deterrence 1:
    The View from Cairo," in Robert Jervis, Richard Ned Lebow and Janice
    Gross Stein, *Psychology and Deterrence* (Baltimore, MD: Johns Hopkins
    University Press, 1984), pp. 34–59.
    "Threat-Based Strategies of Conflict Management: Why Did They Fail in the
    Gulf?," in Stanley A. Renshon, ed., *Political Psychology of the Gulf War:
    Leaders, Publics, and the Process of Conflict* (Pittsburgh, PA: University of
    Pittsburgh Press, 1993), pp. 121–154.
Stern, Fritz, "Bethmann Hollweg and the War: The Limits of Responsibility," in
    Leonard Krieger and Fritz Stern, eds., *The Responsibility of Power: Historical
    Essays in Honor of Hajo Holborn* (Garden City, NY: Doubleday, 1967),
    pp. 271–307.
Stern, Jessica, *The Ultimate Terrorists* (Cambridge, MA: Harvard University Press,
    1999).
Stevenson, David, *The First World War and International Politics* (Oxford: Oxford
    University Press, 1998).
Stiglitz, Joseph and Linda Bilmes, *Three Trillion Dollar War: The True Cost of the
    Iraq Conflict* (New York: Norton, 2008).
Storry, Richard, *Double Patriots: A Study of Japanese Nationalism* (Boston:
    Houghton, Mifflin, 1957).
Strang, David, "Anomaly and Commonplace in European Political Expansion,"
    International Organization, 45 (1991), pp. 143–162.

Strauss, Leo, *The Political Philosophy of Hobbes, Its Basis and Its Genesis*, trans. Elsa M. Sinclair (Chicago: University of Chicago Press, 1952).

Stuart, Douglas T., *Creating the National Security State: A History of the Law That Transformed America* (Princeton, NJ: Princeton University Press, 2008).

Suganami, Hidemi, *On the Causes of War* (Oxford: Oxford University Press, 1996).

"Explaining War: Some Critical Observations," *International Relations*, 16, no. 3 (December 2002), pp. 307–326.

Sun, Youli, *China and the Origins of the Pacific War, 1931–41* (New York: St. Martin's, 1993).

Suskind, Ron, *The One Percent Doctrine: Deep Inside America's Pursuit of Its Enemies Since 9/11* (New York: Simon & Schuster, 2006).

Sutter, Robert G., *China's Rise in Asia: Promises, and Perils* (Lanham, MD: Rowman & Littlefield, 2005).

Suzuki, Susumu, Volker Krause and J. David Singer, "The Correlates of War Project: A Bibliographic History of the Scientific Study of War and Peace, 1964–2002," http://sitemaker.umich.edu/jdsinger/files/cow_bibliographi chistory_071202f_04_07_06_.pdf.

Swaine, Michael D. and Ashley J. Tellis, *Interpreting China's Grand Strategy: Past, Present, and Future* (Santa Monica, CA: RAND, 2000).

Swann, Julian, "Politics and the State in Eighteenth Century Europe," in T. C. W. Blanning, ed., *The Eighteenth Century: Europe, 1688–1815* (Oxford: Oxford University Press, 2000), pp. 11–51.

Szulc, Tad, *Fidel: A Critical Portrait* (New York: Morrow, 1986).

Tammen, Ronald L., Jacek Kugler, Douglas Lemke, Carole Alsharabati, Brian Efird and A. F. K. Organski, *Power Transitions: Strategies for the 21st Century* (New York: Seven Bridges, 2000).

Tannenwald, Nina, *The Nuclear Taboo: The United States and the Nonuse of Nuclear Weapons Since 1945* (New York: Cambridge University Press, 2007).

Taubman, William, *Khrushchev: The Man and His Era* (New York: Norton, 2003).

Taylor, A. J. P., *The Struggle for Mastery in Europe, 1848–1918* (New York: Oxford University Press, 1954).

The Origins of the Second World War (London: Hamish Hamilton, 1961).

Taylor, Charles, "The Politics of Recognition," in Amy Gutmann, ed., *Multiculturalism: Examining the Politics of Recognition* (Princeton, NJ: Princeton University Press, 1994), pp. 25–74.

Taylor, Donald M., "Multiple Group Membership and Self-Identity," *Journal of Cross-Cultural Psychology*, 12 (1981), pp. 61–79.

Tellis, Ashley J., "A Grand Chessboard," *Foreign Policy*, no. 146 (January/February 2005), pp. 52–54.

Tetlock, Philip E., "Accountability and Complexity of Thought," *Journal of Personality and Social Psychology*, 45 (July 1983), pp. 74–83.

Thompson, William R., "Cycles, Capabilities and War: An Ecumenical View," in William R. Thompson, ed., *Contending Approaches to World System Analysis* (Beverly Hills, CA: Sage, 1983).

"Uneven Economic Growth, Systemic Challenges, and Global War," *International Studies Quarterly*, 27 (1983), pp. 341–355.

"Polarity, the Long Cycle and Global Power Warfare," *Journal of Conflict Resolution*, 30 (1986), pp. 587–615.

ed., *Great Power Rivalries* (Columbia, SC: University of South Carolina Press, 1989).

"A Street Car Named Sarajevo: Catalysts, Multiple Causality Chains, and Rivalry Structures," *International Studies Quarterly*, 47, no. 3 (September 2003), pp. 453–474.

Thucydides, *History of the Peloponnesian War*, Books I–II (Cambridge, MA: Harvard University Press, 1919).

Tilly, Charles, "War Making and State Making as Organized Crime," in Peter B. Evans, Dietrich Rueschemeyer and Theda Skocpol, eds., *Bringing the State Back In* (Cambridge: Cambridge University Press, 1985), pp. 169–191.

Coercion, Capital, and European States, AD 990–1990 (Cambridge: Blackwell, 1990).

Tocqueville, Alexis de, *Democracy in America*, trans. and ed. Harvey C. Mansfield and Debra Winthrop (Chicago: University of Chicago Press, 2000).

Tolstoy, Leo, *Essays, Letters and Miscellanies* (New York: Charles Scribner's Son, 1911), vol. I.

Toynbee, Arnold, *A Study of History*, vol. 9 (New York: Oxford University Press, 1954).

Treasure, G. R. R., *The Making of Modern Europe, 1648–1780* (New York: Methuen, 1985).

Treitschke, Heinrich von, *Politics*, 2 vols. (New York: Macmillan, 1916).

Tucker, Spencer, *The Encyclopedia of World War I: A Political, Social, and Military History* (Santa Barbara, CA: ABC-CLIO, 2005), vol. 1.

Tucker, Spencer and Priscilla Roberts, *The Encyclopedia of World War II: A Political, Social, and Military History* (Santa Barbara: ABC-CLIO, 2005), vol. 1.

Turner, Stephen, "Introduction," in *The Cambridge Companion to Weber* (Cambridge: Cambridge University Press, 2000).

Turco, R. P., O. B. Toon, T. P. Ackerman, J. B. Pollack and C. Sagan, "Nuclear Winter: Global Consequences of Multiple Nuclear Explosions," *Science*, 222, no. 4630 (December, 23 1983).

Tyler, Tom R., "Psychological Perspectives on Legitimacy and Legitimation," *Annual Review of Psychology*, 57 (January 2006), pp. 375–400.

Ullman, Richard H., "Redefining Security," *International Security*, 8, no. 1 (Summer 1983), pp. 129–153.

United States Arms Control and Disarmament Agency, *The Effects of Nuclear War* (Washington, DC: Arms Control and Disarmament Agency, April 1979), pp. 16–17.

United States Congress, Office of Technology Assessment, *The Effects of Nuclear War* (London: Croom Helm, 1980), pp. 100–101.

United States Congress, Senate, Committee on Armed Services, *Nuclear Winter and Its Implications*, Hearings before Committee on Armed Services, United States Senate, Ninety-Ninth Congress, First Session, October 2 and 3, 1985 (Washington, DC: Government Printing Office, 1986).

Valentino, Benjamin and Nicholas Valentino, "An Army of the People? National Guard and Reserve Casualties and Public Support for War," unpublished paper.

Van Creveld, Martin, "The Waning of Major War," in Raimo Väyrynen, ed., *The Waning of Major War: Theories and Debates* (London: Routledge, 2005), pp. 97–113.

Van Dyke, Carl, *The Soviet Invasion of Finland, 1939–40* (Portland, OR: Cass, 1997).

Van Evera, Stephen, *Causes of War: Power and the Roots of Conflict* (Ithaca, NY: Cornell University Press, 1999).

Van Wees, Hans, *Greek Warfare: Myth and Realities* (London: Duckworth, 2004).

Vasquez, John A., *Power of Power Politics: A Critique* (New Brunswick, NJ: Rutgers University Press, 1983).

The War Puzzle (Cambridge: Cambridge University Press, 1993).

"Why Do Neighbors Fight? Proximity, Interaction, or Territoriality?," *Journal of Peace Research*, 32, no. 3 (1995), pp. 277–293.

ed., *What Do We Know About War?* (Lanham, MD: Rowman & Littlefield, 2000).

"Reexamining the Steps to War: New Evidence and Empirical Insights," in Manus Midlarsky, ed., *Handbook of War Studies II* (Ann Arbor, MI: University of Michigan Press, 2006), pp. 371–406.

Väyrynen, Raimo, "Economic Cycles, Power Transitions, Political Management and Wars Between Major Powers," *International Studies Quarterly*, 27 (1983), pp. 389–418.

"Introduction," in Raimo Väyrynen, ed., *The Waning of Major War: Theories and Debates* (London: Routledge, 2005), pp. 1–30.

ed., *The Waning of Major War: Theories and Debates* (London: Routledge, 2005).

Veblen, Thorstein, *An Inquiry into the Nature of Peace and the Terms of Its Perpetuation* (New York: Macmillan, 1917).

The Theory of the Leisure Class: An Economic Study in the Evolution of Institutions (New York: Modern Library, 1934).

Vermes, Gabor, *István Tisza: The Liberal Vision and Conservative Statecraft of a Magyar Nationalist* (New York: Columbia University Press, 1985).

Volkogonov, Dimitri, *Stalin: Triumph and Tragedy*, ed. and trans. Harold Shukman (London: Weidenfeld & Nicolson, 1991).

Lenin: A New Biography, trans. Harold Shukman (New York: Simon & Schuster, 1994).

Wakabayashi, Bob Tadashi, *What Really Happened in Nanking: Refutation of a Common Myth* (Tokyo: Shuppan, 2002).

Wallensteen, Peter, "Trends in Major War: Too Early for Warning," in Raimo Väyrynen, ed., *The Waning of Major War: Theories and Debates* (London: Routledge, 2005), pp. 80–94.

Wallerstein, Imanuel, *The Politics of the World Economy* (Cambridge: Cambridge University Press, 1984).

Walt, Stephen M., *The Origins of Alliances* (Ithaca, NY: Cornell University Press, 1987).

Walt, Stephen M. and John J. Mearsheimer, *The Israel Lobby and US Foreign Policy* (New York: Farrar, Straus and Giroux, 2007).

Walters, Francis Paul, *A History of the League of Nations* (New York: Oxford University Press, 1952).

Waltz, Kenneth N., *Man, the State, and War* (New York: Columbia University Press, 1959).

Theory of International Politics (Boston: Addison-Wesley, 1979).

"The Spread of Nuclear Weapons: More May Better," Adelphi Paper 171 (London: International Institute for Strategic Studies, 1981).

"The Emerging Structure of International Politics," *International Security*, 18 (1993), pp. 44–79.

"International Relations Is Not Foreign Policy," *Security Studies*, 6 (1996), pp. 54–57.

"Evaluating Theories," *American Political Science Review*, 91, no. 4 (December 1997), pp. 913–917.

"Structural Realism after the Cold War," *International Security*, 25, no. 1 (Summer 2000), pp. 5–41.

Watkins, Shanea and James Sherk, *Who Serves in the US Military? The Demographics of Enlisted Troops and Officers* (Washington, DC: Heritage Foundation Center for Data Analysis Report, 2008).

Watson, Adam, *The Evolution of International Society: A Comparative Historical Analysis* (New York: Palgrave, 1992).

Wawro, Geoffrey, *The Franco-Prussian War: The German Conquest of France, 1870–1871* (Cambridge: Cambridge University Press, 2003).

Weber, Max, *"Objectivity" in Social Science and Social Policy*, trans. and ed. Edward A. Shils and Henry A. Finch (Glencoe, IL: Free Press, 1949 [1904]).

"The Profession and Vocation of Politics," in Peter Lassman and Ronald Speirs, *Political Writings* (Cambridge: Cambridge University Press, 1994).

Wehler, Hans-Ulrich, *Der deutsche Kaiserreich, 1871-1918* (Göttingen: Vandenhoek and Ruprecht, 1977).

Weigley, Russell F., *The Age of Battles: The Quest for Decisive Warfare from Breitenfeld to Waterloo* (Bloomington, IN: Indiana University Press, 1991).

Weinberg, Gerhard L., *The Foreign Policy of Hitler's Germany*, 2 vols. (Chicago: University of Chicago Press, 1970-1980).

A World at Arms: A Global History of World War II (Cambridge: Cambridge University Press, 1994).

Welch, David A., ed., *Proceedings of the Hawk Key Conference on the Cuban Missile Crisis, 5-8 March 1987* (Cambridge, MA: Harvard University, Center for Science and International Affairs, Working Paper 89-1, 1989).

Painful Choices: A Theory of Foreign Policy Change (Princeton, NJ: Princeton University Press, 2005).

Wendt, Alexander E., *A Social Theory of International Politics* (Cambridge: Cambridge University Press, 1999).

Westad, Odd Arne, ed., *Reviewing the Cold War: Approaches, Interpretations, Theory* (London: Frank Cass, 2000).

The Global Cold War: Third World Interventions and the Making of Our Times (Cambridge: Cambridge University Press, 2003).

White, Donald W., "The Nature of World Power in American History: An Evaluation at the End of World War II," *Diplomatic History*, 11, no. 3, pp. 181-202.

Whiting, Alan S., *China Crosses the Yalu: The Decision to Enter the Korean War* (New York: Macmillan, 1960).

Wight, Martin, "The Balance of Power," in Herbert Butterfield and Martin Wight, eds., *Diplomatic Investigations: Essays in the Theory of International Politics* (London: Allen & Unwin, 1966), pp. 149-175.

Systems of States (Leicester: Leicester University Press, 1977).

Wilde, Oscar, "The Critic as Artist," in Richard Aldington, ed., *The Portable Oscar Wilde* (New York: Viking, 1946), pp. 51-137.

Williamson, Samuel R., *Austria-Hungary and the Coming of the First World War* (London: Macmillan, 1990).

Wilson, Charles, *Profit and Power: A Study of the England and Dutch Wars* (Cambridge: Cambridge University Press, 1957).

Wilson, Trevor, *The Myriad Faces of War: Britain and the Great War, 1914-1918* (London: Polity Press, 1986).

Winch, P. G., *Idea of a Social Science and Its Relation to Philosophy* (London: Routledge and Kegan Paul, 1958).

Wohl, Robert, *The Generation of 1914* (Cambridge, MA: Harvard University Press, 1979).

Wohlforth, William C., "Realism and the End of the Cold War," *International Security*, 19 (Winter 1994–1995), pp. 91–129.

"Stability of a Unipolar World," *International Security*, 24, no. 2 (Summer 1999), pp. 5–41.

"US Strategy in a Unipolar World," in G. John Ikenberry, *America Unrivaled: The Future of the Balance of Power* (Ithaca, NY: Cornell University Press, 2002), pp. 98–118.

Wohlforth, William C., "The Comedy of Errors. A Reply to Mette Eilstrup-Sangiovanni," *European Journal of International Relations*, 15, no. 2 (June 2009), pp. 381–388.

Woit, Peter, *Not Even Wrong: The Failure of String Theory and the Search for Unity in Physical Law* (New York: Basic Books, 2006).

Wolf, John B., *The Emergence of the Great Powers, 1685–1715* (New York: Harper & Row, 1951).

Wolf, Matt W., "Stumbling Toward War: The Soviet Decision to Invade Afghanistan," *Past Imperfect*, 12 (2006), pp. 1–19.

Wolfe, Bertram D., *An Ideology in Power: Reflections on the Russian Revolution* (New York: Stein and Day, 1969).

Wolfers, Arnold, *Discord and Collaboration: Essays on International Politics* (Baltimore, MD: Johns Hopkins University Press, 1962).

Wong, J. W., *Deadly Dreams: Opium, Imperialism, and the Arrow War (1856–1860) in China* (Cambridge: Cambridge University Press, 1998).

Woodward, Bob, *Plan of Attack* (New York: Simon & Schuster, 2004).

State of Denial (New York: Simon & Schuster, 2006).

Wright, Quincy, *A Study of War*, rev. edn. (Chicago: University of Chicago Press, 1965 [1942]).

Wyatt-Brown, Bertram, *Southern Honor: Ethics and Behavior in the Old South* (New York: Oxford University Press, 1986).

The Shaping of Southern Culture: Honor, Grace and War, 1760s–1890s (Chapel Hill, NC: University of North Carolina Press, 2001).

Xu, Yao, *Cong Yalujiang dao Banmendian* [From the Yalu River to Panmunjom] (Beijing: Beijing People's Press, 1985).

Yack, Bernard, *The Fetishism of Modernities: Epochal Self-Consciousness in Contemporary Social and Political Thought* (Notre Dame, IN: University of Notre Dame Press, 1997).

Yates, Robin, "The Song Empire: The World's First Superpower?," in Philip A. Tetlock, Richard Ned Lebow and Geoffrey Parker, eds., *Unmaking the West: "What-If" Scenarios That Rewrite World History* (Ann Arbor, MI: University of Michigan Press, 2006), pp. 205–40.

Yee, Albert S., "Realist Analyses of China's Rise: Theory-Specific Derivations of Core Defense and Auxiliary Emendations," unpublished paper.

Yetiv, Steven A., *Explaining Foreign Policy: US Decision-Making and the Persian Gulf War* (Baltimore, MD: Johns Hopkins University Press, 2004).

Zacher, Mark W., "The Territorial Integrity Norm: International Boundaries and the Use of Force," *International Organization*, 55, no. 2 (Spring 2001), pp. 215–250.

Zagare, Frank, "Review of *The War Trap*," *American Political Science Review*, 76 (1982), pp. 738–739.

Zelditch, M., "Process of Legitimation: Recent Developments and New Directions," *Social Psychology Quarterly*, 64, no. 1 (2001), pp. 4–17.

Zelditch, M. and H. A. Walker, "Normative Regulation of Power," in Shane R. Thye and Edward J. Lawler, eds., *Advances in Group Processes* (Greenwich: JAI Press, 2000).

Zeller, Gaston, "French Diplomacy and Foreign Policy in Their European Setting," in *New Cambridge Modern History* (Cambridge: Cambridge University Press, 1970). vol. 5, pp. 68–72.

Zhang, Shugang, *Mao's Military Romanticism: China and the Korean War, 1950–1953* (Lawrence, KS: University Press of Kansas, 1995).

Zuber, Terence, *Inventing the Schlieffen Plan: German War Planning, 1871–1914* (Oxford: Oxford University Press, 2002).

Zubok, Vladislav, "Why Did the Cold War End in 1989? Explanations of 'The Turn'," in Odd Arne Westad, ed., *Reviewing the Cold War: Approaches, Interpretations, Theory* (London: Frank Cass, 2000), pp. 343–367.

INDEX

Adolphus, Gustavus, 215
affect, 83
Afghanistan, 157
  invasion and occupation of (1993–),
    7, 10, 19, 108, 115, 140, 178, 186,
    190, 210, 211, 218
  Soviet invasion of, 115, 159, 164
al-Qaeda, 186–187, 192
Albright, Madeleine, 217
alliances, 19–20, 87
  see also North Atlantic Treaty
  Organization (NATO),
  Warsaw Pact
Angell, Norman, 136, 141
anger, 74, 96, 122–123, 187–188, 201
  see also revenge, spirit
Anglo-Dutch Wars (1652–1654, 1665–
    1667), 150, 155, 172–173, 185
Anglo-French occupation of Egypt
    (1882), 150, 153
Anglo-French occupation of the Suez
    Canal Zone (1956), 153
Anglo-Persian War (1857), 190
Anglo-Spanish War (1739), 149
appeasement, 60
appetite, 6, 15–16, 18, 59, 77–80,
    84–85, 113
aristocracy, 93, 165, 175
Aristophanes, 7
Aristotle, 15–16, 67–68, 74, 81, 85, 108
Armey, Dick, 180
Asquith, Herbert, 176
Assyria, 69
Augustine, 81
Australia, 148
Austria, 20, 40–41, 55, 94, 95, 100, 103,
    106, 108, 110, 113, 116, 118, 122,
    176, 191

Austria-Hungary, *see* Austria
Aziz, Tariq, 151
Aztecs, 10–11, 76

Baker, James, 178–181
balance of power, 25–31,
    96, 121
Balkan War (1913), 191
battle of Borodino (1812), 134
battle of Malplaquet (1709), 134
Belgium, 106, 176
Bentham, Jeremy, 142
Bethmann Hollweg, Theobald von,
    29, 61
Betts, Richard, 219
Bin Laden, Osama, 187, 192
Bismarck, Otto von, 47, 106, 108, 109,
    150, 181, 190
Black, Jeremy, 173–174
Blainey, David, 53, 105, 144
Boer War (1899–1902), 10, 136
bombing, 79
Borodino, battle of (1812), 134
Boxer Rebellion, 117
Brest-Litovsk, Treaty of (1918), 164
Brezhnev, Leonid I., 160, 165
Bright, John, 136, 142, 205
Britain, 20, 42, 93–95, 99–101, 113, 155,
    192, 213, 215
  see also England
Brooks, Stephen, 124, 152–153, 168
Bueno de Mesquita, Bruce,
    49–53, 57
Bull, Hedley, 11
Bullock, Alan, 109
Bush, George W., administration, 108,
    109, 152, 154, 178–181, 182,
    187–188, 192, 214

Printed by Printforce, the Netherl